Sweetening and Intensification

A volume in the SUNY series in Hindu Studies
Brian Collins, editor

Sweetening and Intensification

Currents Shaping Hindu Practices

Edited by

AMY L. ALLOCCO and
XENIA ZEILER

Published by State University of New York Press, Albany

EU GPSR Authorised Representative:
Logos Europe, 9 rue Nicolas Poussin, 17000, La Rochelle, France
contact@logoseurope.eu

For information, contact State University of New York Press, Albany, NY
www.sunypress.edu

Library of Congress Cataloging-in-Publication Data

Names: Allocco, Amy L., editor. | Zeiler, Xenia, editor.
Title: Sweetening and intensification : currents shaping Hindu practices /
    edited by Amy L. Allocco and Xenia Zeiler.
Description: Albany : State University of New York Press, [2025] | Series:
    A volume in the SUNY series in Hindu Studies | Includes bibliographical
    references and index.
Identifiers: ISBN 9798855804058 (hardcover : alk. paper) | ISBN 9798855804072
    (ebook) | ISBN 9798855804065 (pbk. : alk. paper)
Further information is available at the Library of Congress.

Contents

Part 3: Pilgrimage and Festival Practices

Part 4: Narrative and Visual Spaces

Figure I.1. Map indicating the main sites discussed in the volume's case studies. *Source:* Created by Sakshi Sharma. Used with permission.

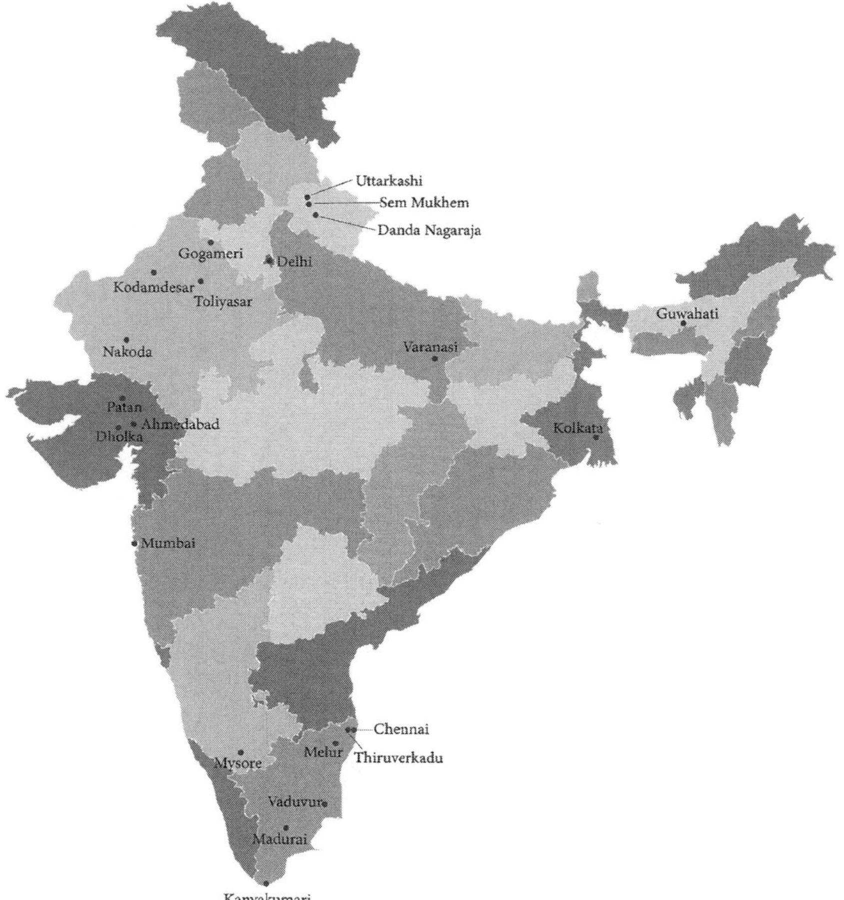

Introduction

Sweetening and Intensification Processes in Hindu Traditions

Xenia Zeiler and Amy L. Allocco

As abiding and often strategic currents in Hindu traditions, sweetening and intensification alternately converge and diverge with respect to Hindu deities, beliefs, narratives, and ritual practices. When putting the two currents—which may at first glance seem mutually exclusive—in relation to each other, we can see that, in fact, these processes are directly connected. Sweetening is itself a form of intensification. In such cases, we can observe a move away from intense or spicy toward benign or bland characteristics. Intensification, by contrast, means a shift from formerly softer toward more extreme tendencies than those that had existed so far. As such, both currents denote an activity, a *change* in how deities, narratives, and practices are defined in Hindu traditions vis-à-vis their position on a perceived scale of sweet—neutral—intense.

Because they have been and continue to be central means of defining the core nature and character of deities and practices, sweetening and intensification not only occur individually but are also often in dialogue. For example, the popular group of goddesses known as the Ten Mahavidya explicitly and deliberately contain members ranging from wholly sweet, to a mixture of sweet and intense, to extremely intense. While it is not entirely clear how or why these goddesses were assembled as a unit, it seems likely that a recognition of the full spectrum of sweet—neutral—spicy played a role (Zeiler 2012b).

In addition to the historical role these processes have played in South Asia and its diasporas, sweetening and intensification increasingly shape the contours of contemporary Hindu worship, temple activities, myth, and visual and material culture. Sweetening trends, on the one hand, and intensification, on the other, occur across diverse Hindu social and geographic contexts, textual and theological traditions, and ritual and media formats. Although reliable evidence related to the precise histories of these currents is often difficult to identify, it is irrefutable that they are currently shifting and developing and their interactions indelibly shape one another. As such, these processes intersect with and may even drive contemporary (re)negotiations, (re)interpretations, and (re)constructions of key Hindu practices, narratives, and symbols.

We understand "sweetening" to include the softening of deities' iconographies, standardization of religious narratives, sanitization of ritual practices, and mainstreaming of theologies. Such efforts may seek to bring diverse Hindu religious elements—from divinities to temple architecture to worship styles to folklore to visual depictions—in line with Sanskritic traditions and upper-caste norms, actual or imagined. In the process, highly local religious practices, divine entities, stories, ontologies, and other phenomena may be identified with and even subsumed by broader, pan-Indian traditions. M. N. Srinivas (1952) referred to this pattern, whereby Sanskritic Hinduism (the "Great Tradition") exerts a dominant and homogenizing cultural influence on local or "little" traditions, as "Sanskritization" (but see Orr 2005 on possible "de-Sanskritization" processes), and many others after him have made use of this interpretive category. Sweetening efforts can also lend support to the reshaping of physical spaces and administrative structures at temples and shrines, leading to new articulations of what constitutes permissible activities in these environments and who is eligible to enter, perform worship in, and exercise control over these sites. Such shifts frequently result in the increased presence of governmental authorities and male Brahman officiants and the concurrent disenfranchisement of women, transgender, and oppressed-caste specialists. Overall, attempts to refine, overwrite, or otherwise clean up specific elements of subaltern traditions may lead to the loss of characteristic regional forms and, ultimately, to homogenization.

Deities themselves are perhaps ground zero for sweetening campaigns, which variously attempt to mute their personalities, subdue their ritual cults, and strip away offerings that some regard as offensive or impure. For instance, we have historically seen and continue to witness movements to temper or even entirely eliminate the fiercer aspects of some Hindu deities' representations, iconography, and ritual practices. Diverse ideologies and aims have inspired softening processes at different times, including indigenous and colonial reformist agendas, the desire to consolidate power in particular sectarian or orthodox circles, and the goal of assimilating originally more capricious and localized deities into elite traditions. In many cases, sweetening tendencies have derived energy from the aesthetic and worship preferences of upwardly mobile and new middle classes. At a practical level, such developments may manifest in, for example, an expansive vegetarianism that entails not only a move away from animal sacrifice but also alcohol and tobacco offerings and the performance of physically arduous vows dedicated to these deities. They may also include incorporating previously independent, local deities into pan-Indian kinship relationships and marginalizing multisensory, embodied practices like possession and prophecy-speaking. In terms of their narrative traditions, oral and vernacular-language texts may be deemphasized, bowdlerized, or identified with Sanskrit and other authoritative sources. The end game of these sweetening trends is the fabrication or reintroduction of seemingly benevolent and nonthreatening divine beings who—divested of tendencies and worship practices that are deemed dangerous, liminal, or impure—are exemplars of a perceived modern and progressive Hindu sensibility. While the sweetening of fierce deities and practices (especially but certainly not exclusively related to goddesses) has a long history in both Hindu text and praxis, this volume demonstrates that we find a new quality and, arguably, quantity of occurrences in contemporary, globalizing South Asia and its transnational communities.

Alongside sweetening streams exists "intensification," a countercurrent that we understand as a heightened insistence on the continuing relevance of rigorous, visceral, and frequently stigmatized religious practices and beliefs. These may include worldviews, narratives, and rituals that originated in Tantric, village, or folk traditions, such as blood sacrifice, firewalking, hook-swinging, bodily piercings, and offering or ingesting intoxicants. We define intensification not solely as the conceptual opposite or reverse of sweetening but rather as a complex and layered process. That is, we take intensification to mean not simply maintaining the fierce characteristics of individual deities and a range of marginalized worship styles, narratives, iconographies, and values, often in the face of resistance to or attempts to modify them, but rather amplifying these elements in response to new circumstances and challenges. Indeed, our framing of intensification foregrounds the question of whether such beliefs and practices are best understood as *re*assertions of historical beliefs and practices that have been understudied by scholars or are, in fact, innovative practices animated by recent developments.

For instance, we see the contemporary (re)emergence of these representations and practices as intrinsic to some deities' theology, character, and proper propitiation and an insistence on continuing them. In terms of iconography, for example, in an era of increasingly cherubic and benign-looking goddess images, intensification may be visible in a fierce visage featuring a protruding tongue, fangs, or loosened hair and her being accompanied by potentially frightening companions, such as ghosts, demons, and guardians. Intensifications in narrative traditions could, for instance, involve refusals to deemphasize accounts of a deity's sexual proclivity, nonvegetarian appetites, or association with misfortunes such as miscarriages.

Intensity related to deities takes many additional forms in diverse strands of Hinduism, but it is perhaps most often expressed through their heated or spiced-up characters and qualities. Intensity can be visible in, for example, gods' and goddesses' volatile natures, their sometimes hard-to-satisfy demands for particular offerings, and their tendency to, under certain conditions, manifest as illness or otherwise torment their devotees. With regard to worship styles, intensification can include ritual items and substances like alcohol, ganja, blood, skulls/bones, tobacco, sacrificial animals, cemetery soil, and cremation ash that may be expensive or otherwise difficult to procure, not to mention coded as impure in what might be described as orthodox or mainstream Hinduism. A deity's afflictive inclinations might manifest as lice or matted hair, pustules or fevers, plagues or epidemics, and fugue states or unrestrained possession.

Much like with sweetening, intensification trends are initiated by varied social, religious, political, and economic developments, either operating on their own or in concert. Such developments might necessitate extending, renewing, or instituting for the first time entirely new worship procedures, ritual materials, visual representations, or textual themes. Some intensifications, for example, may be traceable to the self-assertions of caste-oppressed Hindus who refuse to abandon their distinctive religious forms and instead perform them with a new self-consciousness, pride, or even defiance. At the same time, assertive forms of muscular Hinduism that have emerged in the context of ascendant Hindu nationalism can be analyzed as another sort of intensification. The challenges and opportunities associated with neoliberalism and globalization have given rise to forms of intensification ranging from, on the one hand, rituals to counteract evil eye and sorcery attacks that worshipers believe are thwarting their aspirations for economic thriving and elevated social status, to exuberant temple renovation and creative styles of deity adornment, on the other. These shifting contexts, operative in both South Asian and transnational Hindu contexts, produce heightened ritual responses sparked by the imperatives of heritage and other movements committed to guarding against the disappearance of traditional practices. Other motivations include the difficulties people perceive as linked to the Kali Yuga, families' increasingly scattered or divided lineages, and government development initiatives.

Intensification can also, for instance, be seen in new, revised, or traditional ritual performances informed by the demands of a mercurial deity who communicates through a medium that they do (or do not) want a new shrine and whose reprisals are to be feared if their cravings are not satisfied with the right ritual processes and offerings. Their devotees understand such deities as oblivious to or uninterested in reformist discourses that highlight animal rights, so-called "superstition," or the supposed superiority of traditions that reject such practices, and they tend to believe that these temperamental entities cannot be denied their due without risk. Intensification processes, too, are expressed along a spectrum, and this volume's individual chapters discuss different degrees of ferocity or spicing-up (though instances of extreme intensification are comparatively rare or less documented, or both). In what follows we see cases where intense elements continued or began to coexist with sweeter characteristics or actively resisted sweetening forces, sometimes growing stronger and more pronounced as a result.

Given the significance of these currents, it is now time to present original research from diverse sites, disciplinary backgrounds, theoretical contexts, and methodological vantage points to expand and deepen this important arena of inquiry, advance new questions within it, and offer specific perspectives. What shapes can sweetening and intensification take, and how are they interrelated with society at large, in South Asia and beyond? How are sweetening and intensification—either on their own or working in tandem—relevant for and applicable to the study of Hindu traditions, past and present, and what contribution can their study make to debates about transformations and trends in lived religion?

This multidisciplinary volume is intended to contribute to our understanding of what constitutes sweetening and intensification processes, empirically as well as theoretically, by critically discussing fresh research from various regions with heterogeneous cultural, linguistic, ethnic, and social backgrounds across South Asia and the South Asian diaspora. Likewise, it offers a focused discussion of these trends in Hindu ritual and worship practices over time from multiple perspectives and social, geographic, and academic positions. Whereas softening, sweetening, and gentrification are discussed to some extent in the academic literature (including, for example, Allocco 2018; Harman 2012; McDermott 2001; Padma 2013; Waghorne 2001; Zeiler 2012b), countercurrents that involve a (re)assertion of deities' fiercer characteristics and worship practices have been far less explored (but see Allocco 2020; Allocco 2021; Arumugam 2015; Zeiler 2012a; Zeiler 2019). Moreover, the existing scholarship has tended to focus on these currents vis-à-vis goddess traditions, which have largely been analyzed in terms of "saumyatization" (rendering gentle, auspicious) and has only rarely included male deities. We take a more inclusive approach by bringing these two threads—sweetening and intensification—into sustained conversation to generate insights about these highly significant (yet so far still underresearched and undertheorized) processes. We maintain that these two streams must be analyzed in tandem to account for the diverse ways that Hindu beliefs and practices interact and transform over time.

The present volume is the primary outcome of the two coeditors' collaborative project with the same name, which was awarded a Collaborative International Research Grant by the American Academy of Religion. Although the pandemic thwarted some of our individual and collective presentation and fieldwork plans along the way, several of the contributing authors participated in a double panel focused on the themes of sweetening and intensification that the two editors convened during the online Annual Conference on South Asia in 2021. These and other presentations provided valuable opportunities for contributors as well as those who were ultimately unable to submit a chapter for this volume to test key arguments, gather critical feedback, and generate broader interest in the project. Through its analysis of the converging and diverging currents of sweetening and intensification, we anticipate that the volume will enrich our collective scholarly understanding of the diverse ways that Hindu beliefs and practices have been and are negotiated and contested in historical and contemporary contexts.

The Study of Sweetening and Intensification of Hindu Traditions

As important aspects of Hindu traditions with long-standing significance, the principal themes of this volume have been treated in several prior scholarly studies. Sweetening is, as we noted above, undoubtedly more prominent and visible and has consequently been researched far more. While intensification processes have also very likely existed over the *longue durée* and in diverse spaces in South Asia, they have arguably been present to a lesser degree and have certainly attracted less academic attention. What is unequivocally new and therefore constitutes the declared primary aim of this edited volume is to bring the two currents into a sustained discussion in an effort to understand their exceedingly important (if not driving) roles in many contemporary transformations in Hindu contexts. When reflecting on them as religious, cultural, and social processes, sweetening and intensification are two sides of a coin, so to speak: they are developments attesting to and exemplary of larger negotiations of Hindu authority and identity. For example, they help us gain traction in addressing questions such as which persons, communities, or institutions are actively shaping Hindu ritual practices, modes of worship, and deity representations; who is eligible or authorized to do so (and by whom); and when and where these processes unfold.

This is the first volume to explicitly address the interplay of sweetening and intensification dynamics. Its authors productively draw on important previous scholarship that has been published on either one or the other of these two currents. Existing studies have emerged from various disciplinary and interdisciplinary areas, such as South Asian studies, religious studies, and anthropology, and relevant research has appeared as monographs, edited volumes, stand-alone chapters, and journal articles. More often than not these sources focus on singular case studies, for instance, a deity, text, temple or shrine, community or group, or—more seldom—a ritual or worship practice.

When we survey the existing academic literature on sweetening, several pioneering works deserve mention. Three now-classic studies provide both textual translations and analysis of crucial historical moments of sweetenings in goddess traditions: Thomas B. Coburn's *Devī Māhātmyā: The Crystallization of the Goddess Tradition* (1988); C. Mackenzie Brown's *The Triumph of the Goddess: The Canonical Models of Theological Visions of the Devī-Bhāgāvata Purāṇa* (1990); and Rachel Fell McDermott's *Mother of My Heart, Daughter of My Dreams: Kālī and Umā in the Devotional Poetry of Bengal* (2001). Among studies with a stronger focus on lived religion that discuss sweetening with respect to worship and ritual practice is C. J. Fuller's *The Camphor Flame: Popular Hinduism and Society in India* (1992). This monograph centers on the relationship between Hindu deities and their devotees by privileging ethnographic case studies and comparative anthropological material. We must also name *Revelry, Rivalry, and Longing for the Goddesses of Bengal: Fortunes of Hindu Festivals* by McDermott (2011), which discusses sweetening processes visible in the highly popular Durga Puja and Kali Puja festivals.

The study of sweetening currents has also taken form in journal articles and book chapters. Joanne Punzo Waghorne's "The Gentrification of the Goddess" (2001) focuses on sweetening processes in relation to gentrification for the first time, drawing our attention to shifts in temple architecture and goddesses' iconography (see also Waghorne 2004). In "From Fierce to Domesticated: Mariyamman Joins the Middle Class" (2012), William Harman highlights how this popular Tamil goddess transforms in new and more elite social and economic contexts. Xenia Zeiler (2012b) discusses the radical transformations of a formerly exceptionally dark Tantric goddess into a benign, protective neighborhood goddess in Varanasi in "Transformations in the Textual Tradition of Dhūmāvatī: Changes of the Tantric Mahāvidyā Goddess in Concept, Ritual, Function, and Iconography."

Important contributions to the discussion of both sweetening and intensification have, unsurprisingly, been most often made by edited volumes. While their individual chapters still typically focus on either sweetening or intensification, taken as a whole the volumes nevertheless offer a picture of both currents in one publication. David Gordon White's edited volume *Tantra in Practice* (2000) is one example. It moves beyond the textual dimension of Tantric traditions to highlight changes in the realm of practice. Likewise, the volume *Wild Goddesses in India and Nepal* (1996), coedited by Axel Michaels, Cornelia Vogelsanger, and Annette Wilke, explores the textual and lived traditions of formerly independent goddesses in South Asia. In addition, some edited volumes whose foci lie elsewhere offer perspectives on broader transformation processes, especially sweetening. Among them are, for instance, John Stratton Hawley and Donna Marie Wulff's *Devi: Goddesses of India* (1996) collection; Tazim R. Kassam and Eliza F. Kent's *Lines in Water: Religious Boundaries in South Asia* (2013); P. Pratap Kumar's *Contemporary Hinduism* (2014); and Caleb Simmons, Moumita Sen, and Hillary Rodrigues's *Nine Nights of the Goddess: The Navarātri Festival in South Asia* (2018).

Several existing publications make an effort—to varying extents—to examine the complex interplay between sweetening and intensification, emphasizing how these processes might be embodied in a single deity, place, or text simultaneously. Examples include Amy L. Allocco's "Flower Showers for the Goddess: Borrowing, Modification, and Ritual Innovation in Tamil Nadu" (2018) chapter, which discusses the multifarious worship practices for a popular local goddess in Chennai, whose changing ritual idiom is shaped by broader social and economic shifts in her urban context. In her 2020 article, "Vernacular Practice, Gendered Tensions, and

Interpretive Ambivalence in Hindu Death, Deification, and Domestication Narratives," Allocco also analyzes the competing narratives related to one woman's death, deification, and subsequent domestic ritual cult. In a similar vein, Ehud Halperin underscores one goddess's diverse representations amid ecological changes, the growth in tourism, and debates about animal sacrifice in North India in his monograph *The Many Faces of a Hindu Goddess: Haḍimbā, Her Devotees, and Religion in Rapid Change* (2019). Sree Padma focuses on the appropriation and transformation of the symbolizations of the village goddesses of Andhra Pradesh in her *Vicissitudes of the Goddess: Reconstructions of the Gramadevata in India's Religious Traditions* (2013), while Hugh B. Urban examines the modern transformations of goddess Kamakhya's temple and most important festival, Ambuvaci Mela, in Assam in "The Cradle of Tantra: Modern Transformations of a Tantric Centre in Northeast India from Nationalist Symbol to Tourist Destination" (2019). In "Identity and Divinity: Boundary-Crossing Goddesses in Medieval South India," Leslie Orr (2005) suggests that while the iconography and identity of some goddesses may have been "Brahmanized" (Orr 2005, 24), these and other goddesses may have also undergone a process of "de-Sanskritization" (Orr 2005, 30) and been gradually transformed from great goddesses to village deities. Finally, it is worth citing one particularly relevant source on Hindu deities, temples, and traditions in transnational contexts, namely *A New God in the Diaspora? Muneeswaran Worship in Contemporary Singapore* by Vineeta Sinha (2016).

When it comes to the study of intensification processes, it is evident that fewer publications have concentrated on this topic. This is not to say, fortunately, that research on intense (rather than intensified) Hindu deities, practices, or texts is absent. On the contrary, there are several studies that take up traditions, deities, and communities with darker, more dynamic characteristics than are usually found in mainstream, pan-Hindu settings (including Tantric contexts)—of course and precisely because their dark(er) natures specifically invite studies on these intense aspects. Examples of such scholarship include the comprehensive study of the goddess commonly known as Angalamman, titled *Aṅkāḷaparamēcuvari: A Goddess of Tamilnadu, Her Myths and Cult* (1986), authored by Eveline Meyer, and a number of the chapters in Alf Hiltebeitel's edited volume, *Criminal Gods and Demon Devotees: Essays on the Guardians of Popular Hinduism* (1989). Two articles focusing on Tamil Nadu also illustrate this approach: Allocco's "Bringing the Dead Home: Hindu Invitation Rituals in Tamil South India" (2021) examines the intensified strategies and practices that structure rituals to install deceased relatives in their family home as household deities, and Indira Arumugam's " 'The Old Gods Are Losing Power!' Theologies of Power and Rituals of Productivity in a Tamil Nadu Village" (2015) reviews transforming beliefs and practices related to ritual sacrifice in rural settings. Finally, two pieces of scholarship authored by Zeiler also deserve mention. In "Female Danger: 'Evil,' Inauspiciousness, and Their Symbols in Representations of South Asian Goddesses" (2012a), she deliberates on intense and intensified representations of goddesses who are regarded as malevolent and potentially harmful, while in "Eradicated with Blood: Text and Context of Animal Sacrifice in Tantric and Tantra-Influenced Rituals" (2019) Zeiler analyzes how originally Tantric animal sacrifice intensifies non-Tantric rituals. Yet, apart from such studies focusing on textual, visual, or embodied practices related to these intense or ambivalent deities, studies that explicitly engage the processes and developments that *intensify* them remain few to date.

The scholarship discussed here exemplifies the variety and breadth of existing research on sweetening and intensification related to Hindu traditions, and its strong focus on presenting and discussing case study material. Additional studies, covering other historical periods, world regions, and communities, will continue to widen the scope of available case studies and offer diversified analyses and material that will in turn allow for expanded theorizing. Although some sweetening and intensification movements may share similar backgrounds, catalysts, and developmental patterns, more often they have unique characteristics and manifestations that are directly informed by regional, temporal, and other particularities. It is our hope to contribute to the broader discussion of these developments and theorizing about these processes by presenting this edited volume.

The Structure and Content of This Volume

This edited volume presents different aspects of sweetening and intensification in South Asia and South Asian diasporas with the interrelated goals of broadening our understanding of how these processes unfold in context; relate to larger religious, cultural and social developments; and become a vital part of contemporary lived Hindu traditions. By highlighting this new field and discussing diverse historical, geographic, cultural, spatial, technological, and social settings where these currents materialize, it also endeavors to infuse new content into theoretical and methodological conversations related to researching lived Hindu traditions. In line with these aims, the individual chapters expound different case studies from various historical periods (spanning from medieval times to the present); media genres (ranging from text to film); communities (from lower class to elite upper class and including rural, semiurban, and highly urbanized spaces); ritual, worship, and performance traditions (e.g., Tantric, folk and Smarta); physical spaces of negotiations (such as temples, shrines, households, pilgrimage centers, and cemeteries); and regions in South Asia and its transnational communities. As such, the chapters exemplify the density and variety of sweetening and intensification processes—whether one or the other, or a mix of both—across time, space, and place.

This volume's structure reflects this diversity. The individual chapters are arranged in four thematic sections that highlight the main spaces in which the negotiations and transformations take place. Part 1 is titled "Temples, Localities, and Deities" and includes three chapters. The first is "A Divine Dust-Up: Diverging Trajectories of Local Gods in Garhwal" by Brian K. Pennington. In it he discusses sweetening and intensification as strategies for the renegotiation of the status of deities, rituals, or communities in specific local forms and geographical settings. Specifically, Pennington describes how a centuries-old rivalry between two territorial deities, or *devta*s, in the Uttarkashi District of India's Uttarakhand state recently intensified into open conflict. His chapter explores a physical confrontation between the two *devta*s during the annual Maagh Mela festival in 2020 that also involved their divine guardians and companions, the Dalit ritual drummers who escorted them, and hundreds of their human partisans. Pennington argues that sweetening and intensification exhibit here a complementarity as a rural territorial figure evolves into an urban, Sanskritized deity, sweetened and domesticated in an environment of mass Himalayan tourism but capable of brute force and anger in his local context.

Seth Ligo's chapter, "Your Friendly, Neighborhood Bhairava: Understanding the Role of a Terrifying God in the Form of an Adorable Little-Boy (Batuk)," examines Batuk (Child, Underage) Bhairava, a sweet, friendly, youthful form of the otherwise marginal Bhairava. Drawing upon diverse sources, he articulates several ways to respond to the complex question of where Batuk Bhairava comes from, what role he occupies, and why he is so popular in certain locations and among particular populations. Ligo asks if Batuk is a defanged form of the ferocious deity, a sweeter and more palatable alternative to other forms of Bhairava. Does he fill a perceived gap in the catalog of Bhairava's, and by extension Shiva's, forms? Is he a rejoinder to the popularity of Bala (Little Boy) Krishna in competing schools of Vishnu-oriented Hinduism? To answer these questions, Ligo integrates ethnographic, textual, and material-spatial analyses to consider whether Batuk Bhairava might be an instance of the sweetening of Bhairava forms, which are otherwise associated with liminality, antinomian practice, and apparent transgression. Ultimately, Ligo argues that Batuk is not a gentler Bhairava made more palatable to contemporary, mainstream populations, and less likely to be misinterpreted by outsiders. Rather, Batuk's presence expands access to Bhairava in his many forms. Instead of displacing or distracting from more intense and liminal forms of Bhairava, Batuk's presence in conjunction with such forms results in mutual amplification through contrast. Batuk thus extends the capacity and possibility of Bhairav, from reprehensibility to respectability to venerability to adorability.

The first section closes with Tracy Pintchman's chapter, "This Is a Place Where *Shakti* Dances: Intensifying the Goddess's Power in Michigan," which discusses the role of human and divine actors in establishing a revitalized temple structure. The Parashakthi Goddess Temple in Pontiac, Michigan, was established in 1999 on Vijaya Dashami, a day celebrating the Goddess's victory over demonic forces. The goddess featured at this temple is the Tamil goddess Karumariamman, "Black Mariamman," who is a local goddess in her original South Indian context but takes form in her temple in Michigan as the one Great Goddess who has come to the West for the benefit of all beings. Temple discourse claims that the Goddess commanded the temple be built so she could bring her concentrated energy, or *shakti*, to protect the Western world during the first decades of the new millennium. But in 2018 a fire destroyed most of the temple and it was reconsecrated in an entirely different form in 2022. Pintchman explores how some temple leaders and devotees described the fire as divinely ordained, asserting that the Goddess wanted the site to be destroyed so that a more powerful one could be built to handle stronger demonic forces. In her chapter, she asks and answers the questions: How did the fire change perceptions of temple space? How does a diaspora temple become a "more powerful" vector of *shakti*? What role did humans, the Goddess, and other "supersensual" beings allegedly play in the destruction and regeneration of temple space?

The next section, part 2, is titled "Ritual and Possession Performances" and opens with a chapter by Amy L. Allocco. In "Insistence, Persistence, and Resistance in Tamil Hindu Rituals to Call the Dead," she analyzes these interrelated dynamics in the context of elaborate ceremonies to invite departed relatives back into the world so they may undergo investiture as protective family deities called *puvadaikkari*s. Specifically, the chapter attends to the continued insistence on the necessity of grave soil and crematory ash, tongue-piercing practices, and alcohol offerings by the deified dead and living relatives alike, who persist in regarding these materials and activities as essential to the rite's success and therefore resist sanitized substitutions. Her contribution suggests that the dead's steadfast refusal to be satisfied by anything except rigorous vows and stigmatized substances signals a deliberate resistance to the sweetening trends visible in many contemporary Hindu ritual contexts. The presence of, engagement with, and ingestion of these offerings and practices can introduce dissonance and discomfort in some ritual settings, leading to creative improvisations and negotiations. Allocco thus ascertains that while there is abundant evidence that sweetening and softening currents are influential in numerous Hindu settings today, these tides also pull in other directions. In *puvadaikkari* worship the direction of change identified in gentrification theories may well be reversed, as more intense, "village" ideations provide the frame for bourgeois ones, and not the other way around. New castes are experimenting with rituals to bring home, or domesticate, their dead in dialogue with the challenges of neoliberalism and modern social life, among others. These elaborate, expensive ceremonies are proliferating in urban spaces, including in brahmanical strongholds in the capital city of Chennai. Rather than a homogenizing or gentrifying process, we see in this case an increasing popularity, intensification, and amplification of these divine entities' ritual demands.

Aftab S. Jassal's chapter, "Developing Danda: Aspirations and Transformations of Divine Presence in Uttarakhand," follows. It focuses on the deity Nagaraja, who is commonly identified as a form of the pan-Indian deity Krishna and worshiped across caste, class, and geographical divides in the Garhwal region of the Himalayas. Nagaraja is encountered via deity possession, or divine embodiment, in the context of a ritual performance tradition known as *jagar* ("awakening" the gods) that is traditionally performed by ritual specialists from Dalit communities. Through storytelling, drumming, animal sacrifice, and ritual dance, Nagaraja is made present in embodied form to receive offerings, cure illnesses, exorcise malevolent spirits, give advice in times of difficulty, and intervene in matters of personal and collective importance. In addition, Nagaraja is encountered as a physical image (*murti*) in shrines and temples across the region. In these spaces, Brahman priests mediate contact and exchange between Nagaraja and his devotees. Jassal shows how the Danda Nagaraja temple in the Pauri District of Garhwal has become a critical site through which constructions of regional identity, state discourses on development, and the worship of

Nagaraja are brought together in creative and consequential ways. In addition to describing the moral, affective, and infrastructural labor through which the Danda Nagaraja temple is being transformed into a regionally significant pilgrimage destination, Jassal explores how the god Nagaraja and the practices through which he is known and experienced are sweetened and intensified as the god moves between small-scale *jagar* rituals, on the one hand, and large, public temples such as Danda Nagaraja, on the other. Jassal employs the terms *marg* ("highway"), *desh* ("countryside"), and *nagar* ("town") to delineate the relationship between distinct sites of religious practice in Uttarakhand, namely, the translocally significant Char Dham pilgrimage network; domestic, highly localized *jagar* rituals; and regionally well-known temples such as Danda Nagaraja.

The section concludes with Indira Arumugam's chapter, "Feral Gods: Intimations of a Mercurial Sacrality in Village Tamil Nadu," which engages with three Viranars as evoked by three different lineages within the Kallar caste in central Tamil Nadu. Common deities in rural Tamil settings, Viranars are likely derived from historical ancestors who strove for the betterment of or sacrificed their lives for their communities and were deified upon their death. Over time, they drew worship as guardian deities and a tutelary cult arose around them. In this chapter, Arumugam suggests that while this wild and unwieldy deity is in some cases being subjected to the pressures of domestication, also, as shrines, statues, and regular sacrifices for the Viranars of some lineages grow in number, other Viranars are simultaneously repudiating attempts to streamline, subdue, and orchestrate them. The unpredictability and ultimate unfathomability defining tutelary deities' cults suggests how—even as gentrification threatens to engulf in the form of proliferating fixed shrines, standardized iconography, regular worship, forswearing animal sacrifice, and on occasion recourse to Brahman priests and Sanskritic rituals—one may sense and make sense of a feral numinousness. Mediating between domesticity and ferality, these ambivalent deities trouble the epistemological confinements assigned and enforced by the functional calculus and teleological impetus underpinning prevailing theories of religious transformations such as Sanskritization, modernization, and gentrification.

The three chapters in part 3, "Pilgrimage and Festival Practices," train our gaze on these undertakings in Rajasthan and Karnataka. In "The Changing Flavors of Gogaji Worship," Carter Hawthorne Higgins discusses sweetening, or the standardizing of older ritual formations with more prestigious or widely shared religious styles, and intensification, as what he describes as the "doubling down" on older ritual styles in the face of pressures to change at the rural pilgrimage site of Gogameri, Rajasthan. Building on one of this volume's key terms, sweetening, his chapter extends culinary language and offers *chaat* (literally meaning "licking," "tasting," or "taste")—a celebrated genre of South Asian street food—as an interpretive analogy for the study of religious transformation in Gogameri. More specifically, Higgins presents two priestly efforts to stimulate religious changes and places both efforts in relation to broader shifts in the Gogameri pilgrimage, its public, and their interactions with the wider social field. Namely, he examines an example for intensification, in attempts by the pilgrimage site's abbot and administrative trust to intensify *chhari mela*, festive flagstaff processions, and an example for sweetening, in the form of a ritual called *vaishnav arti* for the resident deity, Gogaji. Higgins argues that just as a chef could alter a *chaat* dish by adding a sweet ingredient or one that would intensify its sourness or spiciness, individual programs of religious change may likewise affect the overall tenor of a festive formation. Yet when such a formation gives rise to many projects of religious change, as Gogameri has in the twenty-first century, then the interrelation of festive ingredients may transform in ways not always capturable in terms of sweetening or intensification alone.

Caleb Simmons's chapter, "Sleep Sweetly Fierce Goddess: Rituals of Intensification and Sweetening of the Goddess Chamundeshwari of Mysore in Navaratri/Dasara and Her Mahotsava," appears next in the section. It examines Chamundeshwari, the goddess of Mysore in Karnataka and tutelary deity of the royal Wodeyar family. In her temple, popular calendar-art-style images of the goddess on signs and posters show her riding atop her tiger and appearing visually synonymous with the pan-Indic goddess Durga, affirming her regal identity in alignment with her association with the royal family of Mysore. Her royal and victorious representations coalesce in her central role in the celebration of Dasara, which refers to the culminating day of the ten-day-long festival Navaratri/Nine Nights of the Goddess and Dasara/Tenth Day. The deity looks very different from the regal Durga in her festival image, which is used when the goddess leaves her temple in procession. Instead, in this depiction she has a sweet face with faint, perhaps nascent, fangs slightly protruding from her lips. This image provides greater insight into the complex, if not paradoxical, identities of the goddess as she is experienced by her devotees. Indeed, Chamundeshwari is a goddess of possibilities, simultaneously capable of compassion and violence, beauty and ghastliness, and—as is perfectly encapsulated in her festival image—sweetness and intensity. In his chapter, Simmons focuses on this tension in Chamundeshwari's identity and how it is managed by her devotees through an annual seventeen-day ritual sequence that extends from the celebration of autumnal Dasara to the goddess's Great Festival, or Mahotsava. In this ritual re-creation of the slaying of the buffalo demon and its aftermath, Chamundi is transformed from her daily role as protector and mother and ritually intensified in order to kill her foe. The process through which the goddess is intensified and sweetened through the festival's ritual cycle is contextualized with a discussion of how Chamundi, the goddess of Mysore, also historically underwent a process of sweetening to become Chamundeshwari, Queen Chamundi. This chapter is supplemented by a multimedia webpage that the author designed specifically to accompany it. At https://tinyurl.com/SleepSweetly, Simmons shares multiple photographs illustrating the different stages of the festival discussed in his chapter.

In "The Sweetening of Bhairav as a Merchants' Miracle Deity," R. Jeremy Saul discusses the popularization of some of Rajasthan's Bhairavs, traditionally regarded as fierce manifestations of Shiva, as examples of both sweetening and intensification. He argues that the most prominent agents of this change in recent decades have been Marwaris, members of mercantile clans who are dispersed throughout India and continue to venerate local Rajasthani deities. By sweetening, the chapter means that Bhairav's long-standing fierce identity in Rajasthani villages has been appropriated and softened to a level that is ritually suitable for the sensibilities of contemporary urban Marwaris. To reflect on Bhairav's sweetening, the author draws primarily on the deity's history and current worship at Nakoda Teerth, a Shvetambar Jain temple complex in western Rajasthan, and on two Hindu Bhairav shrines, Kodamdesar and Toliyasar. Saul suggests that Bhairav's increasing popularity needs to be understood not as a singular Jain or Hindu phenomenon but rather as one element in a broader Marwari interest in Rajasthani "miracle" deities. In addition to noting that Bhairav's sweetening should be understood as a dynamic negotiation between village customs and Marwari patronage and sensibilities, the chapter suggests that Bhairav has been transformed at shrines that receive Marwari donations. Saul argues that the (urban) middle-class desire for increased prosperity, which has become particularly visible in India's current era of economic liberalization and globalization, informs how many urbanites approach miracle deities.

Part 4, "Narrative and Visual Spaces," is the volume's final section and includes four chapters. First in the section is "Envisioning Kameshvari and the Mahavidyas in Women's *Nam* of the Kamakhya Temple and Pilgrimage Site," wherein Patricia Dold analyzes hymns, *Nam*, that are performed by groups of women, with a leader, a *Namati*, in various ritual contexts at the Kamakhya temple site in Assam. Women of all ages and marital status participate as singers and as *Namati* and preserve these hymns from one generation to the next. The goddess Kamakhya and her forms are the focus for many *Nam*, two of which are discussed in detail in Dold's chapter. Similar to other hymns, the lyrics in these two *Nam* describe and unfold the multifaceted layers of Kamakhya and her manifestations, as both pleasant and terrifying; gentle and violent; beautiful and gruesome. Placing each hymn within its performance context, the author juxtaposes each *Nam* and the Sanskritic puranic texts that implicitly or explicitly inform each *Nam*. This analysis demonstrates the complex relationship between intensification and *saumyatization* in play both historically and in contemporary lived religion at Kamakhya. Historically, the analysis provides evidence for the persistence of intensification through centuries-old processes of *saumyatization* as an exoteric and devotional Shakta religiosity emerges in connection with the Kamakhya site and its goddess. That such *Nam* have been preserved and performed by women residents of the Kamakhya site for generations suggests that contemporary religious life at Kamkhya continues to value both *raudra* (fearsome, intense, violent) and *saumya* (pleasant, gentle, and auspicious) qualities.

In "Sanskritizing and Saffronizing the Rabies Goddess: Sweetening and Intensification in the Folklore of Hadkai Mata," Darry Dinnell argues that Hadkai's vernacular folklore has served as a means of sweetening this goddess for the Dalits and Devipujaks who worship her, helping them attest to and perform their own *sattvik* (pure) nature and thereby challenging their exclusion from "proper" Hinduism. Given a paucity of texts and images, he primarily relies on the rich tradition of oral folklore narratives that has developed among Hadkai worshipers like the Dalit Valmiki Samaj and the Devipujaks. He shows how folklore is a realm in which members of these oppressed-class groups can safeguard the goddess while also defending themselves against stereotypes perpetuated by outsiders. Indeed, worshipers' own narratives imagine the goddess as unquestionably *sattvik*, having originated from the efforts of Sanskritic goddesses and devout Brahmans. According to Dinnell, this follows patterns of sweetening or softening seen among other goddesses in Gujarat and beyond, including Sanskritization. But Hadkai's folklore is unique in that it reiterates a *sattvik*, Sanskritic, and even brahmanic character *that always was*. Such claims serve to counteract some of the notoriety around Hadkai and her faithful and also establish a *sattvik* precedent for these groups. Along these lines, Hadkai's shrines demarcate spaces in which Devipujaks, Valmikis, and other marginalized groups can cultivate sensibilities that correspond with those of the supposed elites of mainstream, Smarta-styled Hinduism. While Hadkai's folklore reflects the mix of *sattvik* and *tamasik* (impure), elite and nonelite, and upper-caste and lower-caste sensibilities found in the goddess's iconography and at her worship sites and protests some of the discrimination by caste Hindus and others against her followers, it also promotes elite values.

The following chapter, "Sensational Poetics: The Modern Visual Contextualities of Tiruvalluvar's *Tirukkural*," is written by Amy-Ruth Holt. It analyzes how in Tamil Nadu, one popular source of modern political imagery is the *Tirukkural*, the poetic text of the possible Jain or low-caste saint, Tiruvalluvar, who is credited with composing this sacred collection of *kurals*, or poetic couplets. Today, this probably 450–500 CE text frequently appears contextualized within modern visual narratives, even though most of its verses are without clear visual descriptions or plot-oriented situations, being instead more like proverbs or moral sayings. These more recent visuals either sweeten or intensify the original verses of the *Tirukkural* in an effort to render it more sensationally powerful in its distribution and curation as a model Tamil historical text. With the *Tirukkural's* new visuality, Holt's chapter demonstrates how its modern narratives are often depicted in two opposing manners: through the intensification of the verse's consequences that appear as visual warnings of "what not to do," and through the sweetening of positive outcomes that romanticize this text. Since the agentive context of being in a specific time and space gives material objects their meaning, examples in this study were taken from three different contextualities— national memorial monuments and sculptures sponsored between 1968 and 1999 in Tamil Nadu by the political leaders C. N. Annadurai (1909–1969) and M. Karunanidhi (1924–2018); religious illustrations in three different editions of the *Tirukkural* distributed by the Kauai Hindu Monastery in Hawaii from 1999 to 2005; and Tamil films that include blockbuster hits released from the 1950s to the 2010s. When visually analyzed within these assembled contexts, modern narratives of the *Tirukkural* reveal an underlying sensory teleology, composed of the aesthetic binaries of sweetening and intensification that respond to a growing imaging tradition of nationalistic language devotion.

In the volume's final chapter, "Kali in a Time of Hurt Sentiments," Rachel Fell McDermott examines two related controversies that involved the goddess Kali, one in Toronto and the other in West Bengal, and developed between 2021 and 2023. She asks if the sweetened goddess of Bengal, who in the eighteenth century opened out from her elite, esoteric, fearsome Tantric background to become accessible through devotional movements (*bhakti*) to a wider public, currently makes way for the revitalization of certain fierce practices or beliefs or the creation of new ones. Analyzing two case studies, the short film *Kaali* (2022) and the debates around Kali and her worship in West Bengal's recent elections, McDermott examines the current canonization of the goddess and the broader issues of homogenization and rising majoritarian perspectives. She discusses how Kali's ability to meld seeming opposites—including her darker and sweetened sides, and her antinomian and transcendent characteristics—seems difficult to accept in spaces championing brahmanical values, whether in Toronto, New Delhi, or elsewhere in our interlinked world. She also examines the role of a rhetoric of hurt religious sentiments and the nature of offense in such transformations, showing that intensification at the hands of vocal Bengali devotees and ritual actors, artists, playwrights, and scholars would seem to provoke consternation or worse to a pan-North-India-dominated public. Applying Jan Assmann's cultural memory theory, McDermott concludes that canonization demonstrates the creation of a general rule for theological, iconographic, and historical interpretation that is enforceable and enforced by the culture of offense.

In sum, this volume brings together a broad range of innovative studies on the sweetening of Hindu traditions, on their intensification, and on the interrelation of these currents. The individual chapters do so by presenting new case study material, critically discussing the sweetening and intensification processes involved, and situating this material in terms of broader developments and trends in Hindu traditions. The case studies point to the advantages of researching sweetening and intensification patterns for furthering our broader understanding of the past, present, and potential futures of these traditions. As Hindu traditions continue to expand to new settings, including but not limited to new diaspora and media contexts, the long-established yet ever-changing arrangements of sweet—neutral—intense unfold in new ways as well.

References

Allocco, Amy L. 2018. "Flower Showers for the Goddess: Borrowing, Modification, and Ritual Innovation in Tamil Nadu." In *Ritual Innovation: Strategic Interventions in South Asian Religion*, edited by Brian K. Pennington and Amy L. Allocco, 129–48. State University of New York Press.

Allocco, Amy L. 2020. "Vernacular Practice, Gendered Tensions, and Interpretive Ambivalence in Hindu Death, Deification, and Domestication Narratives." *Journal of Hindu Studies* 13 (2): 144–71. https://doi.org/10.1093/jhs/hiaa007.

Allocco, Amy L. 2021. "Bringing the Dead Home: Hindu Invitation Rituals in Tamil South India." *Journal of the American Academy of Religion* 89 (1): 103–42. https://doi.org/10.1093/jaarel/lfab026.

Arumugam, Indira. 2015. " 'The Old Gods Are Losing Power!': Theologies of Power and Rituals of Productivity in a Tamil Nadu Village." *Modern Asian Studies* 49 (3): 753–86. https://doi.org/10.1017/S0026749X1400016X.

Brown, C. Mackenzie. 1990. *The Triumph of the Goddess: The Canonical Models of Theological Visions of the Devī-Bhāgāvata Purāṇa*. State University of New York Press.

Coburn, Thomas B. 1988. *Devī Mahātmyā: The Crystallization of the Goddess Tradition*. Motilal Banarsidass.

Fuller, C. J. 1992. *The Camphor Flame: Popular Hinduism and Society in India*. Princeton University Press.

Halperin, Ehud. 2019. *The Many Faces of a Hindu Goddess: Haḍimbā, Her Devotees, and Religion in Rapid Change*. Oxford University Press.

Harman, William. 2012. "From Fierce to Domesticated: Mariyamman Joins the Middle Class." *Nidān: International Journal for the Study of Hinduism* 24 (December): 41–65.

Hawley, John Stratton, and Donna Marie Wulff, eds. 1996. *Devī: Goddesses of India*. University of California Press.

Hiltebeitel, Alf, ed. 1989. *Criminal Gods and Demon Devotees: Essays on the Guardians of Popular Hinduism*. State University of New York Press.

Kassam, Tazim R., and Eliza F. Kent, eds. 2013. *Lines in Water: Religious Boundaries in South Asia*. Syracuse University Press.

Kumar, P. Pratap. 2014. *Contemporary Hinduism*. Routledge.

McDermott, Rachel Fell. 2001. *Mother of My Heart, Daughter of My Dreams: Kālī and Umā in the Devotional Poetry of Bengal*. Oxford University Press.

McDermott, Rachel Fell. 2011. *Revelry, Rivalry, and Longing for the Goddesses of Bengal: Fortunes of Hindu Festivals*. Columbia University Press.

Meyer, Eveline. 1986. *Aṅkāḷaparamēcuvari: A Goddess of Tamilnadu, Her Myths and Cult*. Steiner Verlag Wiesbaden GmbH.

Michaels, Axel, Cornelia Vogelsanger, and Annette Wilke, eds. 1996. *Wild Goddesses in India and Nepal: Proceedings of an International Symposium, Berne and Zurich, November 1994*. Peter Lang.

Orr, Leslie. 2005. "Identity and Divinity: Boundary-Crossing Goddesses in Medieval South India." *Journal of the American Academy of Religion* 73 (1): 9–43. doi:10.1093/jaarel/lfi003.

Padma, Sree. 2013. *Vicissitudes of the Goddess: Reconstructions of the Gramadevata in India's Religious Traditions*. Oxford University Press.

Simmons, Caleb, Moumita Sen, and Hillary Rodrigues, eds. 2018. *Nine Nights of the Goddess: The Navarātri Festival in South Asia*. State University of New York Press.

Sinha, Vineeta. 2016. *A New God in the Diaspora? Muneeswaran Worship in Contemporary Singapore*. NUS Press.

Srinivas, M. N. 1952. *Religion and Society Among the Coorgs of South India*. Clarendon.

Urban, Hugh B. 2019. "The Cradle of Tantra: Modern Transformations of a Tantric Centre in Northeast India from Nationalist Symbol to Tourist Destination." *South Asia: Journal of South Asian Studies* 42 (2): 256–77. https://doi.org/10.1080/00856401.2019.157060.

Waghorne, Joanne Punzo. 2001. "The Gentrification of the Goddess." *International Journal of Hindu Studies* 5 (3): 227–67.

Waghorne, Joanne Punzo. 2004. *Diaspora of the Gods: Modern Hindu Temples in an Urban Middle-Class World*. Oxford University Press.

White, David Gordon, ed. 2000. *Tantra in Practice*. Princeton, NJ: Princeton University Press.

Zeiler, Xenia. 2012a. "Female Danger: 'Evil,' Inauspiciousness, and Their Symbols in Representations of South Asian Goddesses." *Nidan: Journal for the Study of Hinduism* 24: 100–117. https://hdl.handle.net/10520/EJC131231.

Zeiler, Xenia. 2012b. "Transformations in the Textual Tradition of Dhūmāvatī: Changes of the Tantric Mahāvidyā Goddess in Concept, Ritual, Function and Iconography." In *Transformations and Transfer of Tantra in Asia and Beyond*, edited by Istvan Keul, 165–94. De Gruyter.

Zeiler, Xenia. 2019. "Eradicated with Blood: Text and Context of Animal Sacrifice in Tantric and Tantra-Influenced Rituals." *International Journal of Hindu Studies* 23 (2): 165–77. https://doi.org/10.1007/s11407-019-09260-5.

Part 1

Temples, Localities, and Deities

1

A Divine Dust-Up

Diverging Trajectories of Local Gods in Garhwal

Brian K. Pennington

A scholarly truism holds that Indian gods are perpetually on the move. This assertion generally refers to physical mobility. Deity procession is a central practice of Hinduism, and Hindu sacralization of space results in the transplantation of Hindu deities across the globe (Branfoot 2007; Jacobsen 2022). Hindu gods, like gods everywhere, however, are also on the move temporally: they transform as they travel across history. Their fortunes ebb and flow. They accumulate new narratives and new characteristics. Technologies and stylistic modes for depicting deities evolve and with them shared conceptions of the gods and goddesses. Some become fiercer while others mellow (see, e.g., Allocco 2018; Arumugam 2015; McDermott 2004; Waghorne 2004). This volume asks us to think about the diverging trajectories that some gods might take as the worldly circumstances with which they intersect shift. What strategies or dynamics does the intensification of a divine figure's personality or a group's ritual practices reveal? Under what conditions and to what ends do gods sweeten their demeanor?

Hindu traditions tell many stories of divine transformations, capturing in myth long historical processes that testify to the gods' plasticity. Often conflict is a central theme in these memories of the deities' rise and fall. Various epic and puranic narratives depict the ascension of Krishna, the most saccharine of all deities, over Indra, cosmic might personified, leaving an emasculated Indra in relative obscurity (Haberman 2006, 111). The confrontation of Shiva and Sati with Sati's father, Daksha, provokes her protest suicide and launches Shiva into a grief-stricken cosmic rampage as pieces of her corpse fall to earth and establish goddess worship within Hindu practice; Daksha is seldom heard from again (Courtright 2011). This chapter tells a story of divine conflict between two locally important territorial deities in Garhwal, a linguistic and cultural region in the Himalayan state of Uttarakhand, that marks an inflection point in their relative status as one asserts dominance over the other.[1]

This story, however, takes place not in mythical time and space but in the present, in a public square in full view of the deities' devotees, who are themselves, of course, implicated in the divergence of the deities' paths and the altercation over a small, delimited space that seals the gods' respective fates. Their physical and legal confrontation over a drab, concrete platform highlights in sharp relief Aftab Jassal's (2016) contention that in Garhwal a deity's seat, its *sthaan*, the place where he or she is most fully and firmly established, is emblematic of a deity's real presence and level of prestige. Deity place-making practices are central to the construction of Garhwali communities, as Jassal notes, and also, as this chapter will show, the reconstruction of those communities and the renegotiation of intergroup relationships. In the encounter that leaves both deities transformed, we observe the dialectical relationship between sweetening and intensification and the manner in which those tendencies may be tempered, modified, or calibrated in response to specific local dynamics. If "sweetening" and "intensification" name broad categories of changes that deities may undergo over time, this chapter helps to show how together they mark out a repertoire of strategies for asserting and negotiating divine power and status. Intensification can entail not just an emphasis on the ferocities associated with some Hindu deities, but also the more blunt exercise of dominance. If the cherubification the editors mention in the introduction is one common form that sweetening may take, in this story we see how it can also imply submission, as deities' respective fortunes rise and fall.

A Divine Conflict

Around noon on Makar Sankranti 2020 (January 15) my phone pinged with a series of insistent WhatsApp messages from Ajay,[2] a close friend in the small city of Uttarkashi, a pilgrimage hub and spiritual center on the main Himalayan tributary of the Ganga River in the state of Uttarakhand. Makar Sankranti marks the passage of the sun into Capricorn (Makara), observed in this region of Garhwal by the march of hundreds of village deities and their human escorts to Uttarkashi to bathe in the frigid Ganga in the predawn hours. In a typical year, at midday, the region's two most powerful local deities, Kandaar Devta and Hari Maharaj, jointly open Maagh Mela, a monthlong festival that features nightly cultural and religious programming and a crowded carnival-cum-market in the Ram Lila (parade) grounds in the center of the city (Negi and Singh 1996).

My phone soon filled with photos and videos conveying images common to Makar Sankranti in Uttarkashi. Festively adorned gods and goddesses bobbed in the streets headed to the river, each borne aloft in a palanquin called a *doli* by barefoot, upper-caste male devotees from the deity's home village (fig. 1.1). Each was accompanied not only by other villagers who had come on foot or by jeep taxi to Uttarkashi but also by a few *bajgi*, men of oppressed Dalit castes carrying ritual musical instruments, the most important of which is the *dhol*, a two-headed drum worn around the neck and played with sticks. Other photos revealed that the atmosphere on this festival day, however, was clearly tense. One divine retinue stood facing off

Figure 1.1. Doli procession across the Bhagirathi River on Makar Sankranti. Uttarkashi, 2016. *Source:* Photo by the author.

against another. Angry faces and raised fists dotted the crowd. In the videos, there was loud shouting and the sound of men issuing a sharp, rising-pitch whistle that projects defiance and invites violence. I texted Ajay quickly to confirm identification: "Are those Kandaar Devta and Hari Maharaj?" Indeed, they are, came the reply.

From my office in North Carolina, I was unable to discern exactly what was happening or the nature of the confrontation, but this was obviously not the usual chain of choreographed events that bring these two deities together to open Uttarkashi's most important annual festival. I was highly intrigued and looked forward to returning to Uttarkashi in a couple of months to follow up on these provocative developments. Kandaar Devta and Hari Maharaj had served as cohosts and patrons of Maagh Mela throughout the living memory of everyone I had ever asked about it. I had studied the evolution of religious practice in this pilgrimage city for over twenty years, and I felt certain that these dramatic developments would reverberate well beyond this festival. COVID-19 was not only to prevent my travel to India for the next three years, but also to close down Maagh Mela itself and effectively cement the day's dramatic developments as the accepted status quo for the foreseeable future. By the summer of 2023, when I was able to visit Uttarkashi again, the regional preeminence of Kandaar Devta, including his conquest of territory once sacred to Hari Maharaj, the legal title to the same, and the resentment-tinged acquiescence of Hari Maharaj and his devotees, seemed accepted facts.

Territorial Deities

Kandaar Devta and Hari Maharaj belong to a class of deities designated by the phrase *devi-devta* (gods and goddesses) or often by just the catch-all *devta*, phrases and terms used all over North India to refer to deities but which, in Garhwal, designate this class of local deities specifically. These figures may sometimes be identified with deities of pan-Indian Hinduism like Shiva, Krishna, and Durga, but even when they are characterized in this secondary fashion, in almost all circumstances their identity as local *devi*s and *devta*s and their association with local stories, sites, and territories are dominant (Berti 2009b, 117–18). The *devi-devta* rule over specific, delimited territories in Garhwal, and they often jealously guard their rights against neighboring *devta*s and involve their devotees in their conflicts (Bindi 2012;

Sutherland 2004). This territoriality is a central defining characteristic of the deities of the Indian Himalayas, particularly in the modern states of Himachal Pradesh and Uttarakhand.

Before the Gurkhas of Nepal conquered these areas of the Himalayas starting in the late eighteenth century and were later expelled by the British, who asserted administrative authority over the mountains in 1815 (Handa 2002, 167–89; Saklani 1987, 29–57), this region was a collection of small independent kingdoms that maintained relationships of rivalry and alliance among themselves, often secured through strategic royal marriage. After Indian independence in 1947, the "princely hill states," as the British called them, joined independent India. Eventually some were gathered into the state of Himachal Pradesh and two of the larger former kingdoms, Garhwal and Kumaon, were joined first to Uttar Pradesh and then, in response to grassroots activism, granted their own independent statehood in 2000 as Uttaranchal, renamed Uttarakhand in 2006 (Elmore 2016; Kumar 2011; Tillin 2013, 95–108).

The territories of those kingdoms were each, therefore, a patchwork of small and large areas over whose residents specific deities exercised their own forms of sovereignty. In the days of the kings, rajas of these hill states could cultivate favor with the *devi*s and *devta*s of their kingdoms through land grants and other means, but the *devi-devta* functioned as a semiautonomous ruler, capable of challenging the king as well as authenticating his authority (Berti 2009a). In local discourse these deities are very often explicitly figured according to various administrative and political metaphors, as god-kings, policemen, or politicians, underscoring their juridical and social functions (Jassal 2016; Sax 2003). The *devi-devta*, therefore, exercised specific, concrete forms of authority over territories with specific boundaries, generally articulating their will through human oracles. The people inhabiting the villages in any deity's territory were, by virtue of their residence in that village, whether through birth or marriage, in well defined, often intimate, forms of sovereign/subject relations.[3] For untold decades our two main antagonists from Makar Sankranti 2020, Kandaar Devta and Hari Maharaj, had ruled in this manner over neighboring territories separated by the main tributary of the Ganga River called the Bhagirathi. Geologic, economic, and political upheaval over the last fifty to one hundred years, however, has entailed the emergence of a fiercer form of Kandaar Devta as the dominant partner in a long-simmering rivalry, a preeminence secured over the course of the COVID-19 pandemic and facilitated by the restrictions on social gathering and interaction it imposed.

Rival Deities and Their Contested Seat

According to local oral tradition, Kandaar Devta's *murti* (image) was discovered during the rule of the Garhwal king, Raja Sudarshan Shah (1815–1857), when a farmer ploughing his fields turned it up in an area now in Uttarkashi and immediately adjacent to a sacred plaza called Chamala ki Chauri. Hearing of the *murti's* discovery, the king ordered it brought to his palace in Tehri and placed it in his temple with his other gods and goddesses, principal among them Rajrajeshwari, the family goddess of the Garhwal royal dynasty. In the morning, when the king went to do his morning *puja* (worship) at the temple, he saw to his surprise that Kandaar Devta's *murti*, which he had placed at the feet of Rajrajeshwari, was now sitting above all the other *murti*s. He moved it back down to its original place but then discovered again the next morning that it had moved itself up above all the others. As this became a daily occurrence, the king recognized the god's power and sent the *murti* to live in a high place—in Sangrali, a village on Varunavat Mountain that rises over Uttarkashi—as he seemed to prefer (Uniyal 2022, 18–19). This story is widely shared in Uttarkashi itself and would seem to have mere local significance as a tale of this minor god's mischief in the royal household. I was surprised, therefore, when a member of the Garhwal royal family I was meeting for the first time in 2023, learning that I was working in Uttarkashi, said in response, "that Kandaar Devta from there—he is a funny guy," and then told me the most detailed version of the story I had ever heard. Many local sources say that Kandaar Devta is a form of Shiva and, whether that association is a long-standing one or an identity acquired more recently, it was fully secured when a new temple was built in the city of Uttarkashi for him in 2007–8 and a local Brahman devotee composed Sanskrit verses praising Shiva that were carved into the marble altar of the temple. We might read those verses and the identification of Kandaar Devta with Shiva they clearly imply as a form of sweetening, an almost literal Sanskritization that elevates Kandaar Devta into the pan-Hindu pantheon, but the power and status of this identification also hints at the intensification that comes to play out.

Hari Maharaj's principal seat, his *sthaan*, sits high atop Kubja, a mountain that stands across the Bhagirathi River from Uttarkashi. Local people identify him as a form of Skanda, son of Shiva and brother to Ganesh, who is also known by the name Kartikeya in North India. His origin story recalls that the powerful god Indra had lived in that remote area. Once when he was being harassed by the great demon Tarakaasura, Indra summoned the deities for their assistance, and Hari Maharaj flew there from Mount Kailash on the peacock vehicle associated with Skanda and defeated Tarakaasura.[4] Indra granted him this *sthaan* and authority over the territory of Baragaddi, extending over the area on the side of the Ganga opposite to Uttarkashi, encircled by high mountains that separate the Bhagirathi River valley from the Mandakini River valley to the east. Compared to the territory of Kandaar Devta, an urbanizing space well connected by a major pilgrimage road to larger cities below, it is relatively wilder and less populated. A ribbon of houses, shops, and schools runs along the river across from Uttarkashi, but beyond them, the mountains of Baragaddi rise steeply. Lovely villages with well-built houses dot the mountainsides, each of them governed and protected by Hari Maharaj.

For the last one hundred to three hundred years, the sacred plaza called Chamala ki Chauri has stood on the opposite side of the Ganga, the area ruled by Kandaar Devta, in the historical core of Uttarkashi called Barahat, which is also the pre-twentieth-century name for the town that would become Uttarkashi. According to some local oral tradition, however, that site previously stood on the other side of the river, in Baragaddi, the territory of Hari Maharaj, and functioned as his *sthaan*. One local etymology of the names, reported also by F. V. Raper in 1810, is based on North Indian words for twelve (*barah*) and market (*haat*) (Raper 1810, 476). By this derivation, Barahat was the market area for the twelve-village territory of Baragaddi, a theory well supported by built history and other evidence, including further British testimony that this small neighborhood was a bustling trading site (Fraser 1820, 494). This oral history holds that a catastrophic flood no one has dated definitively for me altered the course of the Ganga, leaving Chamala ki Chauri on the Barahat/Uttarkashi side of the river.[5] With the shift of the river, Kandaar Devta, whose main temple had stood well above Uttarkashi in the village of Sangrali, moved to assert his rights over this ritually charged public space and to expand his sphere of authority into an area that had been under Hari Maharaj but now sat on Kandaar Devta's side of the river that separated their territories (fig. 1.2). If all of this is true, the shifting of the river and the subsequent growth of the modern city of Uttarkashi has seemingly also entailed an elevation in the authority and status of Kandaar Devta and the relegation of Hari Maharaj to a rule over a poorer, more mountainous, and less accessible region than Uttarkashi, the commercial center and district headquarters where most of the businesses that serve seasonal *yatri*s (pilgrims) in the Himalayas are situated. Against this backdrop, Makar Sankranti 2020 appeared an inflection

Figure 1.2. Map of the gods' approximate territories. *Source:* Created by Sakshi Sharma. Used with permission.

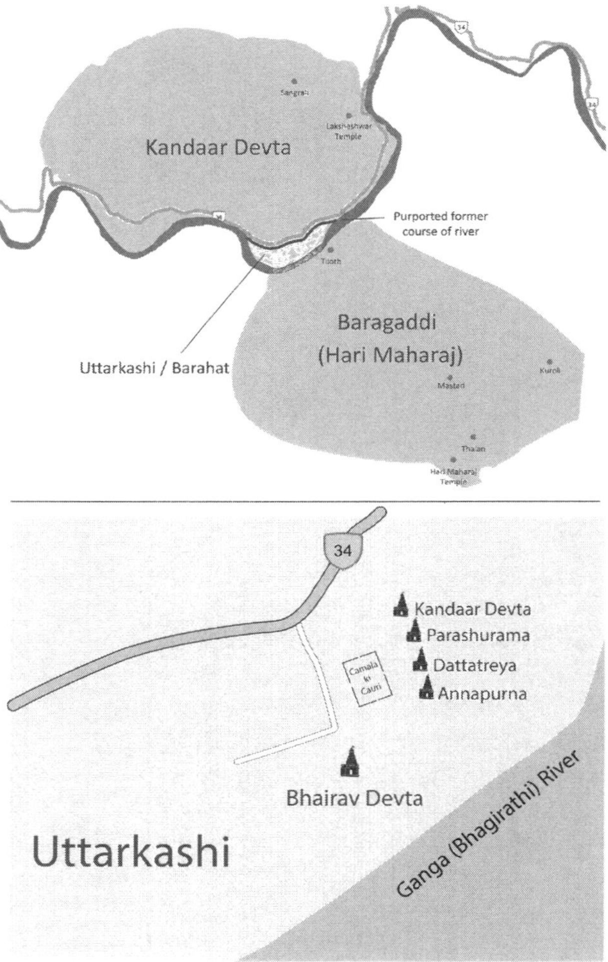

point in the long struggle between these two deities, the moment when tension over rights to this sacred plaza approached its dramatic resolution.

Chamala ki Chauri stands in front of a fifty-meter stretch of small temples that various pieces of evidence suggest are well over three hundred years old in an area of Uttarkashi that forms the heart of Barahat, which was the old name of an important village on this site along the Ganga River before it began to grow in the British period into a modern town later named Uttarkashi to claim ties to the sacred city of Banaras, also known as Kashi, in the plains (Sankrityayan 1953, 1:347). The southernmost of these temples, close to the river, is a small shrine to Bhairav Devta, the area's guardian deity. To his north stands a line of other religious structures: a temple to Annapurna; an old, unoccupied slate-roofed building with a signboard naming it a temple to Dattatreya to which I will return shortly; and a Parashurama temple that some colonial sources suggest was one of the more important temples in town that still features the most impressive antique iconographic and architectural features (Fraser 1820, 494–95; Raturi 1928, 65).[6] Just beyond a structure used for festival staging and cooking rises a temple unlike the others in age, scale, and activity—the Kandaar Devta temple that has played an increasingly important role in the ritual life of this small pilgrimage city since its construction in 2008. While the spacious Ram Lila grounds half a kilometer a way host large public events, Barahat, centered on Chamala ki Chauri, pulses with a distinctly Garhwali ritual energy and cultural significance that local activists and social leaders have invested in it over the past decade.

At the semiurban heart of the modern city, a few hundred meters away, stands the Kashi Vishvanath Temple, rebuilt in 1857 by Khaneti Devi, wife of Maharaja Sudarshan Shah of Tehri Garhwal following the destruction of a temple there in the devastating 1803 earthquake (Handa and Jain 2003, 130–36).[7] Kashi Vishvanath still functions as the patron deity of the town and is well patronized by pilgrims and other visitors to Uttarkashi, but a burgeoning Garhwali heritage movement has elevated Barahat and Chamala ki Chauri as well as Kandaar Devta himself to new levels of importance, projecting them as embodiments of a regional authenticity that exceeds the boundaries of the more nationally normative, Shaiva Hinduism represented in Kashi Vishvanath.

Uttarkashi's Maagh Mela

I participated in Maagh Mela in the Januarys of 2014, 2016, and 2018, and my observations in those years helped establish my understanding of what had been commonly accepted as the festival's regular ritual process and sequence. To summarize briefly, prior to 2020, in the predawn hours of Makar Sankranti, hundreds of *devi*s and *devta*s processed from villages outside Uttarkashi to the banks of the Bhagirathi River, a major tributary of the Ganga at whose source one hundred kilometers upriver from Uttarkashi the descent of the Ganga from the heavens is commemorated at Gangotri. Among those many divine travelers to appear in Uttarkashi with human escorts in the mornings of this annual festival was Hari Maharaj, who arrived in his standard processional form, a silver *dhol*, or two-headed drum played by *bajgi*s, Dalit musicians, and ritual specialists. Hari Maharaj was typically accompanied by a larger retinue of human companions than all the other *devi*s and *devta*s in Uttarkashi on Makar Sankranti morning. Following closely behind him in their *doli*s were two other important deities from Baragaddi, Naag Raja, a deputy *devta* to Hari Maharaj in a pattern not uncommon in Garhwal, and Khand Dvari Devi, whose maternal uncle, or *maama*, is Kandaar Devta. Around noon, Hari Maharaj and his retinue processed to Chamala ki Chauri, where they and the residents of villages from across the river in Baragaddi danced for an hour or so under a sacred peepul tree, some of them experiencing deity possession, in a highly charged ritual atmosphere. Their headdress made from the tail of the *chauri gai*, a Himalayan yak/cow crossbreed that lives at high altitudes, clearly marks devotees of Hari Maharaj, helping to convey an otherworldly ferocity associated with the deity's character (fig. 1.3). During their time on the plaza

Figure 1.3. Hari Maharaj devotees dancing on Chamala ki Chauri on Makar Sankranti. Uttarkashi, 2018. *Source:* Photo by the author.

hundreds of people gathered to watch, including some who had crossed the river with Hari Maharaj as well as many from the Barahat side who were captivated by the visitors' distinctive dress and their emotionally and rhythmically intense dance style. The retinue of Hari Maharaj then slowly processed to the Ram Lila grounds, where they moved through dense crowds, eventually converging with Kandaar Devta and his retinue. Together, they entered the vast tented enclosure where the main cultural and religious programming of the monthlong festival would take place, proceeding deliberately to the elevated stage, where they performed a tense but choreographed standoff that concluded with their jointly signaling the opening of Maagh Mela. By day's end, Hari Maharaj had left the city to stay in a nearby village and the festival's busy schedule of formal programming was underway. The rivalry between the two *devta*s was openly acknowledged and enacted in these moments, but it was patterned and contained. In 2018, one festivalgoer explained the relationship to me this way: "They are rival *devta*s, who sometimes fight, and so do their people, but today everyone comes together."

Traces of Historical Conflict

Why, then, had 2020's opening to Maagh Mela unfolded so differently? Why had the established ritual containment of the neighboring deities' rivalry failed? One set of answers must take account of that dilapidated, seemingly abandoned structure in the very center of Barahat's temple precinct, the building currently identified by a signboard as the "Dattatrey *Sthaanam*," that is, a seat or temple for the Hindu god Dattatrey. Since my early years working in Uttarkashi, the building had always interested me. It was the one structure in this area of the city that had not, like its temple neighbors, had its distinctive Garhwali architectural elements replaced with brick and cement. At the time it had no other identifying features or signs beyond the empty niches in the wall at the entrance, indicating its prior function as a temple. Itinerant *sadhu*s frequently slept there and lounged outside smoking hashish. It was surrounded by contemporary apartment buildings, businesses, and the other temples mentioned above, whose historic central shrines were intact but enclosed by roofs and brightly painted antechambers constructed of modern materials. I regularly asked what the building was and why it was in this condition, but my questions only elicited shrugs or vague conjectures about who owned it.

Much later I discovered nineteenth-century mentions of the Parashuram temple next to Dattatrey in colonial-era sources and began to discern that this small neighborhood was deeply implicated in important historical conflict and change (Fraser 1820, 494; Raturi 1928, 65). Over time, I began to appreciate the violence centered on this spot that had attended shifts in regional power and the social, political, and ecological disruptions that were common to the area. Local amateur historians have told me that in the mid-twentieth century, the great Hindi travelogue writer Rahul Sankrityayan had written that the Dattatrey *Sthaanam* was actually a Buddhist temple that had housed a Buddhist *murti*, perhaps serving the Tibetan and Nepali traders who came to trade in the Barahat market. The local rumor that the government of India removed the Buddha *murti* from the temple in the early Independence period to undercut Chinese claims to the area finds support from at least one regional historian (Handa 2005, 78). One such elderly historian who lived directly behind the Dattatrey *Sthaanam* is among those who have told me that the book in which Sankrityayan developed those claims had been banned in India and remains inaccessible; he said he himself had never seen it. Indeed, as I later discovered, Sankrityayan had written extensively about these sites in Uttarkashi in 1953, systematically laying out evidence that this region had previously been a Tibetan-ruled area and that Buddhism was openly practiced here up until the time he was writing. He reported that the *murti* was actually Dhaatumayii, the Buddhist form of the deity worshiped as Dattatrey in Hinduism, that it was established in the eleventh century by the Tibetan king Naagraaj, and that it was engraved with an identifying inscription in Tibetan (Sankrityayan 1953, 1:62 and 111–12).

There are ample additional reminders in the Uttarkashi District of the robust cultural and economic flows that once connected this region with areas now defined as Tibet or China. The names of towns and landmarks often reflect Tibetan and Chinese presence. Descendants of communities stranded in India when the border conflicts with China broke out in 1960–1962 remain in towns like Dunda, where prayer flags fly and Buddhist temples and practices are widely visible. The *chauri gai* tails that are used as head-dress by Hari Maharaj devotees were presumably sourced through Tibetan traders and suggest ancient ties between those communities. A twenty-six-foot-high trident commemorating the conquest of the region by rulers of the Khas kingdom centered in what is now western Nepal dating to roughly the thirteenth century is a focal point of local worship (Atkinson 2022, 512–13; Handa 2002, 53–57; Sankrityayan 1953, 1:347–49). Today priests at the Shakti Mandir that houses it identify the trident as Durga's weapon in the slaying of Mahishasura and cover over the inscription that indicates its human, rather than divine, origins. Further east in Garhwal the famous Badrinath temple that was closely identified with the Hindu kings of Tehri

Garhwal previously housed a Tibetan deity, and the temple was frequented by Tibetan devotees (David 2017). Traces such as these disclose the long history of conflict over this rather small but strategically situated region that offers passage to the source of the Ganga River and the riches of Tibet. In light of this evidence, we might begin to read the augmentation of Kandaar Devta's power as a moment in the longer trajectory since Independence of the erasure of ethnic and religious diversity and the imposition of more normatively Hindu forms.

An Elephant Parade

This tangled history brings us to the most recent contest between two Garhwali deities and their devotees living on either side of a violent, shifting river that establishes the tense boundary between their respective spheres of authority. I alluded earlier to the possibility that this conflict was related to an increasingly assertive local heritage movement influencing the character of the Maagh Mela festival and its programming schedule by the time I started participating in 2014. Two of the leaders in that local heritage movement were well known to me by then, a regionally famous Garhwali folk singer and a journalist I will call Santosh. Together they formed Lokrang Uttarkashi (The Folk Colors of Uttarkashi), an organization to bring village artists from remote regions to Uttarkashi to perform during festivals and to teach folk performance to Garhwali youth. Santosh, like many others passionate about the preservation and revival of Garhwali language and culture whom I have known, was also an avid amateur historian, and he had dedicated himself particularly to understanding the history of Barahat. He was one of the principal people involved in the reinscription of "Barahat," the historical name of this ancient settlement along the Ganga, back onto modern Uttarkashi and the investment of that name with Garhwali cultural meaning.

Between 2014 and 2018, Lokrang Uttarkashi had effectively reignited interest in the performance of Pandav Nritya (known in the scholarly literature as Pandav Lila; see Sax 2002), an important Garhwali ritual performance tradition in which participants became possessed by the Pandava characters from the epic, the Mahabharata, and other village dance forms. They instituted a raucous annual all-day procession of Kandaar Devta on a cardboard elephant escorted by a dozen Pandava dancers departing from and returning to his glitzy temple near Chamala ki Chauri. Beginning at noon on the day after Makar Sankranti, the procession would wind through the city to the *ghat*s (steps) along the Ganga River, where performers would bathe the Pandavas' weapons and perform *pujas*. The procession would return to Chamala ki Chauri and his temple by evening. The Hathi ka Svang (Elephant Parade) now takes place annually on the day after Makar Sankranti and effectively extends the ritually charged atmosphere a day longer and encourages many of those who had traveled with their *devi*s and *devta*s from villages to prolong their stay in town and enjoy the attractions of Maagh Mela.

With the benefit of hindsight, the annual Hathi ka Svang appears to be a clear effort to assert the uncompromised authority of Kandaar Devta over the whole of Uttarkashi, especially Chamala ki Chauri, his ritual stewardship over Maagh Mela, and his preeminence over Hari Maharaj. Since the building of his temple in Uttarkashi in 2008, it has become a center of the city's ritual life. Prior to its construction, the Parashuram temple immediately adjacent to Chamala ki Chauri had served as the home temple for Maagh Mela (Tiwari and Khugshal 2001, 52–53), but it has now been displaced by the new Kandaar Devta temple, clearly not a neutral or hospitable space for Hari Maharaj. The Hathi ka Svang injects elements of both sweetening and intensification into the atmosphere. Exuberant crowds follow a jaunty cardboard elephant, a bouncy Kandaar Devta riding atop and leading the crowd (fig. 1.4). Underlying the festive mood, however, is an assertion and

Figure 1.4. Kandaar Devta on his elephant during the Hathi ka Svaang. Note the *chauri gai* tail indicating the presence of Hari Maharaj devotees. Uttarkashi, 2018. *Source:* Photo by the author.

projection of Kandaar Devta's dominance. As with processions all over the Hindu world, this parade makes social and political claims to territorial authority in unspoken but unmistakable and, from Baragaddi points of view, confrontational and perhaps menacing ways.

When I began to look into the open conflict between the two *devta*s that began in 2020, I came to understand that a local ayurvedic doctor, who was also the hereditary custodian of the Bhairav Devta shrine, had been a behind-the-scenes organizer and financier of the Hathi ka Svang. I had met Dr. Thapliyar for the first time in late January 2018 to probe his reputed vast knowledge of local history. At that time, he was still deeply grieving the deaths of his son and infant grandchild exactly one year prior, when their car plunged over a cliff into the Ganga, a tragedy I will return to in a moment.

Makar Sankranti 2020

According to firsthand reports, on Makar Sankranti 2020, Hari Maharaj proceeded to Chamala ki Chauri as he typically would, accompanied by Khand Dvari Devi, whom some identify as his consort, and Nag Raja, his deputy. In the previous year, the old peepul tree around which Hari Maharaj would dance that had long stood at the center of the plaza had been cut down and an elevated concrete platform appeared in its place, constructed, I am told, specifically for Kandaar Devta. As Hari Maharaj approached, on the platform stood Kandaar Devta in his *doli*. Departing from the established script, he refused to descend and allow Hari Maharaj and his companion to dance. Given the Garhwali taboo against a woman entering into the company of her maternal uncle, Kandaar Devta's presence intentionally prevented Khand Dvari Devi's ascent. The *devta*'s intransigence was likely expected. In 2019 he had clearly communicated to Hari Maharaj, through ritual gesture and the words of his oracles, that he alone was the custodian of the whole of Maagh Mela and the sole authority over Chamala ki Chauri. The confrontation transmitted directly to my phone in North Carolina in 2020, it turns out, had been brewing for at least a year, and the anticipation of physical conflict was evident in the swelling crowd of Baragaddi residents, regarded as ignorant and rough villagers by those in Uttarkashi, estimated by one eyewitness to number over two thousand.

We have established that Hari Maharaj likely had historical precedent on his side. His case also had a number of sympathizers on both sides of the river. The Uttarkashi folk drama troupe, Samvedna Samuh, was already in dress rehearsals for their new play, *Nara Bijula*, a dramatic retelling of a beloved legend about two folk heroes from Baragaddi that featured on the stage at Maagh Mela a few nights later and helped to generate positive feelings for the people of the area. Kandaar Devta, however, had discovered a new and powerful tool for asserting his authority: the law. The timing of the next set of events is in some doubt, but in early 2020 Ajay reported to me by phone that he had learned that sometime in 2019, the legal owner of the land on which both the Dattatrey *Sthaanam* and Chamala ki Chauri stood, whose Rajput name was revealed in court documents, had deeded the site to a new legal owner, Kandaar Devta. The timing of that filing suggests that he and his collaborators were inspired by the Indian Supreme Court's 2019 ratification of Hindu deity Ram Lalla as a "juridical person" in Ayodhya's Ramjanmabhumi/Babrimasjid case (Siddiq vs. Das and Ors 2019, 164–67). On previous Makar Sankrantis, Kandaar Devta would have vacated the premises before Hari Maharaj and his entourage approached, but in 2020, emboldened by his recently conferred legal title, he stood his ground. Supporters on either side shouted at one another, and eventually Nag Raja, deputy and enforcer to Hari Maharaj, ascended, his escorts pushing aside those of Kandaar Devta. As the two deities faced off, the Dalit drummer for Nag Raja placed his ritually charged, two-headed *dhol* defiantly on the dais before Kandaar Devta. Dismissively, Kandaar Devta bowed low and brushed the *dhol* aside. A roar arose from the crowd as the drummer rushed to save it before it hit the ground. Had it done so, that friend assured me, a dozen people would have died in the ensuing violence. Instead, authorities sprang into action. A hundred police appeared on the scene, and the district magistrate and subdistrict magistrate directed them to keep the sides separated. With both deities stubbornly positioned on Chamala ki Chauri, the magistrates brokered an all-night negotiation that yielded the following agreement: on future Makar Sankrantis, Hari Maharaj would bring food to offer to Kandaar Devta, a grudging acknowledgment of the hierarchy they were encoding. Hari Maharaj and his entourage would be permitted to dance on Chamala ki Chauri for half an hour, and then they would have to move on, effectively ceding the space to Kandaar Devta.

Later in 2020 the journalist and cultural activist Santosh died suddenly of a heart attack at the age of forty. Uttarkashi mourned. Baragaddi, however, saw not senseless tragedy, but divine vengeance. Intemperate voices heralded an intensification of the conflict, announcing that Hari Maharaj had killed Santosh, just as he had killed Dr. Thapliyar's family members for his role in the plan to take over Chamala ki Chauri.

Alternate Narratives

As we well know, in the later months of 2020 and then with much greater ferocity in 2021, COVID-19 ravaged India. Uttarakhand was especially hard hit. Maagh Mela was canceled in 2021 and no public celebrations of it were permitted in 2022. In that span the virus eliminated any immediate opportunity for either rapprochement or escalation between the divine rivals, and my extended absence from India prevented me from pursuing my many questions about this intriguing development. I returned for the first time in 2023 to conduct interviews with devotees of both *devta*s and discovered a ritual and festival landscape much changed, the balance of power between them decisively altered.

On my first day back in Uttarkashi, I met Manoj Sharma, a leader of the Kandaar Devta supporters and a Sanskrit poet and lyricist who had composed the Sanskrit verses praising Kandaar Devta as a form of Shiva carved in the marble at the deity's new temple. With an easy laugh, he dismissed Hari Maharaj's claim to any rights on his side of the river. "Chamala ki Chauri is from our ancestors only," he insisted. But hadn't the river changed course and therefore the boundary between the territories? "That is the Baragaddi theory!," he laughed playfully again. "They also say that Kashi Vishvanath was in their territory—we reject that theory, too!" He said that Baragaddi people had become increasingly aggressive in forcing their claims in recent years, and Kandaar Devta's people were compelled to respond assertively. Baragaddi is a "demonic" place he said in English, switching to Hindi to clarify: it is a land where *asura*s (demons) live, and Baragaddi people have some reflection of that *asura* in them. Uttarkashi, on the other hand, he reminded me, is the abode of the god Shiva, leaving the obvious conclusion unstated.

Sharma expressed sincere regret that the conflict had reached such a fevered pitch: "We two people are not strangers. Our people marry there, and they marry here. My own sister married into Baragaddi, but now because of this conflict, her husband has cut off our relations." He blamed the two *devta*s, explaining that "when they get together, their egos get very big." He then talked about his efforts to repair the fractured relations. On Makar Sankranti 2023 he led a group of Kandaar Devta devotees to meet Hari Maharaj's retinue and garland them in a peace-making gesture. Greeting them with shouts of "Hari Maharaj ki jai!" (Victory to Hari Maharaj!), he implored them to enter the Kandaar Devta temple, "to end this matter before God," but only one member of their party stepped forward. Sharma then detailed the legal process by which they had ultimately dispossessed Hari Maharaj and rendered prior claims on both sides obsolete, but in his version of events, they pursued the legal strategy only after attempts at negotiating a settlement had failed. They approached the Rajput man in a neighboring town whose ancestor had held legal title to the plot on which Chamala ki Chauri stood and appealed to him, insisting, "It is your duty to register Chamala ki Chauri in the name of Kandaar Devta." Otherwise, they speculated darkly, "You will have great misfortune in your life, and your children's children will be punished." Browbeaten and frightened, he signed the document. Sharma exclaimed with jocular self-congratulations, "We scared him!" Because the current legal title was not entirely clear, they quietly issued a "no objection" notice, giving anyone who disputed their legal claim one month to file an appeal. And then they simply waited. The people of Baragaddi found out what had happened only six months later, long after the deed was legally executed, the matter entirely closed.

My old friend Ajay enthusiastically volunteered to go with me to talk to those from the Hari Maharaj side, where I had never traveled before. We hopped in his small hatchback automobile one warm morning and set off on what he declared, in a mock dramatic tone, as "Mission Baragaddi." We crossed the Bhagirathi River, and the road began to rise steeply. After enlisting help to push the small car up a muddy incline where a downpour had washed out the road, we came to Sara village and located Mukesh Das, the *bajgi* drummer recorded on video confronting Kandaar Devta. He ushered us into the tiny single room dwelling that his elderly parents occupied, his father sitting on the floor behind the manual sewing machine that provides many Dalits in the region a supplementary income. He complained bitterly about the Barahat resident who cut down the peepul tree sacred to Hari Maharaj and predicted his imminent death: "That was *paap* (sin)," he angrily concluded. Then he recalled for us the pivotal moment of the 2020 confrontation, declaring that Nag Raj's *dhol* he had been carrying thrust itself on the platform to confront Kandaar Devta: "It moved by itself!"

As we drove further up into the mountains, passing lush terraced fields growing lentils, potatoes, and wheat, Ajay admired the profusion of crops and the colorful, well-built houses. At Kuroli village high on Mt. Kubja we met a dapper Rajput man in a fine Garhwali wool jacket who showed us Khand Dvari Devi's bright home temple overlooking a gushing spring in the center of the village. Her *murti* was an unusual, sculpted form wearing a *chauri gai* tail for hair. He traced out the myths of all the local gods, recounted tales of *asuras* and mountain spirits, and described miraculous deeds by Hari Maharaj that he had witnessed with his own eyes, like a dry temple pond that was instantly filled. He delineated the precise path that the Bhagirathi River below had followed before it shifted and separated Hari Maharaj's people from their commercial and ritual center, Chamala ki Chauri. "Tibetans used to come to Barahat to trade black salt for millets," he explained. "Baragaddi and Barahat were the same place; Barahat was the big market of Baragaddi."

Halfway back down the mountain we found the house of Amit Nautiyal, a Brahman described to us as the deity's fiercest devotee. The exterior wall of the home was emblazoned with the phrase "Jai Hari Maharaj" in large letters. We had never met before, but I knew his face well from earlier years when I saw him dance on Chamala ki Chauri, and from Facebook, where several pages dedicated to Hari Maharaj often feature him under possession, in headdress, and sometimes inundated by a shower of milk, the substance used for bathing Hari Maharaj. The *devta* also regularly possessed other members of Nautiyal's male lineage before him, including his father, paternal uncle, and paternal grandfather. His social cachet as a Brahman along with his educated manner and public communications savvy have made him something of an unofficial leader of Hari Maharaj devotees.

Nautiyal began our conversation by explaining that Hari Maharaj was a form of Kartikeya and touched on some of the puranic myths about that son of Shiva, but then regularly called him "Shankar," a name for Shiva himself, throughout the afternoon. When I asked directly about the dispute with Kandaar Devta, he replied emphatically and directly, "Chamala ki Chauri is our place." He elaborated along lines that were now familiar to me: Baragaddi is not, properly speaking, adjacent to Barahat; it includes Barahat, and therefore, Chamala ki Chauri itself. "In my grandfathers' time, even Kashi Vishvanath itself was on this side of the river," he said, thereby advancing the claim that all of the most important religious sites in Uttarkashi were previously part of Baragaddi. In his account, Kandaar Devta and Hari Maharaj were "guru bhai," fictive brothers for having studied together under Dattatrey, connecting them both to that mysterious abandoned temple whose *murti* he said the government seized and locked up somewhere. I asked him about what happened on Makar Sankranti 2023, and his face softened. "They put a garland on me and said we were brothers," he said. "I respect Kandaar Devta. He is also our god." He then proudly told me that they had also given him a gift: a framed photo that he called to a relative nearby to fetch. The "photo" was actually a large, printed poster of Hindi stanzas. The title across the top read "Sri Kandaar

Stuti" (Praise to Kandaar Devta). I scanned it quickly; some of the phrases were formulaic devotional expressions, but one quickly jumped out: "You are king of Barahat; Victory to Lord Kandaar." Ajay silently pointed to the signature line so I wouldn't miss it: Manoj Sharma. Nautiyal then pulled out a small photograph taken that day: he himself garlanded in front of the Kandaar Devta temple, his head down, hands folded in supplication with flower petals fallen on his shoulders, flanked by Manoj Sharma and other Kandaar Devta devotees smiling broadly.

Conclusion

The developments described in this chapter demonstrate that sweetening and intensification as strategies for the renegotiation of status for deities, rituals, or communities can take highly specific local forms. Such strategies, therefore, never pursue sweetening or intensification in straightforward and uncomplicated ways. Those terms, rather, suggest a broad range of pathways deities might travel as historical forces take effect, adapting sweeter tactics where effective, manifesting fiercer tendencies at other times. Hari Maharaj's reputation as a fierce and powerful *devta*, living most of the year on his wild and isolated mountaintop, remains intact, but the festival rituals in which he has displayed his power are now constrained, his ancient territorial holdings have been seized, and his subordination to Kandaar Devta has been fully accomplished. In offering Kandaar Devta food at his temple during Maagh Mela and ceding Chamala ki Chauri to his authority, his devotees perform publicly a secondary status that they privately dispute, reluctantly accepting social and legal circumstances that have decisively altered relations between the two deities. If Hari Maharaj's disempowerment and acquiescence to the inevitable is a form of sweetening, it is one tinged with reluctance and resentment.

For their part Kandaar Devta's devotees reveal the more aggressive, even vindictive potential that lay behind the mischievous character that local lore attributes to him. His identification with Shiva was openly declared in the iconography and inscriptions included in the design of his 2008 temple, a Sanskritizing move that has its sweetening elements to help situate him for the religious tourists from all over India that appear before him while traversing the region on Himalayan pilgrimage. Shiva, however, is held at arm's length at the same time, both self and other to Kandaar Devta, whose Garhwali character and local significance is key to the fervent devotion he enjoys. His original temple a thousand feet up a mountainside in the small village of Sangrali remains his true home in the eyes of his devotees, but the ritual, temple, and festival in Uttarkashi that have propelled his ascent by alternately softening and hardening his character are urban practices unthinkable apart from mass tourism, mass media, and contemporary politics that his devotees have leveraged to augment his status. This divine dust-up reveals how local calibrations of sweetening and intensification may advance or impede the cosmopolitan aspirations increasingly at play in India's rural divine economies.

Notes

1. The analysis this chapter offers of a specific episode is based on longitudinal research conducted in Uttarkashi district that began in 2000, including twelve individual periods of field research ranging from two weeks to four months. I am grateful to Elon University and its Center for the Study of Religion, Culture, and Society for the funding that made the work this chapter details possible. Among many who assisted me in Uttarkashi, I wish to especially thank Uttam Mishra, Madhav Bhatt, and Ram Chandra Uniyal. Amod Panwar's assistance and insights inform all of my published work on Uttarakhand and I am deeply grateful for his long-term commitment to these projects.

2. All names in this chapter are pseudonyms.

3. The case of women married into villages was more complicated, as they often maintained, sometimes surreptitiously, relations with the deities of their natal villages (Sax 2009, 78–83).

4. One devotee of Hari Maharaj in 2023 told me an interesting variant that explains why a Shaiva deity has the name Hari, a title for Vishnu: Vishnu lived in that area in the mountaintop sthaan and Tarakaasura was harassing him. After Hari Maharaj flew over and defeated the demon, Vishnu gave him the title Hari Maharaj and left the Himalayas, granting the god his sthaan.

5. Recorded events that could be responsible include what are technically known as "obstruction burst" floods caused by shifts in the Gangotri Glacier in 1895 and 1935–38, one of which is likely also responsible for the submersion of the riverside temples at Dharali, eighty kilometers upriver from Uttarkashi. A local teacher told me in 2006 his father credited the great 1978 flood that also resulted from an obstruction of the river (Sati et al. 2020, 892).

6. In 2024 the priest at that temple told me they had a certificate from the Archaeological Survey of India saying the Parashuram murti was from the eighth or ninth century. I have not seen the certificate.

7. Scholarly sources attribute the reconstruction to the king, but I am inclined to follow local oral tradition that credits the queen.

References

Allocco, Amy L. 2018. "Flower Showers for the Goddess: Borrowing, Modification, and Ritual Innovation in Tamil Nadu." In *Ritual Innovation: Strategic Interventions in South Asian Religion*, edited by Brian K. Pennington and Amy L. Allocco, 129–48. State University of New York Press.

Arumugam, Indira. 2015. "'The Old Gods Are Losing Power!': Theologies of Power and Rituals of Productivity in a Tamil Nadu Village." *Modern Asian Studies* 49 (3): 753–86. https://doi.org/10.1017/S0026749X1400016X.

Atkinson, Edwin T. 2022. *Himalayan Districts of the North-Western Provinces of India: Forming Volume XI of the Gazetteer, N.-W. P. (Classic Reprint)*. Forgotten Books.

Berti, Daniela. 2009a. "Divine Jurisdictions and Forms of Government in Himachal Pradesh." In *Territory, Soil, and Society in South Asia*, edited by Gilles Tarabout and Daniela Berti, 311–40. Manohar Publishers. http://catdir.loc.gov/catdir/toc/fy0903/2009313146.html.

Berti, Daniela. 2009b. "Kings, Gods, and Political Leaders in Kullu (Himachal Pradesh)." In *Bards and Mediums: History, Culture and Politics in the Central Himalayan Kingdoms*, edited by Marie Lecomte-Tilouin. Almora Book Depot. http://hal.archives-ouvertes.fr/hal-00613854.

Bindi, Serena. 2012. "'When There Were Only Gods, Then There Was No Disease, No Need for Doctors': Forsaken Deities and Weakened Bodies in the Indian Himalayas." *Anthropology and Medicine* 19 (1): 85–94.

Branfoot, Crispin. 2007. *Gods on the Move: Architecture and Ritual in the South Indian Temple*. Society for South Asian Studies, British Academy.

Courtright, Paul B. 2011. "Searching for Satī." In *Hinduism in Practice*, edited by Hillary Peter Rodrigues, 37–45. Religions in Practice. Routledge.

David, Hans Jürgen. 2017. "Badrīnāth: A Temple at the Periphery of Cultures." PhD diss., University of Vienna.

Elmore, Mark. 2016. *Becoming Religious in a Secular Age*. University of California Press.

Fraser, James Baillie. 1820. *Journal of a Tour Through Part of the Snowy Range of the Himālā Mountains and to the Sources of the Rivers Jumna and Ganges*. Rodwell and Martin.

Haberman, David L. 2006. *River of Love in an Age of Pollution: The Yamuna River of Northern India*. University of California Press. http://catdir.loc.gov/catdir/toc/ecip061/2005029654.html.

Handa, Omacanda. 2002. *History of Uttaranchal*. Indus.

Handa, Omacanda. 2005. *Gaddi Land in Chamba: Its History, Art & Culture: New Light on the Early Wooden Temples*. Indus.

Handa, Omacanda, and Madhu Jain. 2003. *Art and Architecture of Uttaranchal*. Bhavana Books.

Jacobsen, Knut A. 2022. "Hindu Diasporas and Gods on the Move." In *Wiley Blackwell Companion to Hinduism*, 338–51. John Wiley & Sons. https://doi.org/10.1002/9781119144892.ch18.

Jassal, Aftab S. 2016. "Divine Politicking: A Rhetorical Approach to Deity Possession in the Himalayas." *Religions* 7 (9): 1–18. https://doi.org/10.3390/rel7090117.

Kumar, Anup. 2011. *The Making of a Small State: Populist Social Mobilisation and the Hindi Press in the Uttarakhand Movement*. New Perspectives in South Asian History 2. Orient Blackswan.

McDermott, Rachel Fell. 2004. *Mother of My Heart, Daughter of My Dreams: Kali and Uma in the Devotional Poetry of Bengal*. Oxford University Press.

Negi, R. S., and J. Singh. 1996. "Makar Sankranti in the Garhwal Himalayas: A Study in the Sacred Performances." In *The Himalayas: An Anthropological Perspective*, edited by Makhan Jha, 85–92. M.D. Publications.

Raper, F. V. 1810. "Narrative of a Survey for the Purpose of Discovering the Sources of the Ganges." *Asiatick Researches* 11: 446–566.

Raturi, Harikrishna. 1928. *Garhwal ka itihas*. Dehra Dun: Garhwali Press.

Saklani, Atul. 1987. *The History of a Himalayan Princely State: Change, Conflicts, and Awakening (An Interpretative History of Princely State of Tehri Garhwal, U.P., A.D. 1815 to 1949 A.D.)*. Durga.

Sankrityayan, Rahul. 1953. *Himālay-Paricay*. Vol. 1. Allahabad Law Journal Press.

Sati, S. P., Shubhra Sharma, Y. P. Sundriyal, Deepa Rawat, and Manoj Riyal. 2020. "Geo-Environmental Consequences of Obstructing the Bhagirathi River, Uttarakhand Himalaya, India." *Geomatics, Natural Hazards and Risk* 11 (1): 887–905. https://doi.org/10.1080/19475705.2020.1756464.

Sax, William S. 2002. *Dancing the Self: Personhood and Performance in the Pāṇḍav Līlā of Garhwal*. New York. Oxford University Press.

Sax, William S. 2003. "Divine Kingdoms in the Central Himalayas." In *Sacred Landscape of the Himalaya: Proceedings of an International Conference at Heidelberg, 25–27 May 1998*, edited by Niels Gutschow and Axel Michaels, 177–207. Veröffentlichungen zur Sozialanthropologie 4. Austrian Academy of Sciences.

Sax, William S. 2009. *God of Justice: Ritual Healing and Social Justice in the Central Himalayas*. Oxford University Press.

Siddiq vs. Das and Ors. 2019. Supreme Court of India.

Sutherland, Peter. 2004. "Very Little Kingdoms. The Calendrical Order of West Himalayan Hindu Polity." In *Sharing Sovereignty*, edited by Georg Berkemer and Margret Frenz, 31–62. De Gruyter. https://doi.org/10.1515/9783112402696-005.

Tillin, Louise. 2013. *Remapping India: New States and Their Political Origins*. Remapping India. Oxford University Press.

Tiwari, S. D., and Ganesh Khugshal, eds. 2001. *Mele aur utsāv-paramparā*. Kirtl Navani for Winsal Publishing.

Uniyal, Ramchandra. 2022. *Saumyakāshīti vikhyātam: Bāṛāhāṭ/Uttarkāshī*. Gayatri Computers and Printers.

Waghorne, Joanne Punzo. 2004. *Diaspora of the Gods: Modern Hindu Temples in an Urban Middle-Class World*. Oxford University Press. http://hdl.handle.net/2027/heb.30807.

2

Your Friendly, Neighborhood Bhairava

Understanding the Role of a Terrifying God in the Form of an Adorable Little Boy (Batuk)

Seth Ligo

The Hindu god Bhairava is an intense form of Shiva widely associated with violence, ferociousness, and transgression. He is a fanged skull-bearer, outcaste, and cremation-ground dweller whose name means "The Horrible" or "Cry of Fear" (White 2012; Svacchandatantra 1921, 3). This chapter considers the curious example of Batuk[1] (Child; Underage) Bhairava: a sweet, friendly, youthful form of this otherwise grisly and marginal figure. Drawing upon ethnographic, textual, and material cultural resources, I articulate several ways to respond to the compound question of where Batuk Bhairava comes from, what role he fills, and why he is so popular in certain locations and among certain populations. Is he a defanged (perhaps literally) form of this ferocious deity, a sweeter and more generally palatable alternative to other forms of Bhairava described as "angry," "ghoulish," and "destructive?"[2] Does he fill a perceived gap in the catalog of Bhairava's—and by extension Shiva's—forms? Is he a response to the popularity of Bala (little boy) Krishna in competing schools of Vishnu-oriented Hinduism? I will argue that the example shifts toward the sweet and the intense outlined in the introduction to this volume, such as mollification to increase compatibility with evermore interconnected regional traditions; general trends toward the pacific and high Sanskritic Hindu traditions; or the maintenance, amplification, or reassertion of antecedent tradition. Instead, Batuk and the two other forms of Bhairava present in his temple complex serve to extend, fill in, and further integrate the relevance of Bhairava's person, placement, and potential throughout the spectrum of Sweet to Intense.

It is with these questions and hypotheses that I first started spending time in the Batuk Bhairava temple in the neighborhood of Kamaccha, in Varanasi, northern India. Varanasi is arguably Hinduism's most sacred city, with millions of pilgrims visiting each year. Most visit Kashi Vishvanatha (a Shiva temple and the city's most sacred site) and Kal Bhairava (the city's regent who makes effective the ritual purification pilgrims seek). There are many other Bhairavas visited by pilgrims (Ligo 2022), but Batuk Bhairava is the most popular among full-time residents of the city. His temple lies tucked between residential neighborhoods, with little through traffic but many regulars and repeat visitors. In the autumn of 2016 and the spring of 2017, I spent at least an afternoon a week in the temple and was sure not to miss their festivals and events, such as the celebration of Bhairava's birthday, and regular musical and dramatic performances. I observed people moving through the temple space, and spoke with priests, ritual specialists, and lay members of Batuk's devotional family. The relative size, arrangement, contents, and decorative styles of shrines, the *murtis* (devotional statues) they contain, and how these *murtis* are juxtaposed allowed me to think along with devotees about the stories, deities, and traditions intersecting in these spaces. Finally, I turned to temple epigraphy and Hindi-language collections of praise-poetry and ritual manuals for broader, written context. Taken together, I argue that Batuk is not a sweetened Bhairava more palatable to contemporary, mainstream populations, and less likely to be misinterpreted by outsiders. Rather, Batuk's presence expands access to Bhairava in his many forms; instead of displacing or distracting from more intense and liminal forms of Bhairava, Batuk's presence in conjunction with such forms results in mutual amplification through contrast.[3]

Varanasi and the Kamaccha Batuk Temple

The particularity, even peculiarity, of Batuk becomes evident with further consideration of Bhairava in general. In the fifteenth century *Kashi Khanda* in the *Skanda Purana*—the text most widely referenced in Varanasi when seeking further information about that city's sacredness—Bhairava originates when Shiva forms a being that is terrifying in appearance: "*samutpadyapurusham bhairavarritim"* (Skanda Purana 1906, IV.I.31.41). This being is described as "having matted hairs, who is another form of his (Shiva's) own self" (Tagare 1992; Skanda Purana 1906, IV.I.31.51). Neither matted hair nor a fierce countenance appear in the sweet representations and descriptions of Batuk as noted above, and indeed this initial Bhairava seems to be a fully formed adult figure. This fits with the general understanding that Shiva is self-manifest, meaning that his entrees into the world are typically instantaneous and independent. Stories recounting the earthly appearances of Vishnu, on the other hand, typically describe his birth to terrestrial parents, and provide context for popular narrative threads featuring Little-Boy Krishna, or Rama's youth, siblings, and household life. Given the meaning of the name Bhairava, his common attributes, and his appearance as a fully formed adult, we return to the question of just who Batuk Bhairava is, where he comes from, how he functions similarly and dissimilarly to other forms of Bhairava (Kal in particular), and why he is so beloved by certain communities. Observation, participation, and conversation in Batuk's temple provide insight into his nature, form, and function.

To understand Batuk, it is important to consider the various elements and spaces comprised by his temple complex. A single gate provides entry to the site, and just around the corner is the Kamakhya Devi temple, one of the most potent goddess temples in the city. These are the only two temples in the immediate vicinity, and the neighborhood has grown up around them, each available square meter now a shop, storehouse, or dwelling—a relative architectural chronology evinced by overlapping walls and shifts in material and style. The Batuk complex now includes spaces abutted and enclosed by both intentional walls and encroaching construction.

The temple gate opens into a courtyard with a shallow pit for a ritual fire in the middle. Straight across the courtyard is an administrative building with a broad covered porch. In the far right corner is a passageway leading to smaller, ancillary shrines, and in the far left corner is a gate leading into a "party garden"—a pleasant expanse of lawn used for concerts and other community events. On the right side of the courtyard is a medium-sized shrine room featuring a Shiva *linga* (an aniconic representation of Shiva), and directly across from this *linga*, on the left-hand wall, is the entrance to Batuk's temple.

Located in a residential area and propitiated almost exclusively by locals, Batuk's temple compound nevertheless evinces connections with sites across India as well as across the city. There is the adjacent Kamakhya temple, suggesting a connection with India's primary Kamakhya temple in Assam—a point elaborated upon in my closing remarks. The *linga* in the side shrine is a proxy representation of the Grishaneshvara *jyotirlinga* (a transcendent column of light and representation of Shiva) in Aurangabad, Maharashtra. There are twelve *jyotirlingas* distributed across India, and the *linga* featured centrally at Vishvanatha Temple—the most important pilgrimage site in the city—is a part of this pan-Indian network. The entire network is represented in Varanasi by proxy, creating a mesocosm between the microcosm that is the body of the practitioner, and the macrocosm that is Hindu sacred geography in toto (White 2000). The Batuk complex is then connected to pan-Indian and city-spanning networks of sacred sites.

A set of city-spanning correspondences can be identified in the ancillary shrine down a passageway from the courtyard. The shrine features a *murti* of Krodhana (Angry) Bhairava, sometimes also referred to as Adi (first; primary) Bhairava. This Bhairava is a part of the Ashtabhairava, a protective network of eight Bhairavas that span Varanasi (see Ligo 2022). He is flanked by two niches: one contains a small *murti* of Unmatta (wild) Bhairava, the other is an empty niche designated by a thick vermillion coating. I argue elsewhere that this Unmatta, a local echo of a far-flung Unmatta Bhairava at the far periphery of Varanasi's sacred territory, ties Batuk's temple complex to the margin of Varanasi's sacred territory. Further, the niche recalls Bir Baba sites, where local people take on divine agency postmortem (Ligo 2023). Krodhana, then, is the first Bhairava, who is presented with the farthest-flung Bhairava, and also to hyperlocal Bir traditions, whose iconography most Bhairavas adopt in Varanasi (Ligo 2023). Batuk is thereby associated with the totality of Varanasi's sacred territory, as well as folk traditions with which Bhairava shows iconographic connection (Ligo 2023).

Turning our attention from outward-looking networks to the traffic and activity within Batuk's temple complex, it is clear that this is primarily a local, community temple. Devotees recognized and greeted both priests and other visitors when passing through. Children moved about the space freely, appearing to check whether there might be playmates visiting at the same time. It was common to see retired men sitting in the temple, catching up on neighborhood news, and sometimes showing up with chai. Cycles of domesticity were on display: from astrological readings to approve betrothals and select auspicious wedding dates, to rituals performed in support of successful pregnancy and healthy children. The party garden hosted regular events, with multiple generations in attendance: those with less flexible knees in plastic chairs in the back, younger folks on pillows on the covered lawn, and children keeping *mostly* out of the way. On the first day of January, long lines of community members waited to receive Batuk's blessings for a healthy, bountiful year.

There is something fitting about a Little-Boy Bhairava in this family-friendly and community-minded space. He becomes an implicit member of each family, a child alongside whom generations of devotees can grow up. Here any sweetening of Bhairava's character that might be taking place is not for the sake of toeing a mainstream and expected Hindu line, but is instead in keeping with this temple's family-friendly orientation. And yet alongside this sweetness there are enduring intense elements signaling this is certainly still Bhairava. Most overt among these is the presence of dogs—sculpted, drawn, and living. All the temple's Bhairava *murtis* are flanked by dogs, and it was common to see dogs sleeping in the ashes of a ritual fire on cold winter mornings, or on the cool marble floors during the summer. In puppy season, when litters can be found in just about every corner or crossing, many temple-goers distribute biscuits to the nursing mothers. In 2017 a mother and her seven pups were given an old blanket in the temple's electrical closet, with the door kept just wide enough open for her to come and go while keeping the pups protected. While keeping dogs as pets is ever more common in India, they are still generally associated with ritual pollution as scavengers that live on the margins, scrounging the others' refuse. It was just a few feet outside the gate of the Batuk complex where I saw this illustrated most vividly: an adolescent pup gnawing at the carcass of one of its littermates on top of the pile of garbage into which the body had been tossed. Bhairava, unlike most Hindu gods, is also liminal. In his origin story he is almost immediately enjoined to wander beyond the pale of civilized space, completing the skull-bearing penance (Tagare 1992, IV.i.31.59–60). Though he reenters society when the penance is complete, he retains indications of his liminality and otherness—most consistently his association with dogs. While they would be shooed out of most religious and domestic spaces, living dogs are common in Bhairava temples. They are free to come and go, usually finding a good place to snooze and a snack.

The most striking of Bhairava characteristics still observable in the case of Batuk is his acceptance of alcohol—preferably whisky—as an offering. This is also the case at the Lat, Kal, and Krodhan Bhairava sites in the city, and I would suspect it is the case for more, although I have not personally observed as much.[4] When I commissioned a ritual in the temple in November 2016, I was given a shopping list of items to purchase in advance. All could be procured in the religious-goods stalls near Durga Kund Temple with the exception of a fifth of whisky, which I picked up instead at an

"English wine shop" (as liquor stores are called) on my way from the market to Batuk's temple. I will further note that while there is an offering of the five "forbidden" substances made to Unmatta in this same compound, as is discussed below, alcohol is the only one of these five that is offered to Batuk. Otherwise, his preferred offerings are fairly standard: flowers, sweets, and sometimes fruit. On his birthday, tellingly, he is presented with gift baskets that arrange flowers and Cadbury's chocolate bars around a centerpiece: a fifth of Johnnie Walker, Black Label if possible. Smaller bottles, and smaller chocolate bars, feature in the decorations for his Annual Adornment of the Essence of the Three Aspects (*gunas*) Festival.

Figure 2.1. Whisky and Cadbury's chocolate decorating Batuk Bhairava's sanctum on the occasion of his Annual Adornment of the Essence of the Three Aspects (*gunas*) Festival. Varanasi, 2016. *Source:* Photo by the author.

Investigative Interlocution

Initial observations suggest Batuk is not a sweetened or mollified version of Bhairava, as he displays elements of a heterodox, even antinomian nature. So why have a child form of Bhairav? And why should a beloved child-form be associated with Bhairava and not some other deity? I wanted to know, so I asked.[5]

I want to be clear that the most common response to my questions of how Bhairava has a child form when he debuts as an adult, and why he has an adorable aspect when his iconography and very name indicate that he is terrifying, was incredulity: disbelief that someone would ask such ridiculous questions. These questions were not ridiculous because the answer was available and widely known, but because they were quite irrelevant. With a general sense of plural truth, there was no need to explain exactly why Batuk exists, or is as he is. He is present, important, accessible—that's what matters. This was never articulated explicitly, but baffled responses, or kind redirections, made this impression quite clear.

Keeping in mind that my line of questioning originated from an outsider's desire for a certain sort of uniform coherence, conversations with temple-goers did provided contextual insight into both Bhairava and temple complexes like Batuk's in Kamaccha. I asked about Batuk's origins: Was there a reason he took a childlike form? I was told that this was wholly Bhairava, who was in turn wholly Shiva, and that this was the form in which he was born—hence a child. When I asked after his parents Shiva was always the father, but the mother was sometimes the goddess Annapurna, whose temple is paired with that of Shiva as Vishvanatha; and sometimes Batuk's mother was the goddess Ganga, who is also the river-as-living-goddess (the Ganges) that flows alongside Varanasi and provides invaluable reinforcement and completion of the city's sacred nature. These two goddesses are clearly paired with Shiva, and are particularly resonant with the presence of Shiva in Varanasi. Suddenly this neighborhood temple, well inland from the river and at the edge of the city's southern region, is explicitly tied to the sacred city's two principal dyads. With his unique family relationship Batuk connects differently to Shiva and the Goddess than do other Bhairavas who are Shiva's iterations, and the Goddess's attendants. In this view, he is not a liminal form, but one of both *ghar* (home) and *garbha* (womb), born into the ritual and political center, not fundamentally a denizen of the periphery. Here he has not so much been sweetened, but differently integrated into emplaced systems of articulating meaning and value.

Given Batuk's unique relationality, what function might he serve that the many other forms of Bhairava present in the city do not? Given the juvenile parallel between Batuk Bhairava and Bala (child) Krishna, I wondered whether their general role might also be comparable. Could this network of Bhairavas, associated explicitly with Shiva, have produced a child form in parallel to these Bala Krishna traditions, which are related directly to Vishnu? Bala Krishna is often described as a means for experiencing loving devotion (*bhakti*) to Krishna like unto the love of a parent for a child (*vatsalya*) (Arney 2007). There is something about a child, especially a rapscallion, that invites joyful adoration. Batuk does have similar capacities, but they are articulated in a distinct way. I was repeatedly told, with no priming or comparative mention of Bala Krishna, that Batuk was special because he was adorable. He was easy to love and show loving devotion to. This seemed to fit with my supposition, and there was absolutely an element of *bhakti* present in these understandings. But this dimension was not a focal point, and access, efficacy, and the reduction of risk were more prominently presented as explanatory of Batuk's particular potential. Explanations generally went something like this: *He's a little boy, so there's no need for complex and difficult rituals to get his attention and make him happy. Some biscuits, or sweets, and a few kind words are enough—then you have his attention, and you can ask for his help, his blessings.* I realized over the course of several similar conversations that this approach was not merely a matter of convenience. The complexity of the rituals preferred by other forms of Bhairava could pose a challenge, but they also might involve more, and more problematic, elements—such as liquor. For those who did not want to engage in these dimensions of propitiation, Batuk was an alternative. He might still accept whisky, but it was not expected at all times, and biscuits would do.

This awareness of risk extended beyond the sorts of offerings Batuk might accept. It also applied to his approved *sadhanas*, or intensive contemplative and ritual cycles of practice with the aim of achieving superhuman power or liberation. Tantric dimensions of religious traditions (or tantric traditions within broader religious categories) are concerned with accessing and applying macrocosmic energies from the microcosm of the practitioner's body (White 2000). Tantric *sadhanas* are common in Bhairava-related praxis, and most—such as those associated with Kal Bhairava—are understood to be powerful, expedient, and effective, yet risky. They could only be done with the close supervision of a guru, and any misstep might prove catastrophic. Practices related to Batuk kept a sense of this power and expediency, but were understood to be far less risky. Indeed, I was told that it could be learned almost independently—with text and conversation, and of course interaction with Batuk, but without the intense oversight of a specialist.

This tantra-inflected autodidacticism was put to emphatic use by one of my most frequent interlocutors at the Batuk temple. He goes by the name Tantric Baba, both in person and on WhatsApp, so I use the same here. A former middle-school natural sciences teacher, Tantric Baba taught himself how to perform a catalog of rituals from the *Bhairava Tantra Siddhi* (Shrivastava 2010), a volume that on the cover lists its contents as "Worship, Devotional Contemplation, and Information Pertaining to Treatises on the Austere Practices of Mantra and Tantra." Tantric Baba lives a few neighborhoods away from the temple, and works mostly on the porch of its meeting hall. He was a relative newcomer to the space, a second-career ritual specialist, and without an "in" among the established hierarchy of the temple. The following comes from weekly conversations with Tantric Baba that took place from September 2016 to April 2017.

I asked Tantric Baba why he worked in a Bhairava temple, and what the particular benefit of tantra was compared to other ways to engage Bhairava. He told me that this was Shiva's city, and Bhairava was a both powerful protector of the city and a powerful, true form of Shiva. As for what he thought about Batuk in particular, and what Batuk added to the matrix of Bhairava forms, Tantric Baba mentioned how accessible Batuk is, as he is a child. He also noted that Batuk is of the city, and of the people of the city. He is a resident, from which I inferred that other forms of Bhairava were guards, or attendants, as reflected in their placement and iconography. But Batuk lives in a particular neighborhood, in a particular city. As for his preference for tantra, Tantric Baba said that it was powerful, effective, and accessible—he could learn it, he could perform it, it worked, and it was suited to the city of Varanasi just as was the presence of Bhairava in general. His rationale briefly touches on aspects that could initially suggest trends of intensification (the affirmation of Bhairava's connection to tantric power) and sweetening (the broad accessibility and appeal of Batuk). But they are presented in combination, balancing one another, and both are subsumed by the importance of relevance and relation to a particular place. This might be an example of "folk reckoning" (Ligo 2023) with its focus on a particular place, and the specific articulation of a network of signs and meaning that fits a given context.

Tantric Baba was interested in new clients, and asked what sort of ritual I might want to commission. I wasn't married, and he offered to help fix that. In addition to his most requested rituals for finding a spouse, he also offered services that would help with finding a steady, high-paying job and success on exams. As I was conducting dissertation research at the time, I opted for academic success. I could then select the number of recitations drawn from verses in praise of Kal Bhairava, Batuk Bhairava, and the Navagraha, or nine celestial bodies, understood to shape one's fate. The more recitations he completed the more powerful the effect, and correspondingly the higher the price. I chose 1,001 recitations, a middle-tier package, and was told to come back in ten days with the prescribed supplies—those available at the market in Durga Kund, plus a fifth of whisky. Other than first offering the whisky to Batuk, the rest of the concluding, participatory portion of the ritual took place on the porch where Tantric Baba usually sat. With the manipulation of flowers, rice, Ganga water, camphor, and assorted clay vessels, I read the portions of his personal chapbook (not the *Bhairava Tantra Siddhi* with which he had trained), which included preliminary visual meditation, the Batuk root *mantra,* and the first fourteen verses of the Batuk *stotra* (hymn of praise). Beyond garnering Batuk's attention by presenting him with alcohol, there was nothing about any of these processes that might not be observed in nontantric rituals dedicated to other deities. The content of the recited passages, however, is telling. There is extensive overlap in the ways Batuk and Kal Bhairavas are described, praised, and their potency celebrated, but they are not identical. It is to the texts we now turn.

The Writing on the Wall

The following three textual sources help us better understand Batuk's role and nature. The first is the circa eighteenth-century *Batuk Stotra* mentioned above. The second is the reportedly eighth-century *Kalabhairavashtakam,* or set of eight verses in praise of Kal Bhairava. This is the most common Bhairava text in the city, and can be heard in most Bhairava temples; it is read in chapbooks and referenced on temple walls, where it is often engraved into a marble plaque installed alongside the door through which visitors can view Bhairava. The third is the mid-twentieth-century *Batuk Bhairava arati,* a type of veneration that involves reciting praises and moving a flame in a circular pattern in front of the deity. The particular *arati* verses in question are carved into a marble plaque alongside the door to Batuk's temple, and are dedicated to the temple's previous head priest, Bhagvan Puri, whose leadership is widely credited for bringing about the site's current popularity.

The *Batuk Stotra* opens by praising Batuk as Lord, essence, and creator of beings; the knower and protector of the sacred territory. He is a warrior or king (*kshatriya*), a fitting class for a protector or ruler of the city. So far, the descriptions could apply to many Bhairavas, and do not signal anything about a specifically Batuk form. The next lines are more specific: they describe Batuk as a charnel-ground dweller, a meat-eater, with a skull for a begging bowl. He is an accomplished blood-drinker and liquor-drinker. There are other forms of Bhairava distinguished by their skulls, or living in charnel grounds. These seem to be descriptions of other Bhairavas, or of Kal himself. The middle of the *stotra* describes Batuk as having three eyes and a garland of skulls, a wife (Bhairavi) who is also a ruler over beings, and one who is ever peaceful and dear to peaceful people. He is also described as a child and the lord of children (*batukesha*). He is then described as peaceful, peace-giving, and pure, a friend of Shiva, and an effective if aggressive bestower of liberation. This portion ends with Batuk referred to as the protector of the universe and a source of healing.

We have here a description that is both sweet and intense. It affirms Batuk's capacities for insight, liberation, and success as well as his power and potential, which are often expressed in terms of his antinomian aspects. Though he would not directly confirm as much, I reasoned Tantric Baba had honed in on this particular portion of this Batuk *stotra*—one that is not in the book he said he had primarily learned from—because it simultaneously affirms Batuk's boy form and his capacity for peace, while also affirming the acceptability of his consumption of alcohol and meat, and his more transgressive, charnel-ground-dwelling dimensions. There is again an affirmation of sweetness, an almost immediate statement that Bhairava's capacity, even Batuk's capacity, goes far beyond "sweetness." He is peaceful and can also destroy, is a lord of children and of ghost-monsters, and is a king and an outcaste.

Is it possible that Bhairava is always described as having this range of potential? The *Kalabhairavashtakam* provides insight into the attributes of Kal Bhairava in Varanasi. There are aspects that parallel Shiva in his description, such as a crescent moon in his hair, a blue throat, and serpents in place of a sacred thread and other jewelry. He does have fangs, but they are presented in the service of "rending earthly fetters." Otherwise, Kal Bhairava is described as a king, pleasant in form, powerful, a champion of right action and preventer of unrighteous deviance, who is even said to have bejeweled shoes on his feet and pleasantly tinkling bells around his waist. Perhaps this is also an approachable form: powerful, but protective and liberating, a king connected in iconography with Shiva, called Kal Bhairava, known to be associated with darkness and fear, but here also affirmed to be an appealing and helpful figure. It might be tempting to see

Batuk's description as explaining what his name obscures, as does Kal's: the phrases act against the initial impression given by the names. I think this explanation is too reductive, however, as both instances signal a spectrum of appearance, identity, capacity, and distinguishing features: some directly, and some by symbolic association, such as the echoes of Shiva's accoutrement.

Finally, the *arati* of Batuk reveals what a visitor to his temple might have in mind when engaging this particular instance of this form of Bhairava in this place: Batuk in the Kamaccha temple. In addition to the inscription being presented as "In memory of Mahant Bhagvan Puri," I heard several mentions over the months that the *mahant* had composed this *arati* and many other devotional verses still frequently used in the temple. I was not able to confirm this, but it does reinforce the association of these verses with this particular temple in the minds of devotees. In this *arati*, Batuk is revered as a master who lives in our hearts and minds, bears a skull and crescent moon, holds a trident and an hourglass drum, and transcends the three worlds. Again, these details associate Batuk with Shiva, going so far as to say he is "Siva's true form as skull-bearer." Batuk is further said to have lotus feet, be adorned with jewels, live in the forest, and play little drums.[6] The *arati* then describes Batuk cavorting with ghosts and ghouls, saying he is a tipsy drunkard who drinks many cups. The cycle closes by saying that a little boy is Batuk's essential form, that his praises should be sung, and that he will remove faults and suffering as well as grant happiness and prosperity. While the weight of these verses tends toward aspects befitting adoration, Batuk's association with liminal and even antisocial figures and his propensity for drunkenness are also listed. They are not omitted, much less hidden. These are affirmed dimensions of Batuk, as they are with other Bhairavas. Perhaps his sweeter sides have been emphasized in unique ways in this example, especially compared to general descriptions and names of other Bhairavas. But those, too, are praised for their regal, helpful, liberating aspects. Perhaps they are not sweetened as some of the Batuk details—especially his playfulness—but the *Kalabhairavashtakam* also does not reflect the full potential intensity of Bhairava and his forms.

All three textual sources support the interpretation that Batuk is not a "sanitized" Bhairava. They also make it clear that this is not an absorption of a part or version of Bhairava into another, more orthodox, and homogenous Hindu tradition. His more socially challenging, perhaps off-putting aspects are front and center in these ritual texts recited by active priests and etched directly into temple walls. What, then, is Batuk's role? Why does he endure?

Considering a Foundation Story

One of my first hypotheses was that perhaps Batuk, despite the unlikely nature of his existence, was an articulation designed to parallel Bala Krishna, or Krishna as a little boy (*bala*), effectively fleshing out the range of recognized Bhairava forms and providing an iteration particularly suited to adoration. It is curious, then, that this form is Batuk—and not Bala—Bhairava. Although "batuk" is usually translated as "little boy" or "child," a more specific but less frequent gloss would mean a Brahman (priestly class) boy who is still unmarried, and therefore underage.[7] Why might Bhairava be labeled a young Brahman, when he is usually called a Kshatriya (ruling class of kings and warriors)? A possible answer lies in the foundation story of the Batuk Bhairava temple.

Elizabeth Chalier-Visuvalingam, who conducted fieldwork at this same Batuk temple in the 1980s and 1990s, relays the story told by head priest Bhagvan Puri linking the founding of the temple to the need for the king of Varanasi to have a son (Chalier-Visuvalingam 1996). It begins when an ascetic teacher departed Allahabad after a quarrel and brought his Krodhana Bhairava to Kamaccha, in Varanasi, where he continued his spiritual practice. He gained the attention of Balwant Singh, king of Varanasi, who had no son with his primary wife to inherit the throne. Balwant Singh did father a son—Chet Singh—after receiving a fruit blessed by the ascetic. In return, he granted this devotee of Krodhana Bhairava property and funds. Eventually, this ascetic died and his disciple took over. Through a dream, this disciple discovered a lost *murti* of Batuk Bhairava. Balwant Singh funded the construction of a temple in 1733 to house this *murti* and commemorate the birth of his son. In celebration of a little boy, it seems fitting that this is a temple dedicated to Little-Boy Bhairava.

The question still remains, however, as to why we might use the word Batuk and not Bala. It appears that the production of a male heir was not the only challenge Balwant Singh faced. He did have a son, but not with his primary wife. Instead, Chet Singh was the product of an intercaste relationship: his mother being a Kshatriya called Panna, while Balwant was himself a Brahman (Narayan 2011). Balwant Singh did have a grandson, born to his daughter, and he had also adopted an orphaned nephew. Both grandson and nephew/son were born of Brahman-Brahman couples. Chet Singh's matrilineal heritage nearly prevented him from being king, but his ascendence was eventually approved by sufficient local leadership and the

East India Company, rooted mainly in an idea of patrilineal inheritance, and a disregard of intercaste disqualification (Narayan 2011). It does seem fitting, however, that a temple dedicated to the birth of Chet Singh, an awaited heir, features a god named not only after a little boy but also after a little Brahman boy. Perhaps this signaled, and cemented into the minds of the citizens and into the city itself, the sense that despite confounding details, Chet Singh was a legitimate Brahman—if only on his father's side.

Spatial Analysis and the Spectrum of Bhairava

I would like to return to the layout of the Batuk temple complex, and its many contents. In particular, we will look at Krodhana Bhairava, Unmatta Bhairava, and nearby Kamakhya Devi. Krodhana and Unmatta can be found in the side shrine down a passageway in the Batuk complex, and Kamakhya is in the complex adjacent, attended by her own Krodhana Bhairava. The Krodhana Bhairava in the Batuk complex is recognized as the original *murti* brought to Banaras and installed by the ascetic who left Allahabad and whose blessing is said to have enabled Balwant Singh to sire Chet Singh.

As noted, this side shrine also hosts a small image of Unmatta Bhairava, and an empty niche that echoes Bir traditions. It is here that a five "forbidden" substances[8] service is performed every Tuesday. Interestingly, the temporary ritual space is set up in front of the small image of Unmatta, not the much larger image of Krodhana. The ritual specialist inscribes geometric designs in a blend of orange-red powder, Ganga water, and white liquor on the floor. He uses a string of prayer beads featuring beads of bone whose source he would not identify, but which I believe he was hinting were human, and which he stores in a jar of moonshine. He manipulates and consumes fish, liquor, meat, puffed-grain cakes, and eggs—which I assume are a stand-in for sexual activity or effluvia—in his ritual process. Those participating indirectly, or observing ethnographically, are invited to also ritually consume some of the white liquor with just the right grip, and at just the right juncture in the proceedings. Occasionally, young householder men would stop by the shrine with their families, and then return to reach just into the built-in cabinet where the liquor was kept to take a quick quaff while their wives and children were off in the Batuk temple in the center of the complex. Even this tradition, and these Bhairavas, contribute to this temple's neighborhood, "family-friendly" function.

Figure 2.2. Tantric worship of Unmatta Bhairava, Varanasi, 2017. *Source:* Photo by the author.

Although I have observed alcoholic offerings to Bhairava at many of his temples and shrines, I had never heard of any other regularly scheduled "transgressive" service. It seems, then, that Batuk does not disrupt, cancel out, or obscure some of the more grisly aspects of Bhairava's identity and worship. Instead, he hosts them. His presence then is not a normalizing corrective, but a demonstration of the range of the spectrum Bhairava inhabits and addresses. Rather than a middle-ground Bhairava, we have a child with chocolate, the Wild (Unmatta), and the Angry (Krodhana) Bhairavas worshipped in the same complex. Batuk fills out the spectrum of Bhairava potentiality, and while he may functionally parallel other Hindu figures suited for devotional adoration, he never loses elements of that transgressive or tantric weft that weaves him into this wider Bhairava context.

Though the Krodhana Bhairava in the side shrine might be the original brought by the ascetic, it is not the Krodhana listed among the Ashtabhairava, a set of eight Bhairava that encircle and protect the city. The Krodhana in the Ashtabhairava lists is Kamakhya's attendant, and appears alongside her in her temple just down the lane. The Unmatta Bhairava in the Batuk complex is also not part of the Ashtabhairava set—the traditional Unmatta is many kilometers away in Deogarh Village. Interestingly, both Bhairavas have supplanted their almost certainly antecedent analogues, and are now recognized as official proxies for other important Bhairavas (Ligo 2022). In this way, the periphery of the city's sacred space and the protection of the goddess Kamakhya are brought into the Batuk complex, and by extension into the full-spectrum, community-embedded nexus of Bhairava the Batuk complex provides. This, then, is the functional, if not indeed the intended, effect of the anchor of Batuk.

Transposition of the Goddess:
Conclusion and Further Speculations

There is a final layer of speculation that will require further fieldwork to develop, but which can be generally sketched out now: that of the history of these sites, their interconnection, and their correspondence with the Kamakhya Devi temple site in Assam, which I believe they reproduce in Varanasi by proxy. I wonder whether this part of town was not alongside a tributary to the Assi River, and perhaps a site of cremation. This would explain the presence of a *sati* stone, suggesting ritual self-immolation of a widow on her husband's pyre in a cremation ground (see Ligo 2023). A culvert and what appears to have been a bridge evince a former waterway just beyond the Batuk temple. If interceding, more recent edifices are ignored, Krodhana faces the entrance to Kamakhya's sanctum. Could he have been a part of her complex, before being walled into Batuk's? Was the ascetic who brought the Krodhana *murti* to Varanasi a charnel-ground dweller, and for that reason chose this site to continue his practice? Looking at the primary Kamakhya in Assam, it is clear that her neighborhood also includes Bhutana-tha (a name used in the above texts to describe Batuk) Cremation Ground and a small temple to the south: a temple to Bala Bhairava, or Little-Boy Bhairava. I wonder whether we might not be looking at a miniature, slightly rearranged, reproduction of the Assamese nexus of tantric Kamakhya, with

Krodhana as attendant, and Batuk as Bala, the son of Annapurna, who is herself associated with Kamakhya.[9] While now filling out Bhairava's range of function and access in the city, providing a flourishing social hub, I wonder whether he wasn't originally part of a detailed reproduction of this Assamese goddess site. If this is the case, or even partially so, it would also reinforce the idea that Batuk was a name applied due to the narrative tie to Chet Singh and his desire to produce a Brahman son. Otherwise, why would this not be Bala Bhairava, a form that exists in Assam, and that uses a more general term for a little boy—a term that would put him in more direct parallel with Bala Krishna than the chosen name Batuk?

In the preceding, I have integrated ethnographic, textual, and material-spatial analyses to consider whether Batuk Bhairava might be an instance of the "sweetening" of Bhairava forms that are otherwise associated with liminality, antinomian practice, and apparent transgression. While there are some sweet aspects of this form, namely his adorability and his love of sugary snacks, there is never a decoupling, elision, or displacement of Bhairava's associations with the consumption of illicit substances, especially meat and alcohol, nor with his occupation of polluted or liminal areas like cremation grounds, his more terrifying forms and attributes, and his ability to grant liberation by extreme means. This is evident in the connections between elements of the Batuk temple complex with both central and liminal sites in Varanasi; the explanations of devotees and their offerings of both chocolate and liquor; the self-training of Tantric Baba in a praxis that is both less risky but fully potent; and the co-presence of explicitly antinomian tantric ritual programming alongside the everyday functions a temple fulfills for the support of an attendant community in all states and phases of life, neighborhood, and family. Batuk, then, does not obscure this range of Bhairavas evident within the Batuk complex itself. He is not evidence of any of the example modalities of sweetening and intensification with which this volume opens, but he is still evidence of the usefulness of attending shifts along this spectrum in order to better understand the complexity of deities like Bhairava, and the complex human worlds they protect and serve. In the case of Batuk, he expands and fleshes out the capacity and possibility of Bhairav: from reprehensibility, to respectability, to venerability, to adorability. Even potential historical and political entanglements evince a spectrum of participation from the king to the cremation ground. He is, after all, transgressor, powerful liberator, king and regulator, *and* little boy Batuk.

Notes

1. Batuk in Hindi, this name is Batuka in Sanskrit. His intimate, filial relationship with devotees means he is always Batuk, while other deities sometimes lose, and sometimes keep, their terminal, Sanskrit *a.

2. These are names of certain of the *Ashtabhairava*, a set of eight iterations of Bhairava. See Ligo 2022, appendix.

3. For more on patterns of "sweetening" and "intensification," see Allocco 2018, 2021; Arumugam 2015; Harman 2004; McDermott 2001; Padma 2013; Sinha 2016; Waghorne 2004; and Zeiler 2012, 2019. Kind thanks to the editors of this volume for sharing these cross-references.

4. Kal Bhairava in Ujjain, who is clearly linked with Kal Bhairava in Varanasi (both temples have photos of the other on clear display), drinks liters of liquor a day. Little bottles of whisky are included with flowers, incense, and sugar pellets in the offering baskets that can be purchased outside the temple.

5. Unless a particular individual is mentioned, the following accounts are amalgamations of conversations I had with ritual specialists and devotees during my fieldwork in 2016–2017. Note that while there are narratives that pair Batuk with Hanuman as attendants of the Goddess, and stories about *batuks* (young Brahmans) being worshipped in the *Shiva Purana*, the present study focuses on the Batuk Bhairava temple in Kamaccha and materials directly referenced by my interlocutors.

6. There are kettle drums mounted on stands just outside the door to the temple. They allow visitors to make the sound of his seed-mantra: *bam-bam!*

7. My thanks to Gudrun Bühnemann for pointing this out.

8. A set of five substances considered taboo by most mainstream Hindu ritual standards. In Sanskrit, each word begins with an "M," hence the *panca* (five) *makara* (M-words). They are *madya* (wine), *mamsa* (meat), *matsya* (fish), *mudra* (dry grain), and *maithuna* (sex or menses). The use of these materials is generally associated with transgressive practices of certain tantric groups—the first two appear in Batuk materials.

9. See *Annapurna Vrat Katha* mentioned in Eck 1982, 162–63.

References

Allocco, Amy L. 2018. "Flower Showers for the Goddess: Borrowing, Modification, and Ritual Innovation in Tamil Nadu." In *Ritual Innovation: Strategic Interventions in South Asian Religion*, edited by Brian K. Pennington and Amy L. Allocco, 129–48. State University of New York Press.

Allocco, Amy L. 2021. "Bringing the Dead Home: Hindu Invitation Rituals in Tamil South India." *Journal of the American Academy of Religion* 89 (1): 103–42.

Arney, Paul. 2007. "The Bade Shikshapatra: A Vallabhite Guide to the Worship of Krishna's Divine Images." In *Krishna: A Sourcebook*, edited by Edwin F. Bryant. Oxford University Press.

Arumugam, Indira. 2015. " 'The Old Gods Are Losing Power!': Theologies of Power and Rituals of Productivity in a Tamil Nadu Village." *Modern Asian Studies* 49 (3): 753–86.

Chalier-Visuvalingam, Elizabeth. 1996. "Bhairava and the Goddess: Tradition, Gender and Transgression." In *Wild Goddesses in India and Nepal: Proceedings of an International Symposium, Berne and Zurich, November 1994*, edited by Axel Michaels, Cornelia Vogelsanger, and Annette Wilke, 253–301. Peter Lang.

Eck, Diana L. 1982. *Banaras, City of Light*. Knopf.

Harman, William. 2004. "From Fierce to Domesticated: Mariyamman Joins the Middle Class." *Manushi* 140 (January–February): 2–14.

Ligo, Seth. 2022. "Kashi Kshetra, Kashi Mandala: Digitally Mapping Evolving Interpretations of an Idealized Sacred City." *International Journal of Hindu Studies* 26 (August): 161–88.

Ligo, Seth. 2023. "Bhairava, Hanuman, and the Deified Dead: A Material Study of Vernacular, Official, and Folk Registers of Living Hinduism in Varanasi, North India." In *Living Folk Religions*, edited by Sravana Borkataky-Varma and Aaron Ullrey, 113–25. Routledge.

McDermott, Rachel Fell. 2001. *Mother of My Heart, Daughter of My Dreams: Kali and Uma in the Devotional Poetry of Bengal*. Oxford University Press.

Michaels, Axel, Cornelia Vogelsanger, and Annette Wilke. 1996. *Wild Goddesses in India and Nepal: Proceedings of an International Symposium, Berne and Zurich, November 1994*. Peter Lang.

Narayan, Rochisha. 2011. "Caste, Family and Politics in Northern India During the Eighteenth and Nineteenth Centuries." PhD diss., Rutgers University.

Padma, Sree. 2013. *Vicissitudes of the Goddess: Reconstructions of the* Gramadevata *in India's Religious Traditions*. Oxford University Press.

Shrivastava, C. M., trans. 2010. *Bhairava Tantra Siddhi*. Manoj Publications.

Sinha, Vineeta. 2016. *A New God in the Diaspora? Muneeswaran Worship in Contemporary Singapore*. NUS Press.

Skanda Purana. 1906. *Kashi Khanda—First Half (with Hindi Tika by Siddhinath Trivedi)*. Naval Kishore Press.

Svacchanda Tantra with Commentary by Kshemaraja. 1921. Edited with notes by Pandit Madhusudhan Kaul Shastri. Nirnaya-Sagar Press.

Tagare, G. V., trans. 1992. *Skanda Purana*. Motilal Banarsidass.

Waghorne, Joanne Punzo. 2004. *Diaspora of the Gods: Modern Hindu Temples in an Urban Middle-Class World*. Oxford University Press.

White, David Gordon. 2000. Introduction to *Tantra in Practice*, edited by David Gordon White. Princeton University Press.

White, David Gordon. 2012. "Bhairava." In *Brill's Encyclopedia of Hinduism Online*, edited by Knut A. Jacobsen. Brill. https://referenceworks.brillonline.com/entries/brill-s-encyclopedia-of-hinduism/bhairava-COM_1030080.

Zeiler, Xenia. 2012. "Female Danger: 'Evil,' Inauspiciousness, and Their Symbols in Representations of South Asian Goddesses." *Nidan: Journal for the Study of Hinduism* 24: 100–117.

Zeiler, Xenia. 2019. "Eradicated with Blood: Text and Context of Animal Sacrifice in Tantric and Tantra-Influenced Rituals." *International Journal of Hindu Studies* 23 (2): 165–77.

3

This Is a Place Where *Shakti* Dances

Intensifying the Goddess's Power in Michigan

Tracy Pintchman

In June 2019, I was sitting at my desk at home when I received an unexpected phone call. In 2008, I began studying a Hindu goddess temple in Pontiac, Michigan, called the Parashakthi or "Eternal Mother" Temple. In 2017, I turned my attention away from gathering data to writing a book about the temple, so when that phone call came, I had not been to Michigan on a site visit for about eighteen months and did not know what was going on in Pontiac on a day-to-day basis. The call was from a devotee, Ram, who wanted me to speak with the temple's lawyers.[1] The call took me completely by surprise. Ram told me there had been a serious fire in the temple on April 21, 2018, during a *homa* rite. The central practice of *homa* is the placing of offerings (*ahuti*) into a fire so that Agni, the deity of fire, can transform them into gifts to be offered to deities and other spiritual beings. In April 2018, apparently, the vent above the *homa* pit inside the Parashakthi Temple had suffered a serious creosote buildup that caught fire during the *homa*, destroying the roof and damaging much of the existing temple structure.

Following the fire, the temple board consulted a Hindu architect in Tamil Nadu with knowledge of the rules of traditional Hindu architecture (*vastu*) and design (*shilpa*). This architect created a report based on verses he had compiled largely from the Shilparatna of Shrikumara, an authoritative text on the South Indian Dravida or Maya school of architecture. The conclusion at the end of the report was clear. The fire had irreparably damaged the subtle energy present in the temple, so the structure would have to be completely rebuilt. The *murtis*, consecrated deity images, which had largely survived the fire materially, would almost all have to be replaced by new *murtis*.

Ram told me that the insurance company was balking at covering the high cost of the temple's proposed plan to move forward. They wanted to know why the current *murtis* could not just be cleansed ritually and reinstalled. Ram told me that the president and spiritual director of the temple, Dr. G. Krishna Kumar, was insistent that the Goddess had spoken to him directly on the matter. She demanded not only that everything be replaced, but also that the work be entrusted to specific, spiritually sensitive craftsmen (*shilpis*) who, according to temple officials, the Goddess herself had chosen to do the work. Ram wanted me to talk to the temple's Euro-American temple lawyers, who had no knowledge of Hinduism or Hindu temple issues, to help supply them with arguments they could bring to the insurance company.

I assured Ram that I would do whatever I could to help and told him that I was very sorry to learn about the fire. Ram assured me that I need not be concerned because the Goddess had disclosed, through direct revelation, that she had planned the fire and subsequent destruction of the temple structure because doing so was vital to her larger plans. Ram did not want to discuss the issue over the phone but urged me to return to Pontiac as soon as I could to talk to members of the temple board and devotees about the fire.

After a brief chat and discussion of dates for me to return to Pontiac, I hung up the phone. And I wondered. Why would the Goddess destroy her own temple? What was the purpose of the fire in the minds of temple leaders and devotees? What did the temple leadership believe was in the Goddess's plan that made the fire necessary? And what would happen to the temple now?

The Parashakthi Temple: Setting Context

The Parashakthi Temple in Pontiac, Michigan, is also known in English as the "Eternal Mother Temple." Here, allegedly at the Goddess's behest, the consecration of the temple took place in October 1999. During the first ten years of its existence, the temple was renovated and expanded as its community of devotees grew quickly (fig. 3.1). The Goddess to whom this temple is dedicated is Karumariamman, "Black Mariamman," a form of the Tamil goddess Mariamman. The Parashakthi Temple is modeled on an Indian Karumariamman temple in Thiruverkadu, a suburb of Chennai in the South Indian state of Tamil Nadu (Parashakthi Temple, "Shakthi Worship"). Karumariamman is a local Tamil goddess in her original South Indian context, and her temple in Thiruverkadu serves largely local and regional devotees. The Parashakthi Temple website asserts that Karumariamman has assumed a new form in Michigan as the one, universal Goddess, the Divine Mother of all beings, who has come to the West for the benefit of all beings, especially those in the Americas (Parashakthi Temple, "Shakthi Worship").

Karumariamman's appearance in an American Hindu temple as supreme goddess and the main object of reverence is, as far as I can tell, a relatively

Figure 3.1. The Parashakthi Temple in 2009. Pontiac, Michigan. *Source:* Photo by the author.

new phenomenon, but it fits a global pattern. Elaine Craddock notes that in South Indian Hindu contexts, Mariamman in her various forms has often been a goddess of rural, low-caste communities and a "fierce, angry goddess with a voracious appetite for blood sacrifice" (Craddock 2001, 146). In contemporary India, however, Mariamman has moved out of villages and away from her agricultural roots to capture new, middle-class, and high-caste devotees. Mariamman now draws devotees across caste and socioeconomic lines and from urban as well as rural areas (Craddock 2001, 147). William Harman also traces such transformations in South India, but he notes too that Mariamman temples have also moved well "beyond the boundaries of India" into several diasporic contexts (Harman 2004, 3). Mariamman's forays far beyond her local, rural, Tamil Nadu grounding have been well documented (Sinha 2014, 78).

Joanne Waghorne posits that the globalization of local temple traditions has occurred as migrating devotees transport their originally local deities into new, global contexts (Waghorne 2004, 146, 173). Mariamman and other local Tamil goddesses are especially appealing to diaspora Hindus, says Waghorne, because they are not impersonal or distant but are "living energy, the vibration of the universe and the pulse of the devotee" (Waghorne 2004, 227). Hence, South Indian goddesses emerging from low-caste rural contexts are now "fomenting a new solidarity" that "cuts across caste lines, crosses class distinctions, and bridges the urban-rural divide" (Waghorne 2004, 133–34). Waghorne refers to this process as the "bourgeoisification" of the Goddess, although we might equally refer to it as the "sweetening" of the Goddess as she moves from being a fierce, capricious, meat-eating deity to being a benign deity acceptable to middle-class and high-caste sensibilities (see also Allocco 2018 and Arumugam 2020).

The form that Karumariamman takes in both Thiruverkadu and Pontiac is a "sweetened" one. The temple in Thiruverkadu is today under government administration, with ritual worship performed by formally trained, high-caste officiants, or *pujaris*. Yet the temple has rural, Paraiyar ("untouchable" or "scheduled caste") roots. According to one of the main priests at the temple, who claimed to have served there for twenty-eight years when I interviewed him in January 2009, the shift in control of the temple from a Paraiyar family to the state government occurred in the 1960s. One elderly temple devotee listening in on our interview noted that the temple at that time was very popular and attracted significant monetary donations, which probably contributed to state interest in the temple. The main priest of the Thiruverkadu temple, Nagaraja Gurukkal, reports that until the government takeover, the goddess took form in the temple as an earthen pot filled with water and adorned with turmeric paste and Margosa leaves, a form characteristic of rural, Tamil village goddesses (Srinivasan 2009, 215). After it took over, the state government built a new, concrete structure and adopted high-caste practices. Today the temple houses both a full *murti* of the goddess as well as a *murti* of just her head. Tamil village goddesses are often represented by just their heads, so the inclusion of this latter *murti* in temple space suggests an acknowledgment of Karumariamman's village roots. Yet the full "bourgeosified" and sweetened form of the Goddess claims pride of place and functions as the main temple *murti*.

When I was in Thiruverkadu in 2009, at least two members of the Paraiyar family that had in the past presided over the main Karumariamman temple still lived nearby and continued to preside over their own, albeit smaller and less visited, temples where the goddess entered into their bodies, possessing them to prophesize and to perform healings. During that visit, I and my research associate, Thavamani, interviewed Mariammal Sami, the granddaughter of the Thiruverkadu temple's last Paraiyar officiant. Mariammal ran a small temple within walking distance of the main temple in Thiruverkadu (fig. 3.2). She told us that her great-great-grandfather had

Figure 3.2. Mariammal in 2010. Thiruverkadu, Tamil Nadu. *Source:* Photo by the author.

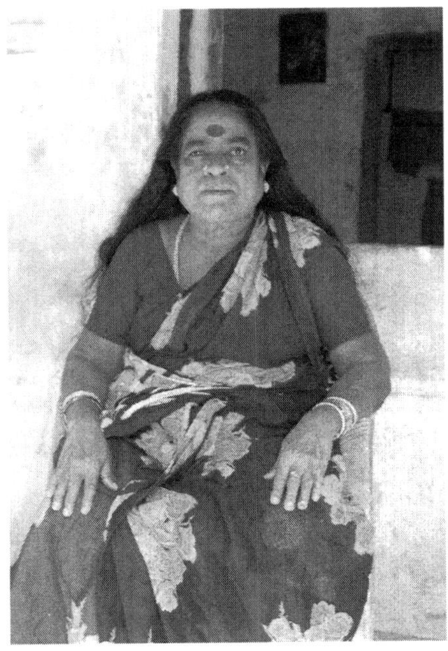

founded the main Thiruverkadu Karumariamman temple. Following his death, her grandfather and then her father had presided over the main temple until the Tamil Nadu government wrested control away from the family. According to Mariammal, prior to the takeover, the temple had been a site of prophecy (*kurimedai*), miracles, and healing, and that the goddess had accepted animal sacrifice. The priest I interviewed in 2009 at the main Karumariamman temple, however, told me that there is no longer any prophesying done at the temple, and animal sacrifice has been banned.

The form that the Goddess takes in Pontiac is, similarly, a sweetened form acceptable to high-caste, middle-class sensibilities. The temple website proclaims that its Goddess is Parashakthi but has elected to appear in the temple as Karumariamman because this is the form that is "closest to earthly creations" and hence most accessible to humans (Parashakthi Temple, "Temple History"). The term *shakti* refers to the feminine, divine power that goddesses embody; the term *parashakthi* means "highest (feminine) power" and refers to the Goddess in her supreme form. Numerous other deities were installed in the temple between its founding and the 2018 fire. But all deities other than the Goddess in her form as Divine Mother are portrayed as manifestations of the Goddess's vibratory energy (*spanda*), with the Goddess serving as their energizing source.

The religious life of the Parashakthi Temple is shaped directly by its religious leader, Kumar, who is also a practicing gastroenterologist. Kumar describes how in 1994 the Goddess appeared to him during his practice of meditation and called on him to build her a temple in the United States so she could radiate to her "children" her blessings for "peace, happiness, and paramount success" and to "protect them from harm" (Parashakthi Temple, "Shakthi Worship"). Many temple devotees recognize Kumar as a mystic and religious visionary, but he claims he is simply a "mailman" who has been elected to deliver directives and truths that the Goddess communicates to him directly through a series of ongoing revelations. Nevertheless, he acknowledges that his "payment" for this service is that the Goddess allows him to read "the mail" before he delivers it to the congregation (see, for example, "Dr. Krishnakumar's Speech on New Year 2021"). The temple community considers Kumar the principal founder of the temple, although Kumar often claims that the Goddess is the actual founder. Many other individuals were active in establishing the temple, and many in the initial group of devotees continue to support the temple financially and remain engaged in temple activities. However, no one else plays the kind of central role that Kumar does in guiding the temple's ongoing religious life (see also Pintchman 2014, 2015, 2018a, and 2018b).

Kumar recounts that when the Goddess first appeared to him during his 1994 meditation, she told him to seek spiritual guidance and help in building "her Western house" from Dr. V. V. Svarnavenkatesha Dikshitar, one of the main priests of the Shaiva Chidambaram Temple in Tamil Nadu (interview, October 2008). Kumar states that this priest initiated him as a disciple and gave him both a *mantra*, the "sound body" or sonic form of a deity or aspect of the Divine (Burchett 2019, 32), and a *yantra*, a diagram imbued with divine energy, as part of his *diksha* or initiation. With these in his possession, Kumar and an inner circle of close spiritual companions began to plan the construction of the Parashakthi Temple, which was finally established in 1999 (see also Pintchman 2014, 2018a, 2024).

The consecration of the *murti* of the Goddess, which established the temple as a living temple, took place at 4 a.m. on October 19, 1999, as that had been deemed to be the most auspicious time for the installation (interview, October 2008).[2] This consecration coincided with the Hindu festival Vijaya Dashami, or "Victory Tenth," which was celebrated that same day. This convergence was not at all a coincidence. Vijaya Dashami commemorates the episode in the Hindu scripture Devi-Mahatmya, or "Glorification of the Goddess," in which the Goddess battles and ultimately vanquishes a buffalo demon, Mahisha, restoring moral order, or *dharma,* to the world.

Parashakthi temple discourse portrays the goddess of the Parashakthi Temple as a deity who not only grants devotees spiritual grace, but also assumes on a universal scale the protective and evil-destroying function associated with the Hindu goddess as she is portrayed in the Devi-Mahatmya. According to Kumar, the temple was constructed at the time of transition between millennia to protect the Western world from danger during the first part of the twenty-first century. Indeed, the abiding mission of the temple is that of divine protection. Kumar has noted on several public occasions that the Goddess orchestrated the construction of the temple because the world would go through a catastrophic period during the first decades of the twenty-first century, and the energy installed at the temple would offer protection from potential disaster. Kumar speaks frequently of demons (*asuras*) as active, malevolent forces that abound in the created universe. He says that when he was planning the temple, the Goddess told him, "When you bring me [to Michigan] in this form, which has never happened before on this earth, all the *asuras* will attack you. They will not want me here" (interview, October 2008). Kumar and other devotees reported to me that as construction on the original temple continued over several years until the 1999 consecration, numerous zoning and building complications arose. Kumar understood those to be the result of destructive *asura* forces. Conversely, the Goddess and other deities established at the Parashakthi Temple are described as supremely powerful, positive forces that can mitigate or even overcome destructive forces.

The grace-giving and protective power embodied at the Parashakthi Temple is said to be available to the entire world but is especially intense at the Goddess's Western home. Kumar recounts that the Goddess herself had been present in the temple's land for millennia before the temple was built. The land's power had thereby attracted in past centuries Native American shamans, whose religious practices then further intensified the land's spiritual power (interview, May 2008). In the temple's first newsletter, published in 2001 after the first portion of the temple was built, devotee Pamela Costa notes, "Local Native American Indians were drawn to the power of the land and selected it for their sacred worship site. . . . It is apparent to many that a vortex of energy exists at the site. We, at the Eternal Mother Temple, believe the Holy Land is aligned with the various planetary and star systems in such a way so as to heighten the energies at the present day site" (Costa 2001, 4). Numerous devotees and visitors have told me over the years that they could sense the presence of the Goddess's power the minute they stepped foot onto temple grounds. One world-renowned *acarya*, or religious teacher, from Vrindavan, North India, who was invited to preside at a Krishna installation at the temple in 2011, told me that while this was his first visit, he could feel that it was a "lively" temple, proclaiming, "This is a place where *shakti* dances."

Matter and Power at the Parashakthi Temple

At the Parashakthi Temple, the Goddess is said to engage material objects and structures to transmit and intensify her grace-giving and protective power. Many devotees perceive religiously significant objects at the temple as possessing unique potency because of their origins, the specific ways they came to be called to the temple and installed, the people who installed them, and the places where they are installed. Their significance and power reside in the amalgamated effect of all the layers of their particularity. Divine power, therefore, resides at the intersection of divine, human, and material worlds. In this regard, David Morgan emphasizes ways that the agency of religious objects is not encased in the things themselves but is instead "made to happen by a variety of enabling circumstances—an encompassing ecology. . . . The shape of materiality is webs. Objects, spaces, and people are nodes within these webs that mediate the relations among individuals, groups, and entire networks" (2021, 20). Morgan argues that a religiously meaningful thing—an object or structure, for example—is actually "a network or assemblage, a gathering of many human and nonhuman actors" that cannot be reduced to the physicality of the thing itself and that is "always more than humans can perceive or control" (2021, 183).

Every object and structure at the temple that wields divine power does so only insofar as the Goddess has chosen it for her "Western house" and had her human agents create or procure it, ritually prepare it, and install it in temple space. Once established, temple objects become, in the eyes of devotees, agents in and of themselves. This is true, for example, of the numerous *murti*s that the temple housed before the 2018 fire. Kumar maintains that the Goddess functions at the Parashakthi Temple as divine curator, deciding which *murti*s to bring to the temple and then revealing those decisions to him. She selects the *murti*s that she allegedly believes to be the most efficacious in responding to both the needs of her devotees for spiritual advancement and calamities, both global and local, which are themselves manifestations of demonic forces. Kumar proclaims that as different *asur*ic (demonic) energies become active in the world, they require the ongoing creation and installation in the Parashakthi Temple of new *murti*s that embody the specific power needed to counter those negative forces. Each new *murti* also enhances the temple's ability to foster spiritual transformation in those who come through its doors. During a conversation we had in Michigan in July 2013, Kumar told me that the *murti*s "are there giving grace, actively. . . . They [also] enhance our receptivity because of our limitations, our sense-based limitations. . . . These objects Mother has granted to us enhance our ability."[3]

E. Allen Richardson (2019) argues that among Hindus in the United States, there has been a cultural trajectory away from perceiving *murti*s as actual embodiments of deity and toward an understanding of them as symbolic, aesthetic, or consumer objects, especially among second- and third-generation American Hindus. He notes, however, that first-generation Hindu immigrants, American Hindu temple priests and leaders, and gurus tend to continue to perceive deity images "through a traditional lens of embodiment" (Richardson 2019, 155). While I have heard devotees at the

Parashakthi Temple express both views, Kumar and other key devotees and temple leaders maintain that all the temple *murtis* are living forms of divine energy that embody the manifold vibrations of the Goddess herself and enhance her grace-giving and protective power. Kumar insists that all the *murtis* emplaced at the temple embody energies that were already present in the land on which the temple stands even before the temple was built, but their embodiment as *murtis* makes those energies much more accessible and available to human worshipers than they would be if they were not embodied. The *murtis* serve as material transmitters and intensifiers of powers that the Goddess wishes to make both more potent and more accessible (interview, March 2008).

Divine protective power is also embodied in a grand, seven-story *rajago-puram* or "royal tower" that was completed in August 2015. George Michell claims that *rajagopurams* originated during the Pallava dynasty (sixth-ninth centuries) in Tamil Nadu and emerged as a dominant temple element by the time of the Pandya dynasty during the twelfth century (Michell 1977, 150). Crispin Branfoot, on the other hand, states that, while *rajagopurams* are present in South India from at least the eleventh century, "their great number and scale are characteristic of the temple complexes built in South India in the sixteenth and seventeenth centuries" (Branfoot 2015, 80). Historical issues aside, today *rajagopurams* can be found at Hindu temples around the world, especially at South Indian temples. Branfoot notes that "the *gopura* is a clear, distinguishing expression of the South Indian identity of the deities and the worshipping community of the temple" at which it is found (Branfoot 2015, 107). At its simplest, a *rajagopuram* functions as a sign indicating the location of the temple, "just like the sign that you put in front of your house to let people know where you live" (Parker 2009, 152). The *rajagopuram* at the Parashakthi Temple, however, is presented in temple discourse as a powerful, protective structure that is unique in the world. Kumar gave a talk at the temple in March 2012 announcing that the Goddess had appeared to him in his meditation and requested that it be built to increase and intensify the temple's protective potency. In his talk, he noted some urgency in getting construction underway because of new destructive forces would be unleashed in the universe starting on December 21 of that year: "So Mother said, 'Bring my *devatas* (deities) who are there [and put them on the *rajagopuram*], and they will stand before the changes, cosmic changes, which may occur on that day, and protect the earth from destruction or the universe from dissolution.' . . . Nothing will happen now because we will succeed in placing, then completing, the *rajagopuram*.

Figure 3.3. Rajagopuram installation. Pontiac, Michigan, 2015. *Source:* Photo by the author.

And these forces will stop the destruction" (Temple talk, March 2012). The occasion of the *rajagopuram*'s installation in 2015 was celebrated in grand fashion, with dignitaries and devotees traveling from India and other parts of the United States to attend.

On its four faces the *rajagopuram* features 520 images, or *vigraha*s, of Hindu deities. Kumar and the temple board oversaw the construction of the *rajagopuram* and the placement of each of the *vigraha*s with a traditional temple architect and several craftsmen executing its production. However, Kumar insists that the Goddess herself identified through direct revelation to him each *devata* to be installed. Kumar also insists the Goddess commanded that the *rajagopuram* be constructed according to her precise instructions in order to circulate her grace-giving and protective energy most effectively. Kumar has declared on several occasions that while ordinarily humans build temples to reach the Divine, the Goddess herself built the temple's *rajagopuram* using human agents only to manifest her wishes. She wanted the *rajagopuram* constructed, Kumar claims, because "she knows the time is bad, and we need protection. This is a temple of protection" ("Importance of Gouri Kund and Its Relevance to Creation" 2021). Kumar is referring here to the idea rooted in the Puranas, an important set of Hindu scriptures, and now widespread among Hindus, that we are living in *kali yuga*, the fourth of four progressively degenerate ages. Because the times are so dangerous, the Goddess has provided a structure of intensified potency to guard against demonic energies.

At the Parashakthi Temple, the Goddess establishes her power in the manifest world and makes it available to humans and other creatures through objects and structures. She accomplishes this through the interventions of humans who act according to her wishes. The divine, human, and material realms are all implicated in an indissoluble web of performative relationships that enable *shakti* to become manifest in specific, divinely chosen substances and structures and to take up residence at the temple and its grounds. The Goddess, the objects she chooses to transmit her power, and the humans she calls to her service all function to anchor her protective energy in the material realm and "make *shakti* dance" at her Western home.

So Why Did the Goddess Destroy Her Own Temple?

When the temple was destroyed in the 2018 fire, the only structure said to have survived unscathed both materially and spiritually was the *rajagopuram*. When I returned to the temple in October 2019, I met with Kumar and a handful of key devotees to ask them specifically about this issue. Kumar told me that the Goddess made sure the *rajagopuram* was constructed entirely in inflammable stone and consecrated in 2015 so that the *shakti* that was present in the temple would have somewhere sacred to which it could retreat while the fire took place. The implication was that the Goddess knew in 2015 that the 2018 fire would occur and had in fact planned for it.

Everyone I spoke with at the temple was convinced that the fire could not possibly have happened if the Goddess had not wanted it to happen. While it might be tempting to attribute the fire to the Goddess's anger or hot temperament given the origins of the Parashakthi Temple's goddess in South Indian village goddess traditions, in fact no one I spoke with offered such an explanation. Instead, the predominant claim I heard was that the temple functioned well for the twenty years it lasted but was not powerful enough for the future given the more intense *asur*ic energy that the universe would now face, so the Goddess had to destroy it to make way for the building of a more powerful structure. The new temple would be much larger and more spectacular than the one that had burned down and would house many more *murti*s. Everyone with whom I spoke assured me the fire was the result of divine intervention, an intervention that the Goddess effected because of the need for a more intensely potent structure that could help more devotees receive Divine Mother's grace and would more powerfully neutralize the intense *asur*ic energies that are to come. Hence, the fire was interpreted in the context of the temple community's existing understanding of the temple and its Goddess: Divine Mother caused the fire to happen because she needed her human agents to rebuild her Western house in a way that would intensify its grace-giving and protective power. Kumar maintains that the Goddess revealed to him directly the thirty-three new deity *murti*s that he says will be installed at the new temple and will render it one of the most, if not the most, spiritually powerful and protective temples on earth. Invoking the *kali yuga* as the age in which we live, and the sanctuaries or *sannidhanams* in which each of the planned deity *murti*s will be placed, Kumar noted the following:

> Mother said this is *kali yuga*. These are dangerous times, and the world will go through various crises. One we are facing right now is the COVID crisis, and that won't end that soon. . . . So, she said, "We need many of my aspects to fight each *asur*ic aspect that is causing this [confluence of crises]." This is one example. There are many other examples. There will be many other attacks. . . . So many attacks are in for us, but we will be protected because Divine Mother is giving us this wonderful temple with various *sannidhanam*s of her, aspects designed by her, energized by her, so they will have the ability to protect us from this onslaught in this *kali yuga*. ("Dr. Krishnakumar Speech About Upcoming New Shrines and Its Significance on Vasantha Navarathiri 2021")

In the months following the fire, the divine energy that had been present in the *murti*s had to be moved ritually into drawings and wooden figures that the temple architect had constructed specifically for this purpose. When a Hindu temple is being renovated or rebuilt, the divine power resident in the *murti*s of the temple must be transferred into a water pot, a wooden image, or a drawn picture to render the space mundane so that anyone can enter it in any state, even an impure one, to complete whatever construction work needs to be done (Sridharan 2019, 80). This transference of power took place over a period of months during the 2018–2019 year. While I was not present for this process, a devotee later described it to me, noting that the temple priests had to go to every shrine, conduct an *abhishekam* (a rite of bathing a *murti* with water and other liquid substances considered pure or auspicious), perform the energy transfer, and move on to the next *murti* until the energy transfer was complete. The drawings, wooden figurines, and the main *murti* of the Goddess were all moved to a shed that was built expressly for this purpose next to the main temple site, which is where I saw them during return visits in 2019 and 2020. A devotee later told me that when Kumar went to India in 2020 and meditated in the Himalayas, the Goddess revealed to him that she wanted the existing *murti* to remain separate from the new temple structure to keep the whole area energized, so she wanted the shed to be turned into a permanent structure. This wish was carried out, and a new *murti* of the Goddess was consecrated in the main temple structure during the 2022 installation. Kumar and others told me that the fire had not touched the original *murti* of the Goddess, even on the subtle level, so it could be retained, but now the Goddess wanted her own space. With several new *murtis* coming to be installed in the new, main temple structure, the Goddess would continue her role as "chairperson of the (divine) board," so to speak, but she preferred to do it from a distance, in her new "office." This arrangement would allow the temple to be even more powerful than it had been before.

By 2019, the rebuilding effort was underway. Kumar told me that even after the energy from the *murtis* had been moved to the shed, the temple priests had continued performing rituals, especially *homas*, in the now physically empty space where the temple had stood right behind the *rajagopuram* "because when you stop doing rituals, the energies might dissipate." These *homas* and other rites helped maintain the divine power in place and kept it active and alive. Kumar noted: "Cosmic energies are all very active at the temple. These cosmic energies, they are very, very fickle. If you don't keep the highest energy continually there, with proper *homa*—if you don't, they dissipate. I have seen that many times" (interview, October 2019). Even though the temple structure had been destroyed, either by fire or by the bulldozers that tore down the remaining structure following the 2018 fire, the subtle, divine energies that constituted temple space and rendered it powerful were continually "fed" so they would remain in the location where the temple had stood for almost nineteen years. In an important way, then, the temple was never really destroyed; only the material shell of the temple was destroyed. Through the practice of ongoing rites, the energies that had always constituted the temple as a lively, powerful place "where *shakti* dances" and not just a "lifeless" structure were made to remain in place. Hence, I was told, the temple continued to protect its community and the world at large even during those years when it was, in a manner of speaking, no longer there. While the new, much larger and more powerful temple building was being planned and then constructed between 2019 and 2022, Kumar told me (interview, August 2022), he and others often sensed the presence of the subtle bodies of deceased temple priests and religious leaders who had spent time at the temple. They were reportedly hanging about because they missed the temple as much as the community of living, human devotees missed it, and they were coming by to check on the progress of the rebuilding effort.

Rising from the Fire

I made a masked visit to the temple site in August 2020, but between that visit and my return to the temple for its grand reopening in August 2022, I followed temple happenings online, especially through the temple's YouTube channel and website. The COVID-19 epidemic and then family issues kept me away during those two years. But I knew I would have to return during the week of rites surrounding the *kumbhabhishekam*, the rites that take place to consecrate a new or, in this case, a newly reconstructed, temple. An email blast sent out on August 7, 2022 made note of the intensified power of the new temple and the pending consecration as follows:[4]

> Devi Parashakthi Temple is Devi's own abode, and all Her transcendent cosmic angels are intensely manifest at our temple for world protection during *Kali Yuga* (difficult times). We are very fortunate and blessed to be given a very powerful place of worship by Divine Mother that is a high vortex of energy as confirmed by many mystics and *siddha*s in India. . . . Divine Mother, out of extreme kindness and affection, has designed and chosen the most effective and important intense cosmic energies to be placed [here] [to] be able to protect the world from the *asur*ic energies so that the world can continue to evolve and keep the *asur*ic energies under control.

The Goddess's decision to intensify her presence at the temple site called for an intensified performance of rites preceding the consecration. Edward S. Casey notes that "there is no knowing or sensing a place except by being in that place, and to be in a place is to be in a position to perceive it" (1996, 18). Knowledge of a place is necessarily experiential or, as Casey describes such knowledge, "placial," since knowledge of places occurs through "knowing them by means of our knowing bodies" (1996, 45). Nonetheless, I offer here a description of the most important practices that took place during the week of consecration rites to give readers a small sense of what being at the temple during that week of intense ritual performance entailed.

The week leading up to the *kumbhabhishekam* began on August 22, 2022, with a Ganesha *homa* in the small temple that the Goddess had commandeered as her new "away" space. By the summer of 2022, the temporary shed that had been constructed to house her *murti* had been replaced with a permanent structure. Ganesha is the deity who removes obstacles, so the temple community needed to seek his blessings before launching the rest of the week's activities. That evening, packets of *navaratna* ("nine jewels") were collected from devotees and transferred to the main temple to be placed under the *murti*s the next day. Collection of the *navaratna* packets continued daily throughout the week, in fact, until the final installation. The second day began with a *homa* to the nine planets (*navagraha*) in the small temple, followed by *abhishekam* to the nine planets and the Goddess herself. In Hindu practice, the *navagraha* are heavenly bodies that can influence human life on the earthly plane, so devotees propitiate them both to seek blessings and to avoid misfortune. The third day began with a *sudarshana homa*, a set of fire offerings made to eradicate negative, demonic energy, and ended with temple *puja* being performed in the evening.

On the fourth day, the temple architect performed the eye-opening ceremony for the *murti*s that were going to be installed on the actual *kumbhabhishekam* day. The opening of the eyes is accomplished when *shilpi*s carve the pupil on the eye of a deity's granite image. Temple priests and devotees also began to decorate the outdoor *yagashala*, the sacrificial "hall" or "arena" in which nine ritual fires would be constructed, to be used in the days directly preceding the consecration. In the evening, temple priests performed a *homa* outside the doors of the main temple for about an hour before performing *vastu shuddhi*, a purification ritual entailing setting fire to a straw effigy and dragging the burning effigy around the new temple complex to remove all evil energies from temple grounds.

The fifth day began with the ritual "charging" of the *yantras* and *navaratna* packets that were to be placed under the *murti*s before installation. Immediately following this rite, a trailer from a local farm and petting zoo pulled into the temple parking lot and released two cows for the performance of cow *puja*. The two cows were coaxed inside the main temple building, where they circumambulated the new *sannidhanam* before being brought back outside to circumambulate the *yagashala* three times before being put back in their trailer and driven around the entire temple complex. Cows are sacred animals to many Hindus, and this rite is seen as removing inauspicious energy and giving blessings to the entire temple complex.

The first large fire sacrifice of the week took place that night outdoors in the *yagashala*. Fires were lit in nine firepits that had been established earlier in the week. The weekend's activities required six additional priests beyond the three already resident at the Parashakthi Temple, so several had been flown in from other Hindu temples in the US and from India. Pots of water into which divine energy had earlier been transferred, called *kalasa*, were brought to the *yagashala* and adorned with mango leaves and coconuts. The water in the pots would come to be charged with divine energy through the hours of *mantra* chanting and fire rites that took place all weekend. Hundreds of *kalasa*s, most of which devotees had sponsored with a financial donation, surrounded the *yagashala* on all sides. Offerings, *ahuti*, are placed into the ritual fire during a *yajna*, with a final, more elaborate offering, the *purnahuti* or "complete offering," taking place at the end of the *yajna*. A *purnahuti* often involves the offering of different kinds of grains, fruits, and fine textiles, such as cotton or silk saris.

Temple activity began to escalate significantly on the morning of the sixth day. Temple crowds also swelled as increasing numbers of devotees flocked to the temple for the weekend's festivities. I was later told that about two thousand people attended the *kumbhabhishekam* that weekend. Many of the attendees were local temple regulars, but there was a surprising number who were not. By the time I made it into the main temple, I saw that several of the *murti*s had been placed in their pedestals overnight and were ready for consecration, including the new *murti* of the Goddess flanked by Ganesha on one side and Karttikeya and his wives on the other. Those of us present for the morning's activities were invited to dab these three *murti*s with sesame oil, which many Hindus believe repels demonic forces. By late morning, we were all ushered out to the *yagashala* for three more hours of fire rites.

The *mantras* chanted in the *yagashala* that morning and afternoon included 1,008 names of the Goddess and long repetitions of a variety of Gayatri *mantras*. When the water in the *kalasas* had been sufficiently charged with divine energy, they were ready to be brought to the temple to transfer that energy to the *murti*s. Kumar, the nine priests, major donors, and members of the board scooped up several of the pots and carried them ceremoniously to the main temple building. Kumar climbed onto a crane that lifted him about thirty feet up into the air and over the *sannidhanams* of Ganesha, the Goddess, and Karttikeya. Kumar dabbed each of the *murti*s with water, sprinkled them with flower petals, and sealed up the very top entry point to each shrine with cement as the congregation below yelled and clapped. When this task had been accomplished, Kumar went to the smaller temple where, exhausted from the week's activities, he stopped at the base of the Goddess's shrine and distributed the consecrating waters to close devotees to pour on the Goddess's *murti*. When all the necessary rites were completed, Kumar announced to those in attendance that, by virtue of attending the *kumbhabhishekam*, we would all now be connected to Divine Mother forever. He also pleaded with the congregation "to be kind and calm for the next two days because we are all semidivine for now." There was another long evening of fire rites performed in the *yagashala*, followed by a dance performance in the main temple.

The day of the actual temple consecration, Sunday, August 28, 2023, began with fire rites in the *yagashala* beginning at 8:00 a.m. When it was time to begin the final consecration, hundreds of devotees processed into the temple carrying *kalasa*s and handed them to volunteers, who placed all the ritual vessels in front of the Goddess's new *murti*. By the time the procession ended, the temple was packed with people crowding in shoulder-to-shoulder. Some late-arriving devotees strained to watch the proceedings from outside the temple doors. The priests poured all the water from the *kalasa*s onto the new *murti* of the Goddess as well as the *murti*s of Ganesha and Karttikeya. The curtains were then closed for about an hour while the priests, aided by Kumar, performed the *prana-pratishtha*, the rite by which *murti*s are brought to life. When the curtains reopened, the temple priests performed a long *abhishekham*, and the nearly two thousand people present swayed, cheered, and chanted. The atmosphere was electric. After the *abhishekam*, the priests performed a *puja* to the freshly installed goddess in her new, more powerful home.

Figure 3.4. The Parashakthi Temple in August 2022, Pontiac, Michigan. *Source:* Photo by the author.

Steven Feld notes that "senses make place," meaning that "the perceptual engagements we call sensing" play a critical role in our "conceptual constructions of place" (Feld 1996, 91). The intensity of sensory immersion entailed in the week of consecration rites reaffirmed devotees' perceptions of the temple as a unique, *śakti*-filled abode that has been specially blessed by the Goddess and had now become, in its new form, even more intensely powerful than it had been before.

Conclusion

In his discussion of Mariamman, Harman observes that while the term "Mari" can refer to disease or rain, it can also mean "change" (Harman 2010, 285). Mariamman is a goddess capable of great change across various divides. Mariamman's rise in popularity over the last several decades and the "growing wealth and importance of her temples" in India and abroad are indicative of her increasing popularity. Within India, Waghorne links a process of sweetening or gentrification of this goddess to political and economic changes of the last several decades, changes that in turn facilitated evolving religious sensibilities that reflect the values of the rising Indian middle class (Waghorne 2004, 135–36). Middle-class South Indian Hindus strive to appropriate the power of the goddess, but they do so by "cleaning her house and purifying or isolating her coarser elements" (Waghorne 2004, 170), thereby making her acceptable to middle-class sensibilities and distancing her from her rural origins. This process of gentrification or sweetening includes practices like employing Brahmin priests in her worship, banning animal sacrifice at her temples, and dissociating her from the violent and unpredictable qualities that prevail in rural, traditional village contexts (Waghorne 2004, 133). While Mariamman is known for her "unpredictable capacity for anger and violence" in traditional rural settings in Tamil Nadu, she is also depicted as a divine mother who is "gracious and loving" (Harman 2010, 185). As she has moved in the past several decades out of villages and away from her very humble rural roots to capture new, middle-class, and high-caste devotees, an emphasis on her latter, "sweet" qualities have risen to the fore and rendered her acceptable to a wider devotional audience. Karumariamman, as a form of Mariamman, participated in the same process of "sweetening" in India before moving across oceans and continents to take up residence in her new home in Michigan. That form also underwent change from 2018 to 2022 when the Goddess, according to Parashakthi Temple discourse, burned down her own temple to bring a newly intensified concentration of protective *shakti* to the Western world.

The Goddess's declared need for an intensified presence in Pontiac is not captured by the sweetening process alone. Robert Orsi has observed that religion entails an "ongoing, dynamic relationship with the realities of everyday life. . . . People appropriate religious idioms as they need them, in response to particular circumstances. All religious ideas and impulses are of the moment, invented, taken, borrowed, and improvised at the intersections of life" (Orsi 1997, 7–8). Lived religion "is shaped and experienced in the interplay among venues of everyday experience" (Orsi 1997, 9). Orsi observes further that inherited religious idioms combined with cultural structures and particular historical moments "give rise to religious creativity and improvisation" and insists that "it is the historicized and encultured religious imagination by means of which, in Marx's famous expression, the frozen circumstances of our worlds are forced to dance" (Orsi 1997, 16–17). The

2018 fire at the Parashakthi Temple, taking place at the specific historical moment at which it occurred and in the context of the temple community's inherited religious idiom, sparked an act of religious creativity "made necessary and possible by particular circumstances in the world" (Orsi 1997, 8). This act of creativity, in the minds of temple community members, was shared between divine and human realms. Both the Goddess and the community that reveres her worked together to create out of the ashes of the temple's destruction a new, more powerful temple that would better serve the needs of the contemporary world. For the temple's devotional community, the Goddess has now become even more intensely present in the patch of earth she claims as her American home. The new land does not simply reproduce the Hindu landscape or "incarnate" it through imitation (Narayanan 2006, 149), but instead supersedes it, surpassing it in sacrality and power. In Pontiac, America is not "foreign soil" but rather is and always has been the site of an enlivened and now intensified *pitha,* earthly seat of the Goddess, that is more *śakti*-filled than many of its Indian antecedents.

Notes

1. "Ram" is a pseudonym. Other conversation partners' given names are used.

2. All interviews were conducted in Pontiac and Troy, Michigan, between 2008 and 2022.

3. I have modified the language slightly for sense.

4. I have corrected grammar and mechanical errors and edited the paragraph slightly for sense.

References

Allocco, Amy. 2018. "Flower Showers for the Goddess: Borrowing, Modification, and Ritual Innovation in Tamil Nadu." In *Ritual Innovation: Strategic Interventions in South Asian Religion,* 129–48. State University of New York Press.

Arumugam, Indira. 2020. "Migrant Deities, Dislocations, Divine Agency, and Mediated Manifestations." *American Behavioral* Scientist 64 (10): 1458–70.

Branfoot, Crispin. 2015. "The Tamil *Gopura*: From Temple Gateway to Global Icon." *Ars Oriantalis* 45: 78–112.

Burchett, Patton E. 2019. *A Genealogy of Devotion: Bhakti, Tantra, Yoga, and Sufism in North India.* Columbia University Press.

Casey, Edward S. 1996. "How to Get from Space to Place in a Fairly Short Stretch of Time." In *Senses of Place*, edited by Steven Feld and Keith H. Basso, 13–52. School of American Research Press.

Costa, Pamela. 2001. "Mystical Origins." *Om Shakthi* 1 (1) (January–March): 12.

Craddock, Elaine. 2001. "Reconstructing the Split Goddess as Śakti in a Tamil Village." In *Seeking Mahādevī: Constructing the Identities of Hindu Great Goddess*, edited by Tracy Pintchman, 145–69. State University of New York Press.

"Dr Krishnakumar Speech About Upcoming New Shrines and Its Significance on Vasantha Navarathiri 2021." 2021. Devi Parashakthi—Eternal Mother Temple. March 26. Video, https://www.youtube.com/watch?v=fivmmebJU8M.

Feld, Steven. 1996. "Waterfalls of Song: An Acoustemology of Place Resounding in Bosavi, Papua New Guinea." In *Senses of Place*, edited by Steven Feld and Keith H. Basso, 91–135. School of American Research Press.

Harman, William. 2004. "Taming the Fever Goddess: Transforming a Tradition in Southern India." *Manushi* 140: 2–16.

Harman, William. 2010. "Possession as Protection and Affliction: The Goddess Mariyamman's Fierce Grace." In *Health and Religious Rituals in South Asia: Disease, Possession, and Healing*, edited by Fabrizio Ferrari, 188–98. Taylor and Francis.

"Importance of Gouri Kund and Its Relevance to Creation." Devi Parashakthi—Eternal Mother Temple. March 26, 2021. Video. https://www.youtube.com/watch?v=u7pXAX714cM&t=1190s.

Michell, George. 1997. *The Hindu Temple: An Introduction to Its Meaning and Forms*. Harper and Row.

Morgan, David. 2021. *The Thing About Religion: An Introduction to the Material Study of Religions*. University of North Carolina Press.

Narayanan, Vasudha. 2006. "Sacred Land, Sacred Service: Hindu Adaptations to the American Landscape." In *A Nation of Religions: The Politics of Pluralism in Multi-Religious America*, edited by Stephen Prothero, 139–59. University of North Carolina Press.

Orsi, Robert. 1997. "Everyday Miracles: The Study of Lived Religion." In *Lived Religion in America: Toward a History of Practice*, edited by David D. Hall, 3–21. Princeton University Press.

Parashakthi Temple. "Shakthi Worship." Accessed May 30, 2023. http://www.parashakthitemple.org/shakthi_worship.aspx.

Parashakthi Temple. "Temple History." Accessed May 30, 2023. https://www.parashakthitemple.org/temple-history.html.

Parker, Samuel K. 2009. "Sanctum and *Gopuram* at Madurai: Aesthetics of *Akam* and *Puṛam* in Tamil Temple Architecture." In *Tamil Geographies: Cultural Constructions of Space and Place in South India*, edited by Marth Ann Selby and Indira Viswanathan Peterson, 143–72. State University of New York Press.

Pintchman, Tracy. 2014. "From Local Goddess to Locale Goddess: Karumariamman as Divine Mother at a North American Hindu Temple." In *Inventing and Reinventing the Local Goddess: Contemporary Iterations of Hindu Deities on the Move*, edited by Sree Padma, 89–103. Lexington Books.

Pintchman, Tracy. 2015. "The Goddess's Shaligrams." In *Sacred Matters: Materiality in Indian Religions*, edited by Tracy Pintchman and Corinne G. Dempsey, 115–33. State University of New York Press.

Pintchman, Tracy. 2018a. "The Divine Mother Comes to Michigan." In *The Oxford History of Hinduism: The Goddess*, edited by Mandakranta Bose, 304–21. Oxford University Press.

Pintchman, Tracy. 2018b. "Shakti Garbha as Ark of the Covenant at an American Hindu Goddess Temple." In *Between Dharma and Halakha*, edited by Ithamar Theodor and Yudit Greenberg, 35–49. Lexington Books.

Pintchman, Tracy. 2024. *Goddess Beyond Boundaries: Worshipping the Eternal Mother at a North American Hindu Temple*. Oxford University Press.

Richardson, E. Allen. 2019. *Hindu Gods in an American Landscape: Changing Perceptions of Indian Sacred Images in the Global Age*. McFarland & Company.

Sinha, Vineeta, 2014. "Bringing Back the Old Ways: Enacting a Goddess Festival in Urban Singapore." *Material Religion* 10 (1): 76–103.

Sridharan, Shriya. 2019. "The Contemporaneity of Tradition: Expansion and Renovation of the Vedanta Desikar Temple in Mylapore, Chennai." In *The Contemporary Hindu Temple: Fragments for a History*, edited by Annapurna Garimella, Shriya Sridharan, and A. Srivathsan, 74–83. Tata Trust.

Srinivasan, Perundevi. 2009. "Stories of the Flesh: Colonial and Anthropological Discourses on the South Indian Goddess Mariyamman." PhD diss., George Washington University.

Waghorne, Joanne Punzo. 2004. *Diaspora of the Gods: Modern Hindu Temples in an Urban Middle-Class World*. Oxford University Press.

Part 2

Ritual and Possession Performances

4

Insistence, Persistence, and Resistance in Tamil Hindu Rituals to Call the Dead

Amy L. Allocco

Standing in an entirely dry Tamil village water tank in early 2019, I watch as a woman named Malar pulls two unlabeled bottles of local liquor out of a bag.[1] She places them among the offerings arrayed in front of a lavishly decorated ritual vessel called the *karagam* that is the focus of this evening's ceremony to invite her late husband Murugan to come home as a family deity (fig. 4.1). The previous night the *pampaikkarar*, the drummer-priests whom Malar hired to officiate at this two-day Hindu invitation ceremony, summoned several deities and dead relatives to dance and speak in her home. Today she and her extended family have assembled at the water tank so the *pampaikkarar* can devote their musical, vocal, and ritual talent to persuading Murugan to take up permanent residence in her home shrine as a protective deity known as a *puvadaikkari*. Although this term literally means "a woman who wears flowers," in colloquial parlance it may refer to any deceased relative who is worshiped as a family god or goddess. As soon as they secure Murugan's consent to return home, the musicians will temporarily locate his spirit in the *karagam*, which they have constructed from neem branches fastened to a bamboo frame and festooned with flowers. The living person on whom the dead man manifests during the ritual will carry the *karagam* to the family's residence at the end of the invitation ceremony so that Murugan may be installed there as a household deity (*veedu sami*).

Figure 4.1. The *karagam* with two bottles of liquor and other offerings in the bed of the dry water tank on the second day of the puvadaikkari *puja*. Note the string (the "thread ladder") that connects the *karagam* to the Ganga and serves as the conduit for the dead to climb out of the waters and into this ritual vessel. Melur, Tamil Nadu, 2019. *Source:* Photo by the author.

Next to the two liquor bottles, a small sterling silver trident glints in the shifting late-afternoon sunlight. The trident's thin shaft will be used to pierce the tongue of whomever the dead selects to speak their prophecy, or *arul vakku*, during tonight's ritual. Such piercings (*alagu*) mark the relationship between the deified dead and their host as permanent and certify the medium's divination as unassailably true. Just before the ceremony's opening drumbeats ring out, a man pulls up on a scooter and hands a small plastic bag filled with earth collected from Murugan's grave to the musicians, who wave camphor and sprinkle flower petals over it before adding it to the display of offerings (*padaiyal*).[2] This cemetery soil will be brought back to Murugan's former home at the conclusion of the ritual and added to the food offerings arranged in his family's domestic shrine. By that point, all the liquor will have been consumed and the silver trident will have pierced and been removed from one of the ritual participants' tongues.

This chapter analyzes the dynamics of insistence, persistence, and resistance operative in Tamil ceremonies to return departed relatives to the world so they may undergo investiture as puvadaikkaris. Specifically, it attends to the continued insistence by the deified dead and living relatives alike on the necessity of grave soil and crematory ash, tongue-piercing practices, and alcohol offerings. These ritual participants persist in regarding these materials and activities as essential to the rite's success and therefore resist "sweeter," sanitized substitutions. My discussion is grounded in long-term ethnographic research conducted within a range of Hindu communities in Tamil Nadu.[3] It operates in conversation with academic literature on the many forms of gentrification—ritual, narrative, architectural, iconographic, and material—and debates regarding practices like animal sacrifice that are impelled by shifting devotional sensibilities and views about what constitutes progressive, modern Hinduism. Theorizing from the 2019 ceremony performed to bring Murugan back into his family's midst and dozens of similar invitation rituals that I have recorded over the last decade, I consider the implications of the dead's demands for these substances and observances when they inhabit and speak through their living kin in extended ritual performances.

The ritual musicians encourage the sought-after dead to enumerate their unfulfilled desires in what are often dramatic and tense exchanges. In the ritual to return Murugan to the world as a puvadaikkari, we encounter a dead patriarch unwilling to settle for fruits, sweets, and vegetarian delicacies, insisting, instead, on "hot" offerings more suited to his appetites and preferences. Although the musicians sometimes urge the deceased to reconsider their demands, especially when the spirit is embodying a young woman for whom it would appear unseemly to consume liquor or have her tongue pierced, these negotiations are rarely successful: the dead usually get what they want. This chapter suggests, then, that the dead's steadfast refusal to be satisfied by anything but demanding vows and stigmatized substances signals a deliberate resistance to the sweetening trends visible in many contemporary Hindu ritual contexts. Indeed, it proposes that the persistence of these materials and activities in defiance of broader sweetening currents is a characteristic indicator of intensification. In Tamil Nadu, sweetening trends manifest in changes such as banning animal sacrifice on temple premises or relegating it to forested peripheries, replacing liquor offerings with rosewater, and softening deities' appearances by removing fierce physical attributes like fangs and extended tongues. As we shall see, piercing practices and alcohol offerings can introduce dissonance and discomfort in some ritual settings, leading to creative improvisations and negotiations.

What Do the Dead Want?

Although the presence of liquor, bodily piercings, and graveyard soil is entirely commonplace in this strand of Tamil vernacular Hinduism, these substances and practices are generally categorized as impure, polluted, and even transgressive in what we might call dominant, elite, or Sanskritic Hindu traditions.[4] They figure among a wide range of offerings and devotional activities that are routinely glossed as "nonvegetarian" and coded as "inferior" in dominant streams of Hindu thought, including animal sacrifice; tobacco and hashish; and rigorous bodily practices like hook-swinging, firewalking, and even divine embodiment (or "possession"). While grave soil is explicitly tainted with the pollution of death and decay and piercings can draw blood (a decidedly impure substance within brahmanic frameworks), alcohol has attracted perhaps more ambivalent meanings in recent years. Alcohol has traditionally been regarded as taboo and treated with moral suspicion in brahmanic contexts, although today its consumption is prevalent in Tamil Nadu (Allocco 2025). In class-privileged circles its use has become associated with globalized cosmopolitanism. Still, alcohol continues to be proscribed in orthodox ritual settings, whether for consumption or as an offering. Indeed, it is unquestionably ranked low in the "gastropolitics" of South Asia, in a cultural tradition that Arjun Appadurai observes "has invested perhaps more than any other in imbuing food with moral and cosmological meanings" (1981, 496).

The enduring and pervasive influence of brahmanical norms on diverse Hindu expressions is hard to overstate. C. J. Fuller, for example, points out that as an indigenous frame of reference, the Sanskritic tradition serves as "the single most important evaluative norm within Hinduism" ([1992] 2004, 27). Consider, for example, Henry Whitehead's century-old observation that the animal sacrifices, cheroots, and alcohol offerings so characteristic of "village" worship are "reviled" by brahmanism, a tradition that codes the shedding of blood as "low and irreligious" ([1921] 1999, 18; cf. Fuller [1992] 2004, 95). The abiding power of brahmanical standards has given rise and lent strength to sweetening efforts, which devalue, marginalize, restrict, and even outlaw ritual practices and substances deemed impure or otherwise problematic. Whitehead's report resonates with Fuller and Haripriya Narasimhan's (2014) more recent summary of Tamil brahmanical views on dietary practices. In their words, "Vegetarianism . . . is equated with ritual purity, coolness, bodily self-control, ascetical self-restraint, and especially nonviolence, whereas meat eating is equated with impurity, heat, aggression, energetic action, and loss of bodily control, and it also necessitates the immoral slaughter of living beings" (2014, 8).

Such categorizations at least partially account for why families sometimes feel the need to be discreet about including items like liquor, chickens, and hand-rolled cigars in their puvadaikkari invitation rituals, especially in temple settings where they may not be sanctioned or may attract opprobrium. Discretion is the norm at the popular Chennai temple dedicated to Goddess Mundakkanni (Allocco 2009, 2018), for example, where I have observed worshipers carefully conceal bottles of alcohol and tobacco among their offerings in puvadaikkari rites to avoid critique or judgment. Rather than capitulations to high-caste sentiments, such tactics should be read as evidence of the persistence of intensifying impulses, where worshipers insist on offering nonvegetarian items regarded as vital to satisfying their dead. Although this temple is nonbrahmanic, it is located in a historically Brahman neighborhood, draws many upper-caste worshipers, and prohibits animal sacrifice on site. Even the eggs that devotees offer to the temple's snake images and anthill generate some uneasiness here: several high-caste and vegetarian interlocutors have told me over the years that they will only visit the temple early in the morning, before too many offensive (and possibly malodorous) eggs pile up (Allocco 2009, 201–2 and 488–89).

Still, it is important to acknowledge that many worshipers here and elsewhere have not internalized Sanskritic norms and do not strive to emulate them. They are therefore relatively unselfconscious about offerings and substances that others might view as regressive, impure, or backward but that they simply regard as their family's or community's customary religious practices. Such worshipers understand these ritual activities and materials as having an established record of satisfying or pleasing their deities and deified dead and believe they should be faithfully followed as far as possible. Likewise, these devotees are often proud of undertaking arduous vows, presenting costly sacrifices, and carefully calibrating their offerings to their deities' capricious appetites.

In at least some cases, however, concern about others' disapproval or worshipers' own discomfort with including potentially stigmatized articles and edibles in their puvadaikkari *puja*s prompts ritual participants to move from discretion to substitution. Significantly, on a few occasions the substitution of "sweeter" items occurred in invitation ceremonies that were performed at home or at open-air water sources, where temple restrictions on specific ritual materials would not apply. Efforts to deny the dead's demands in these settings, too, signals that in some instances participants themselves are apprehensive that certain substances and devotional activities might reflect negatively on their family's reputation in the broader community.

Yet, where I have sometimes observed musicians and family members suggesting that they offer Fanta in place of whiskey, omit tongue-piercing altogether, or smear deep red *kumkum* on the wet interior of a smashed pumpkin to replicate blood sacrifice rather than bite the neck of a live chicken as requested by the deity, it is vital to appreciate that in all these cases the liquor, the piercing implement, and the chicken were already purchased for the *puja*. Except for the grave soil, which is indexed to the deceased person and crucial to inducing their presence, the array of items offered varies from ritual to ritual, based on what the deceased enjoyed most in life. Whether the dead person had a taste for a stiff drink or particularly relished nonvegetarian fare, ritual sponsors had every intention of offering these items as they prepared for the invitation ceremony because recalling and anticipating their departed relative's preferences is part and parcel of enticing these spirits to return. Even if on some occasions hosts balk at allowing their dead to partake of these offerings depending on who these spirits are embodying, the prevailing view is that the specific wishes and cravings of these deceased relatives must be satisfied for them to feel appropriately honored and loved and for the ritual to be efficacious.

Despite the occasional ambivalence about these offerings on the part of living kin, the dead are rarely amenable to revisions of the ritual menu or program. In most instances dead relatives actively—and sometimes angrily—resist suggested modifications. Indeed, they make it clear that they prefer intensity and that their exacting demands must be met. For example, I have seen dead kin complain bitterly about being disrespected in delicate transactions with the *pampaikkarar* about whether the dead should be served their plastic glasses of liquor before or after they advise on the affairs of the living (i.e., give *vakku*). Across dozens of puvadaikkari *puja*s, only in a handful of cases have I witnessed the deceased accept scaled-back portions of liquor or consent to having an alternate ritual participant's tongue pierced, as we shall see below.

In Murugan's case, his living kin maintained that it would be impossible to entice him and their family gods to return to the world or to satisfy these entities once they manifested without alcohol, grave soil, and piercings. Indeed, ritual participants view these potent items and vows as not only essential to meeting the dead's needs and desires but also as *intrinsic to their nature*. Surviving kin derive these understandings directly from the declarations and requests their dead relatives make while embodying and speaking through human hosts. These speech acts constitute one mode of resistance to vegetarian or otherwise sanitized offerings. Worshipers' insistence on retaining these somewhat stigmatized offerings and intense practices, then, is grounded in a sense both of their efficacy and their appropriateness. This example demonstrates that in some contexts, at least, the appetites of the dead and Tamil family gods are neither growing more "refined" or "genteel" nor shifting to align with brahmanic norms and new visions of "modern" religious practice. Instead, it offers evidence of resistance to sweeter substitutes and an insistence on customary rigorous practices and nonvegetarian offerings.

Similarly complex dynamics are reported by Vineeta Sinha (2005) in her study of the Tamil guardian deity Muneeswaran in contemporary Singapore. Some of Muneeswaran's devotees actively critique the "old ways" of worshiping this fierce god with nonvegetarian food, alcohol, ganja, and cigars—and at some established temples he has become completely vegetarian—but others maintain strong attachments to traditional practices (2005, 199–200). These traditionalists worship him at home and at "jungle temples," sometimes under cover of darkness, to ensure that he gets the old-style offerings that "he likes and wants" (201). Likewise, although questions about the appropriateness of alcohol and tongue-piercing sometimes surfaces in puvadaikkari worship, the vast majority of participants regard these substances and activities as indispensable to demonstrating their affection for their dead, meeting their needs, and successfully bringing them home. If religious experience is always conceived as a form of intersection, contact, and coalescence (Nabokov 2000, 8), then it makes sense that supplying the "right" kinds of offerings, the ones that the desired dead savored in life and crave in death, is crucial to facilitating the conjunction with their ancestors that these families seek. Such cases demonstrate the persistence of conventionally stigmatized offerings and more intense modes of transacting with deities, even in the face of various legal and social reform efforts to root out "superstition," abolish animal sacrifice, and valorize nonviolent, "modern" religious expressions (see Berti and Good 2023).

The Ritual Context

As is typical in puvadaikkari invitation and installation rites (Allocco 2021), Murugan's ritual begins in the sponsoring family's home, where the drummers build an elaborate ritual vessel called the *padivilakku* that is dedicated to the family's lineage deity (*kula devam*) on the first night. In addition to the *kula devam*, other deities and departed relatives (*mandavargal*) are encouraged to inhabit and speak through those assembled and urged to facilitate Murugan's return to the world. Then, on the second day, the ritual action shifts from the house to a water source, from which the dead are retrieved before the ceremony culminates back at home with the dead's investiture. The two-day rite to invite Murugan home unfolds in early 2019 in a peri-urban village in Kanchipuram district about two hours' drive from Chennai that I will call Melur. The semirural enclave of Melur is entirely populated by people belonging to the Vanniyar caste, a relatively low-ranked but politically powerful Tamil agricultural community. Murugan died in somewhat mysterious circumstances two years earlier when he was forty-five years old, leaving behind his wife Malar and their two children. At the time of their father's puvadaikkari ceremony, Murugan's son is studying "computers" at a local college and his daughter is in tenth standard. With the family's advance permission, I join their ritual at the invitation of my longtime friends and associates the *pampaikkarar*, the musician-priests who preside over puvadaikkari *puja*s and other nonbrahmanic rites in Tamil Nadu.

The word *puvadaikkari* technically refers to a *woman* wearing flowers, signified by the feminine suffix -*kari*, while the reference to flowers (*pu*) indicates her auspicious status. Although the priests, ritual musicians, and worshipers I consulted during my fieldwork generally concur that the term refers specifically to women who died with living husbands (i.e., as *sumangalis*), deceased young people and even men who are worshiped by their surviving kin are also sometimes called puvadaikkaris today.[5] In the academic literature on Hindu traditions it is well attested that the dead become gods (e.g., Blackburn 1985; Coccari 1989; Knipe 2003), although the scholarship tends to emphasize the deification of those who met violent or heroic ends.[6] Isabelle Nabokov, the only other scholar who has written about puvadaikkari *puja*s, identifies the spirits of the dead as "the elemental figures of South Indian pantheons" (2000, 16; see also Clark-Decès 2007). Although the puvadaikkari appellation was traditionally reserved for auspicious women who lived long lives and died in natural and "good" ways, today it is also applied to an increasing number of people who perished in accidents or by suicide, suffering the kinds of premature deaths that might incline them to become ghosts or troublesome spirits (*pey*). The goal of converting lingering, untimely dead into gods or goddesses is unsurprising, given the potential danger they may pose to the living (Dumont [1957] 1986, 449; Fuller [1992] 2004, 49).

The invitation ritual at hand falls within this expanded framing of puvadaikkari worship not only because the focus of the *puja* is a man named Murugan but also because over the course of the proceedings we will come to learn that he died in an accident that abruptly foreshortened his life. There is another significant element that sets Murugan's rite apart from the prototypical puvadaikkari *puja* performance context. Whereas I was frequently told that invitation ceremonies are performed immediately before auspicious life-cycle transitions such as weddings and children's ear-piercings (cf. Nabokov 2000, 127) and I have attended a small handful that were arranged in conjunction with these rites of passage, the overwhelming majority of those I observed were organized in response to family difficulties and suffering (*sodhanai*) involving illness, economic hardship, and overall failure to thrive or "grow." In Murugan's case, in addition to deep grief and sorrow, his early death generated financial distress and uncertainty. It was in this fraught climate that his *puja* was mounted: rather than a propitious family event, the family's need for healing, sustenance, and support motivated the two-day invitation ritual.

These newer and nontraditional contexts themselves signal intensifications in puvadaikkari worship, where the challenges and precarities of the current moment demand that a wider circle of departed relatives be called back into the world and installed as deified dead. Not only are the ritual accoutrements, activities, and offerings potent, but the rituals themselves bring families into direct and visceral contact with relatives who died in troubling and violent circumstances that leave them poised to become malevolent entities. The desire to transform these spirits into permanent, benevolent household deities drives families' decisions to arrange these expensive ritual performances, which are often undertaken in periods of considerable difficulty when the fewest resources are available. Viramma, the Tamil Dalit agricultural laborer and midwife whose life stories were recorded over the course of a decade by Josiane and Jean-Luc Racine, captures this impulse well: "Good fortune or bad fortune, our dead are like gods to us. We call on them at difficult times, we pray to them to help us" (Viramma, Racine, and Racine 2000, 148).

During the ritual preparations I ask the drummers about the ceremony's relatively unusual context and its focus on a male protagonist. The musicians explain that the overriding desire of Murugan's family to bring their deceased father/husband/brother/son home is a sufficient rationale and point to their procurement of his favorite foods and drinks as evidence of their sincerity. Raja, a drummer, says that since Murugan perished in the prime of his life as the "main" person responsible for sustaining his family, he is urgently needed as a resource for the family he left behind. The ceremony, therefore, will aim to secure protection and support (*tunai*) from the dead patriarch, suggesting that kinship obligations frequently extend beyond the grave in these contexts. In Raja's view, "The ritual will make the family whole again and make it possible for them to prosper." His interpretation underscores family unity as a "fundamental moral and ritual principle that leads to health and well-being," although one that is regularly disrupted by death (Sax 2009, 195). Puvadaikkari *pujas*, then, seek to reconstitute the family by bringing the dead home to dwell permanently among the living as beneficent household deities dedicated to the prosperity and thriving of their surviving kin.

Inviting Murugan

The first evening's domestic ritual is called the *padivilakku puja* because its focus is the flower-swathed ritual assemblage into which a lamp, or *vilakku*, is set. Selvam, the ritual drummer who is the ensemble's decoration, or *alankaram*, specialist, devotes a full four hours to meticulously crafting the *padivilakku*. He sculpts the face and upper body of Murugan's *kula devam*, Ankalamman, from local clay before applying her makeup, dressing her, and adorning her with a crown and jewelry. Other troupe members assist him in artfully winding long ropes of flowers around the bamboo stakes that radiate out behind her image (fig. 4.2). Selvam's brother scrawls a hasty genealogy of Murugan's kin, lamps are lit, and offerings are arranged in front of the resplendent ritual display. Energy courses through the room as bunches of neem fronds are passed around among Malar's immediate and extended family and the musicians ready their percussion instruments—two sets of twin-headed *pampai* drums, an hourglass-shaped *udukkai* drum, and two pairs of *silambu*, oblong hollow brass rattles that resemble anklets. As the lamp offering gets underway, they launch the invocatory song sequence that calls and invites a range of deities. The chief goal of this evening's *puja* is to describe and praise (*varuni*) the *kula devam*, thus "decorating" her with what I term "lyrical *alankaram*" and coaxing her to grant permission (*uttaravu*) for the ritual to call the dead. Whether she conveys her willingness through the movement of the *padivilakku*'s flame or by descending on and speaking through one of the ritual participants, Ankalamman *must* communicate her consent for the family to undertake the ritual.

Figure 4.2. The *padivilakku*, which represents the sponsoring family's lineage deity (*kula devam*), in their home on the first night of Murugan's puvadaikkari *puja*. Melur, Tamil Nadu, 2019. *Source:* Photo by the author.

Over the course of the next several hours, deities and deceased relatives respond to the drummers' exhortations to "come and play" by manifesting on the bodies of family members and neighbors who are packed into the main room of Murugan's home. The goddess Draupadi appears first, followed by two of the family's deceased *sumangali*s, and then Ankalamman, who dances vigorously. All four produce the oracular speech that is so fundamental to the ceremony's success—Ankalamman gives permission for the ritual to proceed, and each goddess in turn confirms her satisfaction with the *puja*, declaring emphatically that Murugan will join them at the water source the following day. After midnight but before the *padivilakku puja* concludes, Subramani, the ritual musicians' leader and guru (*vattiyar*), sings an extended, plaintive song addressed to the dead patriarch. The lyrics trace out Murugan's lineage and implore him to return as a beneficent deity to the house that he built so that he may safeguard his family and help them realize their goals. Subramani uses the analogy of a flowering vine bearing many blossoms to depict the educational success that Murugan should help his children achieve as well as the economic stability, freedom from illness, and future good marriages they should experience. Subramani's improvised song underscores how deeply Murugan's children care for him and entreats the dead man to enjoy the offerings they have assembled for him and serve as a support for his family.

After a brief *puja* at home the next morning, the ritual relocates to Melur's now-dry tank, at whose center is a well containing some remaining water (fig. 4.3).[7] The water sources from which deceased relatives are retrieved during puvadaikkari *puja*s are always identified with the Ganges River and referred to as the "Ganga," where the ritual that recovers the dead from these aquatic depths is called "Ganga *tirattudal*," or "collecting the Ganges." The dead are drawn back into the world of the living via a "thread ladder" (*nul eni*): the ritual musicians lower a decorated lemon attached to a spool of string into the water source and loop the other end around the *karagam*, the ritual vessel in which the invited dead person will take up residence after they climb out of the water (fig. 4.4). Once the dead relative agrees to leave their watery abode and return home, the drummers quickly sever

Figure 4.3. The well in the now-dry village water tank that serves as the Ganga, from which the spirits of the dead will be retrieved. Melur, Tamil Nadu, 2019. *Source:* Photo by the author.

Figure 4.4. The decorated lemon that is dropped into the Ganga and whose string (the "thread ladder") is attached to the *karagam* so the sought-after dead can climb up out of the water and take up residence in this ritual vessel to be carried home and installed there as permanent household deities. Melur, Tamil Nadu, 2019. *Source:* Photo by the author.

the thread connecting the Ganga to the pot, thereby confining this powerful spirit in the flower-decorated *karagam*, which is then carried back home so that the dead person can be ritually installed in the family's domestic sanctuary as a household deity.

When the Dead Will Not Be Denied

Although it can take up to eight hours of spirited playing and singing at the Ganga for the dead to manifest and agree to come home, the ritual musicians have no choice but to toil for as long as it takes, trying different tactics to induce the often-recalcitrant spirits to dance and speak. In Murugan's case, it is not until quite late in the evening that he finally and definitively descends on his own daughter, Ishwari.[8] Inducing the deceased to inhabit the bodies of their relatives is only the first hurdle, though, for the dead often arrive disgruntled and dissatisfied, harboring grudges about how they were treated in life or forgotten in death.

To mollify bad-tempered puvadaikkaris, the drummers sometimes catalog the efforts and expense that the sponsoring family has undertaken to mount the invitation rite and enumerate specific offerings likely to appeal to these spirits. The inclusion of the mud from their graves is frequently mentioned as one signifier of how fervently the deceased is missed and how sincerely their lineage members want them to rejoin the family. When interacting with deceased *sumangalis*, the drummers may describe the colorful saris and bangles that have been assembled on round trays for their enjoyment and implore them to come home to enjoy these accoutrements. With Murugan, however, they take a different approach. Here the musicians announce that if he communicates with them and concedes to come home, there will be "drinks." Although Murugan has refused to answer the drummers' questions up until this point, shortly after this enticement is dangled, he becomes more cooperative. Murugan replies to their queries about the circumstances of his death, revealing that while returning home after a night-time drinking session with two friends in the fields, his motorbike slipped on the bank of a village pond. He rolled down the slope and his head became submerged in the muddy, slushy water at the pond's edge. Unable to raise his head in his intoxicated state (*bodhai*), he suffocated and died there. Murugan's account elicits an emotional outpouring from his relatives, several of whom fall at his feet, weeping piteously. In a particularly gripping moment, the dead man, embodied by his daughter, embraces his wife tightly and the two whirl in grief in the descending darkness, tears coursing down both of their faces. His closest relatives then approach to voice their financial, health, and other concerns and request Murugan's intercession and assistance.

Amid these consultations, Murugan calls out for a bottle of brandy to be brought to him. His family members respond by yelling at the drummers and at the dead man himself. Murugan's mother demands, "Even though it killed you, you just cannot be without it?" His sister chimes in, asking in a scolding tone, "It took you from us, but it is what brings you back to us?" One of the musicians suggests that perhaps his daughter Ishwari should not be the one to consume liquor on his behalf, but Murugan insists that she can and should take the bottle and drink. An older aunt harangues the drummers *not* to pierce Ishwari's tongue, even though Murugan has already demanded it, because doing so would make the girl's oracular relationship with her dead father permanent. The unspoken implication is that although his daughter's embodiment of the patriarch was an unexpected and decidedly less-than-ideal turn of events, it could be finessed later by transferring the dead-man-turned-family-god to a more suitable host.[9] But a piercing will complicate this process since it performatively establishes a reciprocal and enduring relationship that is difficult to withdraw from. Moreover, a permanent possession relationship of this kind might also negatively impact Ishwari's future marriage prospects and—perhaps more disastrously—allow her to take their powerful puvadaikkari with her when she marries out of her natal home, thus depriving her birth family of the protection and benefits these household deities can confer.

At this point the ritual is beset by a cacophony of competing suggestions and unsolicited advice, and the drummers realize they need to regain control of the proceedings. Over the course of the next hour, they work assiduously to pave a middle path, trying to balance Murugan's insistence that he will only cooperate if he is allowed to enjoy the brandy with the family's reluctance to see fifteen-year-old Ishwari consume liquor. Murugan challenges his family about their hesitance, asking forcefully, "How can you deny me? Don't you want me to be happy, even just for a moment?" Eventually the musicians permit Murugan to gulp several swallows of brandy in return for his assurance that he will come home as a puvadaikkari, although they reserve much of the bottle for his dead father, who is embodied by a male relative. Since another family puvadaikkari, an already installed *sumangali*, has also joined their gathering and offered *arul vakku*, the drummers reason that they have to use the one silver trident on hand to pierce her host's tongue, in keeping with a promise made during her original invitation ceremony. They propose that Murugan select his own prophecy-speaking candidate at their *kula devam*'s annual festival and that that person's tongue be pierced then to seal their association. With a finger raised commandingly, Selvam instructs Murugan to only come on/in his daughter when explicitly invited with lit camphor and called by name, but to otherwise allow her to study well and live undisturbed and to select a new person to manifest on before her marriage. With these matters settled, the drummers hastily cut the thread connecting the *karagam* to the Ganga and begin their jubilant procession home, celebrating Murugan's return to the world and his imminent installation in his family's domestic shrine. The ritual is a success. As Selvam commented to me later, "This family has considerable difficulties.

They want comfort and relief, so they did this puvadaikkari *puja*. Although they are not a rich family, they have done it well."

Conclusion

The tendency toward Sanskritization, sweetening, and gentrification has been explored by several scholars, particularly with respect to Hindu goddess traditions (e.g., Harman 2012; McDermott 2001; Padma 2013; Preston 1985; Urban 1999). "Sanskritization" is the term used by M. N. Srinivas (1952) to refer to the ways that Sanskritic Hinduism (the "Great Tradition") exerts a dominant and homogenizing cultural influence on local or "little" traditions. I have written elsewhere about the sanitizing shifts underway at the temple dedicated to Mundakkanni Amman, the Tamil goddess discussed above, where a new "flower shower" (*puchorital*) festival was inaugurated to appeal to upwardly mobile devotees (Allocco 2018). In this event, sweet-smelling flower blossoms are substituted for the pots of milk (*pal kudam*) that devotees carry on their heads as they process around the goddess's precincts. Milk, of course, quickly sours in the sun during these processions and then floods the temple's inner sanctum when it is poured over the goddess's image, attracting flies and soiling participants' clothing. By contrast, the introduction of a festival rite featuring pleasing cascades of fragrant flowers was an intentional move away from messier and less "sophisticated" worship practices. Drawing on work in related Tamil temple spaces, Joanne Punzo Waghorne highlights gentrification processes and suggests that middle class sensibilities and new visual and iconographic forms are effectively overwriting what she calls the "village marks of the South Indian goddess" (2004, 121). She proposes that emerging middle-class devotees who are willing to appropriate the power of the goddess often do so by "cleaning her house and purifying or isolating her coarser elements" (2001, 260; 2004, 170).

Joyce Burkhalter Flueckiger (2020) similarly explores shifts in the narrative and material grammar of village goddesses in Hyderabad, especially in shrine architecture, arguing that enclosing these deities in cement shrines has transformed them from *protector* to *protected* goddesses. She describes efforts to rename a village goddess (*gramadevata*) temple and eradicate animal sacrifice and alcohol offerings so that the site would be "accessible to all" (Flueckiger 2020, 113–14). These decisions were part of a broader campaign to lift this goddess up into a puranic register, to locate her in an entirely new deity kin network that would position her vis-à-vis pan-Indian divinities, and to brahmanize her worship through the addition of *archana* and *abhishekam* (i.e., priest-mediated offerings to and bathing/anointing of the deity) (112–13). Flueckiger demonstrates that a process that began with architectural transformation ultimately led to changes in this goddess's "character" (2020, 115), as Brahman priests replaced the lower-caste family who used to serve her and Sanskrit chanting became a regular feature of her worship while signboards declared animal sacrifice and alcohol offerings to be prohibited.

Although there is less material on sweetening dynamics in devotional contexts centering on male deities in Hindu traditions, Sinha's (2005) work on Muneeswaran, discussed above, provides relevant material. She documents efforts to "clean up" this guardian deity's "folk" elements, such as his meat-eating and smoking, which are perceived as "embarrassing, primitive and debased practices that are not part of Hinduism 'proper'" (2005, 253). Animal or blood sacrifice (*bali*) is an active site of contention in both Hindu god and goddess traditions, sparking vehement insistence on its enduring salience and forceful resistance to its continuation. Several recent sources offer compelling snapshots of what is at stake in debates over whether such sacrifices should be banned or must continue, including Ehud Halperin's (2019) discussion of the controversy related to blood sacrifice dedicated to the Himalayan goddess Hadimba. He traces the history of once-celebrated sacrificial rituals in the Kullu Valley, where former instruments for establishing divine royal power are today disputed practices that attract increasingly vitriolic moral, theological, and legal attacks. Lokesh Ohri (2016) highlights reformist efforts to cast animal sacrifice offered to the four brother deities called Mahasus in the western Himalayas as "regressive" and incompatible with modern Hindu sensibilities, while Hugh Urban (2019) focuses on the deep-seated associations between Goddess Kamakhya's temple in the northeastern Indian state of Assam and "impure" menstrual blood and animal sacrifice. Urban discloses that conservative nationalist groups seeking to position Kamakhya's annual festival as a site for tourism, nationalism, and economic development oppose blood sacrifice as a "backwards perversion of true Hinduism" that threatens their goals (2019, 264). Finally, and much closer to the geographic focus on this chapter, Anthony Good (2023) offers a discussion of animal sacrifice during a Tamil village goddess festival against the backdrop of the debates that swirl around the 1950 Madras Animals and Birds Sacrifices Prohibition Act.

While there is certainly abundant evidence that sweetening and softening currents are influential in contemporary Hindu contexts, I have shown here that these tides also pull in other directions. Indeed, in puvadaikkari worship the direction of change that gentrification theories identify may well be reversed, as "village" ideations frequently provide the frame for bourgeois ones, and not the other way around. In these rituals, in addition to the insistence on the inclusion of crematory ash/grave soil, alcohol offerings, and rigorous tongue-piercing, we see the centrality of divine embodiment and dramatic dialogues with the dead. Two shifts in their performance contexts signals the intensified circumstances that give rise to these ceremonies today, namely that the majority of puvadaikkari *pujas* are now catalyzed by misfortunes rather than auspicious life events and their protagonists are frequently dead relatives who perished in accidents and suicide (Allocco 2025) rather than at the conclusion of long, fulfilling lives. Moreover, I found that families from castes that have not traditionally performed these rituals are experimenting with efforts to bring home, or "domesticate," their dead in dialogue with the challenges of neoliberalism and modern social life, primarily in urban spaces. It appears, then, that rather than a homogenizing or gentrifying process, what we are witnessing is the increasing popularity, intensification, and amplification of these ritual undertakings and, by extension, divine entities' ritual demands.[10]

Although those who worship puvadaikkaris do not explicitly speak of "bringing back the old ways," as Sinha's (2014) interlocutors did when describing their desire to return to the practices they associate with their ancestors' worship of a Tamil goddess in their new diasporic locations in Singapore, they do regularly insist that traditional piercing practices and offering patterns must persist in these ceremonies. In fact, even against the backdrop of broader social and economic changes—including urbanization, migration to cities, and the breakup of joint families—worshipers steadfastly resist significantly changing the terms of engagement with the dead or omitting particular ritual elements. The perceived efficacy of these *pujas* as they are performed now surely fuels this resistance, as does the sense that unwavering devotion will yield the best prospects for recruiting the dead as bulwarks against contemporary uncertainties and instabilities. One of the musicians put it this way: "People worship their puvadaikkaris because it brings good results. It is a popular belief (*aidhigam*) that if this worship is done properly, then the family will improve and develop (*virutti*) and experience satisfaction and fulfillment."

Contrary to the sweetening trends visible in many contemporary Hindu ritual contexts, then, participants' insistence on fulfilling the desires and needs of the dead with intense practices and potent substances understood as intrinsic to their nature stems from the belief that if these entities are successfully summoned and fully satisfied, they will contribute to their family's prosperity, well-being, and growth. In fact, many suggest that these offerings are more essential and relevant than ever precisely because they produce the conditions for the positive interventions of the dead, who become many families' "first gods" after their invitation and installation as household deities. The support of puvadaikkaris is understood as increasingly critical to living kin as they navigate the anxieties and precarities of contemporary social and economic life. That is, relatively fierce and hot practices enlisting the unruly dead are intensifying today because these ancestors are believed to be uniquely positioned to help their families respond to the demands of these particularly troubled times, which are marked by hardships and difficulties as diverse as illness, debt, constrained marriage and employment prospects, and black magic attacks. Their status as gone-but-not-departed family members with an assumed stake in and indeed an *obligation* to their living kin's welfare and prosperity means they are expected to offer not only solace but also crucial support. Given the immense challenges of our times, it seems certain that intense elements of puvadaikkari worship will continue to persist, flourishing against the flow of sweetening streams and continuing to play a critical role in "modern" Hindu traditions.

Notes

1. All names used are pseudonyms. I am grateful to the drummer-priests for inviting me to this and many other ritual performances and for befriending and patiently teaching me over the years. I also appreciate the warm welcome I was shown by the sponsoring family and participants at this puvadaikkari *puja* as well as the perspectives that they generously shared. Earlier versions of this chapter were presented at the Annual Conference on South Asia in Madison, Wisconsin, and the Conference of the European Association for the Study of Religions in Vilnius, Lithuania, where I benefited from excellent questions and conversations. My last set of debts are to trusted readers whose suggestions helped me clarify and improve this chapter: Brian Pennington, Emilia Bachrach, Anya Fredsell, and Jenn Ortegren.

2. Most of the families who engage in puvadaikkari worship bury rather than cremate their dead. Cremation is regarded as an impediment to bringing the dead back into the world as a permanently installed household deity, although not an insurmountable one. Many families who otherwise bury will, however, cremate their first-born to prevent sorcerers (*mantiravadi*s) from exhuming and using eldest children's uniquely powerful bones (especially the skulls) in black magic.

3. My primary period of ethnographic research on puvadaikkari worship in Tamil Nadu spanned 2015 and 2016 and was carried out under the auspices of a Fulbright-Nehru Academic and Professional Excellence Fellowship, an American Institute of Indian Studies (AIIS) Senior Fellowship (funded by the National Endowment for the Humanities), and a Faculty Research and Development Award from Elon University. Follow-up trips in 2018 and 2019 were made possible by Elon University. Prior research periods form the foundation of this work and were also underwritten by Fulbright-Nehru, AIIS, and Elon, as well as by Emory University. I am grateful to each of these institutions for their crucial support and to the Kuppuswami Sastri Research Institute for several periods of affiliation.

4. These and other supposedly "taboo" substances feature prominently in Tantric traditions (Urban 1999), where they are understood to possess transformative power and offer potential for spiritual growth to practitioners who ingest or otherwise interact with them in circumscribed ritual contexts.

5. But see Louis Dumont, who pronounces on the basis of his fieldwork that "the prototype of the deified deceased woman is without any ambiguity a *kanni*, maiden or virgin" ([1957] 1986, 439). For more on eligibility to be a puvadaikkari, see Allocco 2021 (especially 107–9).

6. See Allocco 2021, 130–31, and Allocco 2020, 9, for a summary of this literature.

7. Just a year earlier I visited this village for another family's puvadaikkari *puja* with the same troupe of drummers and found Melur's tank flush with water. Water scarcity is an increasingly significant source of tension in many of the farming communities where puvadaikkari invitation rites are performed. In addition to exerting pressure on rice cultivation and the viability of chilis, peanuts, and other crops, shifting water fortunes have a direct impact on families' ability to access their dead, who are believed to lurk in watery places after their demise (Allocco 2021, 122).

8. As I discuss further below, it is not optimal for daughters—whether outmarried or yet-to-be-married—to host the dead of their birth family. A primary reason is that daughters do not possess the right or entitlement (*urimai*) to embody the dead of their natal family because they will leave this family and join another at marriage.

9. For more on attempts to transfer deities from their selected host to another person and the implications of such reassignments, see Allocco 2020.

10. Indira Arumugam (2015) has observed a similar trend with respect to animal sacrifice dedicated to lineage and tutelary deities in rural Tamil Nadu. She proposes that, despite skepticism about the presence and potency of the old gods in the contemporary milieu, more animals are being killed today than ever before and the scale and spectacle of these sacrificial ceremonies have become ever more extravagant.

References

Allocco, Amy L. 2009. "Snake Goddesses and Anthills: Modern Challenges and Women's Ritual Responses in Contemporary South India." PhD diss., Emory University.

Allocco, Amy L. 2018. "Flower Showers for the Goddess: Borrowing, Modification, and Ritual Innovation in Tamil Nadu." In *Ritual Innovation: Strategic Interventions in South Asian Religion*, edited by Brian K. Pennington and Amy L. Allocco, 129–48. State University of New York Press.

Allocco, Amy L. 2020. "Vernacular Practice, Gendered Tensions, and Interpretive Ambivalence in Hindu Death, Deification, and Domestication Narratives." *Journal of Hindu Studies* 13 (2): 144–71. https://doi.org/10.1093/jhs/hiaa007.

Allocco, Amy L. 2021. "Bringing the Dead Home: Hindu Invitation Rituals in Tamil South India." *Journal of the American Academy of Religion* 89 (1): 103–42. https://doi.org/10.1093/jaarel/lfab026.

Allocco, Amy L. 2025. "Alcohol, Suicide, and Gendered Protest in Dialogues with the Dead." *International Journal of Hindu Studies* 29 (2).

Appadurai, Arjun. 1981. "Gastro-Politics in Hindu South Asia." *American Ethnologist* 8 (3): 494–511.

Arumugam, Indira. 2015. "'The Old Gods Are Losing Power!': Theologies of Power and Rituals of Productivity in a Tamil Nadu Village." *Modern Asian Studies* 49 (3): 753–86. https://doi.org/10.1017/S0026749X1400016X.

Berti, Daniela, and Anthony Good. 2023. "Introduction: The Judicialisation and Politicisation of Sacrifice." In *Animal Sacrifice, Religion and Law in South Asia*, edited by Daniela Berti and Anthony Good, 3–52. Routledge.

Blackburn, Stuart H. 1985. "Death and Deification: Folk Cults in Hinduism." *History of Religions* 24 (3): 255–74.

Clark-Decès, Isabelle. 2007. *The Encounter Never Ends: A Return to the Field of Tamil Rituals*. State University of New York Press.

Coccari, Diane M. 1989. "The Bir Babas of Banaras and the Deified Dead." In *Criminal Gods and Demon Devotees: Essays on the Guardians of Popular Hinduism*, edited by Alf Hiltebeitel, 251–70. State University of New York Press.

Dumont, Louis. (1957) 1986. *A South Indian Subcaste: Social Organization and Religion of the Pramalai Kallar*. Translated by M. Moffatt, L. Morton, and A. Morton. Oxford University Press.

Flueckiger, Joyce Burkhalter. 2020. *Material Acts in Everyday Hindu Worlds*. State University of New York Press.

Fuller, C. J. (1992) 2004. *The Camphor Flame: Popular Hinduism and Society in India*. Princeton University Press.

Fuller, C. J., and Haripriya Narasimhan. 2014. *Tamil Brahmans: The Making of a Middle-Class Caste*. University of Chicago Press.

Good, Anthony. 2023. "Animal Sacrifice, Politics and the Law in Tamil Nadu, South India." In *Animal Sacrifice, Religion and Law in South Asia*, edited by Daniela Berti and Anthony Good, 3–30. Routledge.

Halperin, Ehud. 2019. *The Many Faces of a Hindu Goddess: Haḍimbā, Her Devotees, and Religion in Rapid Change*. Oxford University Press.

Harman, William. 2012. "From Fierce to Domesticated: Mariyamman Joins the Middle Class." *Nidān: International Journal for the Study of Hinduism* 24 (December): 41–65.

Knipe, David M. 2003. "When a Wife Dies First: The *Mūsivāyanam* and a Female Brahman Ritualist in Coastal Andhra." In *The Living and the Dead: Social Dimensions of Death in South Asian Religions*, edited by Liz Wilson, 51–93. State University of New York Press.

McDermott, Rachel Fell. 2001. *Mother of My Heart, Daughter of My Dreams: Kālī and Umā in the Devotional Poetry of Bengal*. Oxford University Press.

Nabokov, Isabelle. 2000. *Religion Against the Self: An Ethnography of Tamil Rituals*. Oxford University Press.

Ohri, Lokesh. 2016. "Rights Versus Rites: *Bali* and Ritual Reform in the Himalayas." In *The Ambivalence of Denial: Danger and Appeal of Rituals*, edited by Ute Hüsken and Udo Simon, 191–219. Harrassowitz Verlag.

Padma, Sree. 2013. *Vicissitudes of the Goddess: Reconstructions of the Gramadevata in India's Religious Traditions*. Oxford University Press.

Preston, James. 1985. *Cult of the Goddess: Social and Religious Change in a Hindu Temple*. Waveland Press.

Sax, William S. 2009. *God of Justice: Ritual Healing and Social Justice in the Central Himalayas*. Oxford University Press.

Sinha, Vineeta. 2005. *A New God in the Diaspora? Muneeswaran Worship in Contemporary Singapore*. Singapore University Press.

Sinha, Vineeta. 2014. " 'Bringing Back the Old Ways': Enacting a Goddess Festival in Urban Singapore." *Material Religion* 10 (1): 76–103.

Srinivas, M. N. 1952. *Religion and Society Among the Coorgs of South India*. Clarendon.

Urban, Hugh B. 1999. "The Extreme Orient: The Construction of 'Tantrism' as a Category in the Orientalist Imagination." *Religion* 29 (2): 123–46. https://doi.org/10.1006/reli.1997.0097.

Urban, Hugh B. 2019. "The Cradle of Tantra: Modern Transformations of a Tantric Centre in Northeast India from Nationalist Symbol to Tourist Destination." *South Asia: Journal of South Asian Studies* 42 (2): 256–77. https://doi.org/10.1080/00856401.2019.1570609.

Viramma, Josiane Racine, and Jean-Luc Racine. 2000. *Viramma: Life of a Dalit*. Translated by W. Hobson. Social Science Press.

Waghorne, Joanne Punzo. 2001. "The Gentrification of the Goddess." *International Journal of Hindu Studies* 5 (3): 227–67.

Waghorne, Joanne Punzo. 2004. *Diaspora of the Gods: Modern Hindu Temples in an Urban Middle-Class World*. Oxford University Press.

Whitehead, Henry. (1921) 1999. *The Village Gods of South India*. Asian Educational Services.

5

Developing Danda

Aspirations and Transformations of
Divine Presence in Uttarakhand

Aftab S. Jassal

The *pahari* ("of the mountains") Hindu deity named Nagaraja is known and made present in a variety of religious settings in the region of Garhwal, in the Himalayan state of Uttarakhand, India. Nagaraja is commonly identified as a form *(rup)* of the pan-Indian deity Krishna. His worship cuts across caste, class, and geographical divides in the region, and many Garhwalis revere him as the *isht dev*, or "chosen deity," of Garhwal, as a whole. Nagaraja is regularly encountered via deity possession, or divine embodiment, in the context of a ritual performance tradition known as *jagar* ("awakening" the gods), wherein religious specialists—who traditionally belong to caste-oppressed, or Dalit, communities—"call" or "invite" deities to inhabit the bodies and homes of devotees. Through storytelling, drumming, animal sacrifice, and ritual "dance" (*nach*), *pahari* deities such as Nagaraja are made present in embodied form to receive offerings, cure illnesses, exorcise malevolent spirits, give advice in times of difficulty, and intervene in matters of personal and collective importance.

In addition to appearing as an embodied actor in *jagar* rituals, which take place in the homes of devotees, Nagaraja also takes on other guises in Garhwal. For instance, in shrines and temples across the region—such as in the regionally well-known temple called Danda Nagaraja—the god is encountered as a physical image (*murti*), or a naturally occurring stone (*shila*), or in some other material form. In these spaces, Brahman priests mediate contact and exchange between Nagaraja and his devotees, unlike in *jagar* rituals that are officiated by Dalit priests.

In this chapter, I show how Danda Nagaraja temple, located in Pauri District in Garhwal, has become a critical site through which constructions of regional identity, state discourses on development, and the worship of Nagaraja are brought together in creative and consequential ways. In addition to describing the moral, affective, and infrastructural labor through which Danda Nagaraja temple (or simply Danda) is being transformed into a regionally significant pilgrimage destination, I explore how the god Nagaraja and the practices through which he is known and experienced are "sweetened" and "intensified" as the god moves between small-scale *jagar* rituals, on the one hand, and large, public temples such as Danda, on the other. Building on the work of Amy L. Allocco (2018), William Harman (2004), Rachel Fell McDermott (2001), Sree Padma (2013), and Xenia Zeiler (2012), I understand "sweetening" as a historical process whereby highly localized, subaltern ontologies and epistemologies are made commensurable with translocal, elite Hindu traditions. In Uttarakhand and elsewhere, this process prioritizes Sanskrit-language texts and concepts vis-à-vis oral and vernacular-language traditions, such as *jagar* narratives, that is, narratives associated with particular deities that are sung to the accompaniment of drumming and divine embodiment during *jagar* rituals in Uttarakhand. Moreover, "sweetening" results in Nagaraja being (re)cast as a remote, purely benevolent—and safe—temple deity, shorn of his dangerous, afflictive tendencies that find expression in *jagar* narratives and rituals. In contrast, I understand "intensification" as a process that culminates in visceral, multisensory, and often volatile engagements between humans and divinities, including practices such as divine embodiment and animal sacrifice, which are generally frowned upon by elite, orthodox Hindu practitioners (Arumugam 2015; Sinha 2016; Zeiler 2012). As instances of "intensification," Nagaraja's *jagar* narratives describe his mercurial temperament and sometimes harmful mode of presence in the world, while *jagar* rituals localize, or concentrate, his presence in private domestic spaces, in or on human bodies.

In the concluding section of this chapter, I employ the terms *marg*, *desh*, and *nagar*—which I translate as "highway," "countryside," and "town," respectively—to think through the relationship between different sites of religious practice and currents of sweetening and intensification in Uttarakhand. While I am wary of the historical uses of *marg* and *desh* as representing the so-called Great and Little Traditions of Hinduism, I suggest that as spatial metaphors they can shed light on the heterogeneous and internally contested character of *pahari* Hinduism/s. However, rather than a binary between *marg* and *desh*, I propose a third concept, *nagar*, to reread these more staid terms. In describing Danda Nagaraja temple as a *nagari*—literally, "of the town"—site, I describe how *nagari* sites draw upon, and sweeten, highly localized traditions of the "countryside," such as *jagar* narratives and rituals, as well as attend to the literal and figurative "highway," which carries pilgrims to and from sites of transregional significance in Uttarakhand, including the religious centers that make up the famous Chota Char Dham ("small four abodes") pilgrimage network, which includes Kedarnath, Badrinath, Gangotri, and Yamunotri.

While I was living in Pauri city in 2010–2011, I heard that there was a grassroots campaign underway for state authorities to recognize Danda Nagaraja temple as the "fifth abode," or *panchava dham*, of Uttarakhand, to cement its reputation as an important pilgrimage destination.[1] Hearing Danda Nagaraja temple described in such glowing terms by my interlocutors, I wondered what it meant to refer to it as the "fifth abode." For whom did this designation matter, and why? What was so special and important about this place? My interlocutors explained that recognizing Danda as the "fifth abode" would confirm that this temple had joined the ranks of the most significant religious sites in the state, that is, Uttarakhand's Chota Char Dham (or simply, Char Dham) pilgrimage network.[2] Including Danda Nagaraja in the Char Dham pilgrimage would, in effect, transform it from a four- to five-abode route.

Danda's fame and stature as an important pilgrimage destination had risen exponentially since the late 1990s. The rise of Danda thus coincided with the neoliberal reforms that transformed the Indian economy in the 1990s as well as Uttarakhand's achievement of statehood in November 2000, after a multidecade struggle for political autonomy and separation from Uttar Pradesh, India's most populous state. According to the Partnership of Resilience and Preparedness, tourism to Uttarakhand has jumped from ten to fifty million annual visitors from 2000 and 2017, with approximately 44 percent of all domestic tourists visiting the state for pilgrimage and religious visits.[3] These millions of pilgrims enrich the state economy and provide employment to large numbers of *pahari* workers and businesses, but also destabilize local ecologies (Whitmore 2018).[4] In recent years, to support the ever-increasing inflow of visitors to Uttarakhand, state and national authorities have invested a great deal of capital into road building and other large-scale infrastructure projects. The pace and scale of such development efforts continue to increase. In October 2017, Prime Minister Narendra Modi visited Uttarakhand and declared, "Through the work we are doing in Kedarnath, we want to show how an ideal *tirth kshetra* [pilgrimage site] should be."[5] Modi visited Kedarnath again in November 2021, stating that "more pilgrims will visit Uttarakhand in the next decade than in the past century and the rapid development in the state will reverse the outward migration of young people" who leave Uttarakhand in large numbers in search of better employment opportunities in other parts of India.[6]

This chapter draws on ethnographic fieldwork conducted in Uttarakhand in 2010–2011, during which time I visited Danda Nagaraja on multiple occasions and spent several weeks in and around the temple. While conducting participant observation at the temple, I lived in a guesthouse on its premises, and later, with a Garhwali friend who resided in a nearby village. I recorded lengthy interviews with numerous influential actors in the temple economy, such as temple priests and patrons, as well as with pilgrims and local devotees of Nagaraja who were familiar with the site. Since 2010, I have also participated in several *jagar* ceremonies across Uttarakhand, recorded multiple variants of Nagaraja's *jagar* narratives, and interviewed *jagar* performers, mediums, and other relevant ritual actors.

In the following section, I draw upon my fieldwork with *jagar* performers and participants to describe how Nagaraja is known and experienced as an embodied actor in *jagar* rituals, in a form that is distinct from how the god is encountered in Danda Nagaraja temple. Following this, I detail how Danda is being transformed into the "fifth abode" and the ways in which Nagaraja and his worship are "sweetened" in this site. Finally, I deploy the terms *marg, desh,* and *nagar* to delineate the relationship between distinct sites of religious practice in Uttarakhand, namely, the translocally significant Char Dham pilgrimage network; domestic, highly localized *jagar* rituals; and regionally well-known temples such as Danda Nagaraja.

Nagaraja as a *Jagar* Deity

In *jagar* rituals, through the performance of narrative song, drumming, and animal sacrifice, *pahari* gods such as Nagaraja are "awakened" (*jagrit karana*) and called into presence in or on the bodies of human mediums in a practice known as "dance" (*nach*).[7] In embodied form, deities not only dance but also "speak" (*bak bolana*), give advice, heal illnesses, mediate disputes, and receive offerings, among other things (Alter 2008; Fiol 2017; Leavitt 1986; Malik 2016; Sax 2009). Individual families who sponsor *jagar* rituals invite religious specialists known as *jagari*s to perform the narrative-songs (*gatha*s) associated with particular deities, play the drums, and mediate contact and exchange between embodied deities and their worshipers.[8] While the vast majority of specialists who perform these religiously significant tasks belong to Dalit communities, they not only cater to the religious needs of Dalits but also mediate relations between *pahari* deities and their caste-privileged Rajput and Brahman worshipers.

Popular narratives associated with the worship of Nagaraja in Garhwal—including narratives that are performed during *jagar* rituals—commonly identify him as a regional form of the pan-Indian god Krishna, as shown in the following short summary of the narrative presented to me by a *jagar* performer in 2010. After the end of the Mahabharata war, Krishna, the divine companion of the Pandavas, saw the beautiful mountains, rivers, and meadows of Garhwal in a dream. He was deeply moved by this sight, and a desire to travel to this place was born in him. On waking from his dream, he began his journey to Garhwal, which he did in disguise, so as not to be disturbed by anyone. On arriving in Garhwal, the god confronted a local ruler named Gangu Ramola and asked him for a *sthan,* or place, to inhabit. Gangu, however, was an arrogant and miserly being, and he denied the god a place. Gangu Ramola's rejection of the god precipitated a condition known as *nagadosh* ("serpent affliction"), which had devastating consequences for Gangu, his subjects, and the natural environment. In time, Gangu realized that the stranger who had come to his door and asked for a dwelling place was no ordinary being, so to save himself and others, Gangu gave the stranger what he desired. On receiving Gangu's offering of place, the disguised god became satisfied (*shant*), and *nagadosh*—which had almost destroyed Gangu Ramola and his kingdom—was also cured or resolved. A temple was built for the god and his disguise melted away; he revealed himself as the god Krishna, who came to be known in Garhwal as Nagaraja, "king of serpents."

As this narrative demonstrates, *pahari* deities are not only experienced as sources of healing but also as agents of affliction. *Nagadosh* is a particular kind of *dosh*, which is literally a "fault" or "blemish";[9] across South Asia, the term *dosh* refers to negative physical, psychological, social, and ecological states that arise out of inauspicious astrological conditions or humoral imbalances within persons, or both (Allocco 2013, 2014). In Garhwal, the word *dosh* also suggests an afflictive or harmful manifestation of a deity. As a ritual medium of Nagaraja explained, *dosha*s materialize the displeasure (*narazagi*) of deities and "attach" (*lagana*) themselves to persons and places, producing disease and misfortune. Based on this latter, region-specific understanding of *dosh*, I choose to translate *nagadosh* as "serpent affliction," rather than the more literal "fault/blemish of a serpent."

I was informed that *nagadosh* usually affects people when they inadvertently injure or kill a snake while engaged in agricultural activity. Because snakes are closely associated with the god Nagaraja, the "king of serpents," harming a snake is also an act of violence against the god, which is turn materializes the god's "displeasure," which takes the form of individual and collective sickness and misfortune. Symptoms of *nagadosh* include physical, psychological, and social difficulties in humans, infertility in humans and animals, disease and destruction of livestock, crop infestations, and more. When a diagnosis of *nagadosh* is found in relation to experiences of personal and collective suffering, the afflicted are prescribed various ritual remedies, including the performance of *jagar* rituals wherein Nagaraja is "danced" (*nachana*) and offerings are made to the god. The goal of such rituals is to heal *nagadosh* by repairing the relationship between Nagaraja and his devotees.

Sometimes, to heal *nagadosh*, the afflicted promise to undertake a pilgrimage journey to an important Nagaraja temple—such as Danda Nagaraja, Sem Mukhem, or Bauk Nag, located in Pauri, Tehri, and Uttarkashi districts in Garhwal, respectively—and perform ritual worship for the god there. In 2010–2011, I had the opportunity to spend several weeks in and around Danda Nagaraja temple. In the following section, I describe my interactions with important actors in the temple economy of Danda, to explicate the relationship between how Nagaraja is encountered in *jagar* narratives and rituals versus how he is known and experienced in the "fifth abode."

Developing Danda

One of Nagaraja's most famous temple dwellings is Danda Nagaraja temple, referred to by devotees as a *nag tirth*, or a "sacred abode of a serpent." Prior to visiting Danda Nagaraja, I heard many reports about the "extraordinary" (*adbhut*) qualities of this place. I was told that visiting Danda enabled devotees to achieve release (*mukti*) from the cycle of life and death and helped them realize (*siddha*) their other spiritual and material desires. Devotees of Nagaraja believe that if one undertakes a pilgrimage (*jat*) to Danda Nagaraja temple and performs ritual worship (*puja*) for the god there, the god will grant his devotees' desires (*manauti*), remove obstacles in their path, and protect and heal them. In exchange for the god's beneficence, devotees vow to sponsor *jagar* ceremonies for the god in their homes and villages or make other kinds of offerings to him. In Danda Nagaraja, devotees' votive offerings include brass bells that hang from trees and other structures in the temple courtyard "like the ripening fruit of karma," as one temple priest described them.

On my visits to Danda Nagaraja, temple priests (*pujaris*) told me that the temple, in its current form, was about 150 years old, even though Nagaraja had been "here" for thousands of years. I experienced Danda's status and popularity in the large numbers of pilgrims who traveled to the temple from across Garhwal and other parts of India. Spending time in Danda, I also learned that urban and expatriate Garhwalis constituted a significant and fast-growing base of support for the temple economy. Because this group of patrons was relatively prosperous, *pujaris* and other temple authorities went to great lengths to cater to them; in turn, they helped provide the significant capital necessary for the continuing renovation and expansion of the temple.

The discursive and infrastructural efforts around the temple were designed to achieve official state recognition for Danda as the "fifth abode" of Uttarakhand. As such, Danda had become part of a larger network of "connected places," to borrow a phrase from Anne Feldhaus (2003). On my visits to Danda, the *pujaris* described how the temple complex had expanded since the mid-nineties, as guesthouses, restaurants, and other facilities had mushroomed around it. Temple authorities—*pujaris*, local landed elites, and other influential patrons who served on the temple committee and managed the financial affairs of the temple—spoke at length about the multiple infrastructure projects and costly endeavors in which they were engaged. One of these projects was establishing a residential college for the study of Sanskrit language and literature, which I was told had been assured accreditation by the state government. The pace of "development"—an English-language term that came up repeatedly in my conversations with temple authorities—had accelerated dramatically since the mid-2000s. Around this time, the paved road that connected Pauri city to Danda Nagaraja temple was also completed. I was told that the completion of this approximately thirty-five-kilometer-long stretch of road had boosted the inflow of pilgrims and capital to the temple. While I was in Danda, I witnessed how local politicians and businessmen who had facilitated the completion of the road capitalized on their association with the temple. Among other things, they regularly sponsored large, well-attended public recitations of the *Bhagavata*

Purana, called *saptah* ("weeklong" ritual recitations), which were covered in all the local newspapers.

One of these wealthy patrons and a member of the temple committee was a man named Mr. Pant,[10] who had been "instrumental in growing and transforming the temple into a major pilgrimage destination (*tirth sthan*)," one *pujari* told me. I rely extensively on Mr. Pant's insights and understandings in the following pages because of his deep knowledge of the temple's history and active, long-term involvement in Danda's "development." Mr. Pant, a middle-aged Brahman man of Garhwali origin, reportedly made his fortune in another North Indian state, where he owned several factories. When he turned sixty, he entrusted the day-to-day operations of his factories to his children. He then moved back to Garhwal and directed all his time, energy, and financial resources to transforming and popularizing Danda Nagaraja temple. As he put it: "I feel that God put me on this earth to <u>develop</u> [Eng.] this place [Danda] and make its benefits available to everyone, so I am happy to play my part." Mr. Pant told me that he was the one who had invited high-level officials in the state government to visit Danda and experience the "practical" benefits of being in this place for themselves. Following their visits, these influential visitors had become convinced of the untapped potential of this temple as a major pilgrimage destination and had agreed to build a paved road to the temple, Mr. Pant reported. This road had made it possible for visitors to travel to Danda from "not only from all over Garhwal, but also from faraway places like Delhi."

According to Mr. Pant, however, much more development was needed in Danda, particularly "to attract devotees from beyond Garhwal." He felt it was important to provide clean water and adequate food and housing facilities for these pilgrims, efforts for which were underway. According to him, the temple had to be "nourished by the waters of faith (*astha*) to become what it is today." However, he added, "there is still a long way to go; we need to spread awareness (*prachar*) about this place all over the country, so that more and more people can come and reap its benefits." For this to happen, even more affective, economic, state, and scientific capital would need to be mobilized in the coming years.

When I asked Mr. Pant how the temple authorities had been able to bring about all these important changes, he acknowledged how new political and economic conditions emerged after Uttarakhand achieved statehood in 2000. Until that point, he said, Garhwal was just a backwater of the most populous state in India, Uttar Pradesh: "Back then [pre-2000], state officials did not pay attention to what was needed in far-flung places like Danda Nagaraja. But now the state capital is close by [in Dehradun city] and all important government officials know us, and we know them, so they are responsive to our needs, providing the <u>facilities</u> to <u>develop</u>" [Eng.], he said.

I soon learned, however, that "developing" Danda in this context also meant creating a separation between *jagar* and temple worship. Mr. Pant contrasted the worship of Nagaraja in Danda Nagaraja temple with how the god was known and experienced in *jagar* rituals; in particular, he identified how the god and his worship had been sweetened in Danda. For instance, Mr. Pant described how he achieved a kind of profound spiritual release, or *mukti*, in Danda, which he contrasted with the "minor," if not wholly illusory, benefits of participating in *jagar* ceremonies. Mr. Pant told me that *puja*—by which he meant the forms of human-divine interaction that were ritually mediated by Brahman priests in temple settings—was the proper and effective way of knowing and worshiping Nagaraja. "Whenever I sponsor a *katha* [a ritual recitation of classical narrative texts such as the Sanskrit-language Bhagavata Purana or Ramayana], perform a *puja*, or simply sit under a tree to reflect upon God (*bhagavan*), I feel great peace," he said. Mr. Pant informed me that performing *puja* for Nagaraja in Danda enabled devotees to "realize" (*siddha*) all their spiritual and material desires. For this reason, he referred to Danda as a *siddha pith* ("place of realization"), "a place that provided many <u>practical</u> [Eng.] benefits for pilgrims." For Mr. Pant, the "development" of Danda was part and parcel of the sweetening of Nagaraja and his worship. Sweetening, among other things, emphasizes brahmanically mediated temple worship and the authority of Sanskrit-language texts over Nagaraja's worship via *jagar* narratives and rituals.

Mr. Pant shared a version of the story of Krishna's arrival in Garhwal that was very different from the key characters or events performed during *jagar* rituals:

> After completing his *lila*s [earthly activities], Krishna decided to travel northward to Uttarakhand. But he knew that Uttarakhand was the land of the gods (*devabhumi*), so he thought, "How can I walk on this land, touching this hallowed ground (*pavitra bhumi*) with my feet?" So, he turned himself into a *nag* [serpent] and slithered on the ground to reach this place [Pauri Garhwal]. Since then, he spends six months of the year in Danda Nagaraja [temple] and six months in Sem Mukhem [temple].[11]

I was surprised that Mr. Pant's version omitted Krishna's critical encounter with Gangu Ramola and the concept of *nagadosh*, the "serpent affliction" that had ravaged Gangu Ramola's kingdom. In particular, I knew that many pilgrims who visited Danda did so as part of a sequence of ritual acts designed to cure *nagadosh*. These pilgrims, who were mostly rural residents of Pauri Garhwal and adjoining districts, were familiar with Nagaraja primarily as a *jagar* deity, that is, they regularly worshiped and interacted with the god as an embodied actor in *jagar* rituals. However, it was clear that the Nagaraja in Mr. Pant's story, and as he was known in Danda, was distinct from how the god was encountered in *jagar* rituals.

When I asked Mr. Pant about these omissions of Gangu Ramola and *nagadosh*, he was dismissive of the narrative of Krishna's encounter with Gangu Ramola, which he characterized as a fanciful tale made up by "unlettered" *jagar* performers who had not studied the "authoritative" (*shastrik*) texts about Krishna, such as the *Bhagavata Purana* and *Bhagavadgita*. According to him, the Gangu Ramola story was not "historical" (*aitihasik*), "because how could a great being like Krishna, who rules over the entire universe and possesses everything in it, stoop to asking for a handful of earth from a minor king like Gangu?" Mr. Pant was also equally dismissive of *nagadosh*, describing it as an example of people's "superstitions" (*andha-vishvas*). While he admitted that *nagadosh* may arise from inauspicious astrological configurations, he denied any connection to Nagaraja-Krishna. He complained that *jagar*-related understandings of *nagadosh* posited that Nagaraja could act in harmful manner toward his devotees, with which Mr. Pant disagreed. Instead, Mr. Pant said that many "lesser" *pahari* deities behaved in this way—demanding extravagant offerings from their devotees and then becoming irate and vengeful if their demands were not met—but Nagaraja "was a different kind of being." Rural Garhwalis were constantly involved in placating "lesser" deities and asking them for help with their petty, everyday problems, he said, such as "mediating a quarrel with a neighbor, finding a job, and of course, curing that headache or fever." In other words, the sweetening of Nagaraja in Danda entailed muting or underplaying his desire for place—or more fundamentally, his desirousness—which finds expression in *jagar* narratives about the god's arrival in Garhwal and encounter with Gangu Ramola. Sweetening (re)cast the god as a detached, desireless, and purely benevolent being. This process also resulted in a denial of any causal link between the god's presence in the world and "serpent affliction," while also devaluing the narrative and ritual expertise of *jagar* performers in favor of brahmanical knowledge and textual authority.

Mr. Pant and the other members of the Danda Nagaraja temple committee reimagined Nagaraja as distinct from other deities in Uttarakhand, to make the argument that Danda could become the "fifth abode." They departed from other, popular understandings of Nagaraja that permeated Garhwal, where he was regarded as an intimate and involved, and sometimes harmful, presence. In contrast, Mr. Pant described how "Nagaraja preferred to live on this high mountain ridge (*danda*), far from the noise and pollution of the world below . . . After all, this is why Krishna came to these mountains, to find some peace and quiet after the end of the Mahabharata war." In other words, in Danda, the god was imagined as a distant, otherworldly renunciant. Representing Nagaraja as a literally and figuratively elevated deity sweetened him, while also elevating the status and prestige of Danda in relation to other *pahari* temples.

In contrast with *jagar* rituals—where Nagaraja's presence is intensified and localized in or on the bodies of human mediums—Mr. Pant described Nagaraja as having a dispersed and depersonalized identity in Danda. Describing the origins of the temple, Mr. Pant told me that it had been constructed "many centuries ago" around a *murti*, or physical image, of a serpent that that had been discovered on a mountainside. I was told that this *murti* was housed in the central enclosure of Danda temple, but while I was in Danda, the central enclosure was not open to visitors. When I questioned Mr. Pant about this, he told me that *murti* was "very powerful" and was only revealed to devotees during special temple festivals. Furthermore, he added, "Nagaraja is present in every part of this temple; all you have to do is close your eyes, silence your mind, and you will feel his presence. . . . In the evenings, just sit quietly under a tree and you will experience deep peace; your thoughts and feelings will not wander; your awareness will become single-pointed (*ekagrat*), and you will stop worrying about everything that distracts you from God." In effect, Mr. Pant was arguing that temple visitors didn't *need* to encounter Nagaraja as a material, localized presence because the god pervaded the temple and surrounding areas. I also noted Mr. Pant's internalized yogic epistemology of "deep peace" and "single-pointed awareness."

Mr. Pant also described how he had invited scientists to "measure the spiritual <u>vibrations</u> [Eng.] in Danda . . . Their measurements confirmed what we had known all along, that this place has tremendous power (*shakti*); it is truly a great place of realization (*siddha pith*)." Mr. Pant's use of the scientific method to affirm the spiritual potency of Danda exemplified the modernist vision that temple developers had in mind for Danda. During my time there, I also observed that the *pujari*s and other temple authorities regularly invoked Western scientific expertise in their interactions with Garhwali temple visitors to bolster their claims about the religious efficacy of visiting Danda, so this form of rhetoric was not limited to Mr. Pant or to me as a non-Garhwali interlocutor.

Despite these concentrated development efforts underway at the Danda Nagaraja temple complex, however, I found that some of my local interlocutors from rural areas were less familiar with the temple; they did not bring up Danda nor insist that I visit it. When I asked them if they had visited Danda themselves, a few described how someone in their family had incurred *nagadosh* and subsequently promised Nagaraja that they would undertake a pilgrimage to the temple if the god would heal them of the affliction. One elderly woman who was a devotee of Nagaraja and who lived in a remote village in Pauri district called Nisni told me that she had visited the temple only once, many years earlier. She said that "because Nagaraja was her family's *isht dev* [chosen deity]," she had gone to see him there. Yet she was disappointed by her first and final visit to the place. Prior to her visit, she had heard that her beloved deity Nagaraja, whom she regularly encountered as an embodied actor in *jagar* rituals, was present in the central enclosure of the temple, in the form of a temple image (*murti*). However, on arriving at the temple she had found that the central enclosure was inaccessible to ordinary visitors and, as such, she was unable to obtain *darshan*, or "sight," of the god there. She was informed by the temple priests that the central enclosure was only kept open for visitors on special days, such as during the religious festival *janamashtami*, which commemorates the birth of Krishna. She reported feeling painfully removed from her "chosen deity"—who, she complained, was "kept under lock and key" by the Brahman priests who managed the temple. During our exchange, she contrasted this unfamiliar sense of distance and separation from Nagaraja with the intimacy of human-divine engagement that she experienced in the performance of *jagar*. For her, Nagaraja was primarily a *jagar* deity, a being who was encountered face-to-face in intimate domestic spaces. In these spaces of intensification, Nagaraja was experienced as a familial and familiar presence: a being who "danced," "spoke," and interacted with his devotees in a direct, immediate, and multisensorial way—whereas in Danda, he was worshipped from afar.

I was compelled by my interlocutor's call to the visceral nature of human-divine relations in *jagar* contexts, but it made me question the growing popularity of Danda Nagaraja temple. How did this woman's experience of Nagaraja as *her* "chosen deity" relate to Mr. Pant's conception of him as a depersonalized, abstract, and sweetened presence? How did these different manifestations of, and relations to, Nagaraja articulate with each other?

Highway, Countryside . . . and Town

In addressing these questions about divergent forms of worship and their implications for religious tourism and development in Uttarakhand, I redeploy the classic binary of *marg* (highway) and *desh* (countryside) and their associations with the so-called Great and Little Traditions of Hinduism, respectively, by adding a third term, *nagar*, which I translate as "town." While the religious prestige of the "highway" can be associated with the Char Dham pilgrimage circuit and *jagar* rituals with practices of the "countryside," I suggest that the worship of Nagaraja in Danda Nagaraja can be understood as "of the town" (*nagari*), and that these terms can help undo enduring binaries between highly localized religious understandings and practices, on the one hand, and pan-Indian, textual, and Sanskritic traditions, on the other (Berreman 1961; Marriott and Beals 1955; Singer 1972; Srinivas 1956).

In his famous work on processes of religious and cultural transformation in South India, M. N. Srinivas distinguished between "Sanskritic Hinduism," or "All-India Hinduism," which includes pan-Indian deities and the importance of ideas such as *moksha* (release from worldly ties and the cycle of birth and death), and "Local Hinduism," which generally involves the worship of deities known only to particular, geographically circumscribed communities (Srinivas 1952). In Srinivas's writings, "All-India" Hinduism—defined as a pattern of brahmanical knowledge and practice with pan-Indian "spread"—is contrasted with local and vernacular forms of Hinduism that are seen as constitutive of the "Little Tradition." Within this framework, Srinivas sees "Sanskritization" as a "two-way process though the local cultures seem to have received more than they have given" (1956, 494). In this sense, the concept of Sanskritization comes to be seen as a process through which All-India Hinduism, or the Great Tradition, spreads at the expense of the Little Tradition, the former acting as a unifying and dominant cultural force.[12]

In "Where Mirrors Are Windows," A. K. Ramanujan takes a playful yet critical approach to the notion of Great and Little Traditions:

One way of defining diversity for India is to say what the Irishman is said to have said about trousers. When asked whether trousers were singular or plural, he said, "Singular at the top and plural at the bottom." This is also a view espoused by people who believe that Indian traditions are organized as a pan-Indian

> Sanskritic Great Tradition (in the singular) and many local Little
> Traditions (in the plural). Older Indian notions of *marga* and *desa*
> and modern Indian politicians' rhetoric about unity in diversity
> fall in line with the same position. (Ramanujan 1989, 7)

Ramanujan further observes that, when employed interchangeably with Great and Little Traditions, the terms *marg* and *desh* are problematically implicated in nationalist paradigms that reify modernist identities and modes of thought by projecting them into the past. In addition to Ramanujan, V. Narayana Rao (1995), Wendy Doniger O'Flaherty (1993), Ann Grodzins Gold (1988), and Sheldon Pollock (2006), among others, have critiqued how *etic* notions of Great and Little Traditions have been misconstrued as civilizational "essences" and conflated with *emic* understandings of *marg* and *desh*. For example, describing the "vernacular revolution" that challenged the hegemony of Sanskrit language and literature in the public sphere during the first millennium, Pollock (2006) discusses how vernacular "Languages of the Place"—*desh*—began to compete with *marg*, or Sanskrit, the prestigious "Language of the Way" (Bronner 2010, 132). Thus, instead of equating *marg* and *desh* with the so-called Great and Little Traditions of Hinduism, Pollock's gloss recontextualizes *marg* and *desh* as terms of literary criticism and premodern intellectual history.

Despite their troubled history as analytical terms, *marg* and *desh* (and *nagar*) as spatial metaphors can illuminate important differences between sites of religious expression in Uttarakhand. More specifically, the literal, spatial connotations of *marg*, *desh*, and *nagar* correspond to the geographical movements of Nagaraja's devotees and pilgrims.

First, in *desh*, Nagaraja becomes associated with experiences of affliction, specifically, *nagadosh*. As the narrative of Nagaraja-Krishna's encounter with Gangu Ramola tells us, affliction is healed, or resolved, when the god is "given place (*sthan*)." These "places" are sites of intensification and include the bodies, homes, and villages of Nagaraja's worshipers. The god heals his worshipers and, in embodied form, also intervenes in other matters of personal and collective importance, such as village governance (Jassal 2024). In *desh*, divinities such as Nagaraja are apprehended viscerally, in and through the senses; divinities appear in *jagar* rituals, which take place in intimate domestic spaces and are mediated by Dalit priests, as well as in larger village rituals—such as *pandav nrtya*, or the "dance of the Pandavas," wherein Nagaraja is "danced" alongside the Pandava brothers, the heroes of the Mahabharata epic (Sax 2002). *Desh* also encompasses the worship of

Nagaraja in countless small shrines and temples that dot the *pahari* landscape. These modest dwellings of the god are known to and frequented by devotees from a single village or group of villages. Therefore, in Uttarakhand, an important quality that distinguishes the spaces of intensification that make up *desh* from *marg* and *nagar* is that, in the former, encounters with the divine are highly localized affairs, catering to small groups of people from circumscribed geographical areas.

Second, we come to *marg*, the "highway." The places that make up the Char Dham pilgrimage circuit, other well-known temples such as Tungnath, and aspiring Char Dham locations like Danda Nagaraja are reached via literal highways that have, in recent decades, succeeded in connecting remote areas in Uttarakhand to the rest of India. Furthermore, these pilgrimage destinations are also connected via a figurative highway, producing an assemblage of concepts, texts, practices, and institutions that are viewed as meaningful or authoritative by a broad swath of the global Hindu community. For instance, Mr. Pant's reference to the concept of *mukti* as the desired goal of temple worship in Danda, or the Bhagavadgita and Bhagavata Purana as "authoritative" (*shastrik*) texts about Nagaraja, gestured to the workings of a figurative Hindu "highway" that connects localized religious traditions to broader, translocal frameworks of meaning and practice. The prestige of the Char Dham circuit also arises from its associations with translocally significant religious figures and textual traditions, such as the philosopher-saint Shankara, the Mahabharata, and the Puranas (Hund and Wren 2018, 16). Importantly, while Char Dham sites are in Uttarakhand and serve as key markers of regional identity for the inhabitants of the state, they are known to, and frequented by, pilgrims from across India and beyond—a feature that sets them apart from the sites that make up *desh* and *nagar*, as I explain below.

Third, Danda Nagaraja temple exemplifies *nagar*, because relative to the Char Dham destinations, non-Garhwalis and some rural Garhwalis are unaware of it and do not visit it en masse. On the other hand, unlike the geographically circumscribed sites that make up *desh*, devotees of Nagaraja from across Garhwal visit Danda. Moreover, in addition to resident Garhwalis, Garhwali expats who live and work outside of Uttarakhand also visit Danda in large numbers. Possessing the financial means to travel to this remote temple, these visitors belong to a relatively prosperous and cosmopolitan segment of Uttarakhand's population. Because urban populations are generally wealthier than rural ones, both in Garhwal and in India, as a whole,[13] temple authorities in Danda endeavor to attract devotees who reside in urban centers.

For instance, the *pujari*s in Danda told me that, in the mid-2000s, the annual temple festival was rescheduled to coincide with schoolchildren's summer holidays, to make it easier for urban and middle-class devotees to travel to the temple with their families. This change was instituted after a protracted battle between two separate factions within the temple committee. One faction was against changing the temple calendar and breaking with generations of institutionalized precedent while the other, winning faction was adamant that this change would allow for more socioeconomically privileged devotees from a wider geographical area to attend the festival and enrich the temple economy. Temple authorities had also renovated the guesthouse on the temple premises, allowing people who lived and worked far away from Danda to visit more frequently and for longer periods of time. These visitors not only spent money on travel to the temple, lodging, food, and various incidental expenses but also donated to the temple's material development, renovation, and construction projects.

Conclusion

While *nagari* sites possess a wider geographical scope than those that make up *desh* and attract a more socioeconomically diverse group of people, they also represent an extension of *desh* by catering to devotees from the "countryside," such as visitors to Danda who know Nagaraja primarily as a *jagar* deity. In other words, *nagar* continues to draw upon pools of knowledge and practice that are grounded in highly localized spaces of intensification. At the same time, my interlocutors in Danda, such as Mr. Pant, indicated how a *nagari* identity was also distinct from *desh*. For instance, temple authorities emphasized Nagaraja's nonafflictive, detached, depersonalized—that is, sweetened—mode of being in Danda, undercutting the narrative and ritual traditions of *jagar* performers and participants. The temple site of Danda Nagaraja thus exemplifies a double vision. On the one hand, it caters to devotees who know Nagaraja primarily as a *jagar* deity. On the other hand, *nagar*'s gaze is increasingly directed outward, to the "highway" and the people who traverse it; a defining characteristic of *nagari* sites is that they aspire to participate in, and belong to, *marg*.

In *The Cultural Role of Cities* (1954), Robert Redfield and Milton Singer analyze the role of urban centers in sociocultural transformation. They argue that, in addition to enabling the consolidation, crystallization, and preservation of localized traditions of the "country," or *desh*, cities also serve as nodes of innovation that expose *desh* to new and unfamiliar forms of knowledge and practice. While the "city" grows out of the "country," the former also draws new influences from the wider world (and the figurative "highway") toward the latter, transforming the latter in the process (Redfield and Singer 1954, 71). The authors note that cities are "creatures as well as creators of . . . cultural change," a description that also applies to *nagar* as a site of religious practice.

While the "city" transforms the "country," and vice versa, as Redfield and Singer observe, in the rural areas of Garhwal where I conducted field-work, people's attitudes toward the rising prominence and cultural influence of *nagari* sites such as Danda Nagaraja were mixed. Some, like the elderly woman from Nisni, had limited engagement with these places; they either did not visit them or felt disappointed when they did. At the same time, *nagari* sites do not cater exclusively to Garhwali expats, urbanites, and non-*pahari* people. During my stay in Danda, temple authorities informed me that resident Garhwalis from local rural communities also visited the temple. Interacting with these visitors, I learned that they were comfortable worshiping Nagaraja both as an embodied actor in *jagar* rituals as well as a temple deity in Danda.

For instance, a local visitor whom I interviewed at the temple mentioned that he had made the pilgrimage to Danda because he had promised Nagaraja to do so while communicating with the god during a *jagar* conducted in his home village. Another visitor mentioned that it was more convenient to visit and worship the god in Danda than to sponsor time-consuming and costly *jagar* ceremonies at home. My interactions with local visitors also confirmed what temple authorities had told me: the temple's growing popularity had provided significant material benefits to the local population of Danda and surrounding areas. To support the increasing inflow of visitors, many new commercial establishments, such as restaurants, guesthouses, and shops, had sprung up along the main road leading to the temple. While the economic benefits of such "development" were distributed unevenly, especially among those at the lower end of the socioeconomic spectrum, they contributed to making locals more favorably inclined toward Danda as a site of religious innovation.

Finally, as I learned during my time in Danda, referring to this temple as the "fifth abode" was not simply a mark of prestige; it also possessed material implications for the growth and development of the temple. Temple authorities had been particularly successful in drawing urban, middle-class, and expat Garhwali visitors, and in mobilizing forms of state and scientific capital, but, as Mr. Pant said, "there is still a long way to go; we need to spread awareness (*prachar*) about this place all over the country, so that more and more people can come and reap its benefits." In other words, in the course of various material and discursive efforts to "develop" Danda and "sweeten" Nagaraja, temple authorities were also transforming the conditions of possibility in which Nagaraja was known and experienced.

Notes

1. See Brian K. Pennington (2016) for a discussion of another "fifth *dham*" in Uttarakhand, and his forthcoming book *God's Fifth Abode: Entrepreneurial Hinduism in the Indian Himalayas*, which analyzes the relationship between processes of economic development and religious transformation in the pilgrimage city of Uttarkashi, Uttarakhand. Additionally, Carter H. Higgins's (2018) article discusses the relationship between processes of neoliberal development and religious place-making in Gogameri, Rajasthan.

2. The concept of a "fifth abode" is analogous to that of a "fifth Veda," which was used to expand the Vedic canon and confer authority and stature on later, post-Vedic textual traditions such as the *Mahabharata* (Hiltebeitel, Adluri, and Bagchee 2011). Similarly, the "fifth abode" designation in relation to Danda Nagaraja draws on the historical success and prestige of the well-known Char Dham pilgrimage network, while at the same time forging a new path for itself.

3. "Tourism in Uttarakhand," Partnership for Resilience & Preparedness. https://prepdata.org/dashboards/uttarakhand-tourism.

4. See Whitmore (2018) for an analysis of the relationship between ecological harm, tourism, development, and religious practice in Kedarnath, one of the "four abodes" of Uttarakhand.

5. "Kedarnath Will Become a Model Pilgrimage Site: PM Modi," *Times of India*, October 20, 2017. https://timesofindia.indiatimes.com/india/kedarnath-will-become-a-model-pilgrimage-site-pm-modi/articleshow/61150280.cms.

6. Kalyan Das, "PM Modi Visits Kedarnath, Says Decade Belongs to Uttarakhand," Hindustan Times, November 6, 2021. https://www.hindustantimes.com/india-news/more-pilgrims-to-visit-char-dham-shrines-in-10-yrs-than-over-last-century-modi-101636114454610.html.

7. A human medium, or vehicle, of a deity is called a *pasva* (beast), *ghora* (horse), or *dangariya* (little horse).

8. These ritual specialists are also called *jagariya*s (*jagar* performers) and *guru*s (experts/guides).

9. William S. Sax (2002) mentions that the failure to perform a collective ritual called *pandav lila* at least once in a generation may lead to ontological diseases

of the social body called *dosh*. According to Sax, this term has a range of meanings, including "fault," "blemish," and "sanction" (2002, 49).

10. All interview names used in this text are pseudonyms.

11. According to Mr. Pant, the "fifth abode" designation was shared equally between Sem Mukhem temple, in Tehri district, and Danda Nagaraja temple, in Pauri district.

12. In *Religion and Society among the Coorgs of South India* (1952), Srinivas complicates the binary of "All-India Hinduism" versus "Local Hinduism" (or Great vs. Little Traditions) by introducing two additional "spreads" of Hinduism. These four categories, arranged in progressively narrowing circles of religio-cultural diffusion, are All-India Hinduism, Peninsular Hinduism, Regional Hinduism, and Local Hinduism (214). Within this framework, "Regional Hinduism" has a more "restricted spread" than both "All-India Hinduism" and South Indian "Peninsular Hinduism" (Srinivas 1952, 214–15). According to Srinivas, while Regional Hinduism "contains some Sanskritic elements," it is also deeply rooted in localized religious cultures—a characteristic that is also true of *nagar*. However, while Nagaraja *is* presented as a "regional" deity in Danda, my understanding of *nagar* diverges from the notion of "Regional Hinduism" as a relatively stable, transhistorical category mediating between All-India and Local Hinduisms. Specifically, by attending to the complex historical realities of neoliberal development, religious tourism, economic migration, urbanization, political statehood, and religious nationalism in contemporary north India, the concept of *nagar* both extends and departs from Srinivas's important work.

13. Chandan Kumar, Piyasa, and Nandita Saikia, "An Update on Explaining the Rural-Urban Gap in Under-Five Mortality in India," *BMC Public Health*, November 16, 2022. DOI: 10.1186/s12889-022-14436-7.

References

Allocco, Amy L. 2013. "Fear, Reverence and Ambivalence." *Religions of South Asia* 7 (1–3): 230–48.

Allocco, Amy L. 2014. "The Blemish of 'Modern Times': Snakes, Planets and the Kaliyugam." *Nidan: International Journal for Indian Studies* 26 (1): 1–21.

Allocco, Amy L. 2018. "Flower Showers for the Goddess: Borrowing, Modification, and Ritual Innovation in Tamil Nadu." In *Ritual Innovation: Strategic Interventions in South Asian Religion*, edited by Brian K. Pennington and Amy L. Allocco, 129–48. State University of New York Press.

Alter, Andrew. 2008. *Dancing with Devtās: Drums, Power and Possession in the Music of Garhwal, North India*. Ashgate.

Arumugam, Indira. 2015. " 'The Old Gods Are Losing Power!' Theologies of Power and Rituals of Productivity in a Tamil Nadu Village." *Modern Asian Studies* 49 (3): 753–86.

Berreman, Gerald D. 1961. "Himalayan Rope Sliding and Village Hinduism: An Analysis." *Southwestern Journal of Anthropology* 17 (4): 326–42.

Bronner, Yigal. 2010. *Extreme Poetry: The South Asian Movement of Simultaneous Narration.* Columbia University Press.

Feldhaus, Anne. 2003. *Connected Places: Region, Pilgrimage, and Geographical Imagination in India.* Palgrave Macmillan.

Fiol, Stefan. 2017. *Recasting Folk in the Himalayas: Indian Music Media and Social Mobility.* University of Illinois Press.

Gold, Ann Grodzins. 1988. *Fruitful Journeys: The Ways of Rajasthani Pilgrims.* University of California Press.

Harman, William. 2004. "From Fierce to Domesticated: Mariyamman Joins the Middle Class." *Manushi* 140 (January–February): 2–14.

Higgins, Carter Hawthorne. 2018. "Hindu Bakaph? Charitable Development and Trust Sovereignty in 'Neoliberal' India." *Muslim World* 108 (4): 652–75.

Hiltebeitel, Alf, Vishwa Adluri, and Joydeep Bagchee. 2011. *Reading the Fifth Veda: Studies on the Mahabharata: Essays.* Brill.

Hund, Andrew J., and James A. Wren. 2018. *The Himalayas: An Encyclopedia of Geography, History, and Culture.* ABC-CLIO.

Jassal, Aftab Singh. 2024. *Gods in the World: Placemaking and Healing in the Himalayas.* Columbia University Press.

Leavitt, John. 1986. "Oracular Therapy in the Kumaon Hills: A Question of Rationality." *Indian Anthropologist* 16 (1): 71–79.

Malik, Aditya. 2016. *Tales of Justice and Rituals of Divine Embodiment: Oral Narratives from the Central Himalayas.* Oxford University Press.

Marriott, McKim, and Alan R. Beals. 1955. *Village India.* University of Chicago Press.

McDermott, Rachel Fell. 2001. *Mother of My Heart, Daughter of My Dreams: Kālī and Umā in the Devotional Poetry of Bengal.* Oxford University Press.

O'Flaherty, Wendy Doniger. 1993. *Purāna Perennis: Reciprocity and Transformation in Hindu and Jaina Texts.* Sri Satguru.

Padma, Sree. 2013. *Vicissitudes of the Goddess: Reconstructions of the Gramadevata in India's Religious Traditions.* Oxford University Press.

Pennington, Brian K. 2016. "Hinduism in North India." In *Hinduism in the Modern World,* edited by Brian A. Hatcher, 31–47. Routledge.

Pollock, Sheldon I. 2006. *The Language of the Gods in the World of Men: Sanskrit Culture and Power in Premodern India.* University of California Press.

Ramanujan, A. K. 1989. "Where Mirrors Are Windows: Toward an Anthology of Reflections." *History of Religions* 28 (3): 187–216.

Rao, V. Narayana. 1995. "Coconut and Honey: Sanskrit and Telugu in Medieval Andhra." *Social Scientist* 23 (10–12): 24–40.

Redfield, Robert, and Milton B. Singer. 1954. "The Cultural Role of Cities." *Economic Development and Cultural Change* 3 (1): 53–73.

Sax, William S. 2002. *Dancing the Self: Personhood and Performance in the* Pāṇḍav Līlā *of Garhwal.* Oxford University Press.

Sax, William S. 2009. *God of Justice: Ritual Healing and Social Justice in the Central Himalayas.* Oxford University Press.

Singer, Milton B. 1972. *When a Great Tradition Modernizes: An Anthropological Approach to Indian Civilization.* Pall Mall Press.

Sinha, Vineeta. 2016. A *New God in the Diaspora? Muneeswaran Worship in Contemporary Singapore.* NUS Press.

Srinivas, M. N. 1952. *Religion and Society Among the Coorgs of South India.* Asia Publishing House.

Srinivas, M. N. 1956. "A Note on Sanskritization and Westernization." *Far Eastern Quarterly* 15 (4): 481–96.

Whitmore, Luke. 2018. *Mountain Water Rock God: Understanding Kedarnath in the Twenty-First Century.* University of California Press.

Zeiler, Xenia. 2012. "Female Danger: 'Evil,' Inauspiciousness, and Their Symbols in Representations of South Asian Goddesses." *Nidan: Journal for the Study of Hinduism* 24: 100–17.

6

Feral Gods

Inklings of a Mercurial Sacrality in Village Tamil Nadu

INDIRA ARUMUGAM

In 2008, the members of the K. K. Vanniyar and Tontani lineages resolved to offer sacrificial worship to their male tutelary deity (*kula deivam*), Viranar. The smaller Tontani lineage had split from the original and larger K. K. Vanniyar lineage decades ago. However, both still shared the same tutelary deity. The tutelary's shrine is under a large tree growing in the shared yard space among the houses belonging to members of the two respective lineages.[1] Their Viranar is in the form of a stone slab. A common deity in rural Tamil Nadu, Viranar's name translates into "The Brave One." While impossible to definitively know, Viranars are probably derived from historical ancestors who strived for the betterment of their communities or sacrificed their own lives to protect others and were deified upon their death. Over time, they became worshiped by the community as guardian deities and tutelary cults arose around them. In this chapter, I engage with three Viranars as evoked by three different lineages within the Kallar caste: (1) the K. K. Vanniyar and Tontani lineages, (2) the Sakkarei Kandiyar lineage, and (3) the Mela Kandiyar lineage . . . Patrilineally reckoned lineages and clans are a feature of kinship groupings among the Kallar caste. Male members of the same lineage or lineage-mates (*pangalis*) trace their descent from a common ancestor. Their households are clustered together

141

in the same vicinity. Lineage-mates share a tutelary deity and ritual cult premised on sacrificial worship.

This chapter is based primarily on twenty months of ethnographic fieldwork between 2006 and 2008 among the Kallars, the dominant caste monopolizing landownership and political offices in Vaduvur, a village of about thirteen thousand people in central Tamil Nadu.[2] Since my family also originates from Vaduvur—although my paternal side has migrated to and are settled in Singapore—most of my ethnographic interlocutors are also my kin (Arumugam 2022). More significantly, my father is a member of the Mela Kandiyar lineage and their Viranar is also his tutelary deity. As a daughter born into this lineage, the ritual actualization of my own rights and obligations (albeit limited by my gender) to this Viranar vivified the insights derived from participant-observation of the sacrificial worship and in-depth interviews with the lineage-mates, their wives, and lineage headmen.

For decades, apart from the odd casual prayer, the K. K. Vanniyar and Tontani lineages had neglected their sacrificial obligations to their deity. They were driven to resurrect their long dormant tutelary sacrifice because of a brutal murder committed by a fellow lineage-mate nicknamed Cell in June 2008. In the aftermath of the horrific murder, K. K. Vanniyar Street where the murderer lived (and I also happened to reside) was rife with indignant gossip. Piecing together several fragmentary accounts from my neighbors, I understood that a severely inebriated Cell had provoked and attacked an innocent lower-caste youth named Ramu.[3] He beat, brutalized, and drowned the injured Ramu in a village canal. Cell then fell into a drunken stupor at a nearby shrine. The next morning, when he awoke to the full horror of his crime, a frightened Cell confessed to his family. The police were informed. Cell was arrested. While this may seem a random confrontation attributable to an individual's drunken rage, I read this homicide as part of the violent implications of historic caste inequities and their contemporary reverberations. After snatching and refusing to return Ramu's new mobile phone, Cell initiated the altercation. When Ramu objected to this offense, Cell retaliated violently. Increasingly prosperous and independent lower castes challenging and undermining prevailing caste hierarchies can lead to vicious responses from privileged castes.[4] For the dominant Kallars—specifically the K. K. Vanniyar and Tontani lineages—however, this murder had a primarily religious significance. Several weeks after the horrific crime, Tontani lineage-mate Subramaniam Vanniyar drew direct links between the prior homicide and proposed sacrifice: "We have not offered a life to Viranar for so long. He must have decided to take the life that he wanted for himself. We must definitely conduct a sacrifice this year. Otherwise, our Viranar might become even angrier."

The life taken was not one of their own, that is, a fellow lineage-mate, but a lower caste youth. Nevertheless, their lineage-mate had killed and could be incarcerated. As mentioned above, the murder and its repercussions were interpreted as punishment but even more so as a warning to the lineage for their failure to observe the sacrificial covenant with their tutelary deity. Since he was not offered a voluntary sacrifice of an animal surrogate by his lineage, Viranar had seized an unwilling human life for himself. In so doing, he had also punished his lineage's desultory neglect, if not willful defiance. In the interest of sustaining their kinship, most tutelaries are believed to be patient with their lineage's lapses and slow to chastise. That is the case until sustained inattention provokes their wrath and invites terrible retributions. Heeding their deity's demands, which had been so forcefully impressed upon them and fearing Viranar's wrath and further divine retributions, the K. K. Vanniyar and Tontani lineages finally organized a sacrificial worship in August 2008. They hired a priest to officiate at the rites and perform the sacrificial decapitations. They bought two goats and a rooster to offer to Viranar. They also invited neighbors from their street to the worship and feast of the sacrificial meat thereafter.[5] Viranar's punitive retaliations reminded his negligent devotees of his presence and powers.

Religious transformations in Hinduism have customarily been theorized in terms of Sanskritization, the process by which groups lower on the caste hierarchy cultivate social mobility by emulating the practices of more elite castes (Srinivas 1952). Other popular explanations include modernization (Srinivas 1996, 101) and Hinduization, that is the gradual incorporation of heterodox practices into a Hindu orthodoxy and the concurrent adoption by alternative traditions of mainstream Hindu features (Ludden 1996). This moderating thrust is mirrored in analyses of deities and ritual cults with the privileging of the ongoing domestication of once fierce, peripatetic, and feral deities, the standardizing of esoteric rituals, and the mainstream-ing of distinctive and perhaps radical theologies (see, e.g., Allocco 2018; McDermott 2001; Padma 2013; Zeiler 2012). Tribal, village, and regional deities mainly propitiated by the lower castes have been rendered local avatars, consorts, or kin of mainstream pan-Indian deities. Folded into high-caste brahmanical genealogies, these once radically different deities are made part of elite Sanskritic theologies. Increasingly fixed in permanent temples, materialized in lithic or metal icons, and venerated with regular worship, these once sovereign deities now become subject to human intentions and actions. When these stridently rural deities migrate with their congregations to the cities or overseas, they become even more gentrified (Harman 2004; Waghorne 2004). Professional Brahmans replace local and part-time priests. Occasional worship becomes daily liturgies. Tamil litanies become Sanskrit mantras. In line with reformist agendas, exacerbated by Hindu nationalist attempts to propagate a homogenized Hinduism, animal sacrifice is often shunned in favor of nonviolent worship (Fuller 2004; Sen 2010). Sacrifice is rendered entirely symbolic with animal and meat offerings replaced by vegetable substitutes like coconuts, gourds, and lemons (Fuller 2004). Feral and ferocious deities who once roamed at their leisure and acted according to their own inscrutable whims are now rooted to a single spot, ensconced in architecture, marooned in iconography, and enveloped by esoteric rites in a dead language (Arumugam 2020a). Their unpredictable and incendiary intensity has become tamed.

Against these prevailing trends, I have documented instances where animal sacrifice is not just surviving but thriving and even increasing as long-abandoned sacrificial worship is resurrected to confront the challenges to production and reproduction that have been intensified by neoliberal and hypercompetitive political-economic circumstances (Arumugam 2015). Resurgent animal sacrifices also speak of a tenacious hostility to brahmanical norms, shifting away from exclusively Sanskritic cultural exemplars and con-current revival of Dravidian, non-Sanskritic values and lifestyles (Arumugam 2015, 773–74; Good 2023). Simultaneously, there are instances where these seemingly subdued deities have retained their capacity to intervene in and act in this world independent of human intentions, machinations, and volition (Arumugam 2020b). Immediately after and sometimes during sacrificial worship, sacred entities are believed to attempt to seize unintended and involuntary human lives for themselves despite the numerous animal surrogates that are willingly and ritually tendered by their devotees. These uncanny appropriations are part of apparently preternatural phenomena that offer, I have proposed elsewhere, a rubric through which divine agency may become discernible to human awareness and understanding or the lack thereof (Arumugam 2023a). These examples of insistence on a sovereign anarchy in the face of theological, ritual, and politico-economic imperatives to curate, abridge, and moderate these deities and their ritual cults have propelled this consideration of the heteroglossic undercurrents constituting a male tutelary deity, Viranar.

This wild and unwieldy deity is being subjected to the pressures of domestication. However, as shrines, statues, and regular sacrifices for the Viranars of some lineages proliferate, other Viranars are simultaneously repudiating attempts to streamline, subdue, and orchestrate them. Discussing how sustained neglect of the sacrificial covenant is believed to cause a tutelary to make his presence and powers known concretely and forcefully, I delineate the constitutive kinship between a lineage and its tutelary. Even as Viranar may appear to be a rather generic guardian deity, I propose that the specific prescriptions and prohibitions characteristic of each ritual cult and especially the unique preferences of each lineage's tutelary manifest the distinctive personas of each deity. These idiosyncrasies, even with respect to the same deity and variances within the same cult, make visible the tensions between devotees' aspirations and their deity's own preferences. These tensions are most apparent when it comes to deciding when, how, and especially if to build a temple to house the deity. To settle down or remain free to roam—this is at the heart of arbitrations between human purposes and a sovereign sacred. Charting the shifting dynamics of standardizing mellowness and fierce forcefulness underpinning rural tutelary cults, I make perceptible assertions of a divine agency that chafes against human intentions and often elides easy social, political, and economic explanations (also Arumugam 2023a). The unpredictability and ultimate unfathomability defining tutelary deities' cults suggests how, even as gentrification threatens to engulf—in the form of proliferating fixed shrines, standardized iconography, regular worship, forswearing animal sacrifice, and on occasion recourse to Brahman priests and Sanskritic rituals—one may still sense and make sense of a feral numinousness. Tamed or still wild, all deities demand some reverence, as signs of their devotees' deference. The more feral deities just want this ritual attention to be on their own terms—sporadic worship as testaments to their presence and power and then to be left largely alone to simply be. Mediating between domesticity and ferality, these ambivalent deities trouble the epistemological confinements assigned and enforced by the functional calculus and teleological impetus underpinning prevailing theories of religious transformations such as Sanskritization, modernization, and gentrification. In so doing, they challenge us to recognize, theorize, and represent their very real presence—with all its energy, excess, and above all eerie enigma—in their devotees' lives.

Kin and Deity: Co-Constituting and Cohabiting

In 2008, at the end of the Mela Kandiyar lineage's sacrifice, as the hired butchers were processing the decapitated goat carcasses, Murugan Kandiyar, a young Mela Kandiyar lineage-mate, explained why he had made sure to attend this worship. Murugan had moved away from his native Vaduvur to the neighboring district of Tondaiman Pudukottai. Citing the inconvenience, he stopped attending his deity's annual sacrifice. In 2007, Murugan had undertaken a pilgrimage to the Ayyappan temple in Sabarimalai, Kerala, which he was forced to abandon. Having undertaken the vow (*vratam*), he scrupulously observed the expected austerities for the forty-one days preceding his pilgrimage. Throughout his vow, he bathed twice daily and donned the characteristic *rudraksha* bead necklace and plain black clothing. He renounced meat, alcohol, smoking, and sex. He refrained from displaying anger and uttering profanities. He visited the local temples regularly (see, e.g., Osella and Osella 2003). And yet, he sighed, "When I arrived at its base, I was unable to climb the steep hill and walk the forest path to the temple. Ayyappan would not allow me to. He decides who and if one can approach him. He stopped me. He told me to worship my lineage deity first and only then come and see him." So, in 2008, even though he had to rush off to work early the next morning, Murugan attended and remained for the duration of Viranar's late-night worship. Having concluded that he had failed to ascend Ayyappan's hill because he had not secured Viranar's blessings before embarking on his pilgrimage, Murugan told me that he had resolved from then on to religiously attend his lineage worship. Approaching one's lineage god before embarking on any major endeavor secures the deity's permission, cooperation, and protection so that obstacles are removed, and success is facilitated. For example, when Upputanni lineage-mate Govindasamy Vanniyar bought a new tractor, he had "With the Protection of Sri Ravuthar Ayyan" ("Revered Ravuthar Father") inscribed on the nameplate. The first stop in Vaduvur on the tractor's long trip from the sales lot was Ravuthar's shrine. Only after he sought Ravuthar's blessings did Govindasamy drive the tractor home and begin ploughing his fields. One's tutelary god is one's primary deity and should be approached before all others.

Tutelaries and their congregations mutually constitute and continually cohabit with each other. This affinity is materialized in and through the covenant of sacrifice. Lineages should offer regular sacrifice to their tutelary deities. And yet, most have not. Taking one's tutelary deity for granted also defines their kinship. According to Maurice Bloch (1973, 75–77; also see Clark-Decès 2014), kin are expected to accept imbalances in the relationship, at least briefly. Too exact a tallying, too immediate a repayment, too perfect an equilibrium makes this relational equation more of a blatantly calculative, instrumentalist, and transactional contract. Kin are obliged to bear immediate deficits in the short term in the interest of a long-term commitment, that is, their enduring kinship. To this end, tutelary deities too tend to tolerate their lineage's delays in honoring sacrificial obligations or neglecting regular worship. Until, that is, as we saw with the K. K. Vanniyar and Tontani lineages' Viranar that I began with, they do not.

Prescriptions and Prohibitions: Manifesting Preferences and Making Personae

As related by Sakthivel Kandiyar, a member of the Mela Kandiyar lineage, with vast experience in organizing sacrificial worship for his tutelary deity, Viranar is one of the more exacting tutelary deities. Viranar's stringency is evident in the rigorous protocols and prohibitions framing his sacrificial worship. While other lineage deities may be more lenient, the Viranar ritual cults are some of the strictest in their exclusion or marginalization of women. Women cannot be full members of a lineage enjoying all the rights and observing the obligations this demands. Women who are (1) born into a lineage (*poranta ponnus*), that is, sisters and daughters and those (2) married into a lineage (*pukunta ponnus*),[6] that is, mothers and wives, are merely associates. While sisters and daughters do have more rights in their natal lineage than mothers and wives, both are secondary to and subsumed by their male kin. More significantly, postpubertal but premenopausal women—women in the reproductive prime—are excluded from witnessing animal sacrifices and even approaching the lineage deities' sanctums. For example, during the Mela Kandiyar lineage's worship in 2008, the women stood at the margins of the field where Viranar's shrine is located so that they could not even see the rituals properly. The exclusion of women in their reproductive prime from the lineage cult has been theorized as part of the counterintuitive male appropriation of responsibility for fertility through ritual that necessitates the exclusion of actual organic fertility (Arumugam 2023b; Bloch and Parry 1982; Nabokov 2000). These prohibitions are being gradually relaxed or renegotiated and women are venturing closer to the deity. Nevertheless, most women have internalized these rules and adhere strictly to them for fear of being seized (*pidichu*) or possessed or smote (*adichu*) by a wrathful deity (Arumugam 2015).

Along with determining who can worship or even approach them, Viranar is also fastidious about the animal he will accept as an appropriate sacrifice. As Veerasamy Kandiyar, the Mela Kandiyar lineage's headman, explained to me, the male goat to be sacrificed must have sufficiently large horns to underline its virility. It must also be perfectly black without any white or rust-colored patches. Otherwise, Viranar may reject the sacrifice offered. This is why an ad hoc committee of lineage-mates inspects the goats thoroughly before purchase. During the Mela Kandiyar lineage's tutelary worship in 2008, five live goats were led toward and presented before Viranar, their necks garlanded with flowers and foreheads daubed with turmeric and vermilion. The goats were forced to bend their heads—to signify their "consent" to be the sacrifice. As turmeric-infused water was splashed over their heads, the goats shivered, spraying yellow water droplets. While purifying the goat, this ablution also renounces ownership and severs any other persisting ties between the sacrificer and the sacrificial animal. The goats were then led away from Viranar's main shrine. Before Viranar's subordinate and guardian deity (*kaval deivam*) Munnadiyan ("Forerunner"), one Mela Kandiyar lineage-mate caught hold of a goat's head and another its back legs to pull so that its neck became stretched. With a single stroke of his saber, the ritual priest decapitated a goat, then moved on to the next until all five were summarily dispatched. The heads were kept aside. The writhing carcasses were tossed aside so as not to get the spurting blood on anyone. Then the butchers took over, skinning, disemboweling, and chopping the carcass and proportioning the meat into seventy-six equal shares to be distributed to each of the sponsoring lineage-mates. Even after the sacrifice, Viranar does not relax his strictures.

Varied taboos surrounded the now sanctified meat. Rules about how any meat not consumed immediately (in the form of a communal feast or the next morning in the form of individual shares in each household) must be treated vary across different tutelary deities and ritual cults. Other lineage cults, like that of the Northern Mannaiyars' Val-Muniswarar, forbid the sacrificial meat's consumption by anyone other than the requisite lineage members. Another Viranar, that of the Southern Mannaiyars, allows nonlineage members to consume the sacred meat, but it must be consumed within the lineage territory itself. None of this meat can be given even to families living outside the territory concerned. The Viranar cults expressly forbid this sacred meat from being sun-dried and kept aside for later use. However, the Northern Mannaiyars' Val-Muniswarar cult only forbids the drying of the meat out in the sun in full sight of everybody. The meat can be dried out of sight, in the shade. Such prescriptions and prohibitions render sacrificial flesh unlike any routine meat and constitute its sacrality. At the same time, these rules serve to craft the distinctiveness of various deities and their ritual cults.

The particular places from where they are wrought and continue to protect, theogonies retelling their birth, the corpus of myths, legends, and stories narrating their presence and powers and characteristic appearance, attire, and weaponry, as well as attending deities, animals, or humans, chart the specific persona of tutelary deities like Viranar (Eck 2011; Hawley and Wulff 1996). The plethora of ritual and postritual protocols that are expected, including the types, sex, forms, and colors of the live sacrificial animals demanded, make known deities' specific desires and expectations. The varying degrees of stringency with which the protocols are enforced and the differing severity with which infringements are punished constitute their varying temperaments. Grounding these deities in particular places, among particular peoples, and in specific ritual tastes and taboos makes transcendent deities immediate and intimate. More significantly, they render a generic, even vague sacrality into a specific and singular deity, highlighting their idiosyncrasies to fashion their distinctive identities. In the process, they also assert the distinctive will (and willfulness) of these deities. Assertions of divine agency are even more compelling when it comes to if, when, and how such deities decide between persistent itinerancy and eventual settlement.

Between Feral Roaming and Tamed Dwelling: Manifesting Sovereignty

The Viranar of the Sakkarei Kandiyar lineage assumes the unremarkable form of a tree branch stuck into the ground under a tree in a nondescript field. Even these basic elements of stone, wood, and metal from which the sacred is wrought are later attempts at materialization (Arumugam 2021). The very first repository of the tutelary god is actually the soil itself. This reality is borne out by the method of relocating a lineage deity—taking "a handful of earth from the original site and carry[ing] it to the new one" and building a new shrine on this old foundation (Dumont 2000, 371; Mines 2005, 131–34). According to Andal, a woman married into the Sakkarei Kandiyar lineage, this method was also how their own Viranar had come into being. An intralineage conflict had provoked the Sakkarei Kandiyar lineage to split from the larger encompassing Mela Kandiyar lineage to form an independent segment. The Sakkarei Kandiyar lineage built a new shrine, installed their own Viranar icon, and instituted their specific sacrificial worship. Encapsulating the substantial affinity between a people, their place, their kin, and their gods, tutelary deities are immanent in the soil itself (Daniel 1984; Mines 2005; Sax 2009, 51–92). Being unenclosed by architecture and unencumbered by iconography leaves these elemental deities free to roam across the landscape. Rudimentary representation, minimal ritual syntax, and irregular worship paves the way for these deities to be ambulatory and free to act on their own impulses (Arumugam 2021, 2023a). Even as he began as a handful of elemental earth, the Sakkarei Kandiyar lineage's Viranar is now in the process of being given a permanent shrine (Flueckiger 2020, 99–132).

Siva, a wealthy businessman who owns a company providing marquees, lighting, and decorations for large meetings, specifically during political campaigns, is a member of this lineage. Attributing his prosperity to their Viranar's grace, Siva usually sponsors the communal feast after their annual lineage sacrifice. Lineage membership is premised on a strident equality among all the constituent male members, which is strenuously enforced. Given that taxation means representation, all lineage-mates must contribute equally to common lineage pursuits (Arumugam 2025). Nevertheless, Siva was willing to sponsor the more peripheral aspects of constructing their deity a permanent shrine. Two lineage-mates were willing to donate part of their fields to site the proposed shrine. The lineage is in the initial stages of raising the considerable funds necessary to build this new and permanent structure for their Viranar.

The Sakkarei Kandiyar lineage's sizable membership, their gradually increasing wealth and prestige, and especially the spectacular success of one of their kinsmen is simultaneously reflected in the regularity and increasing sumptuousness of their sacrificial worship to their tutelary deity. Tutelary deities, as mentioned earlier, are at the apex of a socio-ritual calculus that seeks to govern the potency of the land and channel it toward politico-economic purposes and are accorded ultimate responsibility for generativity (Arumugam 2015). Villagers recognize that wealth, productivity, and life itself are not contingent on human labors and technologies alone but are ultimately enigmatic, being subject to arbitrary divine interventions. The agricultural economy consists of relations between producers and the sacred (Sahlins 2017). Lineages are obliged to acknowledge their debt to their tutelary deity for their success, hence the imperative to offer sacrifice. Successful lineages demonstrate their gratitude and hopes for further prosperity through permanent and spectacular shrines, imposing iconography, and more regular and lavish lineage worship, changes that pave the way for the gentrification of these deities and their ritual cults.

Even so, decisions to root their peripatetic deity are not solely made by the lineage-mates. To illustrate this, I describe the dynamics preceding building a shrine by another lineage for their tutelary deity who is not a Viranar but has similar attributes and demands. In 2006, I asked several Upputanni lineage-mates in Vaduvur why they had decided to build a permanent shrine for their lineage deity, Ravuthar. One lineage member, Govindasamy Vanniyar, reported a troubling omen: "Our old shrine was a large tin can—like the ones used to store oil—under a tree out in the fields. On a shelf fitted through a hole in the can, we placed a lamp. We lit the lamp to evoke Ravuthar. We also had a trident . . . this is the mother goddess (*amman*), Durgai. During a storm, the tree sheltering the shrine fell. We rescued the lamp and the trident. But the shrine was no more."

Another Upputanni lineage-mate, Rajendran Vanniyar, recounted how they had been troubled by misfortune for some time: "Marriages that had been more or less finalized broke down at the last hurdle. Crops failed. Livestock died unexpectedly, or did not multiply as they should. Our lineage-mates themselves suffered health problems or had business failures and debt problems." The Upputanni lineage-mates consulted several astrologers who offered startlingly similar diagnoses: they had a powerful lineage god who continued to be by their side, but he was on the verge of abandoning them due to their neglect. Not experiencing the desired outcomes of marriages, parturitions (both human and animal), harvests, and business enterprises alludes to a decline in fertility that can be interpreted as symptomatic of deeper problems in the bond between a lineage and its deity. Along with these dire omens and signs of stifled fertility, Rajendran Vanniyar related some compelling dreams he had had as the lineage was contemplating building a temple: "My daughter was standing at the old shrine and an elephant was bearing down on her. You were also there.[7] I shouted at you to run. Another lineage-mate was also running away from the advancing elephant. . . . In another dream, I was cooking and serving food in Ravuthar's newly built temple." The Upputanni lineage's headman, the elderly Doraikannu Vanniyar, also recounted a dream where he was approached by a remarkably persistent man on a white horse who grumbled, "While you are all sleeping comfortably indoors, I am being burned by the sun and buffeted by the rains!" Ignoring this complaint, the headman sunk into a deeper slumber. The apparition returned and roared, "I am talking to you, and you dare to continue sleeping!" The headman reported bolting upright as he realized that the vision was their lineage deity, Ravuthar. This dream was the final impetus: in 2005, the Upputanni lineage began building the temple.

Figure 6.1. Ravuthar's just completed first temple. Vaduvur, Tamil Nadu, 2007. *Source:* Photo by the author.

Levying an equal tax on all the constituent households, the Upputanni lineage slowly raised the necessary funds.[8] They hired artisans to build and paint the shrine and craft their deity's statue.

In 2007, with the temple completed, they engaged a Brahman priest to conduct the consecration ceremony to inhere the deity to the shrine space and vivify the icon. After the forty-eight-day *mandalabhishekam* rituals to amplify this site-specific divine power, the lineage conducted the first sacrificial worship to their deity at his new shrine. They bought two black goats and engaged a local priest/medium to dedicate and decapitate the animals. They hired butchers to process the postsacrificial carcasses into exactly equal shares of meat for each of the sponsoring lineage households. Several days after this first sacrificial worship at their new temple in 2007, I listened to Sami Ammal, Upputanni lineage-mate Govindasamy Vanniyar's wife, making several resolutions: "Since we have a temple, we must make sure that we offer sacrifice every year from now on. Having a temple and statues means that we must treat them carefully. We cannot be casual like before. We must fear as much as we worship (*baya-bhakti*). Not doing the

Figure 6.2. New statue of Ravuthar. Vaduvur, Tamil Nadu, 2007. *Source:* Photo by the author.

rituals properly may make things go awry. We cannot anger Ravuthar again." At the behest of their deity, allusive ambulation gave way to literal fixity via architecture, iconography, and standardized veneration.

A permanent shrine with fixed iconography may pave the way to the constraining and mellowing of a once untamed and intense deity. However, most of the time, it is the deity itself who is believed to desire this rootedness and resplendence. The Upputanni lineage's Ravuthar chides his lineage for leaving him to brave the elements while they live comfortably indoors. Visitations of misfortunes and suffering, uneasy omens, and reproving dreams and prophetic visions articulate the deity's desires volubly and impel devotees to fulfill them in the material world. Even as they augur gentrification, dynamics of rootedness, architecture, iconography, and regular liturgies can also manifest the deity's will and whims. No shrine can be built without the presiding deity's permission as communicated through its priest, medium, or god-dancer (*sami-adi*). These visitations and visions encapsulate the deity's capacity to cause actions to happen and indeed act in this world: that is their agency.

Between Devotees' Aspirations and Deities' Willfulness: Divine Agency

This divine agency becomes even clearer when we consider the persistent obduracy of the Mela Kandiyar lineage's Viranar. Where the Upputanni lineage's Ravuthar has insisted on being housed comfortably indoors in his own shrine, this Viranar is unyielding about his freedom. During a brief visit to Vaduvur in 2012, I asked the Mela Kandiyar lineage's then headman, Veerasamy Kandiyar, a retired professor from Poondy College in nearby Thanjavur, about their plans for their deity:

> We have repeatedly asked Viranar's permission to build him a temple [through his priest/medium]. But he continues to vehemently decline our request. He absolutely refuses. He prefers to live out in the open, basking in the sun and soaking in the rain. He likes to roam. He wants to be free. In 2008, the field where he resides became severely waterlogged and practically impassable. Only then did he even allow us to lay down a concrete floor, erect a corrugated tin canopy, and build a basic niche to shelter him. And that is all we have been able to do. He still refuses a temple. We ask him repeatedly, but he is adamant. He will not allow a temple.

This Viranar remains, as he always has been, a large stone slab in the minimally sheltered open air.

That he receives an annual sacrifice at all, given that there are seventy-six households in the Mela Kandiyar lineage, is almost miraculous. Deferments of or failure to offer sacrifice, as we have seen, can anger deities enough to retaliate against and severely punish their own lineage members. Nevertheless, the internal divisions, fierce competitiveness, and protracted conflicts typical of relations among lineage-mates means that consistent worship can never be assumed (Arumugam 2025). An example of a conflict that prevented regular offerings is the dispute over land ownership among two Mela Kandiyar

Figure 6.3. Viranar, in his niche, out in the field. Vaduvur, Tamil Nadu, 2023. *Source:* Photo by the author.

lineage-mates that was tied up in litigation for nearly twenty years. During this time, the lineage did not offer the expected sacrificial worship to their Viranar. According to Sakthivel Kandiyar, a Mela Kandiyar lineage-mate, "We were just too divided." The performance of a tutelary sacrifice—contingent on the coming together and cooperation of the constituent members of a lineage—is often thwarted by friction among the lineage-mates themselves. In some circumstances, lineage-mates cannot agree enough to come together to even perform them. Ritual may not resolve, transcend, or triumph over but rather succumb to politics. Even successfully performed sacrifices, however, are no guarantee that the tutelary deity for which they are performed will be pleased or at least appeased and therefore be obliging.

In 2008, the Mela Kandiyar lineage did manage to come together to sacrifice five male goats that were portioned into seventy-six equal shares for distributing among the lineage-mates. Their Viranar repudiates permanence, architecture, iconography, and intricate ritualization—all processes presaging gentrification. Additionally, unlike the mellowed deities ensconced within gentrified ritual cults, he refuses to be placated with mere symbolic sacrifices or vegetarian substitutes. This Viranar continues to demand the ritual killing of actual living animals. Even as his lineage has now been able to sacrifice animals every year without fail, he is not amenable to their aspirations for him and their ritual cult. Through his spirit mediums and ritual priests, he informs his lineage about and insists upon his own inclinations. Lucid about his own preferences and loquacious about what he will and will not accept, this Viranar must be cajoled, convinced, and implored for even the most basic changes to his abode. Even as his adherents persist in trying to change his mind, this Viranar continues to resist their grand plans for him.

Before the onslaught of COVID-19 in 2020, the Mela Kandiyar lineage once again revived their plans to build a temple for their Viranar. They engaged a reputedly powerful priest from neighboring Kerala state who managed to decipher Viranar's most recent demands. After decades of refusing, Viranar finally (but perhaps reluctantly) conceded to having a permanent shrine built for him. However, he was categorical about not having an anthropomorphic statue to represent him. While he may reside in a shrine, Viranar insists on remaining an aniconic stone slab.

Viranar's unexpected change of mind was followed by the death of the elderly landowner who owned the small plot where their Viranar's makeshift shrine is sited. She had been allowing them to use the land for the annual rituals. Even though her sons were amenable, she had been adamant about not selling it to the lineage outright. The lineage-mates could not build a permanent temple simply based on a verbal understanding. Her death meant that they could now own the land and build the temple. Preliminary discussions had begun. But the project's impetus proved short-lived. As the pandemic was gathering force and its attendant social distancing and lockdowns were intensifying, the headman, Veerasamy Kandiyar, called my father, his fellow lineage-mate, to discuss raising funds for the proposed new temple. Just as some momentum was gathering—after a protracted struggle with the landowner and, more importantly, with their lineage deity—the headman unexpectedly succumbed to the coronavirus. His untimely death once again frustrated the temple-building plans. As of 2022, according to the new headman nicknamed Pulavar (Poet), the temple-building plans remain nebulous. Their Viranar, as per the deity's preference, remains a slab of stone, in a rudimentary niche, out in an open field. His congregation's grand plans have once again been foiled. Viranar remains free to roam as he pleases.

Figure 6.4. Aniconic Viranar. Vaduvur, Tamil Nadu, 2023. *Source:* Photo by the author.

Conclusion: Uncanny Deities, Unsettling Explanations

Comparing the differing materials and processes through which different gods are fabricated and enlivened in a village in Tamil Nadu, Soumhya Venkatesan (2020) notes that the stone-bodied Sanskritic gods require constant tending to become and especially to remain animated. The Sanskritic gods themselves may be omnipotent. However, to install in and continuously inhere them to a lithic icon requires brahmanical ritual procedures and Sanskrit recitations. Brahman priests understand their Sanskrit mantras are what turn icons into deities and maintain them as such. Conversely, the clay-bodied village deities are "self-sufficient and self-sustaining," requiring "no further ritual action beyond . . . [their] enlivening" (Venkatesan 2020, 452). Indeed, after the installation ritual, many village gods are left alone, their clay bodies becoming weathered, disintegrating, and returning to the soil from which they were initially wrought. "Animated and fetishized, they are alive and can act on their own behalf. Characterized as quick to anger, village deities are often best respectfully avoided" (Venkatesan 2020, 452). According to one of Venkatesan's interlocutors, a potter, "He [the village deity] is there and will do his work. Why unnecessarily attract his attention?" (452).

Accordingly, it is clear that village tutelary deities like Viranar flourish, in all their ferocious ferality, when left largely untended. Ferality thrives when abandoned by humans, when left to its own devices, to simply be. Ferocity reigns when people do not attempt to pin down, manage, and manicure it to fit their own purposes. When inhabiting the margins, haunting fields, yards, and shadows, these deities were untamed. When they were simply aniconic rocks, branches, and termite mounds, they roamed whenever and wherever they wanted. When worshiped only as and when their adherents could, they were uninhibited. When offered animal sacrifices, they were wildly intense. When only sporadically attended to, these deities were free to be exactly what they are. Contrary to the hitherto benign neglect, pronounced, prolonged, and unwavering attention is now altering the form, nature, and force of these deities.

As the village gods are made to assume increasingly brahmanical aesthetics and adopt gentrified ways as part of people's social mobility projects, they come to warrant the consistent attention and tending to that the temple-dwelling, stone-bodied Sanskritic deities require. Keeping their gods at the margins, as far as to avoid them unless absolutely necessary, liberates not just people (from regular ritual obligations) but also the gods (from having to accommodate themselves to human frameworks). Drawing them closer together, gentrification enmeshes people and their gods more thoroughly in a complex of expectations, commitments, and transactions. This increased entanglement paves the way for once largely self-sufficient, even sovereign, deities to become more subject to human intentions and actions with their forceful intensity moderated, even muted.

However, within Viranar's heteroglossic being, deeds, and demands are also inklings of a persistent and intense uncanniness. Some Viranars may be accepting and themselves even demanding temples, icons, and spectacular rituals. Simultaneously, other Viranars are stridently repudiating their increasingly affluent devotees' aspirations to reform them in the pursuit of "more prestigious" religiosities. Refuting the teleological thrust—where what was tumultuous is ultimately tamed, the heterodox purified, the ambiguous rationalized, and the unruly institutionalized—underpinning prevailing theories of religious transformations such as Sanskritization, modernization, gentrification, and sweetening, some deities remain enigmatic (Uchiyamada

2008). Even as they disdain routine, spectacular, and institutionalized worship, the more feral deities do insist upon periodic ritual attention. Occasional worship is critical to reiterate, nourish, and renew the fertility premised on kinship among people, their deities, and the land. Most of the time, however, these deities prefer to be left alone, to come and go as they please, and to be as they choose. By troubling explanations that decipher and describe deities primarily in terms of their symbolic weight, functional significance, and politico-economic resonance, such ambivalent deities continue to confound. The divergent, even paradoxical demands of such deities unsettle anthropocentric categories centering human intentions, actions, and interpretations to offer a glimpse of the inscrutable unearthliness constituting the sacred. Such equivocations evoke a still enigmatic world, where one may liaise with the gods but do not and, indeed, can never really know them.

Notes

1. In 2024, the lineages built and consecrated a permanent shrine for their deity on this site.

2. Additionally, I made brief visits in 2012 and 2015. During the pandemic (2020–2022), when I could not travel, I kept abreast of the developing situation via phone and video calls.

3. The names of the victim, the murderer, and the murderer's lineage-mates have been anonymized. All other names have been retained as they are.

4. The unjust aftermath of this appalling crime underlined the caste inequities in Vaduvur. Ramu's lower caste parents, agricultural laborers working for Kallar landlords, could not afford to press their case or protest too much. Via his family's canny machinations, Cell was released shortly after.

5. While looking forward to the free goat and chicken curry, several villagers were also uneasy about the sacrificial feast following so closely after the brutal murder. In Hindu metaphysics, eating and especially digestion are means to process sin, to make it disappear (Parry 1985, 625–27; Parry 1980; Calasso 2014, 213; Arumugam 2021). Mahindran, a priest at a nearby mother goddess shrine, asked, "Were they spilling the blood of goats to atone for the sin of murder? A life for a life?" This reading was rendered plausible by the K. K. Vanniyar and Tontani lineages not having the communal goat sacrificed and portioned as individual shares for each of the sponsoring lineage-mates, as is more usual, but instead hiring cooks and laying on a feast for the entire street. Villagers wondered if this feast intended for their neighbors to help the K. K. Vanniyar and Tontani lineages consume, excrete, and expiate their fellow lineage-mate's homicidal sin.

6. Since descent is paramount in tracing lineage membership, only women born into a lineage are structurally recognized, can claim kinship rights, and have

ritual significance. Women who are married into a lineage are so subsumed into their husbands' and sons' lineage membership as to be rendered almost categorically invisible. My interlocuters have no equivalent term for them. Instead, I have employed a term commonly used in other contexts to refer to virilocally married women entering/being incorporated into their marital households.

7. My mother was born into this Upputanni lineage. Rajendran is my classificatory mother's brother and has known me since I was born.

8. To supplement these taxes, they accepted donations from their sisters and daughters who had married out and moved away. These additional funds were only used for peripherals. For example, as a daughter born into the lineage, my mother donated money for the painting of the shrine and statues. This was to emphasize that these were simply voluntary donations, not obligatory taxations, and therefore did not render any rights to the deity or claims upon the sacrifice.

References

Allocco, Amy L. 2018. "Flower Showers for the Goddess: Borrowing, Modification, and Ritual Innovation in Tamil Nadu." In *Ritual Innovation: Strategic Interventions in South Asian Religion*, edited by Brian K. Pennington and Amy L. Allocco, 129–48. State University of New York Press.

Allocco, Amy L. 2021. "Bringing the Dead Home: Hindu Invitation Rituals in Tamil South India." *Journal of the American Academy of Religion* 89 (4): 103–42.

Arumugam, Indira. 2015. "'The Old Gods Are Losing Power!' Theologies of Power and Rituals of Productivity in a Tamil Nadu Village." *Modern Asian Studies* 49 (3): 753–86.

Arumugam, Indira. 2020a. "Migrant Deities: Dislocation, Divine Agency, and Mediated Manifestations." *American Behavioral Scientist* 64 (10): 1458–70.

Arumugam, Indira. 2020b. "Gods as Monsters: Insatiable Appetites, Exceeding Interpretations, and a Surfeit of Life." In *Monster Anthropology: Ethnographic Explorations of Transforming Social Worlds Through Monsters*, edited by Yasmine Musharbash and G. H. Presterudsteun, 44–58. Bloomsbury Academic.

Arumugam, Indira. 2021. "Touchable Gods: Improvised Icons, Irreverent Rituals and Intimate Kinship with Deities in Village Tamil Nadu." *Religions of South Asia* 13 (2): 230–51.

Arumugam, Indira. 2022. "Kin but Not Kind: An Anthropologist Among 'Her People.'" Member Voices, *Cultural Anthropology Fieldsights*, October 25. https://culanth.org/fieldsights/kin-but-not-kind-an-anthropologist-among-her-people.

Arumugam, Indira. 2023a. "The Sacred Unbound: Insufficient Rituals, Excess Life and Divine Agency in Rural South India." *Hau: Journal of Ethnographic Theory* 13 (1): 53–67.

Arumugam, Indira. 2023b. "Centering Women, Countering Killing: Women Sacrificing, Sacralising Maternity and Substantiating Intimacy with a Tamil Hindu Goddess." *Anthropological Forum* 33 (1): 27–49.

Arumugam, Indira. 2025. *Visceral Politics: Imaginaries of Power in South India.* Cambridge University Press.

Bloch, Maurice. 1973. "The Long-Term and the Short-Term: The Economic and Political Significance of the Morality of Kinship." In *The Character of Kinship*, edited by Jack Goody, 75–87. Cambridge University Press.

Bloch, Maurice, and Jonathan Parry. 1982. Introduction to *Death and the Regeneration of Life*, edited by Maurice Bloch and Jonathan Parry, 1–44. Cambridge University Press.

Calasso, Roberto. 2014. *Ardor.* Farrar, Straus and Giroux.

Clark-Decès, Isabelle. 2014. *The Right Spouse: Preferential Marriages in Tamil Nadu.* Stanford University Press.

Daniel, Valentine E. 1984. *Fluid Signs: Being a Person the Tamil Way.* University of California Press.

Dumont, Louis. 2000. *A South Indian Subcaste: Social Organisation and Religion of the Pramalai Kallar.* Oxford University Press.

Eck, Diana L. 2011. *India: A Sacred Geography.* Harvard University Press.

Flueckiger, Joyce Burkhalter. 2020. *Material Acts in Everyday Hindu Worlds.* State University of New York Press.

Fuller, C. J. 2004. *The Camphor Flame: Popular Hinduism and Society in India.* Princeton University Press.

Good, Anthony. 2023. "Animal Sacrifice, Politics and the Law in Tamil Nadu, South India." In *Animal Sacrifice, Religion and Law in South Asia*, edited by Daniela Berti and Anthony Good, 1–30. Routledge.

Harman, William. 2004. "From Fierce to Domesticated: Mariyamman Joins the Middle Class." *Manushi* 140: 2–14.

Hawley, John Stratton, and Donna Marie Wulff, eds. 1996. *Devi: Goddesses of India.* University of California Press.

Ludden, David, ed. 1996. *Making India Hindu.* Oxford University Press.

McDermott, Rachel Fell. 2001. *Mother of My Heart, Daughter of My Dreams: Kālī and Umā in the Devotional Poetry of Bengal.* Oxford University Press.

Mines, Diane. 2005. *Fierce Gods: Inequality, Ritual, and the Politics of Dignity in a South Indian Village.* Indiana University Press.

Nabokov, Isabelle. 2000. *Religion Against the Self: An Ethnography of Tamil Rituals.* Oxford University Press.

Osella, Filippo, and Caroline Osella. 2003. "Ayyappan Saranam: Masculinity and the Sabarimala Pilgrimage in Kerala." *Journal of the Royal Anthropological Institute* 9 (4): 729–54.

Padma, Sree. 2013. *Vicissitudes of the Goddess: Reconstructions of the Gramadevata in India's Religious Traditions.* Oxford University Press.

Parry, Jonathan. 1980. "Ghosts, Greed and Sin: The Occupational Identity of the Benares Funeral Priests." *Man*, n.s., 15 (1): 88–111.

Parry, Jonathan. 1985. "Death and Digestion: The Symbolism of Food and Eating in North Indian Mortuary Rites." *Man*, n.s., 20 (4): 612–30.

Sahlins, Marshall. 2017. "The Original Political Society." *Hau: Journal of Ethnographic Theory* 7 (2): 91–128.

Sax, William Sturman. 2009. *God of Justice: Ritual Healing and Social Justice in the Central Himalayas*. Oxford University Press.

Sen, Ronojoy. 2010. *Articles of Faith: Religion, Secularism, and the Indian Supreme Court*. Oxford University Press.

Srinivas, M. N. 1952. *Religion and Society Among the Coorgs of South India*. Clarendon.

Srinivas, M. N. 1996. *Social Change in Modern India*. University of California Press.

Uchiyamada, Yasushi. 2008. "Kurati and Kali: The Dead-End of Hierarchical Finality and the Moving Body That Assembles the Unthinkable Series." Paper presented at "The Unthinkable—Thinking Beyond the Limits of Culture Symposium," Institute of Ethnology, Academia Sinica, Taiwan, December 13–14.

Venkatesan, Soumhya. 2020. "Object, Subject, Thing: Tamil Hindu Priests' Material Practices and Practical Theories of Animation and Accommodation." *American Ethnologist* 47 (4): 447–60.

Waghorne, Joanne Punzo. 2004. *Diaspora of the Gods: Modern Hindu Temples in an Urban Middle-Class World*. Oxford University Press.

Zeiler, Xenia. 2012. "Female Danger: 'Evil,' Inauspiciousness, and Their Symbols in Representations of South Asian Goddesses." *Nidan: Journal for the Study of Hinduism* 24: 100–117.

Part 3

Pilgrimage and Festival Practices

7

The Changing Flavors of Gogaji Worship

Carter Hawthorne Higgins

Over the eleven months that I conducted fieldwork at the rural pilgrimage site of Gogameri, Rajasthan, between 2010 and 2016, I typically ate lunch with Hindu and Sikh devotees at the free cross-caste refectory (*bhandara*) of Gorakhtila, the village's monastic temple of Gorakhnath.[1] A legendary postclassical ascetic who is popularly regarded as the founder of the Nath order of yogis, Gorakhnath is also celebrated in Gogameri as the divine guru of Gogaji, the oral-epic hero-deity whose tomb-shrine (*meri*; literally, "mound") provides the village with its name. I occasionally lunched with either hereditary priestly clan at the mausoleum: the Chayals, Muslim Rajput attendants of Gogaji, whom they claim as an ancestor; and the Sharmas, Brahman attendants of Naharsinghji—Gogaji's priest and military advisor in the epic—from whom they claim descent. Unlike Gorakhtila's refectory, though, their kitchens are not well-known pilgrimage institutions. After pilgrimage activities wound down, I would eat dinner with employees of the Shri Gogaji Tea Stand at the intersection of the highway and the one-kilometer road between the train station and the Gogaji mausoleum.

The Shri Gogaji Tea Stand provided me with an ideal vantage point from which to observe the rhythms of Gogameri's pilgrimage traffic. From the far side of the highway, it looks out over the "festival grounds" where one of Rajasthan's largest annual *mela*s, or pilgrimage and livestock fairs, is staged. Every morning I would arrive at the stand for coffee as the day's first pilgrims were disembarking from their buses. Throughout the year a trickle of pilgrims flows through the village daily. This trickle swells into a stream on the ninth day of each month of the Vikrami calendar, when devotees celebrate minor holidays (*chhoti naumi*) in Gogaji's honor. During the annual festival across the month of Bhadua (August–September), Gogameri becomes flooded with pilgrims, traders, performers, ascetics, ritual specialists, police, bureaucrats, and beggars. The largest crowds appear on the ninth days of Bhadua's waxing and waning lunar fortnights, marking the annual celebration of Goganaumi ("Gogaji's Ninth") in ritual systems found to the east and west of Delhi, respectively. In the months before Bhadua, residents chatting at the Shri Gogaji Tea Stand often comment on indications of the impending festival. Likely the two most remarked-on of such signs are travelers dressed in yellow clothes and popup snack-food stalls.

Complex processes of religious change have gripped Gogameri in the twenty-first century. Before reflecting on these processes, this chapter begins with yellow clothes and snacks because these signs respectively evoke one of my focal points and an interpretive metaphor that I will propose. Advocates for religious change often use yellow clothes as a metonym to represent the pilgrimage practices that they hope to reshape. For instance, Surya Sharma is a Brahman guru from Agra who coordinates forms of Gogaji worship with forms of Vaishnava practice. Explaining the rationale for his efforts, on June 7, 2010, Surya told me that in the absence of scholarly Hindu leaders (*vidvan*) and brahmanical fire-sacrifices (*yajna*), "all pilgrims do is wear yellow clothes, offer liquor and goats, and beg Gogaji [for miracles]." Another far more prominent guru is Balyogi Rupnath, the charismatic and politically active *mahant* (monastic abbot) of Gorakhtila. Rupnath expresses great support for yellow clothes and associated styles of festive practice, albeit not the now-banned offering of intoxicants and animal sacrifices. Yet Rupnath seeks to dignify these ritual styles by proposing a new hagiographic explanation of their symbolism, stitched together from reworked patches of Gogaji's epic, Gorakhnath's lore, and Hindu nationalist accounts of post-classical Hindu-Muslim encounter.[2] If yellow clothes evoke iconic styles of pilgrimage practice, then snack food suggests a metaphor for the simultaneity in Gogameri of the processes interrogated in this volume: *sweetening*, or the standardizing of older ritual formations with more prestigious or widely shared religious styles, or both; and *intensification*, or the doubling down on older, "fierce" ritual styles in the face of pressures to change—a process that in some cases can include the rearticulation of such styles within muscular modes of Hindu practice. Extending the culinary language of sweetening, this chapter poses *chaat*—a celebrated genre of South Asian street food—as an interpretive analogy for the study of religious transformation in Gogameri.

The word *chaat* literally means "licking," "tasting," or "taste." As a name for snack foods its sense is comparable to the 1956 advertising slogan, "finger-lickin' good," of the US fast-food corporation, Kentucky Fried Chicken. Diverse regional and local varieties of *chaat* abound in India's street-based cuisine, and many are now available far from their homes thanks to migration, cultural flows, and the acceleration of both since India's market reforms in the early 1990s (Baviskar 2021; Solomon 2015).[3] Just as *chaat* constitutes a genre of locally and regionally developed cultural forms that are now being elaborated by fast-paced circulation, so too would there appear to be a *mela*-form that changes in interaction with local, regional, and transregional celebrations as well as traffic among them. More importantly, the *chaat* metaphor draws attention to issues of diversity and assembly at festivals. Consider the dish *alu papri chaat*. Vendors combine the eponymous boiled potatoes (*alu*) and fried wheat-flour crackers (*papri*) with boiled chickpeas, chopped onions, fresh cilantro, yogurt, tamarind and mint chutneys, spice mixtures, etcetera. Perhaps paradigmatically among mobile regional styles, *alu papri chaat* thus combines a wide range of colors, flavors, and textures on a single plate.

The *chaat* analogy is designed to suggest that at a given time it is the singular assemblage of constituent ingredients—ritual, narrative, semiotic, material, bodily, libidinal, social, economic, political, and suprahuman elements—that accounts for the present shape and religio-aesthetic *taste* (*rasa*) of a festive formation.[4] Below, I introduce two priestly efforts to stimulate religious shifts by examining their engagements with one ritual form each. In these engagements the efforts may be described respectively as *intensifying* and *sweetening*, but beyond the ritual forms in question things become complicated. In exploring this complication, I place both efforts in relation to broader shifts in the Gogameri pilgrimage, its public, and their interactions with the wider social field. Just as a chef could alter a *chaat* dish by adding a sweet ingredient or one that would intensify its sourness or spiciness, it is certainly possible for individual programs of religious change to affect the overall tenor of a festive formation. Yet when such a formation gives rise to many projects of religious change, as Gogameri has in the twenty-first century, then the interrelation of festive ingredients may transform in ways not always capturable in terms of sweetening or intensification. Where these categories aid in an analysis of Gogameri is at the localized level of individual projects, or even—when projects exhibit both types of transformation, as in the cases below—in select components thereof.

A Model of Continuous Religious Transformation

Celebrations in honor of Gogaji once punctuated North Indian ritual life across spectra of religious and socioeconomic belonging. Toward the periphery of Gogaji's devotional public in the nineteenth and early twentieth centuries, demographically speaking most anyone might have celebrated Goganaumi, attended performances of Gogaji's epic, or sought his miraculous aid by worshipping at replica tomb-shrines with varied ritual forms that colonial ethnographers and later scholars tied alternately to Hindu practice, Islamic tomb veneration, and combinations thereof (Higgins 2022, 255n8–n9). A smaller number of hereditary devotees closer to the center of Gogaji's devotional public—many of them hailing from lower-status groups along the margins of elite articulations of India's "religions"—additionally sponsored and attended devotional gatherings and made pilgrimages to Gogameri and Gogaji's birthplace temple in Dadreva, Rajasthan. Some of them also maintained long-term relationships with the Chayals in Gogameri (Oman 1889, 72–73), to whom pre-twentieth-century records in the Rajasthan state archives refer as the hereditary priestly attendants of the Gogaji mausoleum, and whom bardic genealogical texts depict as Chauhan Rajputs whose forebears had converted to Islam (Sarsar 2011, 107–8; Sarsar 2013, 324, 326–27; Higgins 2022, 225). Dispersed across northern India, Gogaji worship was characterized by a diversity of narrative and ritual practices. In order to gain a sense of such narrative diversity, consider how Anglophone scholars have described the epic. Colonial ethnographers identified "Hindu" and "Muslim" variants (Higgins 2022, 256n11)—the first in which Gogaji dies in battle against an imperial army, and the second in which he yogically inters himself and (half-)converts by uttering the first half of the Islamic declaration of faith. Late-twentieth-century folklorists classified the epic alternately as "martial," "romantic," and "magical" (Blackburn 1989; Hiltebeitel 1999), depending on whether the versions with which they were familiar focused on Gogaji's battle against his insurgent cousins and their imperial ally, on Gogaji's family drama and his subsequent yogic quest to perform "living self-entombment" (*jivit samadhi*), or on his control of snakes and other miraculous feats, respectively. Today devotees continue to celebrate diverse narratives praising Gogaji as a Rajput king, a cow-protecting hero, a village god of snakes, a miracle-working yogi, a Hindu convert to Islam, an avatar of Vishnu, a Hindu war hero who died fighting "Muslim invaders," and many combinations thereof. Is there a historical model of religious transformation that might help make sense of the Gogameri festival's ability to nurture such diverse celebrations and more recent transformations alike?

Across the past three decades Kenneth Dean has developed a powerful understanding of temple festivals in southeast China and its networks in Southeast Asia. Building on Gilles Deleuze and Félix Guattari (1987), he suggests that each "ritual event" constitutes a singular channeling of forces—affective, libidinal, economic, and so forth—that facilitates the continuous production of persons, cultural formations, and religious movements. For instance, Dean (1998) traces the way that the Three in One movement has ceaselessly developed new institutions, ritual forms (or "machines"), and affective potentials by improvising with inherited materials in new historical contexts. The result is an ever-expanding pool of molded capacities to interact with festivals and the world at large, a pool that Dean terms the "syncretic field of potential" (1998, 58–60; 2016). On his understanding it is the actualization of these potentials at festivals—through the intermediate zone of preindividual intensity and transcorporeal affect—that serves to individuate persons, communities, and religious formations anew. I find this historical model of religious transformation helpful in thinking through recent changes in Gogameri because Dean's interpretation of ritual events insists on the continuous and cumulative elaboration of religious formations—in interaction with an open and coevally changing social field—and because it connects processes of historical development to the affective registers of subject formation and community formation in ritual celebrations. However, given Dean's focus on ritual events within village communities and urban neighborhoods, his model of festive individuation must be adjusted to fit the scattered public of Gogameri's pilgrimage festival.

The archive of written documents pertinent to the history of Gogaji worship is limited and late. Yet as I have conjectured elsewhere (Higgins 2022), perhaps a Gogaji narrative, a pilgrimage and livestock fair in Gogameri, and their overlapping martial-ascetic symbolism arose between the thirteenth and fifteenth centuries along routes traversed by the largely itinerant communities of the Thar Desert, traveling low-status performers, Rajput-Afghan warrior-ascetics, and lower-status ascetic practitioners of tantric yoga—the forerunners of today's Nath Yogis. From their points of intersection there would have coalesced a variable ensemble of mythemes and ritual forms that could be employed to praise Gogaji as well as a range of ritual aptitudes and preferences among celebrants. The ensemble would have circulated across North India through the travels of performers, ritual specialists, pilgrims, and itinerant communities. After the better-known figure of Gorakhnath was appended to Gogaji's narrative and Gogaji became known as a wonder-working figure (Blackburn 1989), settled individuals and families would have begun importing components of the ensemble in order to strengthen their requests for Gogaji's assistance. In some cases where Gogaji was seen to respond favorably, new devotees would have emerged and incorporated elements of the ensemble into their local ritual milieux, creatively reaggregating them with existing components in their changing configurations of practice and life.

Over time larger shifts in the social field would have made it possible to see elements of Gogaji worship in new ways. Devotees would have refashioned them variously in response to new resonances and dissonances with contemporaneous cultural flows. After the conjectured emergence of Gogaji celebrations between the thirteenth and fifteenth centuries, four periods of dramatic social change would have brought the diffuse Gogaji formation to successive turning points, leading to new phases of historical development (cf. Dean 1998, 39–40, 43–45, 282–87). A Rajput-Mughal phase between the sixteenth and mid-eighteenth centuries witnessed the rise of landed polities, settled living, genealogical narrations of inherited status, and the royal patronage of Vaishnava religious institutions. Gogameri was incorporated into the new Bikaner state, and higher-status groups eulogized Gogaji as a Kshatriya-Rajput king. Between the late eighteenth and early twentieth centuries a British-Rajput phase introduced post-Enlightenment discursive and empirical practices related to religion, caste, and history. As colonial ethnography bi-individualized separate "Hindu" and "Muslim" epics and depicted Goganaumi processions as a low-caste affair (Higgins 2018, 663–64), the Bikaner state patronized upkeep and renovations at the Gogameri mausoleum, including the installation of a devotional icon (Higgins 2018, 664–67; Sarsar 2013). And it was only after the early twentieth-century state-sponsored renovations that government records start to mention the Brahman priests of Naharsinghji in addition to the Chayals (Sarsar 2011, 107–8; 2013, 324, 326–27). In a mass-nationalist and nation-building phase between the 1920s and 1990s, the discourses of religion, historiography, and "Hindu trauma" (Thapar 2004)—attributed to raids by the ninth-to-tenth-century Turko-Persian warrior-king, Mahmud Ghaznavi—were deployed in literature renarrating Gogaji's self-sacrificial defense of Hindu India from Mahmud's "invasions" (Munshi 1976; Charan 2000). When Bikaner joined the new Indian state of Rajasthan in 1949, the management of Gogaji's mausoleum was transferred to its Devasthan Department, which manages ex-royal-temple endowments.

Building on the characterizations of my conversation partners in Gogameri, I take the turn of the millennium as marking the transition to a new and current phase in the historical development of Gogaji veneration.[5] By then India's entrance into the global market, the widespread availability of affordable transport technologies, and new religious and cultural-historical trends in leisure travel all fed into a dramatic expansion of Gogameri's pilgrimage public, now including many lower-middle-class Hindu families and very few Muslims. Alongside Hindu nationalism's ascent to the mainstream, these changes shook up social relations among devotees and created new opportunities for innovation and contestation. Devotees, priests, and local elites began lobbying government agencies for development services, which were lacking in the village and inadequate for the growing number of festival celebrants. In line with ongoing market reforms, the Devasthan Department enacted a public-private development scheme that enabled devotees to organize public trusts and provide such services themselves. Hindu nationalist and state actors joined the abbot of Gorakhtila in spurring pilgrims into philanthropic action. The Gorakhtila temple board, state agencies, and pilgrim-led trusts sponsored the construction of new religio-touristic sites whose spatial forms are explicitly coded as Hindu, including a new Gogaji Temple that engulfs the architecturally Islamic mausoleum. Concomitantly, resident Devasthan workers partnered with the Sharma priests of Naharsinghji in efforts to wrest the mausoleum from the Chayals and the department itself. In the process, these collaborations formulated and publicized a controversy over religious inheritance and jurisdiction. Had Gogaji been Hindu or Muslim, pro-Hindu or pluralistic? And what should the answer to such questions mean for devotional practice, the Chayal priesthood, and the socioreligious ethos of devotees?

The remainder of this chapter considers two priestly projects that have helped to articulate and spread the controversy over Gogaji's hagiography and its import for pilgrimage practice. The analysis focuses on the way that these efforts treat a given ritual form and its connections to larger concerns. The next section examines attempts by Gorakhtila's abbot and administrative trust to intensify *chhari mela*, or festive flagstaff processions, while the section thereafter explores efforts by the Sharma and Devasthan priests to sweeten Gogaji worship with *vaishnav arti*, or daily lamp-offerings. Although these groups intensify or sweeten a form of practice, they tie their efforts to hagiographic innovations that selectively sweeten, intensify, critique, and reject various narrative practices—against the backdrop of demographic shifts in the pilgrimage public, the multiparty push to rebuild Gogameri's landscape in Hindu spatial forms, and novel claims of Hindu belonging and territory. Thus, stated in the terms of the *chaat* analogy, my analysis of the new flavors of Gogaji worship focuses on notable elements of a changing composite scene, rather than isolating single ingredients in a stable recipe.

Intensifying Flagstaff Processions

The most iconic form of festive practice is *chhari mela*—or flagpole procession—especially when processors from east of Delhi don yellow clothes (an uncommon sartorial practice west of Delhi). *Chhari*s are bamboo stems bearing flags, coconuts, peacock feathers, groom-style headpieces (featuring turbans, flower garlands decoratively veiling the "face," or both), or some combination of these decorative items. Many groups worship Gogaji as embodied in their *chhari* before offering the standard itself at the mausoleum. Processions may also feature drummers and singer-musicians, while members may carry fireplace tongs (*chimta*) and *chabuk*s—iron horsewhips with faux blades at their ends. Occasionally processors become possessed and flog themselves relatively lightly with horsewhips. If members of a procession prostrate themselves at regular intervals, then another member may brush them with a *chabuk* each cycle.

Similar to plates of *chaat*, both *chhari* processions and their reconception by the Gorakhtila temple board comprise patterned arrangements of diverse elements evoking distinctive religio-aesthetic tastes and senses of festive inheritance. Processional objects emit affective forces that shape pilgrimage encounters and devotional repertoires (Higgins 2022, 235–59). These objects also operate as technologies of saintly presence and commemoration. Devotees often understand them to be styled in remembrance of Gogaji and his companions, and when an item helps to facilitate divine presence or action it is usually that of the personage it memorializes. However, interpretations of their symbolism oscillate between war, nuptials, and asceticism. Pilgrims alternately associate yellow clothes with the uniforms of warriors or ascetics, and the processions themselves with Gogaji's army, his wedding party, or Gorakhnath's ascetic caravan. With their various martial, ascetic, and nuptial associations, the processional objects overlap with a broader cluster of ritual implements that Alf Hiltebeitel calls Afghan-Rajput

Figure 7.1. An elaborate processional flagpole, or *chhari*, seen above the foot traffic around Gorakhtila. Gogameri, 2019. *Source:* Courtesy of Kalyan Bista. Used with permission.

"militant-ascetic puja weapons" (1999, 362). Once used ritually and as arms by warrior-ascetics both "Hindu" and "Muslim" (Green 2009, 44, 163n49; Pinch 1996, 144), tongs in Gogameri are typically said to memorialize Gorakhnath's yogic fireplace (*dhuna*) at Gorakhtila. Goganaumi processions share their most prominent *puja* weapons with Islamic festivals that were also long celebrated by Hindus. Articulating with mobile standards found in festive commemorations of Muslim paragons (e.g., Amin 2015, 136–39), flagstaffs are treated as Gogaji, the bridegroom, when their bearers form a stylized wedding party, and as Gogaji's military flag when they comprise a commemorative army. Stylistically reminiscent of the bladed chains with which some Shia mourners flagellate themselves during Muharram, horse-whips are linked to various companions of Gogaji in view of their use in different types of possession.[6] Disagreement over the symbolism of these objects does not usually bar mutual celebration because—judging from my observations and conversations with devotees who accounted differently for pilgrimage practices—their value as mediators of saintly presence outweighs demands for homogeneous interpretation.

Since Rupnath was consecrated as Gorakhtila's abbot in 2004, he has transformed the temple's administrative board, the Gorakhtila Dhuna Trust, into a prominent agent of wide-ranging changes in Gogameri (Higgins 2022). Yet Rupnath also throws his weight behind abiding styles of festive practice. Even as Gorakhtila organizes public ritual performances of "Sanatani" (or orthoprax Hindu) and "Vedic" flavor—including recitations of Vaishnava texts and fire sacrifices—its representatives routinely highlight the diversity of devotees and their forms of practice, praising *chhari* processions in particular. However, their support stops short of hagiographic diversity, which is a central target of the Dhuna Trust's multiply publicized critiques—especially the claims that Gogaji converted to Islam and that non-Hindus have an equal share of inheritance and jurisdiction in Gogameri. As Sarvan Suthar,

Figure 7.2. A *chhari mela* of saffron-clad pilgrims takes a break. Gogameri, 2019. *Source:* Courtesy of Kalyan Bista. Used with permission.

one of the two journalists employed by the trust, asked me rhetorically on January 12, 2013, "Why would Gogaji, who lived and died to protect Hindu *dharma* [here: "religion"] from Muslim invaders, convert in the end?"

In elucidating their understanding of the symbolism of *chhari* processions and encouraging pilgrims to see their practices anew, Rupnath and Dhuna trustees use diverse media—including polemical tracts, liturgical chapbooks, two twice-monthly periodicals, nightly public audiences with the abbot, public celebrations, the spatial design of new pilgrimage facilities, and passing conversations with visitors to the temple—to redescribe Goganaumi as an annual commemoration of Gogaji's martyrdom in battle against Mahmud Ghaznavi. Their narrations run along the following lines. As an avatar of Shiva, Gorakhnath foresaw the enduring trauma that "Muslim invaders" would cause Hindus, beginning with Mahmud. He therefore arranged for a selfless Rajput hero, Gogaji, to be born and become king of the northern Thar Desert—the gateway between the Persianate world and Hindu India—in time to confront Mahmud (on this reckoning, in the late tenth and early eleventh centuries). Once Gorakhnath intuited that Mahmud had set out for India, Gogaji readied his troops while his father-in-law, a Rajput ruler in the Gangetic plains, sent rations to Gorakhnath's camp in Gogameri. As Gogaji was departing Dadreva, he learned of atrocities that Mahmud was committing against Hindus: murder, forced conversion, and the enslaving of those who refused to convert as human-waste transporters—whose descendants would thence become untouchable. The indignant Gogaji gave his military flag to his police chief and lifelong companion, the untouchable Bhajju Kotval, and raced into battle. After fighting heroically, he fell at the site of the future mausoleum. In the words of one hagiographic text commissioned by the Dhuna Trust, when devotees wear saffron military uniforms, hoist the flagstaff, donate foodstuff to Gorakhtila's refectory, or celebrate alongside Dalit pilgrims, they "revivify the memory of Rajputs' valorous waging of religious wars (*dharmayuddh*)" and "effectuate what was appropriate to the event of that time": a supply of dharmic troops who will secure the victory of Gogaji and Hindu India over Mahmud and foreign Islamic rule (Sharma and Sharma 2005, 109).

At first blush this can sound like an invented tradition inspired by Hindu nationalism. However, when one approaches such claims as experiments with the inherited pool of festive resources—which now reverberate in new ways with contemporary cultural flows—it becomes possible to see a more delicate compound of continuities and innovations. In tracing the prehistory of twentieth-century claims that Mahmud's 1026 raid of the

Shiva-Somnath temple in Gujarat left intergenerational scars accounting for contemporary Hindu-Muslim antagonism, Romila Thapar (2004) has shown that elite Indic-language literature makes little reference to Mahmud beginning a few generations afterwards, only to revive his memory at the end of the nineteenth century. Yet Thapar also finds Mahmud's name preserved ambivalently in the oral epics of plebian classes (cf. Amin 2015). And in the first English-language reference to Gogaji from the Thar Desert, in the 1830s James Tod reproduced the Mewar court's sense that Gogaji died fighting Mahmud (1920, 807, 843–44, 1027n1). Colonial ethnographies noted narrations of Gogaji's wars with several late-medieval emperors (e.g., Prithviraj Chauhan and Muhammad Ghori). Given the geographical dispersion and diversity of Gogaji devotees, this is unsurprising. Nor is it surprising that devotees like Rupnath and Gorakhtila journalist Sarvan Suthar, who both grew up in the 1970s and 1980s celebrating Gogaji's self-sacrificial battle against Mahmud—and both of whom have worked in collaboration with Hindu nationalist organizations and politicians (Higgins 2022)—should make connections between this hagiography and majoritarian historical representations mobilized amid Hindu nationalism's rise since the 1980s. What Rupnath has directed researchers and writers to do, as Sarvan told me on June 10, 2010, is to "systematize" the diverse narrative practices of pilgrims in conversation with scholarship and historical records. And given the complex matrix of sensibilities, access to resources, and scarcity of written documents in which Sarvan and his colleagues pursue this mandate, they have mostly worked with systematizing-resources that accord with Hindu nationalist visions of Indian history.

Although the ascetic militarism of the Dhuna Trust's representations of *chhari mela* may be tamer than many of the other fierce practices studied in this volume, I would argue that these reenvisionings constitute an intensified and transformative commitment to rearticulated older styles of strenuous festive celebration and serve as an example of the assertiveness of muscular modes of Hinduism, which the introduction to this volume suggests may be amenable to analysis as a type of intensification. Yet while the Dhuna Trust aims to intensify the investments of pilgrims in practices of flagpole procession, it does so by sweetening martial hagiographic practices with Hindutva-adjacent public history, by downplaying romantic and magical narrative themes (e.g., Gogaji's family drama and his control over snakes), and by rejecting such epic scenes as Gogaji's yogic self-entombing and his conversion to Islam. To speak here only of sweetening and intensifying would not do justice to the Dhuna Trust's projects. Yet when these terms are rerouted through the *chaat* metaphor—encompassing the assembly of diverse ingredients in the festive formation, in the Dhuna Trust's program of religious change, and in their interactions with accelerated traffic across the social field—they can assist in clarifying the extent to which specific components of the trust's efforts draw on and modify inherited practices under wider pressures and appeals. If this argument is plausible in an analysis of new engagements with an older ritual form, then how might it hold up in an exploration of a newly imported form?

Sweetening Gogaji Worship

As a great many priests, residents, and long-standing devotees told me, every day since the early 2000s a growing number of pilgrims has participated in a new form of Gogaji worship at the mausoleum. As the sun rises and sets, a locally resident low-level employee of the Devasthan Department emerges into the circumambulatory path around the sepulcher, or *garhi* (literally, "small fort"). Dressed conspicuously in priestly attire, he directs a small cohort of Sharma priests, other department workers, and volunteers in preparation. They scrub the Gogaji tomb and tile floors with water, light incense, and place candlewick oil lamps and other offerings on a silver tray. A cohort member then sounds a conch shell, and the Devasthan worker shouts out for devotional attention in a call-and-response style. Standing before the tomb, the Devasthan employee waves the tray of lamps in alternating clockwise and counterclockwise circles while singing the hymn *Om Jay Jagdish Hare* ("May the Lord of the Universe Be Victorious, O Vishnu/ Krishna"). Worshipers sing along, clap, and ring bells. Halfway through the hymn, the Devasthan worker offers the flames to the other nine sancta in the mausoleum—associated with Gogaji, his wife, his mother, Gorakhnath, and Naharsinghji. Upon returning, he adorns and feeds the anthropomorphic images carved into the tomb and leads worshipers in chants praising well-known Hindu deities, the chanter's parents and guru, and Sanatan Dharm—"the eternal religion," or so-called orthoprax Hinduism. Thereafter pilgrims touch, massage, and perfume the tomb before receiving *prasad* (blessed leftovers). Finally, they circumambulate the "small fort" counterclockwise, as one would an Islamic funerary site but not usually a temple.[7]

This ritual form—known as *vaishnav arti* in Gogameri but elsewhere simply as *arti*—works first and foremost as a collective mode of daily worship.[8] Yet *vaishnav arti* operates in several additional ways as well. While *arti* names a mode of practice coordinating material objects, modes of bodily action, ideal inner states, ritualized space-times, and relations to divinities, it is also a "semiotic form" (Keane 2007). Thanks to cultural flows and processes of social education, participants and observers are often able to recognize performances both as "*arti*" and as a "Hindu" practice. For many Hindus *arti* also serves as an important context of subjectivation, one that repeatedly molds devotional repertoires and thereby generates conditions of receptivity to certain truth-claims (Meyer 2010). For a worshiper whose devotional capacities have been shaped partly in contexts of *arti*, an act of offering can modify the atmospheric mood of the present and provide a temporary center of orientation (Deleuze and Guattari 1987, 311–12, 479). When such a center is stabilized and encircled by boundaries—say, when a *murti* (deity image) is established in a temple—then each offering regenerates the devotional site by reinvesting it with new energies of life and attention (Deleuze and Guattari 1987, 315). And as *arti* is routinely offered to the Gogaji tomb as if the tomb were the *murti* in a temple, it redraws the site's constituent components into a new interrelation, evoking a different sense of place. If on the whole one effect of *vaishnav arti* in Gogameri seems to be a sweetening of Gogaji worship, then adopting a *chaat*-like view of the mausoleum as a patterned interrelation of composite ingredients makes it possible to see that the narrative practices of the Sharma and Devasthan priests—as well as earlier precedents for the importation of publicly circulating ritual forms and brahmanical conceptions of Gogaji's divinity—involve processes of intensification that would complicate any picture of straightforward sweetening.

According to every priest, pilgrim, and village resident whom I asked, there was no set collective mode of daily worship in the mausoleum prior to the popularization of *vaishnav arti* in the early 2000s.[9] Rather, individual groups of pilgrims proceeded through the mausoleum's ten sites of devotional offerings either alone or to the accompaniment of partial epic performances by hereditary singers based in Gogameri or traveling with the pilgrims. At each site a priestly attendant oversaw their acts of worship and received their offerings.[10] Sarsar (2011, 113–14, 116–17; 2013, 325–26) quotes from eighteenth- and nineteenth-century archival documents recording the public purchase and private donation of supplies to be offered in the mausoleum by the Chayals during the festival and on other celebratory occasions (e.g., Divali), including coconuts, *guggal* incense (the fragrant resin of the Indian bdellium tree, for which Gogaji is named), oil, and ghee. While these quotes do not elaborate on the ritualized ways in which the Chayals presented such offerings, in the twenty-first century my Chayal fieldwork friends claimed routinely that the men of their family are committed to facilitating the devotional acts of all pilgrims regardless of the diverse religious styles that they may use—a commitment that many Chayal men cast as a prime example of what they called their clan's characteristic openness to devotees across lines of religious and caste difference. When I was in the field, some pilgrims laid colorful flag-sized shawls over the exposed tomb, just as one would see at the funerary memorial shrines of Muslim holy men; others offered ritual prestations commonly seen in Hindu *puja* to the image carved into the tomb; and many made offerings of both sorts to Gogaji in addition to embracing, massaging, and perfuming his tomb.

On most accounts it was the Devasthan "peon" (*chaprasi*), a man I will call Mishrimal Swami, who first brought *vaishnav arti* into the mausoleum. As a young rural Brahman, Mishrimal arrived in Gogameri in 1986 on a short-term construction contract before being hired by the department. Although he found the mausoleum poorly suited to his own devotional interests, hearing miracle stories and witnessing exorcisms eventually materialized Gogaji's divinity for him. Unable to inhabit the modes of worship led by the Chayals, he asked his Devasthan supervisor if he could approach Gogaji with *vaishnav arti*, his preferred method of daily worship. On February 12, 2013, Mishrimal told me that his supervisor denied his request because "the Muslims would take offense." Disappointed, he sat in meditation in front of the tomb and asked Gogaji how he should proceed. In Mishrimal's meditative state, Gogaji "commanded" him (*adesh kiya*) to worship with *vaishnav arti* and promised that no one would interfere. Yet "over the next six or seven years," Mishrimal claimed, his boss and the Chayals "repeatedly threw [him] out of the mausoleum" for doing so. (My Chayal interlocutors contest this claim. Indeed, between 2008 and 2016, rather than view the collective performance of Gogaji's *arti* as a threat to their position, the Chayals I knew encouraged Hindu pilgrims to worship in the manner they preferred, including through the offering of *arti*.) Then in the early 2000s his supervisor was arrested for stealing donations but released from police custody without a charge. Feeling doubly betrayed by Gogaji, Mishrimal foreswore the mausoleum. Eventually, as he told me on May 12, 2013, Gogaji visited Mishrimal in a dream, demanding that he resume offering *vaishnav arti* at the tomb. As soon as Mishrimal did, he insisted, Gogaji had his supervisor charged and convicted, and the Sharma-Devasthan priestly alliance fell into place.

In response to the pilgrimage's transformations in the early 2000s, the Sharma priests and resident Devasthan employees formed a strategic partnership in pursuit of three aims: inspiring broad recognition that the mausoleum is a Hindu temple rather than a para-Islamic space; displacing the Chayals as its hereditary priests; and reining in what they allege to be the Devasthan Department's corrupt superintendence.[11] In 2008 they jointly sued the department and the Chayals in the Rajasthan High Court, asking the bench the back all three aims.[12] Upon receiving the suit, the court ordered the department temporarily to relieve the Chayals of their jurisdiction over the tomb,[13] effectively transforming the department's resident employees into Gogaji's "governmental priests" (*sarkari pujari*), as I typically heard them called between 2008 and 2016. Although the court rejected both the 2008 petition and the multiple appeals that followed, the case galvanized some sections of the pilgrimage public into support for its aims. In this regard, though, *vaishnav arti* has arguably outshone the suit.

Modifying Webb Keane's (2007, 67–76) analysis of creed recitation and its role in the globalization of Protestant Christianity, one could highlight linguistic and subjective dynamics in *vaishnav arti* that may help to reorient some worshipers toward claims of Hindu affiliation and dominion. First, the play of linguistic de- and re-recontextualization in the Hindi-language hymn *Om Jay Jagdish Hare* figured centrally into Mishrimal's ability to incorporate *vaishnav arti* into the mausoleum (Keane 2007, 14–15, 181n2, chap. 9). Composed by Shardha Ram Phillauri (1837–1881), the lyrics praise Vishnu, Krishna, or "god" in general as the universal lord. However, they do so without explicitly referencing their local context of composition or any mythic content, thereby rendering the hymn moveable across diverse Hindu locales. They also distill Shardha Ram's interventions in nineteenth-century religious debates into easy-to-remember, devotionally compelling verse. Perhaps the first activist to focus on the defense and spread of Sanatan Dharm in Punjab, Shardha Ram was a Brahman priest, polyglot, and author who also worked as a translator for Christian missions and the colonial government (Jones 2006, 106–9). Stirred by Christian and "reformist" challenges to brahmanical "orthodoxy," he traveled northern India, combining his priestly training with aspects of Christian proselytism and emergent practices of institution-building, and urging audiences to embrace brahmanical-Vaishnava orientations and practices (Jones 2006). Hence, while a lack of contextual specificity makes *Om Jay Jagdish Hare* portable, Shardha Ram's lyrics can introduce a novel theological perspective where *vaishnav arti* is imported.

Above I referenced the range of Gogaji's hagiographic personalities, from cow-protecting hero to Muslim convert and wonder-working yogi. In the colonial period a Bikaner prince commissioned a collection of bardic panegyrics, one of which praises Gogaji as a cosmic brahmanical divinity (Tessitori 1918, 79). *Vaishnav arti* develops this innovation by inviting pilgrims to address Gogaji as "the cosmic Lord" (*Jagdish*), "the knower or director of inner states and actions" (*antaryami*), and "the all-pervading *brahman*." Worshipers singing the hymn also use Shardha Ram's words to implore Gogaji to act in their lives. Some of this language articulates with requests commonly made of Gogaji, such as "a mind-heart free of grief" (*dukh bina se man ka*), domestic "happiness and prosperity" (*sukh-sampatti ghar ave*), and allayed "bodily sufferings" (*kasht mitem tan ka*). Yet when singers ask Gogaji to "clear away [their] misperceptions" (*vishay vikar mitao*), "defeat [their] sin" (*pap haro*), and "intensify [their] reverence and love" (*shraddha prem barhao*), they employ nineteenth-century brahmanical-Vaishnava concepts that seem new to Gogaji worship. Indeed, several first-person verses appear to shift Gogaji worship onto a new devotional terrain, as when pilgrims sing, "I take refuge in [and] desire none apart from you."[14] How might the collective singing of these lyrics in Gogameri affect the sorts of relationship that pilgrims cultivate to Gogaji?

Alongside linguistic dynamics, certain operations of subjectivity can also assist *vaishnav arti* in arousing a sense of Hindu belonging and territory. The social and affective context of worship can create a pull that encourages some pilgrims to inhabit the lyrics they sing (Keane 2007, 67–70; Deleuze and Guattari 1987, 78–89, 107–9). In such cases addressing *Om Jay Jagdish Hare* to Gogaji—in the presence of his tomb, his priests, one's co-traveling family, and other devotees, and in a devotional space sensorially intensified by candlelight, music, incense, and ritual implements—may provoke momentary "alignments" between the singer's devotional orientations toward Gogaji and the hymn's treatment of Jagdish (Keane 2007, 71). This transformation may be miniscule during a single attendance of *vaishnav arti*, but part of the experience will be registered in self-consciousness as one observes oneself worshipfully addressing the hymn to Gogaji (Keane 2007, 75–76). Even more of the experience will be archived in habit, memory, and implicit expectation. If pilgrims repeatedly offer *vaishnav arti* to Gogaji at home as well as in Gogameri, then all the archived micro-alignments will compose a new layer in their cumulative abilities to interact with him, gradually expanding the collective pool of resources for Gogaji worship.

Dominique-Sila Khan (1997, 222–23) has suggested that before the 2000s Gogaji's mausoleum was largely home to stylistically Hindu acts of pilgrimage worship. Still, such acts existed alongside stylistically Islamic acts such as the laying of shawls on the tomb. Expanding on the *chaat* metaphor, one might say that the mausoleum's characteristic *flavor* results from the contingent interrelation of all such ritualized acts, the atmospheric moods they precipitate, and their contrapuntal relations to ritualized (and nonritual) acts and ensuing mood shifts beyond the mausoleum (Deleuze and Guattari 1987, 317–23). By adding *vaishnav arti* into the mix—at a time when *arti* and *Om Jay Jagdish Hare* have become grand performances at prominent pilgrimage temples—the Sharma and Devasthan priests have reassembled the components of the mausoleum's flavor in a way that can feel (or *taste*) even more "Hindu." And after the Rajasthan government and its private partners built the new Gogaji Temple in 2018—hiding the minarets and Nastaliq-script plaques within a larger fort-style structure (Higgins 2018, 664–65)—the mausoleum's feel has also been de-"Islamized."

If *vaishnav arti* is sweetening pilgrimage practice as the result of gradual developments, then the Sharma and Devasthan priests also superadd territorial claims to its offering. In publications, court filings, and conversations with pilgrims, the Sharmas argue for Hindu affiliation and brahmanical jurisdiction

Figure 7.3. Pilgrims waiting in line for entry into the Gogaji mausoleum, whose minarets are hidden within the structure of the New Gogaji Temple. Gogameri, 2019. *Source:* Courtesy of Kalyan Bista. Used with permission.

by highlighting their claims to descent from Naharsinghji, by renarrating Gogaji's epic, and by invoking the daily offering of *vaishnav arti*—and not *namaz* (Islamic prayer)—within the mausoleum. Hagiographically, they follow the Dhuna Trust in suggesting that Gorakhnath was an avatar of Shiva and that Gogaji fought Mahmud Ghaznavi. Yet they additionally claim that Gogaji was an avatar of Vishnu who descended in order to defend Hindu *dharma*—or cosmo-political order—from the counter-*dharma* of Islamic conquest. The Sharmas also double down on the widely celebrated oral-epic episode in which Gogaji perishes not by an enemy's sword but, rather, by his own yogic performance of "living self-entombment" (*jivit samadhi*). Like the Chayals, they narrate this scene partly to account for the tomb's potency. However, they further relate it to Gogaji's plan for revenge. After entombing, writes O. P. Sharma in the clan's central polemical text, the immaterial *shakti* (power) of Vishnu-Gogaji "ravaged Ghaznavi, the non-Indian barbarian (*malechchh*), just as Lord Ram extinguished Ravan's rule and *shri* Krishna ended Kansa's evil administration" (Sharma n.d., 21).

Similar to the Dhuna Trust's intensification of *chhari mela*s, what initially looks like a priestly effort to sweeten Gogaji worship through *vaishnav arti* turns out to entail a more involved distribution of inheritances and innovations. On the one hand, as a widely circulating form of daily Hindu worship, *vaishnav arti* is a crucial resource in the multiparty program to recast the pilgrimage in a more explicitly Hindu mold. To curious Hindu newcomers who are unfamiliar with potentially confusing styles of pilgrimage practice, it can offer a comforting way to find one's bearings. To pilgrims with historically deeper ties to Gogameri, it may gradually extend their devotional repertoires, enabling them to relate to Gogaji as a great divinity. And in the mausoleum morning and evening *arti* not only bookends all the other, stylistically varied ritual activities but is also the only scheduled daily worship. Hence, when the Sharmas suggest that the mausoleum is a temple because temples feature *arti*, mosques house *namaz*, and the mausoleum includes the former but omits the latter, they articulate an apparently commonsensical argument that resonates with many people's experiences.

On the other hand, while *vaishnav arti* is a recent import, its treatment of Gogaji as Jagdish has at least one precedent in a late nineteenth-century royally sponsored bardic composition eulogizing Gogaji as a great brahmanical divinity. Moreover, if my conjecture regarding the history of Gogaji worship has any merit, then the incorporation of a new ritual form and attendant modes of linguistic praise would be in keeping with long-term developmental patterns. Yet perhaps the most surprising intensification may be the renarration of Gogaji's living self-entombment. In many ways the Sharmas are prime advocates of what colonial ethnographers would call the *Hindu* epic variant, or what late twentieth-century folklorists would call the *martial* one, both narrating Gogaji's death in battle. Yet here the Sharmas adapt the conclusion of the so-called *Muslim, romantic,* or *magical* epic variants—in which Gogaji entombs himself yogically—to a novel revenge fantasy. And while Hindu nationalist currents are an important ingredient in this fantasy, so too are the historically deep resonances of martial-ascetic narrative materials, Vaishnava tales of divine violence, and heroic-epic celebrations of resistance to imperial incorporation—on which Hindu nationalist narratives themselves draw (Hiltebeitel 1999; Khan 1997; Pollock 1993; Thapar 2004). Hence, while the introduction of *vaishnav arti* may represent a sweetening that intensifies long-established developmental patterns, it is coupled with a hagiographic innovation that rethinks older epic scenes and character traits—on the basis of felicitous reverberations with contemporary cultural flows—before redrawing them into a new narration that both celebrates Gogaji and argues for brahmanical dominion over the tomb.

Proportion and Manner of Assembly

I have tried to suggest that the terms *sweetening* and *intensification* are helpful additions to my analysis of Gogameri, on two conditions: that they inform my approach to subcharacteristic projects of religious change, and that at the overall level they be filtered through the *chaat* metaphor. This metaphor evoked the *mela's* ability to assemble a gamut of sundry travelers, activities, and devotional styles into a patterned celebration with a distinctive religio-aesthetic flavor. It also oriented my gaze toward the sort of complex a-centered processes of religious formation that Dean (1998, 2016) has described in the Sinosphere. It is once one's interpretive lens is trained thus on the festive assembly in Gogameri, I proposed, that one can identify localized projects of sweetening, intensification, or both. However, this argument leaves two questions unanswered.

First, if a single ingredient can sweeten a dish of *chaat* or intensify its spiciness or sourness, then might an individual project of religious change not sweeten or intensify the Gogameri festival? I see this question as one of proportionality. Admittedly this is where the *chaat* analogy breaks down.

It is much easier for a chef to add more pomegranate, chili, or tamarind to a *chaat* dish than for a priestly group to persuade a pilgrimage public to reinterpret or change their practices. The Dhuna Trust and Sharma priests work with print, social media, and public celebrations in efforts to reach increasingly larger audiences, and time will show the impacts. Yet at least through 2013 the growing number of pilgrims who attended *vaishnav arti* was still relatively small, whereas most pilgrims offered prayers, donations, and reverence in assorted variations on what Khan described as Hindu worship adapted to a para-Islamic environment. The number of pilgrims who sought out the Sharma priests also paled in comparison to those who sought out the Chayals. Of course, most devotees primarily seek religious direction not from pilgrimage priests but, rather, from family, community members, and specialists back home. Given all this, plus the involvement of government agencies and pilgrim trusts in efforts to reshape Gogameri, and the fact that pilgrimage worship is just one—albeit prioritized—component in the mix of festive and commercial activities at the *mela*, by themselves the Dhuna Trust's hagiographic re-explanations of *chhari mela* and the Sharma-Devasthan leadership of *vaishnav arti* seem poorly equipped to transform the Gogaji formation wholesale.

Secondly, why focus on specific projects of religious change rather than on transformations dispersed across large swaths of the pilgrimage public? Could one not discuss the intensification or sweetening of Gogaji worship at the latter scale without the *chaat* analogy? I do understand the current phase of historical development to be characterized by a convergence of forces that are pushing to make Gogameri and Gogaji more "Hindu." Yet they do so in such variegated ways, and with such different conceptions of what being "Hindu" entails, that it is difficult to see with any clarity an overall process of either sweetening or intensification. By starting with a *chaat*-style view of the festive formation and then tracking the emergence, efforts, and claims of localizable projects, I have tried to learn from a broader methodological move in the study of South Asian religions—one that takes texts, ritual innovations, claims to inheritance and belonging, and landscape alterations as argumentative interventions in polemical contexts (Blackburn 2024). The two projects introduced here participate in larger, ongoing debates and contestations. Seeing their productions as conjectural proposals to be evaluated by the pilgrimage public—and as performatives that are always liable to misfire—opens the way to further study of their reception and the multiform responses that they engender.

Notes

1. The research on which this chapter draws was supported in 2010 by the Graduate School of Cornell University, in 2013 by an International Dissertation Research Fellowship of the Social Science Research Council, and in 2016 by the Asia Research Institute of the National University of Singapore. All the interviews referenced here were conducted conversationally and documented by hand. Except for authors and public figures, I use pseudonyms for my interlocutors. I wish to thank Amy L. Allocco, Xenia Zeiler, and the three anonymous reviewers for their helpful comments on earlier drafts of this chapter.

2. I use the term *postclassical*—rather than, say, "medieval"—capaciously to refer to the period between the tail end of the first millennium and the middle of the second millennium CE.

3. I thank Hayden Kantor (pers. comm.) for calling this literature to my attention.

4. Risking confusion (Phillips 2006), I here flatten the difference between Deleuze and Guattari's (1987) concept of *agencement*, rendered as "assemblage" in English, and the combination of ingredients in cooking, often termed *assemblage* in French.

5. This paragraph summarizes arguments that I have made in more detail in Higgins 2018 and 2022.

6. When employed in exorcisms of malefic spirits, *chabuk*s are often interpreted as the disciplinary tool of Bhajju Kotval (Gogaji's outcaste head of royal police) or Naharsinghji. In benevolent possessions by Gogaji—when, like other deities, he is said to "mount" (*charhna*) his mare or steed—horsewhips are sometimes tied to Gogaji's relationship with Nila (his flying blue horse).

7. In most Hindu contexts a feedback loop between embodied dispositions to practice and theories of purity and impurity inclines worshippers to circumambulate deities, temples, and so forth clockwise, presenting the purer right side of their bodies to manifestations of divine power while keeping the potentially less pure left sides of their bodies at a distance. The archetype for circumambulating Islamic pilgrimage sites counterclockwise is ostensibly the practice of circumambulating the Kaaba during the Hajj (Bellamy 2011, 135). Given the construction of the sepulcher in Gogameri, devotees enter through a front door, make their way clockwise around the tomb, and exit through the right door, where a metal railing directs them leftward. As pilgrims circumambulate the sepulcher counterclockwise, they also present devotional offerings at the structure's pinnacle (offered at the base of a ladder), the well of Naharsinghji, a fire pit, and a martial kettledrum before arriving back at the entrance.

8. While the Hindi adjective *vaishnav* literally indicates a devotional orientation toward Vishnu, it is sometimes also used to refer to brahmanical modes of living, as in vegetarian restaurants called *vaishnav dhaba*s. I understand the name *vaishnav arti* in both senses.

9. Although I do not understand the Gogaji mausoleum to be a *dargah* (or Sufi tomb-shrine) per se—taking *meri*, instead, as a proper noun for this ritual site and other Gogaji shrines styled in its likeness—it is helpful here to recall Bellamy's (2011) observation that ritual practice at many *dargah*s does not feature the collective offering of liturgical worship.

10. Between the early twentieth century and 2008, all priestly attendants would have been Chayal men during the eleven-month off-season each year, whereas during the festival in Bhadua month Sharma men would have tended to the two sites dedicated to Naharsinghji, state representatives would have tended to the tomb itself, and the Chayals would have tended to the remaining seven sites. After the Sharma priests joined the resident Devasthan manager of the Gogaji mausoleum in suing both the Chayals and the Devasthan Department for control of the whole site in 2008 (see below), the Sharmas began tending to the two Naharsinghji sites year-round, and judicial and bureaucratic orders stationed Devasthan workers at the tomb full time.

11. My characterization of the Sharma-Devasthan partnership and its central aims is based on my conversations with members of both groups (spanning months and even years in some cases), on the publications that the Sharmas have sponsored (including Sharma n.d.), and on their legal filings against the Devasthan Department and the Chayals (see the following note for one such case).

12. Pandit Shyam Lal v. State of Rajasthan & Ors. S.B. Civil Writ Petition No. 6836/2008 (Rajasthan High Court in Jodhpur).

13. "Interim Order" issued by Justice Govind Mathur on September 8, 2008, in connection with *Pandit Shyam Lal*; quoted in State of Rajasthan & Ors. v. Abdul Hamid & Ors. D.B. Spl. Appl. Writ No. 1216/2019 (Rajasthan High Court in Jodhpur), 4.

14. Sharan gahum main kis ki? / Tum bin aur na duja / as karum jis ki.

References

Amin, Shahid. 2015. *Conquest and Community: The Afterlife of Warrior Saint Ghazi Miyan*. Orient BlackSwan.

Baviskar, Amita. 2021. "Street Food and the Art of Survival: Migrants and Places in Delhi, India." *Food, Culture & Society* 21 (1): 142–55. https://doi.org/10.1080/15528014.2020.1859903.

Bellamy, Carla. 2011. *The Powerful Ephemeral: Everyday Healing in an Ambiguously Islamic Place*. University of California Press.

Blackburn, Anne M. 2024. *Buddhist-Inflected Sovereignties Across the Indian Ocean: The Pali Arena, 1200–1500*. University of Hawai'i Press.

Blackburn, Stuart H. 1989. "Patterns of Development for Indian Oral Epics." In *Oral Epics in India*, edited by Stuart H. Blackburn, Peter J. Claus, Joyce B. Flueckiger, and Susan S. Wadley, 15–33. University of California Press.

Charan, Chandradan. (1962) 2000. *Gogaji Chauhan ri Rajasthani gatha*. Bharatiya Vidyamandir Shodh-Pratishthan.

Dean, Kenneth. 1998. *Lord of the Three in One: The Spread of a Cult in Southeast China*. Princeton University Press.

Dean, Kenneth. 2016. "Conditions of Mastery: The Syncretic Religious Field of Singapore and the Rise of Hokkien Daoist Master Tan Kok Hian." *Cahiers d'Extrême-Asie* 25: 219–44.

Deleuze, Gilles, and Félix Guattari. 1987. *A Thousand Plateaus: Capitalism and Schizophrenia, Vol. II*. Translated by Brian Massumi. University of Minnesota Press.

Green, Nile. 2009. *Islam and the Army in Colonial India: Sepoy Religion and the Service of Empire*. Cambridge University Press.

Higgins, Carter Hawthorne. 2018. "Hindu Bakaph? Charitable Development and Trust Sovereignty in 'Neoliberal' India." *Muslim World* 108: 652–75.

Higgins, Carter Hawthorne. 2022. "The Evocative Partnerships of a Monastic Nath Temple in Contemporary Rajasthan." In *The Power of Nath Yogis: Yogic Charisma, Political Influence and Social Authority*, edited by Daniela Bevilacqua and Eloisa Stuparich, 249–79. Amsterdam University Press.

Hiltebeitel, Alf. 1999. *Rethinking India's Oral and Classical Epics: Draupadī Among Rajputs, Muslims, and Dalits*. University of Chicago Press.

Jones, Kenneth W. (1989) 2006. *Socio-Religious Reform Movements in British India*. Cambridge University Press.

Keane, Webb. 2007. *Christian Moderns: Freedom and Fetish in the Mission Encounter*. University of California Press.

Khan, Dominique-Sila. 1997. *Conversions and Shifting Identities: Ramdev Pir and the Ismailis in Rajasthan*. Manohar.

Meyer, Birgit. 2010. "Aesthetics of Persuasion: Global Christianity and Pentecostalism's Sensational Forms." *South Atlantic Quarterly* 109 (4): 741–63. https://doi.org/10.1215/00382876-2010-015.

Munshi, K. M. (1937) 1976. *Jaya Somanatha*. Translated by H. M. Patel. Bharatiya Vidya Bhavan.

Oman, John Campbell. 1889. *Indian Life: Religious and Social*. T. Fisher Unwin.

Phillips, John. 2006. "*Agencement*/Assemblage." *Theory, Culture & Society* 23 (2–3): 108–9.

Pinch, William R. 1996. "Soldiers, Monks, and Militant Sadhus." In *Contesting the Nation: Religion, Community, and the Politics of Democracy in India*, edited by David Ludden, 140–61. University of Pennsylvania Press.

Pollock, Sheldon. 1993. "Rāmāyaṇa and Political Imagination in India." *Journal of Asian Studies* 52 (2): 261–97.

Sarsar, Sarita. 2011. "The Cult of Goga Pir: Folklore and Popular Appeal in Medieval Rajasthan." Master's thesis, Jawarharlal Nehru University.

Sarsar, Sarita. 2013. "Economic Contours of Hero's Den: Untalked Dynamics of Gogamedi Shrine in Medieval Rajasthan." *Proceedings of the Indian History Congress* 74: 323–27.

Sharma, Chananmal, and Savatri Sharma. 2005. *Gorakhnath evam Gogaji ka shodh-purn itihas*. Mahila Ayog Prakashan.

Sharma, O.P. N.d. *Shri Gogaji bhagavan ka sachcha darbar: Mandir ke pushtaini pujariyom dvara paripusht pramanik pustak*. N.p.

Solomon, Harris. 2015. "'The Taste No Chef Can Give': Processing Street Food in Mumbai." *Cultural Anthropology* 30 (1): 65–90. https://doi.org/10.14506/ca30.1.05.

Tessitori, L. P. 1918. *Bardic and Historical Manuscripts. Section II: Bardic Poetry. Part I: Bikaner State*. Asian Society.

Thapar, Romila. 2004. *Somanatha: The Many Voices of a History*. Penguin.

Tod, James. (1829–1832) 1920. *Annals and Antiquities of Rajasthan or the Central and Western Rajput States of India*. 2 vols. Edited by William Crooke. Oxford University Press.

8

Sleep Sweetly, Fierce Goddess

Rituals of Intensification and Sweetening of the Goddess Chamundeshwari of Mysore in Navaratri/Dasara and Her Mahotsava

CALEB SIMMONS

In recent years, Mysore (also spelled Mysuru), a city in the southern Indian state of Karnataka, has become an increasingly popular tourist site for both Indian and international tourists.[1] The city, located between the Deccan plateau and the Western Ghat mountain range, has a pleasant temperate climate that makes it a welcome getaway from other regions with more extreme temperature fluctuations. Its royal history as a successor state and regional imperial power in the seventeenth and eighteenth centuries, the legacy of its famous Muslim ruler Tipu Sultan, and the colonial prestige garnered by the Wodeyar (also spelled Wadiyar) kings who developed their capital as a center for arts and governed the "model princely state" draw people of all backgrounds to the city to enjoy its architecture, visual arts, and music. In recent decades, due primarily to the reputation of Pattabhi Jois's Ashtanga Yogashala, the city has also emerged as an international destination for yoga training, drawing thousands of yogis every year to study yoga in the epicenter of the modern yoga movement. No matter the reason for visiting Mysore, at one point during one's visit almost all make the pilgrimage up Chamundi Hill, where a sign on the road to the top of

191

the hill reads: "One of the Sixteen Most Holy Sites in All of India." The primary purpose of the pilgrimage is to see Chamundeshwari, the goddess of the city, tutelary deity of the royal Wodeyar family, and, as another sign on the roadside hill proclaims, "Queen of the Universe."

Owing to the great popularity of the site these days, the temple is almost always very crowded, especially on Tuesdays and Fridays, which are both days associated with goddesses in Hinduism. While waiting in one of the entry queues (different donations or *dana* can expedite access), the visitor sees popular, calendar-art-style images of the goddess on signs and posters. In these images, she rides atop her tiger and appears visually synonymous with the pan-Indic goddess Durga, affirming her regal identity in alignment with the roadside signage and her association with the royal family of Mysore. Once visitors enter the temple, they wind through the maze of steel barriers that snake the queue through the temple and ultimately enter the central apartment (*garbha griha*) of the goddess where her primary image is seated. Given the brevity of their time in this antechamber, visitors only have a moment to participate in the ritual exchange of sight (*darshan*) with Chamundeshwari. She is dressed head to toe in the finest silk saris, ornamented with jewelry made of precious metals with gem inlays, and garlanded with jasmine, marigolds, and other fragrant flowers. Offerings of sweets, money, saris, and many other things are laid at her feet while the rich scents of camphor, incense, and coconut sit heavily in the air. Even with this symphony of sensory stimulation, her eyes—painted white and covered with metal—draw the gaze of even the most casual visitor. Other than small portions of her face, one can see very little of the stone image of the goddess, perhaps masking the violence that is at the core of her identity. The image—as has been described to me by the temple's priests—shows the goddess in her most victorious moment slaying Mahisha, the infamous buffalo demon of classical Indian mythology (see *Devi Mahatmya*).[2] This violent and cosmos-saving act is central to her identity, and local lore claims that Mysore was the site of Mahisha's kingdom (etymology: Mahisha Mysore) and that the hill was the physical location where the goddess killed the demon. Her royal and victorious representations coalesce in her central role in the celebration of Dasara, which refers to both the tenth and culminating day of the ten-day-long festival (Navaratri/Nine Nights of the Goddess + Dasara/Tenth Day) and more generally refers to the entire festival. Dasara celebrates the goddess's victory over the buffalo demon. Indeed, it is in this context that Chamundeshwari is most known throughout India and how she is most frequently discussed in Western scholarship.

Once visitors leave the temple, they encounter a variety of entrepreneurs capitalizing on the experience by selling photos of the goddess in various media, including laminated 8 × 10 prints, plaques, and even on jewelry. If one examines the image closely, it is not the image that is in the central apartment of the goddess, but it is a smaller metal image, called the "festival image" (*utsava vigraha*), that is used when the goddess leaves her temple on procession around the top of the hill. In this representation, she looks very different from the regal Durga. Instead, she has a sweet, almost plump face of an infant or toddler with faint, perhaps nascent, fangs slightly protruding from her lips. This image provides greater insight into the complex, if not paradoxical, identities of the goddess as she is experienced by her devotees. Like many other Hindu goddesses discussed in this volume, Chamundeshwari is a goddess of possibilities, simultaneously capable of compassion and violence, beauty and ghastliness, and—as is perfectly encapsulated in her festival image—sweetness and intensity.

In this chapter, I focus on this tension in Chamundeshwari's identity and how it is managed by her devotees through an annual seventeen-day ritual sequence that extends from the celebration of autumnal Dasara to the goddess's "Great Festival" (Mahotsava). This ritual cycle of intensification and sweetening constitutes a complex process of energetic metabolism in which the goddess's power is transformed and redistributed. During Dasara, Chamundeshwari's energy is intensified through the reenactment of her martial exploits, culminating in an unleashing of her *shakti* to slay the buffalo demon. This phase serves not merely to display the goddess's intensity but to activate a dynamic state of potency that enlivens her devotees and the city. As the festival progresses into the Great Festival, this accumulated energy undergoes a ritualized transformation. Bathing, procession, and sleep rituals serve a sweetening function that metabolizes this intensity, converting her raw martial power into a more diffused and sustainable nurturing presence. Through this process, the goddess's intense aspects are not suppressed but rather harnessed, enabling her to transition from a fierce protector to a nurturing mother. This annual cycle underscores the dialectical relationship between intensity and sweetness, revealing how rituals process these seemingly opposite forces, thereby reaffirming the goddess's multifaceted nature.

My research on this topic includes over a decade of participation in the festival both in person and virtually, via social and other media; however, the bulk of my observations are based on formal fieldwork conducted in Mysore during the 2013 Dasara and Great Festival.[3] During the festival period, we see the intensification of the goddess leading up to the killing of the buffalo demon and her ensuing victory laps in her chariot and float festivals before she is ritually calmed and put to bed, only after which she can be recrowned to return to normal functionality for her devotees. It is through this essential ritual cycle that devotees experience her cosmic significance by reliving her mythic exploits and affirming reciprocity in their relationship. In this ritual re-creation of the slaying of the buffalo demon and its aftermath, Chamundi is transformed from her daily role as protector and as mother and ritually intensified in order to kill her foe. While the goddess commits the ultimate cosmic act of safekeeping and salvation for her devotees in this festival, her devotees, in turn, provide her with the support to be victorious via offerings and adulation. The devotees also offer the means to disperse her intensified energy and calm her murderous rage, helping the fierce goddess to once again be sweet. Before discussing the process through which the goddess is intensified and sweetened through the festival's ritual cycle, it is important to contextualize how Chamundi, the goddess of Mysore, also historically underwent a process of sweetening to become Chamundeshwari, Queen Chamundi.[4]

Chamundi Becomes Chamundeshwari:
The Mythological Sweetening of a Fierce Goddess

While Chamundeshwari of Mysore is iconographically and mythologically connected to the pan-Indian goddess Durga, her name is derived from that of another goddess from pan-Indic lore, Chamunda (aka Chamundi). Chamunda shares many characteristics with the fierce goddess Kali, and only slight iconographic features distinguish the two in most of their iconic representations (Donaldson 1991). The first extant literary account of Chamunda is found in a Sanskrit text from the sixth or seventh century, *Devi Mahatmya* (Glorification of the Goddess), in which the name is linked directly to Kali. While the Durga-esque goddess (called Ambika or "Mother" in this text) fights the demon generals Chanda ("Fierce") and Munda ("Bald"), her anger emanates from her face and personifies as a fierce goddess called Kali ("Dark One") (Simmons 2022, 43–54). Kali in her potent rage kills the powerful demon generals and presents their heads as offerings to Ambika. The text explains that since the generals were named Chanda and Munda, Kali is given the name "Chamunda" when Ambika sees the gift. Of interesting note for our discussion, the scene in which Chamunda's name is mentioned is in the third episode of *Devi Mahatmya*, following the second episode that features the killing of the buffalo-demon Mahisha, through which Chamundeshwari of Mysore is connected to Durga.

While the *Devi Mahatmya* makes a compelling, if not etymologically accurate, case for Chamunda being a derivative identity of the goddess Kali, most scholars agree that the cult of Chamunda was independent of the association with the Great Goddess and closely aligned with more terrific cults, such as the Great Wisdom Goddesses (*mahavidyas*) or the Seven Little Mothers (*saptamatrikas*) (Kinsley 1998, 32; Coburn 1988). As part of this fearsome group, Chamunda was often the final goddess of the sequence, and, unlike the others, appears as an emaciated elder goddess. Known for her ferocity and lust for blood, Chamunda was cast in the Sanskritic tradition as an outsider deity whose cult resisted normative ritual culture. For instance, in the *Malatimadhava* (ca. seventh or eighth century CE) of Bhavabhuti, Chamunda devotees are referred to as "skull bearers" (*kapalika*) who conduct ritual sacrifices of virgin girls to their goddess in cremation grounds (Kale 1967).

By the twelfth century, a significant shift had taken place in the representation of the Great Goddess tradition from earlier texts like the *Devi Mahatmya* and *Malatimadhava*, which depicted fearsome goddesses with a taste for blood and flesh, to the later *Devibhagavata Purana*. This evolution, described for example by C. Mackenzie Brown and occurring around the twelfth century, saw a transformation in the Great Goddess's characterization and is epitomized in the *Devibhagavata Purana* (Brown 1990, 11 and 214). *Devibhagavata Purana* emerged amid sectarian turbulence and aimed to reaffirm Great Goddess *shakta* theology while responding to the Vaishnava *Bhagavata Purana*. The text reflected a systemized theology of the Great Goddess's superiority over other deities, especially Vishnu, and portrayed her as a mother figure and embodiment of materiality (*prakriti*), emphasizing compassion. This transition involved revising older martial and erotic myths to present the Great Goddess as a "mother of infinite compassion." As a result, the once visceral and potent stories of the Goddess and her various fierce forms became more transcendent and metaphysical, with fierce deities like Chamundi marginalized in brahmanical ritual practices (see Coburn 1988). Central to this process was the development of normative ritual culture based on manuals (*agama*) in which purity and pollution became highly regulated. Rituals that included flesh-offerings or other substances were regarded as polluting and vegetarian rituals and deities were elevated in status. This process continually unfolds in local contexts, much like the transformation experienced by Chamundi of Mysore (see Mahalakshmi 2011; Padma 2013, 2014).

The history of how this ferocious, intense hag goddess came to be associated with the Great Goddess in the form of Durga in Mysore is unclear, although there are hints that point to a slow transformation over time. In our earliest extant records, the hill of Mysore was not known as Chamundi Hill; instead, it was called Shiva (Mahabalachala) Hill because of an older Shiva temple located at the top of the hill (situated just south of the Chamundeshwari temple).[5] It is common in South India for Shiva temples to have a small shrine to the Seven Little Mothers on the northern periphery of the temple grounds. It is possible that the cult of Chamundi grew from this subordinate shrine into something much, much larger. If so, this would align with similar trends found throughout India where fierce local goddesses are gradually associated with the pan-Indian Great Goddess and the regal Durga cult (Coburn 1988; Mahalakshmi 2011; Padma 2001 and 2013, 2).

The growth of Chamundi's temple and cult in the region most likely originates from its relationship with the Wodeyar kings of the region. Nowadays, Chamundeshwari is the dynasty's family and royal goddess, and tradition holds that this relationship grew from a vision that the legendary fourteenth-century progenitors of the kingdom, Yaduraya and Krishnaraya, received from the goddess (Wodeyar 1916). Oher dynastic records attribute this relationship to a life-saving miracle in which the goddess protected Chamaraja, the Bald (Bolu), from a lightning strike when he was climbing the hill. Regardless of the exact event that caused this relationship to flourish, Chamundi was associated with the hill and the Wodeyar clan by the sixteenth century, and through this relationship her status was elevated within the Sanskrit mythological tradition through association with the goddess Durga and slaying the buffalo demon Mahisha by the seventeenth century.[6] The final push that elevated the goddess to her current status took place in the early nineteenth century, when Wodeyar king Krishnaraja III renovated the temple and installed Tamil Dikshita Brahmans as the temple's head priests.[7] At this point, the rituals of the temple were regulated by *agamic* ritual manuals, and the goddess became a vegetarian and motherly. From this time forward, the intensity of the goddess was subdued . . . at least for most of the year.

Intensity and Sweetening in Chamundi's Seventeen-Day Ritual Cycle

While the goddess is typically calm, regal, and maternal, during her annual ritual cycle that takes place during a seventeen-day period in September–

October her latent intensity is awakened. The ritual cycle begins according to the traditional lunar calendar during the festival of Navaratri or the "Nine Nights" (Simmons, Sen, and Rodrigues 2018). This festival celebrates the Great Goddess of India and culminates in Vijayadashami or the "Tenth [day] of Victory" (Dasara, also means the "tenth [day]") during which her victory over the buffalo demon Mahisha is celebrated. The festival is celebrated differently throughout India, but in most regions the festival has fostered an association between the goddess and kingship, as the medieval, early modern, and even modern and contemporary Indian kings derived their authority to rule and sovereign power from the goddess and her ritual accoutrement (Hüsken, Narayanan, and Zotter 2021; McDermott 2011; Simmons 2020 and 2021a). It is during this festival that the goddess is roused from her docile state to the embodiment of the power and frenzy necessary to defeat her mighty demon foe.

In Mysore, this festival is followed shortly thereafter by Chamundeshwari's local Mahotsava. This festival continues the celebration of her victory and her sovereignty over the space, but it also functions to purify the goddess from her violent and necessarily polluting act of spilling blood through ritual bathing. It also helps to calm her by pacifying her intensity, dispersing her power through processions and soothing her into a much-needed sleep. Within in this seventeen-day cycle, Chamundeshwari is ritually aroused to unsustainable levels of violent, intense energy reminiscent of her mythic backstory and then pacified to resume her role as the stately mother goddess, who watches over, protects, and provides for her city and her loving devotees.

Navaratri and Dasara: Unleashing the Intensity of the Goddess

The Dasara festival in Mysore unfolds as a grand spectacle, intertwining the ritual worship of the goddess Chamundeshwari with the ceremonial duties of kingship and state that involve the maharaja of Mysore, the descendent of the former royal family who ruled over the region, and modern politicians (Simmons 2021b). This ten-day cultural and religious festival commences with fervor and reverence, involving intricate rituals, processions, and performances that transform the city into a tableau of mythic proportions. The royal and religious rituals coincide to intensify the power of the goddess and the king, who in premodernity would launch military campaigns at the culmination of the ten-day festival through which his sovereignty would be confirmed. The first day of Dasara kicks off with a flurry of activities. The moveable festival image of Chamundeshwari, usually enshrined in the Mysore Palace, is carefully transported to her temple located atop Chamundi Hill. Here, the temple's head priest adorns the goddess with fragrant jasmine and rose garlands in preparation for the inauguration ceremony, attended by prominent political figures and VIPs. Inside the temple, daily rituals commence according to precise celestial alignments and are repeated at the same time for the first nine days of Navaratri/Dasara (see table 8.1). The day begins

Table 8.1. Approximate Timetable of Regular Navaratri Events at Chamundi Hill in 2013

Time	Goddess Ritual	Time	Royal Ritual
6:00–7:30 a.m.	Anointing of the primary image	6:12–6:28 a.m.	Maharaja ritual anointing and the fixing of the throne
9:10–9:15 a.m.	*Puja* at the sacrificial place	7:30–8:40 a.m.	Throne *puja*
9:15 a.m.	Procession of the "Perpetual Celebration" image	8:46–9:09 a.m.	Tying of the thread bracelet
10:30 a.m.	Procession of the festival image	11:15 a.m.	Throne ascension for morning *darbar*
5:00 p.m.	Large festival image procession with *puja* at various external shrines	12:30–1:25 p.m.	The palace image of Chamundeshwari taken from *darbar* hall to mirror (*kannadi*) hall
8:15 p.m.	*Puja* at the sacrificial place	6:00 p.m.	Throne ascension for evening *darbar*
8:30 p.m.	Procession of the "Perpetual Celebration" image		

Source: Created by the author.

with the sacred anointing/bath of the primary deity followed by regular daily *puja* (worship). The priests then perform *puja* at the sacrificial place (*bali pitha*), offering cooked rice to deities representing different directions. Subsequently, the image of the "perpetual celebration" (*nityotsava vigraha*), a very small special image of the goddess, is brought out for a procession around the temple accompanied by musicians. *Puja* at the sacrificial place and "perpetual celebration" image processions are repeated both in the morning and evening. After each procession, the temple's primary image receives lamp (*arati*) *puja*. Simultaneously, down the hill and in the palace, the maharaja conducts similar rituals, drawing parallels between his authority and the goddess's divinity. Each day, the maharaja begins his Navaratri rituals, mirroring the goddess's sacred bath with his own anointing ceremony. He then worships the royal throne and ties a sacred thread bracelet (*kangana*) around his wrist demarcating both good fortune and protection, proceeds to his golden throne in the palace's *darbar* (court) hall, and holds two *darbars* (ceremonial court sessions) each day. The mirroring of the rituals for the goddess and the king is central to the cycle as each are simultaneously intensifying in order to harness the power to effectively carry out their (martial) duties.

For the goddess, the intensification can be seen in the progression of forms through which she manifests throughout the festival. The larger festival image, specially adorned for each day, is placed on one of her nine processional vehicles and taken on a procession around the hill at noon. This procession is repeated twice daily, with the evening iteration being more elaborate, including special *puja*s along the way. Throughout the festival, Chamundeshwari is portrayed in different forms and mounted on various vehicles (see table 8.2). The different vehicles and forms align with the different manifestations of the goddess known as *Matrikas* or "Little Mothers" found in the *Devi Mahatmya*, who are known for their intensity, protection, and propensity for destruction. The vehicles ritually embed Chamundeshwari and the landscape into the goddess's heroic battles against her demonic foes. Notably, on the seventh day, she transitions from regal to more intense forms of the goddess in preparation for her battle with the buffalo demon, marked by a special and secretive tantric Kalaratri or "Dark Night" *puja*.

The rituals of Kalaratri at Chamundeshwari on Chamundi Hill in Mysore are unique and stand out in the context of the larger festival framework as they mark the transition of the goddess, bringing to the surface her fierce and uncontrollable intensity. Whereas most nights follow a standard, public ritual program described in the *agamic* ritual manuals, during Kalaratri

Table 8.2. Forms of the "Little Mothers" Taken by Chamundi During Her Processions Around Chamundi Hill for Each Day of Dasara

Day	Form of the Goddess	Vehicle
Day One	Brahmi	Hamsa (swan)
Day Two	Maheshwari	Rishibha (bull)
Day Three	Kaumari	Navilu (peacock)
Day Four	Vaishnavi	Garuda (eagle)
Day Five	Varahi	Simha (lion)*
Day Six	Indrani	Gaja (elephant)
Day Seven	Sarasvati	Bhuta (ghost) [Navilu (peacock) with *vina*]
Day Eight	Chamundi	Simha (lion)**
Day Nine	Chamundeshwari	Shesha (snake)

*Prior to the procession, I was told that the vehicle for the day would be a *kona* (water buffalo). It is unclear how this would be connected to Chamundeshwari in her form as Varahi.

**The night before is Kalaratri, during which the fierce goddess is worshipped behind the closed door of the temple. The head temple priest, Shashisekhara Dikshita, informed me that she retains this form in the procession the subsequent day so "that people can see the beauty of the fierce goddess." I was also informed that the *bhuta* or "ghost" ridden by the goddess is that of Mahishasura himself.

the temple doors are closed to all but the priests and temple workers, who take part in nonnormative rituals that are ritually dangerous but extremely powerful. Due to the secretive nature of the Kalaratri rituals, I was unable to observe them and none of my informants were at liberty to tell me which rituals were performed. Those of us outside the temple could hear the echo of drums and gunshots vibrating against the temple's large stone walls. I was told by several people outside the temple that it was closed at this time because on this night, to heighten the goddess's power and ferocity, the goddess accepts blood offerings. The next day the processional form of the goddess remains in her fierce form as Chamunda with matted hair and a garland of skulls. Crowds of devotees flock to the temple to take *darshan* and catch a glimpse of her in this ornamentation because it is believed that in this moment she is at her most powerful.

On the final day of Navaratri, weapon (*ayudha*) *puja* or worship of the weapons takes place. In Western scholarship, my own included, discussions of weapon *puja* have focused on its connection to kingship (Dirks 1993,

Figure 8.1. Chamundeshwari's processional form in Kalaratri ornamentation. *Source:* Photo by the author.

38–42; Simmons 2021b; Stein 1984, 313; Zotter 2018). Indeed, in the palace fort complex weapon *puja* garners a great deal of media attention as the maharaja performs rituals of gratitude in front of traditional weapons, like swords and shields, and for his vehicles, which range from horses, camels, and elephants to Mercedeses and BMWs. The goddess's role, however, is clearly visible in these rituals, especially in the culminating *puja* to the *banni* tree (*Prosopis cineraria*). *Banni puja* celebrates and reenacts the *puja* performed by the Pandava brothers in the *Mahabharata*. In this story, the brothers worship the goddess at a *banni* tree, after which the goddess protects their weapons during the year of exile when they hide incognito.[8] Upon her hill, the goddess is worshipped in more traditional forms, including a fire ritual (*chandi homa*), and she is placed atop the cosmic serpent Shesha—denoting her role as the all-powerful goddess undefeated in battle—for her last procession before going back down the hill for Dasara.

Dasara or "tenth" is the final day of the festival whose intent is to heighten the power and ferocity of the goddess needed to kill the buffalo demon. The Kannada term "Dasara" is related to the Sanskrit *dashami* ("tenth"), part of the longer name of the culminating festival day *vijayadashami* or "the tenth day of victory" in celebration of the goddess's triumph. In premodernity, the day marked the beginning of the military campaigns for the kingdom and was and continues to be a day associated with competition and physical power that is intensified by the goddess. Therefore, the royal rituals of Dasara begin with a wrestling match in the palace grounds that display the intense physicality of the day and provide an offering to the goddess. This battle between traditional wrestlers (*jattis*) is short but intense, ending only when one of the wrestlers' spiked brass knuckles draws blood from their opponent. When this blood hits the earth, the ritual program is in full swing, and the now goddess, who has been empowered, begins her descent from her temple down into the city. Once at the palace, she is placed atop an elephant mount (this time a real elephant, not a metal facsimile) and triumphantly processes through the streets of the city displaying her intensity to all its inhabitants.

Mahotsava: Sweetening the Goddess

With the conclusion of the popular state-sponsored Dasara festival, the pomp of the celebration dies down, and hordes of tourists and visitors leave Mysore. Residents and civic employees hurriedly return the city to normalcy, removing the decorations that had transformed Mysore into a carnivalesque spectacle. Local devotees, however, begin preparing for the next round of indispensable rituals that starts two days later. These rituals, collectively known as Chamundeshwari's "Great Festival" or Mahotsava, welcome the goddess home from her military exploits. In Dasara, the goddess is celebrated for her victories, but she also remains bloodthirsty, insatiable from the fight and craving more. It is through this Great Festival—composed of various other smaller festivals—in honor of the goddess that the devotees help cool the goddess's anger, sweetening her ferocity and subduing her violent rage until she can ultimately take rest and fall asleep. Counterbalancing Dasara, during which the goddess comes to the aid of her devotees, in the Great Festival it is her devotees who come to the aid of the goddess to soothe her back into the goddess of possibilities.

Rathotsava: Victory Laps

Chamundeshwari's Mahotsava begins with a grand chariot (*ratha*) festival (*utsava*) or *rathotsava*, wherein an elaborately adorned image of the goddess is pulled through the streets atop an enormous chariot. The public ritual begins at the small shrine called the *darbar mantapa*, a significant focal point of the ceremony, which is decorated with an abundance of aromatic flower garlands. At the center of this stage, a processional image of the goddess holds court bedecked with the regal jewels belonging to the palace and the royal family. After the maharaja takes *darshan* of the goddess, she is affixed atop an equally ornate chariot. The initiation of the chariot festival, a pivotal element of the festivity, is inaugurated by the maharaja through a symbolic act of holding the chariot's rope after which thousands of devotees collectively participated in the ritual by taking turns pulling the chariot. While the chariot is circumambulated around the temple, devotees fervently proffered fruits, coconuts, and flowers as tokens of their reverence to the deity.

This time is especially valuable for devotees since the goddess is still in her powerful state following her transformation through the rituals of Navaratri. Following this procession, the *ratha* remains stationed in

Figure 8.2. Chamundeshwari's chariot pulled through the streets of Chamundi Hill. *Source:* Photo by the author.

proximity to the temple premises, near its gates, until the evening hours, affording devotees the opportunity to engage in further prayers and offerings and receiving supercharged *darshan*. The goddess remains so potent that newlywed couples participate in the festival, making devotional offerings during this auspicious occasion to ensure a harmonious, obstacle-free, and bountiful marriage. By evening time, most visitors have left the hill and the inhabitants of the small village atop Chamundi Hill take the goddess around the village, worshipping at different halls. Through this process, the villagers, primarily priests and other ritual professionals, help to dissipate the power of the goddess, imbuing the hill's sacred landscape with divine power, or *shakti*.

Snanotsava/Teppotsava: Cleansing and Cooling

Having invigorated the surrounds of her earthly abode with her overflowing power, through the ritual processions of the chariot festival, on the subsequent day the process of cooling and sweetening the goddess begins. According to local lore, part of what makes Chamundeshwari so powerful after Kalaratri is that she has been energized by the blood offerings and the blood of her foes on the battlefield (Simmons 2022, 27–55). To cool her intensity and to return her and her priests to a pure state, the polluting blood must be washed away in the bathing festival (*snanotsava*).

The bathing festival ritual begins in the temple, where one specially selected priest is ritually bathed through symbolic pouring of purifying water (*teertha*), sacred chants, and the offering of fragrant flowers and herbs in front of the goddess's processional image. The bathing ceremony itself involves pouring water, often infused with auspicious substances like milk, curd, honey, sandalwood paste, and scented oils, over the deities. Then, the temple priests, along with the small "perpetual celebration" (*nityotsava*) image of the goddess, march from the temple down to the goddess's tank (*devikere*), a short walk from the temple. The entire ceremony is conducted with great meticulousness and ritual precision, as priests recite powerful *mantras* and utilize breathing techniques that purify the priests and the goddess internally and externally. Additionally, through the communal ritual bath, the goddess power is diffused into the materiality of the water in the tank and not only extended into the bodies of the priests but also invigorates the tank, which traditionally was the primary source of water for the village of Chamundi Hill and still remains the source for ritual purposes.

Devotees gather around to witness the ritual bath, singing devotional songs and generally enjoying the festivities. They eagerly wait to receive from the temple priests a few drops of the water that has been used to bathe the goddess. Taking a few drops of water in their palms, devotees then touch it to their lips and foreheads, receiving both the purifying potential of the water and the residual leavings of the goddess's power in the process.

That evening devotees and onlookers return to the goddess's tank for her float festival (*teppotsava*). Unlike the highly ritualized bathing festival earlier in the day, the float festival is a vibrant and captivating celebration during which the processional image of Chamundeshwari is taken around the temple tank several times in a small boat (*teppa*) beautifully decorated with flowers and colorful LED lights. The festivities begin with typical rituals and processions conducted within the temple premises. As dusk sets in, the beautifully adorned processional image of the goddess is ceremoniously carried back down to the *devikere* tank near the temple. Amid chanting and the sound of temple instruments, the goddess is gently placed on the float and, once aboard and secured, the procession around the small body of water commences, guided by priests and accompanied and observed by a joyful crowd of devotees, journalists, and tourists. The float is slowly maneuvered through the water in a large circular pattern, accompanied by the loud, rhythmic beating of drums, cymbals, and flutes and by devotional songs piped through loudspeakers.

Figure 8.3. Chamundeshwari's float launches in the temple pond. *Source:* Photo by the author.

Like the chariot, the float festival is a visual spectacle that attracts devotees and tourists alike who can gaze upon the goddess as she imbues them and the landscape surrounding her earthly abode with her power. During the float festival, however, the goddess, after having her bath, is now back to her purified state and her power is more accessible to devotees, mediated through the unique ritual properties of water. While her intensity has been alleviated and her power somewhat diffused, she remains in a state of volatility with her power difficult to control, so further mediation is necessary for the goddess to return to her typical temperament.

Shayanotsava: Sleep Sweetly, Fierce Goddess

The nighttime festival or *shayanotsava* marks the ultimate and profoundly symbolic stage in the process of cooling the ferocity of the goddess Chamundeshwari. It serves as the culmination of a meticulously choreographed journey—a journey from untamed ferocity to a state of tranquil pacification, protection, and profound compassion. Though the crowd is smaller than during most of the other festivities for the Mahotsava, everyone gathers in eager anticipation, aware that they are about to witness both beautiful decoration and a profound transformation—a transition that takes Chamundeshwari from her fierce, unstoppable form to one of serene benevolence. The essence of the nighttime festival lies in its ability to soothe and calm the goddess, allowing her to rest, symbolizing her return from the fiery throes of ferocity to the gentle embrace of compassion, encapsulating the multiplicities inherent in the goddess.

Preparations for the nighttime festival begin much earlier in the day as priests and temple workers prepare the small antechamber (*ardhamantapa*) outside of the temple's main sanctum (*garbha griha*), preparing a bed for her much-needed sleep. This resting place sits opposite the devotional images (*bhakti vigraha*) of a former ruler of Mysore, Krishnaraja Wodeyar III (r. 1799–1868), and three of his wives.[9] The room is adorned with the most exquisite saris made of fine Mysore silks, fragrant petals, and delicate garlands and is surrounded by all her favorite sweets. After the conclusion of the temple's regular ritual program, the processional image of Chamundeshwari, adorned in resplendent attire, is carried to the antechamber. Before laying the deity down, the temple priests perform a series of rituals. Incense wafts through the air, as *arti* lamps are waved, and the temple resounds with the recitation of devotional hymns and Sanskrit *mantra*s.

As the image of Chamundeshwari is gently placed on her resting spot, a palpable shift in the atmosphere occurs. The priests, in a symbolic act of lulling her to sleep, sing soothing lullabies and devotional songs as they swing the bed, soothing the goddess into slumber. In this moment, the deity's ferocity dissipates. Chamundeshwari, only days before full of uncontrollable wrath, now becomes a sweet, childlike deity, coddled by her priests, soon to awaken as their guardian, protector, and a symbol of compassionate motherhood. The nighttime festival is a poignant reminder of the vast range of possibilities of goddesses in the Hindu traditions, ranging from intense to sweet, and that even the most fierce and powerful deities have and need moments of tranquility and rest.

The nighttime festival is not only a religious ritual but also an opportunity for devotees to express their love, devotion, and gratitude toward the goddess. Devotees—primarily Chamundeshwari's priests, temple workers, and their families—are not only witnesses but participants in this transformation. Since the antechamber is so small, in 2013, the year I participated in the ritual, the temple livestreamed the ritual on television monitors set up within the temple grounds just outside the main temple walls. After the ritual is

Figure 8.4. Head priest Shashishekhara Dikshita attending to Chamundeshwari during the *shayanotsava*. *Source:* Photo by the author.

completed, everyone in attendance has the opportunity to enter and view the goddess in her most serene form, give her more sweets, and speak and sing sweetly to help her sleep. Many in attendance, myself included, stayed at the temple into the early hours of the morning, enjoying the opportunity to dote upon the goddess. By the time we finally left the temple, my heart was filled with a sense of profound peace and community.

Mahabhisheka: Anointing the Queen

After awakening from her night of slumber, the penultimate day of the festival is marked by the anointing ceremony (*mahabhisheka*) of the goddess. While not a public ritual like the others described in this chapter, this ceremony is a captivating and elaborate ritual that holds profound significance in Hindu traditions. During the anointing, Chamundeshwari, the fierce goddess—who is now cooled and awakened in her role as the protector of Mysore—is bathed through the pouring of sacred substances, including milk, yogurt, honey, ghee, and sandalwood paste, and accompanied by recitations and ritual gestures performed by temple priests.

Although the ritual is short and performed outside of public view, the annual ceremonial anointing of the goddess is a vivid reflection of the connection between Chamundeshwari's divine authority and earthly kingship, drawing parallels to medieval kingship rituals. Medieval kings, too, underwent similar ceremonies, often by religious authorities, to legitimize their rule and seek divine authority for their reign. The act of anointing in both contexts underscores the belief in a divine origin of sovereignty—the notion that rulers and deities alike derive their authority and power from a higher, transcendental source—in this case, the Great Goddess (Simmons 2021a). It reflects the idea that earthly rulers govern with the divine's sanction and protection and as a metonym of the divine sovereign. Furthermore, the grandeur and pomp surrounding the anointing mirror the extravagance of medieval kingship rituals. Both events are marked by ornate decorations, sumptuous offerings, and ceremonial regalia, creating a spectacle that highlights the significance of the moment. In the context of Chamundeshwari's annual ritual cycle, the anointing marks her full transition back into her regal state and her readiness to resume her role as the queen of the universe.

Mudiyutsava: Crowning the Queen of the Universe

The final day of Chamundeshwari's Great Festival is marked by the crowning festival (*mudiyutsava*).[10] The culmination of the annual ritual cycle, on this day Chamundeshwari's processional image is coronated with a crown full of precious gemstones and wears necklaces that are equally richly ornamented. As the crowning event (pun intended) of the Great Festival, throngs of onlookers fill the street that encircles the hill and watch and photograph as the goddess in her finery befitting the queen of the universe is taken on procession around the hilltop. Like the chariot and float festivals, the crowning festival is a time of spectacle and merriment with a cacophony of sounds from the temple musicians and blaring loudspeakers and sights from the spiraling LEDs on the goddess's palanquin to the glow of thousands of smartphone screens snapping photos and livestreaming on various social media platforms.

At the culmination of the procession, the goddess returns to her place in the temple and the regular daily life of the temple resumes. Now situated within her earthly abode, the seventeen-day journey of intensification into ferocity and subsequent sweetening and cooling is concluded, from queen and mother to fierce and bloodthirsty and back again. Those fortunate enough to witness the transformations were given insight into the full range of the goddess's power condensed into two and a half weeks.

Conclusion

The Navaratri/Dasara and Great Festival cycle in Mysore provide a fascinating insight into the intricate and multifaceted nature of goddess Chamundeshwari. The festivals unfold as a grand spectacle, blending ritual worship and public participation. The ritual cycle's initial stages during Navaratri involve unleashing the intensity of the goddess. She is celebrated in various forms and vehicles, reflecting her heroic battles against demonic forces. The transition to her violent form during the special Kalaratri *puja* marks a moment of heightened power and intensity. On the final day of Navaratri, the battle-ready goddess descends into the city, symbolizing her readiness to combat the buffalo demon.

Subsequently, the festival shifts toward the sweetening and calming of the goddess. The Mahotsava, which follows Dasara, plays a pivotal role in cooling the goddess's fury. The chariot festival (*rathotsava*), where the goddess is pulled on an ornate chariot, shares her potency and allows devotees to bask in her powerful presence as she imbues the physical landscape with her *shakti*. The bathing (*snanotsava*) and boat (*teppotsava*) festivals ritual cleanses and cools the goddess, symbolically washing away the impurities of her battlefield exploits, and diffuses her power into the ritual waters. The goddess is finally fully calmed and sweetened in the nighttime festival (*shayanotsava*), which culminates in the transformation of Chamundeshwari. In this peaceful ritual, her fierce form is soothed, and she is put to bed, transitioning from intense rage to serene benevolence. Devotees play an active role in this transformation, expressing their love and devotion through rituals, offerings, and even singing her to sleep—all preparing the goddess to resume her role as the queen of the universe and protector mother of Mysore and its people.

Chamundeshwari's ritual cycle is a rich tapestry of rituals and festivities that intensify the ferocity of the goddess and then sweeten and calm her, highlighting the multiplicity and complexity of her nature. It serves as a ritual embodiment of the range of the goddess's power that is harnessed, experienced, and ultimately cherished by her devotees. This cycle of intensification and sweetening creates a dynamic process wherein the goddess's power is not only exhibited but also transformed. The initial intensification during Navaratri, with its martial symbolism and ferocious manifestations, amplifies Chamundeshwari's energy to its peak. This phase acts as a catalyst that both provokes and harnesses her *shakti*, drawing the devotees into a heightened state of devotional attachment. The goddess's intense aspects serve to reaffirm her role as the protector and vanquisher of enemies, a necessary prelude to her subsequent sweetening. As the festival progresses throughout the Great Festival, the ritual acts of sweetening—cooling baths, chariot processions, and nighttime ceremonies—metabolize the released energy, distributing her blessings throughout the community. These calming rituals do not merely pacify the goddess; they transform her intense, martial power into a nurturing force, symbolically feeding and nurturing the land and its people. This cyclical process, repeated annually, perpetuates the goddess's dual aspects of intensity and sweetness, ensuring her continued prominence and the renewal of her devotees' faith. It also reinforces the interconnectedness of both aspects of the goddess, demonstrating how divine intensity is ultimately channeled into sweetness for societal welfare. Through this annual journey, she reveals herself as a fearsome protector, a motherly figure, and a symbol of compassionate divinity, embodying the diverse facets of Hindu goddess worship.

Notes

1. Accompanying multimedia webpage: https://tinyurl.com/SleepSweetly.

2. The image of the goddess is normally heavily decorated with large silk *saris* and garlands of flowers that obscure all but the goddess's face. She is only

uncovered during her twice-daily ritual anointing/bath (*abhisheka*), which is not open to the public.

3. This fieldwork was conducted with the support of the American Institute of Indian Studies Daniel H. H. Ingalls Memorial Junior Fellowship. For their generosity and unparalleled access to all the rituals, I am greatly indebted to the priests and temple workers of the Chamundeshwari temple, the Chamundeshwari Temple Executive Trust, the Karnataka State Department of Museums and Archaeology, the Office of the Royal House of Mysore, and the late maharaja of Mysore, Shrikantadatta Narasimharaja Wodeyar.

4. I am maintaining the local name Chamundi in reference to the goddess of Mysore; however, in Sanskrit, she was often referred to as both Chamundi and Chamunda, with Chamunda being the most common. Chamundeshwari is a combination of the title *ishwari*, which I have translated as queen, and Chamunda.

5. *EC Volume III.1*, My 16: 11.9–10. The first clear reference to the name of Chamundi Hill does not enter into epigraphic records until the nineteenth century. *EC Volume V,* My 148.

6. Gōvindavaidya, *Kaṇṭhīravanarasarāja Vijayam*, I.10. For more information, see Simmons 2014.

7. There is no consensus on the exact date that the temple priests were replaced. Morab states that Wodeyar king Krishnaraja III gave land grants to Tamil Brahmans in 1819, which served as the official invitation to the Brahman priests (Misra 1990, 62). However, in a book-length study of the temple coauthored with B. B. Goswami, Morab says that it was in 1848 that the Shivarchaka priests were officially replaced by the Tamil Dikshita Brahmans (Goswami and Morab 1991, 2). Epigraphic evidence supports both claims. The other priests (in descending order of ritual hierarchy) are Hoysala Karnataka Brahmans, Smarta (Ayyar) Brahmans, and Lingayatas.

8. *Banni* is the Kannada term. It is called *shami* in Sanskrit.

9. For a fuller discussion of this image and its placement, see Simmons 2016.

10. The festival is also known as the *jawahiri utsava* or "festival of the gemstones."

References

Brown, C. Mackenzie. 1990. *The Triumph of the Goddess: The Canonical Models of Theological Visions of the Devī-Bhāgāvata Purāṇa*. State University of New York Press.

Coburn, Thomas B. 1988. *Devī Mahātmyā: The Crystallization of the Goddess Tradition*. Motilal Banarsidass.

Dirks, Nicholas B. 1993. *The Hollow Crown: Ethnohistory of an Indian Kingdom*. University of Michigan Press.

Donaldson, Thomas Eugene. 1991. "The Śava-Vāhana as Puruṣa in Orissan Images: Cāmuṇḍā to Kālī/Tārā." *Artibus Asiae* 51 (1/2): 107–41.

Epigraphia Carnatica (EC). 1898–1905. Vols. 1–12. Government Press.

Goswami, B. B., and S. G. Morab. 1991. *Chamundesvari Temple in Mysore*. Anthropological Survey of India.

Gōvindavaidya. 1971. *Kaṇṭhīravarasarāja vijayam*. Edited by R. Sharma Sastry. University of Mysore Press.

Hüsken, Ute, Vasudha Narayanan, and Astrid Zotter, eds. 2021. *Nine Nights of Power: Durgā, Dolls, and Darbārs*. State University of New York Press.

Kale, M. R. 1967. *Bhavabhuti's Malatimadhava with Commentary of Jagaddhara*. Motilal Banarsidass.

Kinsley, David R. 1998. *Tantric Visions of the Divine Feminine: The Ten Mahāvidyās*. Motilal Banarsidass.

Mahalakshmi, R. 2011. *The Making of the Goddess: Korravai-Durga in the Tamil Traditions*. Penguin.

McDermott, Rachel Fell. 2011. *Revelry, Rivalry, and Longing for the Goddesses of Bengal: Fortunes of Hindu Festivals*. Columbia University Press.

Misra, P. K. 1990. *Cultural Profile of Mysore City*. Anthropological Society of India.

Padma, Sree. 2001. "From Village to City: Transforming Goddesses in Urban Andhra Pradesh." In *Seeking Mahādevī: Constructing the Identities of the Hindu Great Goddess*, edited by Tracy Pintchman, 115–44. State University of New York Press.

Padma, Sree. 2013. *Vicissitudes of the Goddess: Reconstructions of the Gramadevata in India's Religious Traditions*. Oxford University Press.

Padma, Sree. 2014. *Inventing and Reinventing the Goddess: Contemporary Iterations of Hindu Deities on the Move*. Lexington Books.

Revised Epigraphia Carnatica. 1972–2009. Vol. 1–16. Institute of Kannada Studies, University of Mysore.

Simmons, Caleb. 2014. "The Goddess and Vaiṣṇavism in Search for Regional Supremacy: Woḍeyar Devotional Traditions During the Reign of Rāja Woḍeyar (1578–1617 CE)." *Indian History* 1 (Spring): 27–46.

Simmons, Caleb. 2016. "Creating Royalty: Identity-Making and the Devotional Images of the Woḍeyars of Mysore." In *Archaeology of Bhakti: Royal Bhakti, Local Bhakti*, edited by Emmanuel Francis and Charlotte Schmid, 209–35. Institut Français de Pondichéry, Ecole Francaise d'Extreme Orient.

Simmons, Caleb. 2019. "Dynastic Continuity and Election in Contemporary Karnataka Politics." In *The Conundrum of Worldly Power: Sovereignty in South Asia*, edited by David Gilmartin, Pamela Price, and Arild Ruud, 136–49. Routledge.

Simmons, Caleb. 2020. *Devotional Sovereignty: Kingship and Religion in India*. Oxford University Press.

Simmons, Caleb. 2021a. "Devotional Foundations of Earthly Sovereignty: Conceptualizing Sovereignty and the Role of Devotion in Narrative Political Theology

in Premodern India." *Religions* 12 (11): 911. https://doi.org/10.3390/rel
12110911.

Simmons, Caleb. 2021b. "Domains of Dasara: Reflections on the Struggle for Significance in Contemporary Mysore." In *Nine Nights of Power*, edited by Ute Hüsken, Vasudha Narayanan, and Astrid Zotter, 221–48. State University of New York Press.

Simmons, Caleb. 2022. *Singing the Goddess into Place: Locality, Myth, and Social Change in Chamundi of the Hill, a Kannada Folk Ballad.* State University of New York Press.

Simmons, Caleb, Moumita Sen, and Hillary Rodrigues, eds. 2018. *Nine Nights of the Goddess: The Navarātri Festival in South Asia.* State University of New York Press.

Stein, Burton. 1984. *All the Kings' Mana: Papers on Medieval South Indian History.* New Era Publications.

Woḍeyar, Śrī Mummaḍi Kṛṣṇarāja. 1916 and 1922. *Maisūru Saṃsthānada Prabhugaḷu Śrīmanmahārājaravara Vaṃśāvaḷi.* Vols. 1–2. Edited by B. Ramakrishna Row. Government Branch Press.

Zotter, Astrid. 2018. "Which Durgā? What Navarātra? Remarks on Reconfigurations of Royal Rituals in the Kathmandu Valley." In *Nine Nights of the Goddess: The Navarātri Festival in South Asia*, edited by Caleb Simmons, Moumita Sen, and Hillary Rodrigues, 39–62. State University of New York Press.

9

The Sweetening of Bhairav as a Merchants' Miracle Deity

R. Jeremy Saul

The popularization of some of Rajasthan's enshrined Bhairavs, generally considered as fierce manifestations of the god Shiva, could be regarded as exemplifying a process of initial "sweetening" and subsequent "intensification." As I will argue in this chapter, some of the most prominent agents of this change in recent decades have been Marwaris, mercantile clans that trace their descent to Rajasthan and continue to revere this state's local deities but nowadays reside in cities throughout India. By "sweetening," I mean that Bhairav's long-standing fierce identity in Rajasthani villages has been appropriated and softened to a level that is ritually suitable for the sensibilities of contemporary urbanites, especially Marwaris. Moreover, within the last thirty years or so, Marwari patronage has funded the installation of numerous images of Bhairav and other Rajasthani miracle deities (*chamatkarik devata* in Hindi), in other words, deities with reputations for great wish-granting efficacy, in various Jain and Hindu temples throughout India. This recent geographical expansion could be interpreted as an "intensification" of these deities' earlier worship in Rajasthan. Working within this two-step framework, in this chapter I will mostly focus on the process of Bhairav's sweetening within Rajasthan itself, leaving a more in-depth discussion of his subsequent intensification throughout India for a future study, which would necessarily bring in various additional sites.

215

Figure 9.1. A replication of Nakoda Bhairava at a Shvetambar Jain shrine in Ratlam, Madhya Pradesh, 2022. *Source:* Photo by the author.

In tracking Bhairav's sweetening, I primarily draw on his history and current worship at Nakoda Teerth (*teerth* means a pilgrimage site), a Shvetambar Jain temple complex in western Rajasthan (fig. 9.1). I will also briefly consider two Hindu Marwari-favored Bhairav shrines, Kodamdesar and Toliyasar, to broaden that discussion to Marwaris as a whole. From this examination of Bhairav's recent transformation in both Jain and Hindu settings, I suggest that his increasing popularity needs to be understood not as a singular Jain or Hindu phenomenon but rather as one part of a broad urban Marwari preoccupation with deities in Rajasthan who provide miracles for those who approach them in sincere worship. Although the research for this discussion arose from ethnographic fieldwork initially conducted in 2011, with additional short stints supplemented by archival research between 2016 and 2023, it will be presented within a historical framework, since I approach sweetening as a temporal process taking place over decades. Furthermore, as I will elaborate, Bhairav's sweetening need not be analyzed as a linear trajectory, but rather as a fluctuating negotiation between village customs and the Marwari patronage, priests, and temple administrators who would appropriate them. This chapter will thus emphasize that divine sweetening may be discerned in a diverse range of ritual outcomes.

Marwaris are most commonly considered to comprise three Rajasthan-descended mercantile groups: Oswal Jains (Oswal signaling their allegiance to a lineage goddess in the town of Osiyan, in the same area of Rajasthan as Nakoda), and Hindu Agrawals and Maheshwaris. A fourth group, Brahmans descended from Rajasthan who often also engage in trade, typically associate with Marwaris in cities throughout India, hence they effectively live as Marwaris too. Despite the nominal sectarian division between Oswal Jains and Hindus, in my observation when attending Marwari public events in cities around India, these merchants generally share more or less the same lifestyle and cultural outlook, hence they are all easily called Marwaris in Indian public life in recognition of their commonality. Most importantly for this chapter, they also share an intense interest in finding deities reputed to provide worldly miracles.

In considering mercantile or Marwari patronage of such deities, I find a useful starting point in John Stratton Hawley's (2001) introductory article for a thematic journal issue on the pivotal role of the "middle class" in influencing contemporary Indian religious practice, which in my formulation amounts to ritual sweetening. A definition of the middle class commonly identifies urbanites with business or professional jobs who aspire to upward mobility and have some financial resources; this essentially describes Marwaris. Any number of scholars have analyzed the rising influence of the middle class in India in recent decades, but fewer have discussed bourgeois interventions in religious practice. Milton Singer (1972), however, provides an examination of the innovations of urban Indian religiosity, and, more recently, Tulasi Srinivas (2018) and Deonnie Moodie (2019) offer further investigations. Pertinent to our discussion, Hawley (2001, 224) states that the middle-class embrace of previously obscure or regionally specific deities (such as Bhairav in Rajasthan, I would add) has elevated those deities to broader importance, potentially with geographically expanded publics (hence intensification). The implication is that financial resources and access to urban socioeconomic networks (as is the case with Marwaris) predispose upgrading. Taking this premise further, Lawrence Babb (2004) and Anne Hardgrove (2004) present cases of pan-Indian Marwari funding of shrines in Rajasthan, and its substantial effect on these shrines' subsequent material and ritual development.

Putting these factors together, I surmise that Bhairav has been similarly transformed at shrines receiving Marwari donations. Indeed, the middle-class desire for increased prosperity, which has become particularly visible in India's era of economic liberalization and receptivity to globalized capitalism since the national reforms of 1991, describes the mindset in which many urbanites approach miracle deities. It is a truism affirmed by devotees that faith in a deity will be rewarded with a desired miracle. Marwaris and other merchants, for whom daily financial gain and loss is an unavoidable concern in life, tend to also be among those most inclined to demonstrate their devotion in the form of financial donations to religious institutions to hedge their chances of success. This practice is evident in the many Marwari names among donors listed in wall inscriptions in temples of Rajasthan (Saul 2022).

The aim of this chapter, then, is to highlight the sweetening effects of the Marwari devotional patronage of Bhairav, and by extension other miracle deities of Rajasthan. To that end, I have organized this chapter as several sections supporting this thesis, namely: a comparison of presweetened Bhairav in Rajasthan with his sweetened outcome at Nakoda; the historical Marwari relationship to Rajasthan that informs this sweetening; the similarity of Jain and Hindu Marwari devotion to miracle deities such as Bhairav across sectarian identities; Kodamdesar and Toliyasar Bhairav as examples of Hindu Marwari sweetening; the historical narrative of Nakoda Bhairav, which illustrates a Marwari-driven process of sweetening; and a conclusion, with lingering questions for further research. This discussion thereby lays the foundation for a future study addressing the intensification of sweetened Bhairav's devotion at sites outside Rajasthan.

Bhairav, Unsweetened to Sweetened Miracle Deity

I begin this discussion with a sketch of Bhairav in both unsweetened and sweetened forms to introduce the premise that he is subject to temporal change, with his eventual sweetening represented by Nakoda Bhairav. Although now less visible than was the case some decades ago, "unsweetened" Bhairav nonetheless persists in Rajasthan at some shrines that apparently have not been receiving pan-Indian mercantile attention. These village manifestations have been little documented apart from some useful studies that I will mention in this section. A consideration of Bhairav's presweetened disposition is important for understanding his sweetened iterations because his presweetened fierceness, most vividly exemplified by ritually impure animal sacrifice and preference for alcohol offerings, has been transmuted into an enhanced perception that his capacity for miracles draws from a reservoir of supernatural powers deeper than simply auspicious blessings. While sacrifice for Bhairav has declined in recent decades in favor of vegetarian offerings, hence sweetening, the older ritual regime persists in some settings that have not yet gotten attention from distant urbanites. For example, in 2023, in a small village in the Bikaner area, I came across a tree locally described as a "Bhairav shrine." It was decorated with pieces of cloth, apparently indicating wishes made, not unlike small items that Hindu worshippers commonly leave as tokens of wishes made at miracle deities' shrines (Bellamy 2011), and a freshly offered goat leg hanging from a branch, signaling that this god favors flesh offerings. This small vignette points to a formerly more pervasive culture of sacrifice for Bhairav.

For a detailed examination of Bhairav's formerly more widespread presweetened worship, the closest we have is Yogesh Atal's (1961) decades-old study of local Bhairavs in villages of southern Rajasthan and adjacent Madhya Pradesh. As Atal shows, many of these deities regularly accept sacrifice. At these shrines, ritual specialists, known as *bhopas*, go into trance to call forth Bhairav to respond to assembled devotees' prayers. These practices are especially prominent on Sundays, a day that today persists as the deity's preferred day for miracles in Nakoda and elsewhere. In Atal's village study, Bhairav is typically worshipped as an aniconic stone, often painted vermillion. In 2023, Nakoda's temple employees and devotees similarly reported to me that their Bhairav had originally been worshipped in an aniconic form many decades ago, before that stone was replaced with the figural image now seen. And according to some temple employees, the original aniconic Nakoda Bhairav was somehow inserted into his current carved iconic image at the time of its installation, suggesting the importance of his former, presweetened identity for empowering his postsweetened form.

A key aspect of Bhairav's presweetened village identity, relevant to his postsweetened worship in Nakoda, is the god's frequent (although not universal) bifurcation into white and black forms. Atal refers to the deity's bifurcation but does not elaborate on its significance. Further on this point, Lindsey Harlan's (2003, 135–48) study of hero worship in Rajput society provides confirmation of Bhairav's traditional bifurcation in the village setting, noting that in Rajput practice white Bhairav is ritually pure (*satvik*) and cool-tempered, while the black one is fierce (*rajasik*) and hot-tempered. Thus, white Bhairav is coded as auspicious and black Bhairav as demonic. As Harlan adds, the blood of Rajputs fallen in battle constitutes a blood offering for the goddess, their lineage protector, with whom Bhairav is often worshipped; but how a fallen hero would become transmuted into black as opposed to white Bhairav has yet to be detailed. My own Rajput respondents have characterized Bhairav as one of three possible divinized outcomes for an exemplary individual, but have not yet fully explained to me how one's life or manner of death leads to one or another of these three. This point aside, Harlan tells us that Rajput Bhairav, whether black or white (or perhaps both), often serves as a guardian, if not the main deity, in temples where sacrifices are offered—a presweetened precursor to his present-day role as a *rakshak* or protector specifically dedicated to Parshvanath, one of Jainism's twenty-four world-transcending *jinas* or spiritual saviors. As I have seen at the Kodamdesar and Toliyasar Bhairav shrines (to be discussed), the distinctions between white and black manifestations have often become muddied. When I questioned devotees about the two Bhairavs' difference, typical responses showed uncertainty, venturing only that the two deities are "brothers" with no obvious difference.

Still, Bhairav's presweetened two-color polarity has found revived significance in the sweetened Marwari context of Nakoda Teerth. The famous image of Nakoda Bhairav, although seemingly the most popular deity there, is not the only Bhairav, but rather forms part of a white-black pair. Nakoda Bhairav is considered by devotees as white (*gora* or pale in Hindi), although he is actually light brown-colored (inasmuch as the stone used for his image was brought from nearby Jaisalmer, where it is common). As devotees have said, white Nakoda Bhairav provides miracles of wealth and other rewards consistent with Jain ritual purity, all the more so since he divinely protects Parshvanath. Meanwhile, an occult—that is to say, demonic-natured—black (*kala*) Bhairav was installed in Nakoda at his own shrine in 1951, perhaps around two hundred meters from white Bhairav, outside the walled complex of Jain temples where white Bhairav resides (Jain 2006, 58). Black Bhairav handles personal problems in which malevolent spirits may be culpable, and in general he offers a wilder, "tantric" approach to resolving intractable problems. Thus, black Bhairav's onetime fierce village disposition involving sacrifice has effectively morphed into a sweetened version that is still somewhat demonic but suitable for Jains, a role that upholds white Bhairav as a manifestation that works entirely within the norms of scriptural Jain doctrine.

Since black Bhairav in Nakoda is kept physically distant from white Bhairav, his occult associations will not taint the main temple complex. But he is nonetheless close enough for devotees to visit both Bhairavs each day for priest-led standard services of morning and evening *arati* or public worship with a lit lamp. The precise timings of the two Bhairavs' daily *arati* are sequentially coordinated so that the black Bhairav's service does not start until some minutes after the white Bhairav's service has finished.

Further, Nakoda Teerth's administrators provide a free shuttle vehicle after each *arati* to pick up devotees in front of white Bhairav's temple complex and take them to the entrance of black Bhairav's temple, demonstrating how they have adopted the deity's bifurcated past within Jain protocol. The two deities are also rendered visually distinct: Nakoda's white Bhairav is depicted only from the waist up, as he supposedly appeared in that form in a dream to an influential Jain ascetic many decades ago. He also always appears in this easily recognizable form when replicated in Shvetambar shrines around the country. By contrast, Nakoda's black Bhairav is shown full-bodied and riding on a dog (Bhairav's traditional vehicle), a form that has long been associated with older, tantric (occult) depictions. But these distinctions aside, the two Bhairavs in Nakoda each in his own way derives efficacy from the devotional public's perception of their village-level origins.

Rajasthan as a Marwari Ancestral Homeland

Having introduced the essential dynamic of merchant-favored sweetening, as seen in Rajasthan, I will say more about how Marwaris have been important agents of this change. A key point for analyzing Marwari reverence for Rajasthan's miracle deities is that these merchants not only value the deities' efficacy but also consider it their hereditary duty to worship them because these deities are associated with Marwaris' ancestral land in Rajasthan and look after the prosperity and well-being of their lineages. In the current era of Marwari patronage, which the administrators and priests of temples materially benefit from and thus desire, as I have discussed at length elsewhere (Saul 2022), this beneficence has been a driving force for sweetening. Marwaris' sense of connection to deities in Rajasthan may not mean that their ancestors originated in the exact location of such a deity, but at least from the region. For instance, no current-day Jains are known to be descended from the vicinity of Nakoda, but since Nakoda is close to the border between Rajasthan and Gujarat it attracts a broad range of Jains linked to those two states. Meanwhile, as I have observed at Rajasthan's various Hindu temples, a large number of nonmerchant groups, such as farmers, are also attracted by the prospect of miracles. But a crucial difference is that these other groups do not reliably give donations, whereas big-spending merchants do. Nonmercantile groups more likely show their devotion through ritualized fasting (*vrat*) in conjunction with long pilgrimages for miracle deities, often on foot as a physical testament of faith. As told to me at such Hindu shrines as Salasar and Khatu Shyam, where I have done fieldwork, ordinary devotees may be ambivalent about priests, hence they do not give donations to them, because priests often allegedly privilege higher-paying "VIP" visitors. In effect, then, Marwaris, who typically arrive by vehicle and stay in somewhat more luxurious lodgings, are cultivated among temple authorities as valued patrons, and ritual regimes are overseen with the interests of these devotees in mind.

Reverence for Rajasthan's miracle deities also serves as an antidote for the widespread perception, as told to me by pilgrims (in Salasar, Khatu Shyam, and elsewhere), that globalization and other modern changes threaten traditional Indic spiritual life. By this logic, devotees describe the people of Rajasthan as "innocent" (*bhola*), that is to say lacking in the cunning, competitive methods that urbanites supposedly employ to get ahead, insofar as rural Rajasthanis seemingly represent a way of life closer to premodern Indic spirituality. This viewpoint of Rajasthan as a vestige of premodern village virtue also easily blends into the Hindu nationalist narrative that Hindu Indians need to reclaim their ancient heritage to help them reinstate classical societal values after centuries of degrading Muslim and British colonial rule (Thapar et al. 2016). In our present era, known in Hindu cosmology as the Kali Yug (Kalyug), destined to be a time of moral downfall throughout the world (Lutgendorf 2007), Rajasthan's various miracle deities are thus at times lauded by devotees as local *avatars* or earthly manifestations of Hinduism's higher deities, having arrived in our modern world to offer moral guidance and hope through the miracles they perform. Based on my frequent observation of Marwaris' grand devotional events in cities throughout India, where religious songs and frequent speeches by esteemed singers remind us that devotion to deities is a solution for our era's problems, Marwaris have embraced this mindset, which merges their particular veneration of Rajasthan's deities with pan-Indian trends in devotion.

In contrast to this vision of rural Rajasthan as a morally upright ancestral homeland, Marwaris have not found a firm sense of belonging in the cultural milieu of their adopted cities. Hardgrove (2004, xiii) observes this predicament in Kolkata's Hindu Marwaris' long-standing efforts to formulate a dignified public image for themselves by association with the premodern Rajasthan of heroic Rajputs. Marwari-backed publications often emphasize this connection, as seen in romanticized book illustrations of life in Rajasthan (such as Kaushik Barua 1973), not to mention handbooks of village customs and songs published in Kolkata (the Marwari cultural capital) and sold at shrines in Rajasthan that Marwaris visit. As Hardgrove shows, this rhetoric of Rajasthan serves as a counterargument against local Bengali distrust of Marwaris, echoed in cities throughout India, as untrustworthy, culturally insular moneylenders. Hardgrove sees Marwaris' reaction to this perception in their enthusiasim for Rani Sati, a Rajasthani goddess. Rani Sati is said to have been a Marwari merchant woman in medieval Rajasthan who became deified when she committed *sati*, immolating herself in the manner of a Rajput woman on her husband's funeral pyre. This account aligns with Hindu Marwaris' frequent assertion that their ancestors had once been Rajput-like warriors who, through historical mishaps (perhaps, some locals suggest, because they married beneath their caste), were obliged to adopt a mercantile identity centuries ago. And as Jains commonly tell me, adopting pacifist Jain doctrine likewise prompted some Rajputs to become vegetarian Jain merchants. This selective appropriation of Rajput culture as a marker of heroic premodern life, now adapted to Marwari sensibilities, is exemplified in the sweetening of Bhairav.

I think it is instructive, then, to consider Nathaniel Roberts's statement (2015, 237) that in order to understand urban religion in India we need to be aware of the ideological construction of village practices as its necessary "other," endowing rurality with cultural authenticity and moral authority from an urban perspective. This kind of urban-rural symbiosis has long been seen in Oswal Jains' periodic visits from afar to their ancestral goddess shrine in Osiyan (Cort 2007), and also of course in Hindu Marwaris' visits to Rani Sati since colonial times. Hence, Nakoda Teerth itself, located in a sparsely populated semidesert area near Rajasthan's border with Gujarat, seems ideally positioned to represent urban mercantile desire for a remote location embodying the survival of ancient spiritual wisdom. Indeed, as I will recount, despite the fact that Nakoda now has no permanent Jain community, it claims an illustrious, highly embellished ancient history centered on a local Jain kingdom (as described in handbooks for pilgrims). Nowadays, in the vicinity of Nakoda we find only one small village two kilometers away, inhabited by tribal Bhils, other lower castes, and a few Rajputs (and no Jains).

Not Just Jain but Also Marwari Patronage

Pan-Marwari devotional enthusiasm for miracle deities has become more pronounced in the last thirty or more years, which has arguably hastened the sweetening process of Bhairav. Consider, for example, that although

Nakoda Bhairav's history officially goes back many centuries, he has gained great popularity only since around 1990. This is evidenced by the installation of his images in most Shvetambar Jain temples along the west side of India, and possibly farther afield (a kind of intensification), from around 1990 onwards, which I have been surveying. This expansion represents the consolidation of pilgrimage networks based on Nakoda among dispersed Shvetambar Jain communities, who have maintained family and business relationships among themselves, and to a large extent share a social milieu with Hindu Marwaris. I should note, though, that Digambar Jains, the other major sect of Jainism besides Shvetambars, follow a different, seemingly stricter ritual protocol focused more particularly on Jainism's twenty-four *jinas* (see, e.g., Dundas 2002, 45–59, for a discussion of sectarian differences) and revere living ascetics in lieu of miracle deities. As Shvetambar Jain respondents in Nakoda and at other shrines concurred, Bhairav is not significantly worshipped in Digambar practice, apparently because of these doctrinal differences, and therefore does not appear in Digambar temples. But a Marwari sensibility centered on miracle deities nonetheless straddles Rajasthan-descended Shvetambar Jain and Hindu identities.

In line with this pan-Marwari sensibility (excluding Digambar Jains), we can correlate Nakoda Bhairav's expansion throughout western Indian Shvetambar devotion with the coeval ramping up of Agrawal, Maheshwari, and Brahman patronage of certain other Bhairavs in Rajasthan, and the more recent establishment of some Rajasthani Bhairav-centric Hindu sites in various cities with Marwari communities (such as Delhi and Kolkata). This intensification in the worship of Rajasthan's various miracle deities is evident in the many new temples for them that have been erected or materially enhanced since the early 1990s, more often with mercantile (particularly Marwari) funding, as I have documented (Saul 2022). This growth is paralleled in the burgeoning industry for religious song (*bhajan*) books for these deities, as sold at their shrines in Rajasthan. As of now, Nakoda Bhairav is apparently in the earlier stages of this trajectory, considering the large number of texts already sold for some local manifestations of Hanuman and Krishna, but I have come across a *Nakoda Bhairav Chalisa* (Sureeshwar 2014, 37). Its title emulates the *Hanuman Chalisa*, a much older hymn that has long been preeminent across northern India for invoking Hanuman's protection. Hence, I suggest, Nakoda Bhairav's sweetening needs to be analyzed within the frame of a broader, pan-Marwari devotional turn that has supported the popularization of selected village deities in Rajasthan who provide miracles.

In proposing pan-Marwari agency, I find Michael Carrithers's (2000) theory of "polytropy" to be useful. By this term, he means that Jains freely draw from Hindu *bhakti* or deity devotion as a model for Jain practice that transcends sectarian boundaries. It is reasonable to say that for Marwaris, as for many Hindus, divine efficacy is more compelling than sectarian affiliation, as also witnessed, for example, in Hindus' ready adoption of long-standing Sufi shrines as sites for miracles (Bellamy 2011). Thus, Jain and Hindu Marwari religious identities exist on a continuum.[1] For that matter, in Shvetambar practice, a large number of local deities from the village-level Hindu cultural matrix, such as Ghantakarn, Manibhadra, and Padmavati, said by devotees to have originated in rural Gujarat, were "converted" to Jainism (hence sweetened) as protectors over the centuries, reminiscent of how various Hindu miracle deities of rural Rajasthan are now invoked as having come to earth to support pan-Indian higher scriptural morality.[2]

As I referenced earlier, in India's era of economic liberalization, miracle deities have gained heightened importance for both Jain and Hindu merchants as a means for rapid economic advancement and well-being. Fittingly, then, Jain Marwari devotees and Nakoda's temple administrators frequently observe that the main image of Bhairav in Nakoda is especially sought for his role in wealth production (Aukland 2013). Deities in Rajasthan that are most highly acclaimed by Hindu Marwaris likewise have reputations for enhancing prosperity, which has led to an uptick in donations from hopeful Marwari devotees over the years (Saul 2022). Inasmuch as Nakoda Bhairav is also responsible for upholding the doctrine of the *jinas*, he thus grants his miracles in their name.[3] This role is analogous to local manifestations of Hanuman, for example, who represent Ram, a scriptural deity of higher authority (Lutgendorf 2007; also see Cort 1997 for direct comparisons between Hanuman and Bhairav). Consistent with this role of representing a higher entity, Nakoda Bhairav's image is typically positioned in physical proximity to Parshvanath, the *jina* that he protects. Replications of Nakoda Bhairav's image have in recent decades been similarly positioned adjacent to or near Parshvanath in various other Shvetambar temples too.[4]

Further affirming a pan-Marwari identity, Jain devotees in Nakoda told me that Oswal Jain Marwaris, like Hindu Marwaris, had been Rajputs who long ago converted to Jainism. Hence, both Jain and Hindu Marwaris feel some attraction for Rajasthani miracle deities that Rajputs would traditionally favor, such as Bhairav, since Rajput associations mark those deities as authentically "Rajasthani." In pre-Independence days, Rajput nobility were the primary benefactors of shrines, but in the more egalitarian post-Independence era, as Rajput political power in Rajasthan has declined, Marwaris have largely replaced them (Harlan 2003, 39). But as Babb (2004) notes, notwithstanding their long-standing idealization of Rajputs as chivalrous representations of premodern Rajasthan, Marwaris' ethic of teetotaling vegetarianism and mercantilism makes them opposite to the public perception of Rajputs as engaged in "manly" activities like drinking alcohol, eating meat, and going to war. Hence, the Marwari embrace of reconfigured—sweetened—Rajput deities expresses Marwaris' sense that they and these deities represent Rajasthani heritage in terms made congenial to them.

We could equate such sweetening with Hindu "Vaishnavization," a diversely interpreted term that in Lutgendorf's (2007) explanation entails the reconfiguration of local systems of worship in line with pan-Indian scripturally sanctioned doctrine emphasizing Vishnu and his *avatar*s and vegetarianism. As Vaishnavite vegetarians with financial resources, Hindu Marwari merchants have been supportive of Vaishnavization in Rajasthan, especially in the last several decades, as they acclaim Rajasthan's miracle deities. One can track this trend in the ongoing campaign, championed by Brahman priests and their Marwari patrons, to replace blood sacrifice with vegetarian brahmanical (or Jain) ritual, a devotional regime that has become increasingly normative throughout Rajasthan in the last century.[5]

Alcohol offerings, a longtime mainstay for Bhairav, have become correspondingly more stigmatized in Rajasthan, not to mention elsewhere in northern India at least, as impure according to scriptural Vaishnavite doctrine. I noticed this, for example, when priests at a Bhairav shrine near Jodhpur, Rajasthan, discouraged me from taking photographs of devotees offering alcohol, apparently so as not to publicize and thereby put shame on them for following old-style worship. The same priests encouraged me to take photographs of non-alcohol-giving worship. Despite these subtle tensions, as I have witnessed elsewhere, alcohol offering is often still allowed, even if discreetly, at some Bhairav sites in recognition of the god's underlying fierceness and persistent appetite for impure offerings, even in his postsweetened state.

Bhairav as a Hindu Marwari Miracle Deity

I have proposed that Nakoda Bhairav's ascent should be analyzed not as a stand-alone Jain issue but rather as part of a broader cultural transformation of Rajasthan's miracle deities driven by Marwari patronage. To further illustrate this point, I will briefly examine what are locally described as the two most prominent Bhairavs of Hindu temples in Rajasthan. Not coincidentally, they have recently gained Marwari acclaim for miracles, hence each plausibly demonstrates a process of sweetening to varying degrees. One of these two Bhairavs is white and resides in the village of Kodamdesar, near the city of Bikaner, while the other is black, and is found in the village of Toliyasar, likewise in the Bikaner area but more distant from the city (figs. 9.2 and 9.3). Temple administrators at the two sites have said that these two Bhairavs constitute a white-black pair, much as we have seen in Rajput practice (and in Nakoda). As told to me by multiple villagers at these sites, these two Bhairavs were brought at the same time by Rajputs from a village in the Jodhpur area around 450 years ago and subsequently enshrined in their respective present-day villages.

Figure 9.2. Kodamdesar Bhairava. Rajasthan, 2019. *Source:* Photo by the author.

Figure 9.3. Toliyasar Bhairava. Rajasthan, 2018. *Source:* Photo by the author.

Locals at both sites acknowledge that Rajputs were formerly the pre-eminent patrons, and add that over the last century, or at least decades, they disappeared from the scene. Rajput authority was replaced by the priests or administrators who had formerly served them, and in this changed regime the deities eventually attracted Marwari backing. While it remains unclear to me whether the Bhairavs had ever been considered as deified Rajput heroes, in the current devotional setting they are understood to be *avatar*s of Shiva. Bhairavs as deified heroes do nonetheless persist in at least some shrines in Rajasthan where Rajputs remain in control and Marwaris are not a significant factor. The most famous instance could be the colossal pair of black and white Bhairavs in Mandore that are associated with Jodhpur's royal Rajput patronage (Harlan 2003). I suggest that the emphasis on Bhairav as an *avatar* rather than as a deified hero at Kodamdesar and Toliyasar may have been strengthened by the transition from Rajput to Marwari patronage.

This has marginalized customary Rajput privilege in favor of pan-Indian interpretations of village deities, construing those deities as *avatars* of Indian scriptural deities, as also commonly embraced by middle-class urbanites.

Visiting Kodamdesar Bhairav in 2020, I observed that this deity, situated in an open-air shrine and shaped as a large aniconic white cone-shaped head without a body (hence, conceptually reminiscent of Nakoda's white Bhairav), still regularly receives alcohol from devotees. However, currently only vegetarian offerings, not blood sacrifice, may be offered at the shrine. Still, as Carter Higgins (2016) has witnessed here, sacrifice nonetheless takes place out of public view in a clearing at some distance from the shrine. As I have seen at some goddess shrines (such as Kaila Devi in Rajasthan), this distancing is a strategy for continuing to make blood offerings for deities receptive to sacrifice when officially forbidden. An administrator in charge of the Kodamdesar shrine told me, "All the Rajputs formerly involved here moved to Bikaner City by around 1990," and since then sacrifice in front of the shrine itself has been stopped. And Marwaris have since then become influential patrons, as became apparent when the administrator showed me a hefty guest book and proudly pointed out the names and addresses of many Marwari visitors from around the country. I conclude that Kodamdesar Bhairav now occupies a middle space between village worship and Marwari-favored sweetening, substantiating my earlier point that sweetening is not necessarily absolute but responsive to situational shifts in patronage and resulting ritual relationships. In this fluid situation, Kodamdesar Bhairav is white, and yet his divine nature does not (and possibly never did) neatly conform to the white-black divine binary that Atal and Harlan observe in the village setting.

Shifting to the black Bhairav of Toliyasar, we might initially expect him to be more overtly demonic because of his color coding, as we saw in Nakoda, but, like Kodamdesar Bhairav, Toliayasar Bhairav may represent a transitional state between village and sweetened sensibilities. Toliyasar Bhairav formally appears as an iconic figure riding a dog (like Nakoda's black Bhairav), and he has seemingly received substantial patronage, since he resides in a richly decorated, expansive temple. According to some among Toliyasar's dominant Rajpurohit Brahman clan, they took control of the temple from Rajputs well over a century ago (hence earlier than at Kodamdesar). And, I was told, when they came into power, in order to enforce brahmanical rules of ritual purity they arranged for Toliyasar Bhairav's previous Rajput regimen of blood sacrifice to be henceforth transferred to a preexisting Bhairav in a nearby village, where Rajputs have remained dominant and where even today relatively few merchants come.

Compounding these changes in Toliyasar, in recent decades Marwaris descended from the surrounding region have been reaffirming their ancestral connections here, becoming major donors for this black Bhairav. Attending Toliyasar Bhairav's grand annual festival in 2018, I observed that a group of Marwaris now living in Guwahati, Assam, partly or entirely sponsored this event, and were listed on promotional posters as the main contacts for information about the festival. During the festival, they were given certain privileges as honored visitors, such as pouring sacred water over one of black Bhairav's two images (one being more recently added, possibly to make the god's image more easily accessible for worshippers), while Brahmans chanted Sanskrit mantras in the background. This reconfiguration of black Bhairav as a brahmanical scriptural deity, despite his impure Rajput background, points to a process of ritual sweetening.

However, upon further observation, some aspects of Toliyasar Bhairav indicate the persistence of darker associations. Rajpurohit locals noted that this Bhairav still sometimes receives offerings of alcohol, similar to Kodamdesar Bhairav, albeit never blood sacrifice. And, at the annual festival I observed a few devotees, possessed by Bhairav, moving around in a trancelike state, and even swinging chains (potentially for self-flagellation) while facing either of the two black images. This indicates the survival of some practices associated with village worship of the sort that Atal had described. My takeaway from Kodamdesar and Toliyasar, then, is that they both show the outcome of sweetening paralleling increased Marwari patronage, mediated through Brahman priests or other religious authorities, in place of onetime Rajput dominance. But neither Bhairav has entirely shed his fiercer associations, insofar as that fierceness underscores the god's all-important capacity to provide miracles by means beyond the realm of conventional blessings. I therefore suggest that miracle deities' rural associations and particularly Bhairav's sweetened fierceness are attractive to Marwaris' looking for efficacy arising from ancient village conjury. Hence, in the setting of Nakoda Teerth, there has been a turn to accentuate Bhairav as two clearly opposite forms, with the white one representing Jain doctrinal purity and the black one unrestrained village-level efficacy.

Nakoda Bhairav's Sweetening

Returning to Nakoda Bhairav, I will now recount his historical narrative of sweetening, which essentially tracks the progress of Jain Marwari influence.

The most straightforward source for this history is to be found in various Hindi booklets (e.g., Jain 2006 and Sureeshvar 2014) produced in Nakoda for visitors, which I will refer to as the collective "standard history," since they are very similar. Some booklets may be more detailed than others, but they all agree on the basic points that I narrate. As we will see, Bhairav's story is not one of linear sweetening, but rather of contending forces pulling him in various ritual directions at different times, ultimately leading to the reinstatement of Jain doctrinal supremacy within the last century. Even so, the standard history leaves us with some gaps at critical junctures, only partly ameliorated by devotees' and temple administrators' anecdotes. We can also gain some insight on the present-day worship of white Bhairav from Knut Aukland (2013), whose ethnographic article on the god's possession of devotees at Nakoda remains the only extended discussion about him up to now. However, Aukland's approach is synchronic and narrowly focused on possession and white Bhairav, largely omitting the historical-cultural dimensions that I have emphasized.

The standard history tells us that in the third century CE a Jain king ruled over a city named Virampur near present-day Nakoda Teerth, but, some centuries later, an iconoclastic Muslim king ordered the destruction of Virampur's temples. Anticipating this threat, some inhabitants buried their Jain images, such as the *jina* Parshvanath, next to a lake near another town, nowadays considered the "original" Nakoda, after which the current Nakoda Teerth has been named. Still later, Parshvanath's buried image was recovered and reinstalled in Virampur, but further Muslim attacks necessitated the image's reburial. Nakoda Teerth's standard history further informs us that in 1455 Bhairav made his first local appearance in the dream of a wandering Jain ascetic who had arrived in Virampur, directing him where to find the *jina*'s buried image. As the ascetic's entourage carried Parshvanath's unearthed image back to Virampur, Bhairav miraculously materialized as a boy dancing in the road in front of them, thereby leading the way and asserting his role as a protector of the *jina*.[6] The ascetic honored Bhairav's crucial assistance by installing him as an aniconic stone image to guard Parshvanath's revived temple. The god thus became known as Nakoda Bhairav because he had led the Jain devotees from that place.

These early events reflect a contemporary Jain reconstruction of Nakoda's history, with Bhairav appearing from the start as a Jain protector. However, a major gap remains, as this history needs to account for the fact that there was a long hiatus between the area's ancient glory and its modern reconstructed importance in Jainism. Addressing this point, the standard history goes on to say that, in the seventeenth century, local non-Jain disgruntlement against Oswal Jains, due to their wealth and supposed pride (alluded to, but not elaborated in the historical accounts), compelled all Jains living in the Nakoda area to flee to Jaisalmer (apparently seeking refuge there), after which Virampur apparently ceased to exist. This reference to the Jains' exile from the Nakoda area hints at the common stereotypical anecdote among some non-Jains in Rajasthan's villages today (as I have heard) that Jain Marwaris are prone to usurious moneylending (for example, see Ellis 1991, 76n2). Without any Jains left, the standard history implies that Bhairav was claimed from this point on as a deity of the non-Jain villagers of the area, and his worship turned to blood sacrifice and alcohol. Local respondents affirm that this was the case. But this situation later shifted again, as the standard history tells us that in 1903 a wandering female Jain ascetic and her followers arrived. These devotees renovated Parshvanath's temple with the assent of the local Rajput chieftain, and with funding from Jain merchants in cities of western Rajasthan (Jain 2006, 35). This marked Nakoda Teerth's inauguration as a contemporary pilgrimage destination.

As the standard history tells us, during the centuries-long interregnum when there was no Jain worship in Nakoda, the Parshvanath image had remained intact but neglected in its original place. However, the location of Bhairav's aniconic image during that time remains unaddressed in historical accounts, and not well understood among locals. But all sources, both the written histories and local respondents, concur that Bhairav appeared in 1933 in a dream to a Jain ascetic named Himachalsuri at the Nakoda site, commanding that he be reinstalled as Parshvanath's divine protector. This reinstallation took place the following year, in 1934. Critically, before Bhairav's reinstallation could take place, Himachalsuri demanded of the god that he promise to stop accepting impure offerings, such as blood sacrifice, and start taking only Jain-sanctioned offerings, like fruit and sweets, and henceforth wear a *janeu* or sacred thread typical of a high-caste Hindu. In henceforth adopting a *janeu*, Bhairav was recast as a ritually pure Hindu deity, thus fit to serve a *jina* representing Jainism's spiritual ideals. In this sense, the god was ritually sweetened.

I heard an additional revealing anecdote, not mentioned in the written history, from several employees at Nakoda Teerth and from locals in Mewanagar, the nearest village, where no Jains live. In this other account, as a villager said, "Not long before Bhairav's reinstallation in 1934, the local population, being entirely non-Jain, was stricken with a terrible pestilence that killed many. Himachalsuri thereupon told Mewanagar's inhabitants that the pestilence was Bhairav's way of punishing them for having worshipped him with blood sacrifice and alcohol. From then on, the ascetic said, they would need to fall in line with the new ritual regime." In this way, we might say, Jains appropriated and reconfigured the wild village deity. The locals followed accordingly, and their descendants have since taken up service jobs supporting Jain pilgrimage at the temple complex, where they commute daily from Mewanagar. But not surprisingly, as is common at pilgrimage sites in Rajasthan, the locals also continue to follow their own customs in worship, quite apart from the Jain Marwari-supported temple. That is, I observed, their primary shrine is not in Nakoda itself but at a memorial to a local ascetic a bit closer to their village.

Conclusion

As I have mentioned, Bhairav's case demonstrates that ritual sweetening is not necessarily a linear development, but rather can be discerned in a negotiation of sorts between shrine authorities, devotees, and the local population, resulting in multiple possible outcomes, which I have correlated with Jain and Hindu Marwari patronage. In discussing the various paths of sweetening at Kodamdesar, Toliyasar, and then Nakoda, although Marwari involvement is implicated, numerous episodes in the historical process remain to be addressed. These gaps will require additional research to gain a better understanding of the actual timeline of events pertaining to Bhairav's transformation. At Kodamdesar and Toliyasar, for example, the past dominance, beliefs, and customs of Rajput rulers and the way in which they worshipped Bhairav need to be better documented, and a more precise narrative of the advent of Marwari activity at the shrines would be useful for analyzing a ritual transformation. At Nakoda, the relationship between the white and black Bhairavs still needs further investigation. In my observation, for example, black Bhairav presides over possession, and yet Aukland reports it happening only in proximity to white Bhairav and does not mention the existence of black Bhairav.

Furthermore, several important details in Nakoda Bhairav's history remain to be discerned, which would clarify white Bhairav's physical relation to the site's development. For instance, all respondents agree that an aniconic image of the god had previously been installed as a protector immediately outside the temple, to the side of the entrance, but it is not clear how long the image had remained outside the temple before being moved inside, where it is today, and how it had been worshipped in its outdoor position. Was Bhairav ever "impurely" worshiped in front of the temple, seemingly before Himachalsuri exacted his demands for purity from the deity at the time of the temple's restoration in 1934? Also, various administrators and visitors alike have told me that the god's image had been moved inside the temple (and thereupon reconfigured in iconic form, either in 1934 or sometime later) because too many devotees were coming only to see Bhairav (in front of the temple) on account of his growing reputation for miracles, which overshadowed Parshvanath.[7] Temple authorities thereupon not only moved Bhairav inside but also positioned his image so that all visitors entering the temple would be compelled to worship Parshvanath before proceeding to adjacent Bhairav, their divine resource for miracles. By this move, the temple reenforced the scriptural supremacy of the *jina* over Bhairav's burgeoning miracle cult.

Interestingly, a Jain employee of the temple, who had grown up in Gujarat and was once brought by his grandfather to visit Nakoda as a child in the early 1990s, stated that Bhairav was still situated outside at that time, which would not match the standard history. And Caroline Humphrey (1991, 221) likewise says in passing that white Nakoda Bhairav's image was outside the temple at the time of her research, but it is not clear if her brief account relies on personal observation or hearsay. Moreover, a relevant subtext in this story is that an image of Hanuman now occupies Bhairav's former outdoor niche, perhaps registering Hanuman's own increasing popularity as a miracle provider in Marwari society by the early 1990s. If Hanuman's image was set up at that time, as at least one respondent and Humphrey apparently opine, it may have been an attempt to provide a commensurate substitute for Bhairav as a miracle deity in front of the temple to broadcast the promise of miracles awaiting visitors.

Again, we are left to conclude that ritual sweetening as a process is fraught with detours, resulting in a wide spectrum of outcomes. Despite such uncertainties, I have argued that Marwari devotees from outside Rajasthan, bringing an urban sensibility consistent with broader pan-Indian religious currents, and identifying with Rajasthan's miracle deities, have increasingly made their presence felt through their patronage. Some Marwaris were presumably coming to these shrines many decades earlier, but only by the early 1990s does empirical evidence of their financial influence become overt, such as the coalescence of numerous Marwari devotional organizations in cities throughout India dedicated to Rajasthan's miracle deities, funding for the establishment of new temples for miracle deities, and the installation of Nakoda Bhairav images in Shvetambar shrines throughout western India.

Meanwhile, local Bhairavs that have remained outside Marwari attention may also have evolved in line with broader social change, but not necessarily so perceptibly, since they have not yet attracted notable outside patronage.

Notes

1. Caroline Humphrey (1991, 215) sees socioeconomic interchangeability between Jain and Hindu Marwaris, who traditionally had similar occupations and competed for trade rights from local leaders in Rajasthan.

2. John Cort (1997) extensively discusses Ghantakarn, and secondarily other Jain protector deities, including Nakoda Bhairav, as having Tantric associations, meaning that they are able to bestow mystical powers on devotees. However, Cort emphasizes, this darker aspect of divinity was necessarily brought into conformity with Jain doctrine by the twentieth century.

3. Regarding Bhairav's acclaim as a miracle deity, we might ask where people were going for miracles before his ascent in recent decades. Specific to Shvetambar Jainism, deified deceased Jain ascetics were revered for providing miracles, as Lawrence Babb (1993, 3) has shown in the case of the Khartar Gacch lineage of ascetics in Jaipur. Unlike *jinas*, who had attained liberation from the cycle of earthly existence and were therefore no longer available to serve humanity except as models of salvific behavior, the deified ascetics remained in the world of rebirth, hence they were accessible to the faithful through their images.

4. Jaini (1991, 194) states that Parshvanath traditionally had a close relationship with protector deities because of his longtime association with serpent deities (*nagas*), who guard land and also protect his seated image.

5. See Gold 2008, 176n24, for an instance in which a Rajasthani goddess who had been receiving sacrifice was recently replaced with a ritually vegetarian image of Hanuman himself.

6. This description of Bhairav as a little boy might relate to his currently popularized childlike depiction in poster art throughout northern India (see Ligo, this volume).

7. Anticipating Bhairav's modern-day rise as a more compelling alternative to Parshvanath, Jaini (1991, 196–97) observes that in early Jain history the worship of village *yaksha*s (chthonic deities) became so popular that they similarly rivaled the *jina*s.

References

Atal, Yogesh. 1961. "The Cult of Bheru in a Mewar Village and Its Vicinage." In *Aspects of Religion in Indian Society*, edited by Lalita Prasad Vidyarthi, 140–50. Kedar Nath Ram Nath.

Aukland, Knut. 2013. "Understanding Possession in Jainism: A Study of Oracular Possession in Nakoda." *Modern Asian Studies* 47 (1): 109–34.

Babb, Lawrence Alan. 1993. "Monks and Miracles: Religious Symbols and Images of Origin Among Oswal Jains." *Journal of Asian Studies* 52 (1): 3–21.

Babb, Lawrence Alan. 2004. *Alchemies of Violence: Myths of Identity and the Life of Trade in Western India*. Sage.

Bellamy, Carla. 2011. *The Powerful Ephemeral: Everyday Healing in an Ambiguously Islamic Place*. University of California Press.

Carrithers, Michael. 2000. "On Polytropy: Or the Natural Condition of Spiritual Cosmopolitanism in India: The Digambar Jain Case." *Modern Asian Studies* 34 (4): 831–61.

Cort, John. 1997. "Tantra in Jainism: The Cult of Ghantakarn Mahavir, the Great Hero Bell-Ears." *Bulletin d'Etudes Indiennes* 15: 115–33.

Cort, John. 2007. "Devotees, Families and Tourists: Pilgrims and Shrines in Rajasthan." In *Raj Rhapsodies: Tourism, Heritage and the Seduction of History*, edited by Carol Henderson and Maxine Weisgrau, 165–81. Ashgate.

Dundas, Paul. 2002. *The Jains*. Routledge.

Ellis, Christine Cottam. 1991. "The Jain Merchant Castes of Rajasthan: Some Aspects of the Management of Social Identity in a Market Town." In *The Assembly of Listeners: Jains in Society*, edited by Michael Carrithers and Caroline Humphrey, 75–107. Cambridge University Press.

Gold, Ann Grodzins. 2008. "Deep Beauty: Rajasthani Goddess Shrines Above and Below the Surface." *International Journal of Hindu Studies* 12 (2): 153–79.

Hardgrove, Anne. 2004. *Community and Public Culture: The Marwaris in Calcutta*. Oxford University Press.

Harlan, Lindsey. 2003. *The Goddesses' Henchmen: Gender in Indian Hero Worship*. Oxford University Press.

Hawley, John Stratton. 2001. "Modern India and the Question of Middle-Class Religion." *International Journal of Hindu Studies* 5 (3): 217–25.

Higgins, Carter. 2016. "Ritual Recognition of Divine Presence in North India." *Journal of Ritual Studies* 30 (2): 1–11.

Humphrey, Caroline. 1991. "Fairs and Miracles: At the Boundaries of the Jain Community in Rajasthan." In *The Assembly of Listeners: Jains in Society*, edited by Michael Carrithers and Caroline Humphrey, 201–25. Cambridge University Press.

Jain, Bhurchand. 2006. *Jai Shri Nakoda*. Jodhpur: Arihant Prakashan.

Jaini, Padmanaibhi. 1991. "Is There a Popular Jainism?" In *The Assembly of Listeners: Jains in Society*, edited by Michael Carrithers and Caroline Humphrey, 187–99. Cambridge University Press.

Kaushik Barua, Rishi Jaimini. 1973. *Main apne Marvari samaj ko pyar karta hun*. Jaimini Publications.

Lutgendorf, Philip. 2007. *Hanuman's Tale: The Messages of a Divine Monkey*. Oxford University Press.

Moodie, Deonnie. 2019. *The Making of a Modern Temple and a Hindu City: Kalighat and Kolkata.* Oxford University Press.

Roberts, Nathaniel. 2015. "From Village to City: Hinduism and the 'Hindu Caste System.'" In *Handbook of Religion and the Asian City: Aspiration and Urbanization in the Twenty-First Century,* edited by Peter van der Veer, 237–54. University of California Press.

Saul, R. Jeremy. 2022. "Merchants, Ritualists, and Bifurcated Hanumans: A Cultural History of Rajasthan's Miracle Deities." *International Journal of Hindu Studies* 26 (3): 363–91.

Singer, Milton. 1972. *When a Great Tradition Modernizes: An Anthropological Approach to Indian Civilization.* Praeger.

Srinivas, Tulasi. 2018. *The Cow in the Elevator: An Anthropology of Wonder.* Duke University Press.

Sureeshvar, Vijay Jinottam. 2014. *Shri Nakoda Bhairav Dev.* Jain Shasan Seva Trust.

Thapar, Romila, A. G. Noorani, and Sadanand Menon. 2016. *On Nationalism.* Aleph.

Part 4

Narrative and Visual Spaces

10

Envisioning Kameshvari and the Mahavidyas in Women's *Nam* of the Kamakhya Temple and Pilgrimage Site

Patricia Dold

Women residents at the Kamakhya temple site in Assam preserve and perform a repertoire of hymns that describe, celebrate, and express devotion (*bhakti*) toward numerous gods and goddesses. These hymns, *Nam*, are performed by groups of women, with a leader, a *Namati*, in various ritual contexts in homes and at or inside temples and shrines of the Kamakhya site and community. Women preserve these hymns from one generation to the next and women of all ages and marital status—including widows—participate as singers and as *Namati*. The goddess Kamakhya and her forms are the focus for many *Nam* and two of these are my focus in this chapter. Like many *Nam*, these two hymns highlight both the distinctness of specific forms of the goddess and their unity within and as the goddess Kamakhya. Further, these *Nams'* lyrics present Kamakhya and her forms as both pleasant and terrifying; gentle and violent; beautiful and gruesome. Also, each of these two *Nam* has an identified or identifiable source or background text, which provide a basis for comparative discussion of intensification and saumyatization, that is, the preservation and development of *raudra* (fearsome, intense, violent) *and saumya* (pleasant, gentle, and auspicious) elements.

Located in Guwahati, the capital of the state of Assam in northeastern India, along the southern bank of the Brahmaputra river on Nilachal, "the dark hill," the Kamakhya temple and pilgrimage site is home to a large number of temples and open-air shrines as well as a community of several thousand residents (Maa Kamakhya Devalaya 2023, and see fig. 10.1). An even greater number of pilgrims visit the site each year for Kamakhya has long been identified as one of *Shakta pitha*s, "seats of the goddess," and as a major center for tantric practice (Urban 2010, 31–50; Van Kooij 2022, 3–4). At Nilachal, this "seat" is in the main temple of the goddess Kamakhya, which also houses other images of the goddess and some of her forms and associates. Some smaller temples, such as the Tokureshvar temple, are dedicated to forms of the god Shiva while several others enshrine various goddesses, including the Mahavidyas, ten tantric goddesses who are locally considered to collectively represent Kamakhya herself. The resident

Figure 10.1. Section of a lithograph titled "Kamakhya, the sacred site (*tirtha*) of Sati in [the district of] Kamarupa" from the Kamakhya site. Lithograph purchased at Kamakhya in 2009; photo taken in 2023 in St. John's, Newfoundland and Labrador, Canada. *Source:* Photo by the author.

community of Kamakhya not only includes the families of those who work in the site's temples and serve its thousands of pilgrims, but also those with little or no connection to its religious life.

Groups of women residents of Kamakhya gather daily, weekly, or for special family and festival occasions in homes, at small shrines, and at or within temples of Kamakhya to perform *Nam*. Often, groups of women perform *Nam* as part of their offerings to a deity in a *puja*, a common form of devotional ritual whereby a deity is honored with food, drink, flowers, light, incense, and other offerings. As is also typical for *pujas*, the women share some of these offerings, food especially, as *prasad* (the deity's blessing, more literally their pleasure or gratitude). *Nam* lyrics and the *pujas* that are their performance context express *bhakti*, and therefore emphasize the relationship between deity and devotee. At a pilgrimage site like Kamakhya, the relationship between deity *and place* is also essential, and I have argued elsewhere (Dold 2011, 2013) that women's *Nam* performance represents a liturgical tradition that ensures the ongoing *presence* of deities at the Kamakhya site.

Women's *Nam* performances belong to the lived religion of residents of the Kamakhya site, which is one dimension of the broader religiosity of Kamakhya. It is informed by pilgrimage and tantra, but is not identical with them. As Urban (2010, 2–4) has argued, scholars must avoid sensationalizing or exoticizing the site and its religious phenomena. I contend that we must also avoid trivializing and infantilizing religious forms and all the more so when discussing women's religious practices or goddess-centered texts and practices (Dold 2013, 116–20).

To avoid both sensationalizing and trivializing *Nam*, the women who sing them, and the goddesses they worship, this chapter considers intensification and "saumyatization" as potentially converging, diverging, or complementary currents in contemporary Hindu traditions. "Saumyatization" is appropriate for *Nam* because *Nam* lyrics very rarely use adjectives translatable as "soft" or "sweet" about the goddess or her characteristics: her smile might be sweet (*mridu*), but she is not. *Nam* do, however, use many of the synonyms of the Assamese and Sanskrit word *saumya*, translatable as benign, pleasant, gentle, auspicious, attractive, cool, and calm.

This approach facilitates representation and discussion of the theology of Kamakhya women's *Nam*, and helps make visible some of the complexities of these hymns and their connections to Kamakhya lived religion. Comparative analysis of select *Nam* with Shakta puranic texts provides a broader historical perspective on the *persistence of intensification through centuries-old processes of saumyatization* as an exoteric and devotional Shakta religiosity emerges in connection with the Kamakhya site and its goddess.[1]

My work on Kamakhya women's *Nam* began in January 2008, when I began collaborating with Jayashree Athparia,[2] a resident of Kamakhya whose knowledge of Assamese, the Kamarupi dialect, local "folk" religion, and many of the women who sing *Nam* proved indispensable. With women's permission, we recorded, translated, and discussed our translations together and with *Namati*.[3] Our collection of *Nam* focuses on the goddess Kamakhya, but also on Kali and the Mahavidyas.[4] We did not conduct formal interviews with singers or with *Namati*.

My analysis begins with a Kameshvari *Nam* composed by Parvati Devi (1919–2019) and described to us by her as her commentary on a *dhyana* (visualization) from the *Kalika Purana* (tenth-eleventh centuries; Urban 2010, 5; Van Kooij 2022, 3–4). Later, I discuss a Sati-Mahavidya *Nam*, which narrates Sati's transformation into the ten Mahavidyas, a scene that has in its background narratives of the *Mahabhagavata* and *Brihaddharma Puranas*.[5] In both cases, I highlight the raudra and saumya character of the lyrics, juxtapose the *Nam* and its Sanskritic and puranic background, and discuss the significance of performance contexts. Both *Nam* provide cases of intensification continuing within the development of *bhakti* to and worship of a single supreme goddess who inspires *bhakti* in part *because* her nature comprises multiple distinct identities. The *bhakti* of these hymns is itself varied: the Kameshvari *Nam* offers explicit expression of a highly emotional devotion. In the Sati-Mahavidya *Nam*, a protective devotion is only implied. For each, the performance context provides further nuance regarding worshipers' relationships with divine being(s). For the Sati-Mahavidya *Nam* in particular, the *Deodhani* festival performance context points to the *Nam*'s role in preserving intense or raudra elements. Finally, each hymn offers a different response to the *bhakti* devotionalism already present in the *Nam*'s source text, and therefore, in each case, we have evidence that currents of saumyatization and intensification have been in progress for several centuries. Such engagement and creativity of oral tradition in relation to puranic sacred narratives is not unusual in lived Hinduism (Flueckiger 2015, 19–30, 46–62) in part because the *Puranas*, a large and complex genre of religious text, are an important source for mythic sacred narratives and for *bhakti* (Michaels 2004, 59–60).

The Kameshvari *Nam* and the *Kalika Purana*

Based on my observations and as confirmed by Athparia, Parvati Devi was a highly respected *Namati* who possessed great dedication to learning and preserving local traditions. On August 16, 2009, Athparia and I requested a private performance of the Sati-Mahavidya *Nam*. Parvati Devi began the afternoon's performance with her own composition, a Kameshvari *Nam*. That this was her composition makes it unusual, as *Namati* typically insist that these hymns have no known author. Instead, they have been passed down orally through generations such that women refer fondly to "old" (*purana*) *Nam*. Parvati Devi's authorship was clearly important to her: denied access to formal education as a child, she made her brothers teach her how to read, she said, because she wanted to read Sanskrit texts about Kamakhya.

By virtue of its focus on Kameshvari and her *Kalika Purana dhyana*, this *Nam* deals with phenomena of great significance for the Kamakhya site. The *Kalika Purana* is inevitably discussed in scholarship and contemporary media about the site, and the Kameshvari *dhyana* describes the Calanta, the movable form of the goddess Kamakhya carried in processions (Deka 2004, 44, 55).[6] Kameshvari, with her six heads and seated on a red lotus growing from the navel of a white corpse lying on the back of a lion, is a form of the goddess Kamakhya frequently shown on local lithographs (see fig. 10.1). That Parvati Devi identified a *dhyana* as the basis for her *Nam* is significant also. A *dhyana* is part of preparatory ritual instruction to enable visualization of a divine being who will be a focus for subsequent ritual procedures and whose presence within or near the worshiper is achieved through the *dhyana* and other tools, such as *mantra* recitation. To compose a commentary on such a text, and a Sanskrit text at that, is to assume an authoritative stance on ritual. Recitation of Sanskrit texts is a significant aspect of male priests' daily ritual routines at Kamakhya. So, with her composition, Parvati Devi is positioning herself within the priestly ritual domain and prescriptive Sanskritic textual tradition.

Here is our translation of the *Nam*, in full. Italics indicate parallels with the *Kalika Purana*'s Kameshvari *dhyana* and other similar passages, as discussed below.

> Come, O Mother, Goddess Kamakhya to the temple that is
> my heart
> I offer to your feet the tears of my eyes and these fragrant
> flowers,[7] O Mother.
> Whose Beauty are you, O Mother, whose color is red?[8]
> *Sitting on a lion upon which there is a red lotus*, O Mother
> *Six-faced, twelve-armed, with eighteen eyes*, O Mother.[9]
> Whose Beauty are you, whose *own throne is Narayana*, O Mother?

Whose Beauty are you, who *sits on a red lotus*, O Mother,
Under whose feet is Shiva in the form of a corpse, O Mother?[10]
O Mother, *adorned with kumkum, of golden color*, you *enchant the minds* of the sages.
O Mother, with four hands, *holding the Rudraksa, and offering gestures of fearlessness and boon-granting.*[11]
O Mother, your *hair lying free*, your *smile gentle*, with a sweet lower lip, a lolling tongue, and *three eyes*; you are to be worshiped by all.
The sun and moon are hiding the ears of Vama,[12] O Mother.
O Mother, you have five-faces and five forms.[13]
She sits upon five ghosts, O Mother, always sitting she is happy.
Kamakhya is the supreme Queen; the Supreme Prakriti, O Mother.
Brahma, Vishnu, and Shiva do not know her real form, O Mother.
She *who takes whatever form is desired*, she is Kameshvari, Queen of Desire, O Mother
Desired and inspiring desire, O Mother.[14]
The Goddess loves her devotees tenderly (*bhakata vatsala*); *her hands offer fearlessness and boons* (*abhaya barada*)
O Mother, your form is peaceful (*achita*), your greatness unsurpassed.
O Mother, you are endless, the Vedas do not know your limits.
O Mother, you sit on the mountain that is the Dark Hill (*nilachal*)
Your feet give fearlessness, rescue all (*rakha kara*), O Mother.
O Mother, we, with so little intelligence, do not know [how to offer] devotion (*bhakati*)!
O Mother, we do not have the strength to sing about your greatness.
Not knowing, we have sung your verses, O Mother, do not blame us for our flaws.
At the time of death, give us a place under your feet, O Mother.

Throughout, the Kameshvari *Nam* emphasizes *bhakti*, using vernacularized equivalents for devotion, devotee, and the goddess's tenderness (*vatsala*, literally calf-love, the affection of a cow for her calf) for her devotees. Both the singer and the goddess herself are attributed strong affection, and the goddess inspires various emotions and responses typical for *bhakti*, including longing for the deity's presence, humility and awe before the incomprehensible mystery and greatness of the goddess, gratitude for the goddess's proximity, and confidence that she will rescue from fear and provide solace in death. She is "peaceful," since she wields no weapons, according to Parvati Devi, and is therefore, perhaps, approachable. *Bhakti* was also evident in the gentle timbre of Parvati Devi's voice and also in this *Nam*'s flowing—saumya—melody. She adopted a much harsher (raudra) tone in her performance of a Kali Karalavadani *Nam*, matching its focus on "Kali, whose face is gruesome," and its choppy, rhythmic—raudra—melody (Dold 2013, 140–41).

The *Kalika Purana*'s Kameshvari *dhyana* has no explicit emphasis on *bhakti* or its emotions and the context of its *dhyana* is tantric *sadhana* (prescribed ritual and meditative practice) rather than an overtly devotional practice, such as a *puja*. However, the *Kalika Purana* knows and depicts *bhakti* in various ways. It uses the word *bhakti* to describe ideal practice (e.g., the adept should practice with devotion, devoutly) and recommends specific procedures for a tantric *bhakti*.[15] Further, Kameshvari's *gayatri mantra*[16] has an overtly devotional tone similar to the tone of Parvati Devi's *Nam*: "O Kameshvari, come here, be before me, into my presence, (72) let us make thee, Kameshvari, the aim of our knowledge, let us contemplate Kamakhya, O Kubji, O Mahamaya, and thereafter: 'may She inspire us.' (73) Come, come, O noble Mother, causing grace to the world . . . have mercy upon me" [*prasida me*] (KP 64.72–74 in Van Kooij 2022, 212).

Furthermore, the *Kalika Purana* depicts *bhakti* on the part of those who follow its instructions on the use of *dhyana*s, *mantra*s, and so on for worshiping the goddess. It is Shiva who delivers these ritual instructions to his sons, Vetala and Bhairava, so they will be released from their current mortal form, itself the result of a curse from the goddess, their mother. They complete a *dhyana* and she appears before them as visualized: standing on a white ghost, her body is "completely lovely" and "shines like a red lotus," and she has full and firm breasts and wields a sword. The boys close their eyes and repeatedly ask her to save them. She touches them "with the tip of her boon-giving hand," thus restoring their divinity (*Kalika Purana* 76.91–93, as translated in Van Kooij 2022, 190–91). As with Kameshvari's *gayatri mantra*, the dynamics and emotions of *bhakti* are evident here, although they are not explicitly called *bhakti*.

Both the *Kalika Purana*'s Kameshvari *dhyana* and Parvati Devi's *Nam* use relatively few raudra elements, though I will later show that Parvati Devi adds raudra features, thus intensifying her representation of the goddess. That the *Nam* not only preserves but intensifies raudra qualities is noteworthy given the *Nam*'s emotional devotionalism, itself a saumyatization of the *bhakti* of the *Kalika Purana*.

The *Kalika Purana*'s Kameshvari *dhyana* already implies that this goddess could be a focus for *bhakti*. It instructs the tantric adept to imagine this goddess's "enchanting" (*manohara*) form, which has both raudra and saumya features. She "shines like collyrium," has dark blue glossy hair, six faces, twelve arms, and eighteen eyes. She is "adorned with all ornaments" and has a "wreath of rubies and pearls." Though she holds several weapons (a bow, arrows, sword, spear, and trident), she also carries nonviolent objects (e.g., a book, rosary, and lotus) and offers a benevolent gesture of fearlessness (*abhaya mudra*; *Kalika Purana* 64.16–21 in Van Kooij 2022, 210–11). She stands on "a white ghost (*preta*) upon a lion, upon this a red lotus," has "a little smile round her mouth," and wears "a many-coloured cloth and a tiger's skin" (*Kalika Purana* 64.25–26 in Van Kooij 2022, 211). The stated results of the visualization do not include *bhakti* but neither do they include any overtly tantric goal. Instead, the visualization, with its raudra and saumya elements, promises success in "righteousness (*dharma*), love (*kama*) and wealth (*artha*)" (*Kalika Purana* 64.27a in Van Kooij 2022, 211).

As previously noted, Parvati Devi indicated that carrying weapons would be incompatible with Kameshvari's peaceful character. Her *Nam* includes only two other raudra elements also found in the *dhyana*: the corpse that forms Kameshvari's seat and, perhaps, the goddess's fearlessness gesture. However, Parvati Devi has added other raudra features to her Kameshvari *Nam*, such as the five ghosts that are the goddess's seat (line 8), her lolling tongue (line 13), and her loose hair (line 12), which Van Kooij (2022, 186–8) notes is a feature of the goddess Kali/Kalika in the *Kalika Purana*. Loose hair and a lolling tongue are typical features of Kali in *Nam* and five ghosts also form the seat of Shorashi/Rajrajeshvari, one of the Mahavidyas, according to the Sati-Mahavidya *Nam*. Whatever their source, Parvati Devi deemed it fitting to attribute to Kameshvari raudra elements not in her source *dhyana*, even as she is composing an explicitly devotional hymn to a "peaceful" goddess. One begins to wonder if *bhakti* is intensified through the combination of saumya and raudra elements. Certainly, both the *Kalika Purana* and Kamakhya *Nam* celebrate the complexity of the goddess in various ways. One of these, perhaps, is through the use of both saumya and raudra elements. Another is that she is at once one and many.

While both the *Nam* and the *dhyana* state that Kameshvari has six heads, the *dhyana* offers detail on each of the six forms, including their names. These details have no parallel in the *Nam*, though Parvati Devi later identified the six goddesses referenced in line five as Kamakhya, Shorashi, Tirpurasundari, Sharada, Shiva, and Kamala—and so conveyed awareness of Kameshvari's multiple identities. Parvati Devi's *Nam* does explicitly describe the goddess's multiplicity even as it focuses on her specific form as Kameshvari. The *Nam* repeats some of the *dhyana*'s descriptive detail about the goddess's multiple forms: her six heads, twelve arms, and eighteen eyes. However, other details in the *Nam* have significant parallels elsewhere in the *Kalika Purana*. The Kameshvari *Nam*, in lines nine through fourteen, uses specific vocabulary from another *dhyana*, that of the goddess Kamakhya. It describes her as having a corpse as her seat, ears adorned with the sun and moon (*ravishashiyutakarna*), coloring that is yellow like saffron (*kumkumpita-varna*), a rosary (*akshasutra*), and offering the fearlessness and boon-granting *mudra*s (*Kalika Purana* 62.141–44 in Van Kooij 2022, 197). Other details in the *Nam* such as the smiling face, loose hair, and three eyes as well as the fearlessness and boon-granting gestures occur in many *Kalika Purana dhyana*s. The five forms and five faces of line fifteen have no single parallel but might refer collectively to the *Kalika Purana*'s five forms of Kamakhya.[17] Perhaps the *Nam* asserts the identity of Kamakhya and Kameshvari or that the goddess transforms from one identity—with six heads—to another, with five heads. Or perhaps the *Nam* conflates multiple goddesses as Kameshvari while still preserving details distinct to each.

I suggest that any of these readings is possible in part because the *Kalika Purana* itself has a *deliberately* complex theology. Its goddess is one *and* many and the text insists there is multiplicity within the divine unity and sometimes even the multiple forms have multiple forms. Shiva instructs Vetala and Bhairava at considerable length about the goddess Mahamaya's ability to take on different forms to serve different needs and desires, including her own. When appropriate, she is fierce, wields a sword, and stands on a ghost. In her erotic mode or mood, she wears a garland and sits on a red lotus. When she grants wishes, she stands on a lion. In her own form, she rests on all three. This Mahamaya is the source of all other goddesses, including Kamakhya, just as the sun is the source of rays. Yet Kamakhya is the root form of Mahamaya and, of course, Kamakhya herself has five forms. She is, as the *Kalika Purana* says, *kamarupini*, assuming forms as she wishes. This *Kalika Purana* passage concludes by reaffirming that the goddess is one and many: "In this way, Mahamaya Kamakhya, always having just one form, but being different in vision and form—therefore one should worship her accordingly" (*Kalika Purana* 58.48–71 in Van Kooij 2022, 192–93). I suggest that this theological perspective that sees multiplicity within a single divine being is retained if not also enhanced in Parvati Devi's Kameshvari *Nam*. Further, the *Nam* develops its *bhakti* orientation toward this goddess by drawing on devotional language from elsewhere in the *Kalika Purana* while also enhancing raudra and saumya elements from the Kalika's *dhyana*, from elsewhere in that text, and from other *Nam* of the Kamakhya site.

To conclude the discussion of the Kameshvari *Nam*, I return to the nature of its source text as a *dhyana*. As discussed above, the *Nam* is clearly a devotional hymn. Yet Parvati Devi's decision to sing it first implies that it retains something of its character as a tantric *dhyana*, since such visualizations are among the preliminary steps in a tantric ritual procedure. Part of the *Namati's* role is to select appropriate *Nam* for a given ritual context and determine the order in which they should be sung. Parvati Devi seemed to have such duties in mind even in the private and informal setting of her performance that day. That is, Parvati Devi explained that she needed to sing a *Nam* to Annapurna prior to the Sati-Mahavidya *Nam* because the goddess lived first as Annapurna (she who is "full of food"), and was born as Sati only later. Thus, the order of *Nam* performance was important in her view. Perhaps, then, it was also important to begin the performance with an appropriate tool for starting a ritual: a *Nam* based on a puranic *dhyana* celebrating a complex representation of the goddess as Kamesvari, the main anthropomorphic form of the goddess in the main temple, before offering hymns focused on other forms like Annapurna and Sati. Such attention to the details of *Nam* performance highlights the importance of the entire *Nam* tradition for the women who sing, including these hymns' representations of complex, saumya/raudra deities.

The Sati-Mahavidya *Nam*

The Sati-Mahavidya *Nam*, of unknown date and authorship as is typical for *Nam*, provides another example of the nature of the goddess as one and many. This *Nam* also features both raudra and saumya elements in its descriptions of goddesses. Furthermore, it has the *Deodhani* festival as one of its performance contexts, and for this festival the individuality of the goddess's many forms becomes embodied in individual *Deodha*s, the men who each become a "voice of a deity."

The narrative of Sati is well known at the Kamakhya site as a sacred narrative explaining the origin of the site as a *pitha*, a seat of the goddess (Urban 2010, 34–37; Rajan-Misra 2004, 26–29). The narrative explains that the *pitha*s were established at sites where pieces of Sati's corpse fell.

Oblivious to all else, the grief-stricken Shiva carried the body of his beloved wife Sati, whose death was a result of a conflict with her father, Daksha. The gods intervened to remove her body and restore order. The *yoni* (vulva) fell on Nilachal, establishing the Kamakhya *pitha*, the cave in the main temple where the *yoni* rests (see fig. 10.1).

The Sati-Mahavidya *Nam* narrates one scene from the narrative and as much as the Sati narrative provides a myth of origin for Kamakhya, this scene is the myth of origin for the ten Mahavidyas as the goddess Kamakhya (Dold 2004). The *Nam* begins by referring to the argument between Shiva and Sati about whether they should attend a ritual (*yajna*) that Sati's father Daksha is sponsoring, but to which he has not invited them. Shiva, taking a firm stance in proper etiquette, insists that attending without an invitation would only invite disrespect. Sati, perhaps adopting the attitude of a wife dutifully asking her husband's permission, states her request to go:

> Lord Shiva heard the request:
> "I will go to see the *yajna* at my father's home"
> Shankar says, you will go to your father's house without invitation!
> If you go, you will receive disrespect (*apaman*).
> Hear this story, Daksha is doing the *yajna*
> He will not give us our share, this is his karma.[18]

Sati insists on attending on the basis of a daughter's loyalty and rights, as she does also in the *Mahabhagavata Purana*'s version (8.27b–28): "She says to her husband, 'don't speak like that.' A daughter [just] goes to her father's house, where is the need for an invitation?" The *Nam*, like the Purana, says that Shiva stands firm in refusing to give her permission. Sati, in anger, transforms:

> At this moment, Shiva does not give permission to Sati
> Angry, Sati becomes Kali,[19] with a fear-inspiring face,
> Hair loose, like a great cloud, with teeth like fangs
> With corpselike form, she appears in all the directions.
> Wearing a garland of heads, dripping blood
> In one left hand, a severed head, dripping blood
> In her other left hand, a curved knife.
> Her two right hands make the "fear not" and "ask a boon" *mudra*s
> Her tongue lolling, blood streaming from the corners of her mouth

> Her third eye, a half moon, shining on her forehead.
> Seeing her, he is afraid, and turns his face away.

To this point, the *Nam* closely parallels the *Mahabhagavata Purana*'s version of this scene, which is itself in the background of the *Brihaddharma Purana* (36.19–77). In both, Sati and Shiva argue at length. In the *Mahabhagavata Purana* (8.47–53), Sati is insulted and angry. Her eyes turn red, and she observes that where he once devoutly requested that she become his wife, Shiva now insults her so she must show him her "power":

> Seeing her, the goddess, her lower lip trembling with rage, the pupils of her eyes resembling the doomsday fire, Shiva shut his eyes. She laughed loudly, her mouth full of terrible fangs. Bewildered and terrified, he looked upon her, the terrible one who appeared old, naked, her hair flying, her tongue lolling, bearing four arms. She whose roar was dreadful, was adorned with a garland of human heads. Brilliant like a great host of suns, her head blazing with its tiara, she looked like a rising star. Assuming her horrible form, Sati was burning violently through her own power. Smiling broadly, rising up with a great roar, she shone before him. (8.47–52, abridged translation by Dold using Kumar 1983)

Sati becomes Kali, though the *Mahabhagavata Purana* does not use this name here (as the *Nam* does). Shiva flees from her, so the goddess tries to restrain him by adopting ten forms and appearing in all directions. Again and again, he runs, but wherever he flees he confronts another of her fearsome forms. Eventually he stops, asks where Sati has gone, and is told she is right there as the ten Mahavidyas who are then briefly introduced by the goddess (*Mahabhagavata Purana* 8.62–63, 65–71; *Brihaddharma Purana* 36.126, 128–30).

By contrast, as the scene unfolds in the *Nam*, the appearance of each of the Mahavidyas is described in detail and, consistent with many other descriptions of these ten goddesses,[20] the *Nam* typically attributes both *raudra* and *saumya* elements to each. Nevertheless, as he encounters each Mahavidya, Shiva becomes increasingly agitated, and even when he faces relatively *saumya* forms he averts his face, feels fear, trembles, closes his eyes, or attempts to run away, only to find his path blocked. His reactions are, arguably, intensified.

Becoming Tara, Sati stands before Shiva
Blue in color, with a lolling tongue, her face gruesome
Her single lock of matted hair forming a cobra's hood over her head
A half-moon behind her hair, shines its light on her forehead.
Three-eyed, with a big belly, she wears a tiger's hide.
Her four hands adorned with a blue lotus and an undulating
    sea snake;
On the left, a bow and arrow.
Seeing her, Pashupati [Shiva] is afraid and wishes to run away.

The *Nam* continues in this vein, describing Sati's transformation into the rest of the ten Mahavidyas. As with these first two transformations, the *Nam* always says it is Sati who transforms, thus repeating in most cases the juxtaposition of the predominantly saumya wife of Shiva and these alternate forms that frighten or repulse him, and which are therefore predominantly raudra. The *Nam* thereby reaffirms her singular identity even as it describes each of the ten Mahavidyas as distinct goddesses.

Sati, appearing as Rajrajeshvari,
Red-colored, three-eyed, making good luck and purity
In her four hands, she is adorned with a noose, a goad, bow,
    and arrow.
Brahma, Vishnu, Hara, Ishvara, Rudra, these five are
Five ghosts set under her platform.
Seeing her, Shankar turns his face away.
. . . .
As Chinnamasta, Sati became most transformed
Being filled with desire, she transforms as she pleases
Naked, with two arms, supported on a red lotus
A snake on top, wearing a garland of heads
She is walking holding her own head in her hand
Three streams of blood are spurting from her neck
One stream of blood she is drinking, feeding herself blood
On either side of her, her friends Dakini and Yogini are feeding
    on two streams of blood.
Her three eyes have the brightness of the moon, the sun and fire.
She is radiant, the brightness of the sun and moon is on her
    forehead
Siva, seeing her, is afraid and shuts his eyes.

According to the *Mahabhagavata Purana* (8.73, also *Brihaddharma Purana* 36.132–33), the Mahavidyas grant all wishes and fulfill "intentions to cause control, paralysis, hatred and so on and death, quitting, agitation, bewilderment, and flight of enemies." Although the power of the Mahavidyas to take action against a worshipers' enemies is known to texts and lived practice at Kamakhya (Dold 2011, 59–61; Van Kooij 2022, 140–47), the *Nam* itself is not explicit about this. Some of these effects are experienced by Shiva in both the *Nam* and the puranic narrations. The *Nam* does suggest, in its closing lines, that the Mahavidyas protect their worshipers:

> In Bharata, Mother is these ten forms
> That are in the ten directions. Protect us, great king Krishna.[21]

Certainly, the *Nam* could be seen to express the power of the Mahavidyas against enemies and thus their ability to protect worshipers. But is such a power fearsome (raudra) or benign (saumya)? For the worshiper, it is benign, but this benevolence requires fearsome power. Perhaps this dual quality, this simultaneous ferocity and benevolence, is reinforced by the mixed character of the group of Mahavidyas, with some, like Kamala, highly saumya, and others, like Chinnamasta, highly raudra. If so, then in a *Nam* such as this and the Sanskrit text in its background, intensification and saumyatization converge. Certainly, the *Nam* clearly displays and asserts the presence of all ten forms of the goddess, one in each of the ten directions.[22] There can be no doubt about the importance of the divine presences at a pilgrimage site like Kamakhya. Indeed, the presence of divine beings in living human bodies is a major dimension of the *Deodhani* festival, which is one ritual context for performance of *Nam*, including the Sati-Mahavidya *Nam*.

The Sati-Mahavidya *Nam* and the *Deodhani* Festival

One of the major annual festivals of Kamakhya is the *Deodhani* festival held over three days in August (Dold 2011; Garigliano 2018; Rajan-Mishra 2004, 55–59). During the festival, *Deodha*s, men who have been selected by a god or goddess, embody their deity. These embodiments allow their god or goddess to dance, to receive various offerings including garlands of flowers and the flesh of sacrificed animals, and, at specified times, to hear and respond to requests from worshipers (Garigliano 2018, 199n30, quoting Goswami 1960, 51–52). For several hours each day in and around the main temple, large crowds watch the *Deodha*s dance to the accompaniment of several drummers and two men playing brass horns (*kaliyas*). The music and the *Deodha*'s's visits to the image of Manasa (a snake goddess) in the main temple (and perhaps also the hashish they smoke) energize the *Deodha*s as they dance, gesticulate, and offer facial expressions characteristic of their deity (Garigliano 2018, 208–18). Some goddess *Deodha*s dance barefoot on the sharp edge of a sword and receive offerings of live pigeons. I witnessed *Deodha*s bite off birds' heads, chew, and spit out the remnants (Dold 2011, 55). The atmosphere is dramatic and intense and the intensity seems to be appreciated by the assembled crowds. Irene Garigliano notes that among the most popular *Deodha*s are those who embody deities like Kali and Chinnamasta, fierce goddesses whose *Deodha*s' dances are the most dramatic and energetic (2018, 214), or like the *Deodha* of Bagala who "exults, over-whelmed with joy, completely thrilled and intoxicated by bliss" (2018, 212).

Women's *Nam* singing also "energizes" or "divinizes" *Deodha*s in that it helps bring the deities into their human *Deodha*. Garigliano (2018, 205–6) describes a three-hour *Nam* performance crucial for the descent of the goddess Raksha (Protective) Kali into her *Deodha*. I attended a similar performance where women's *Nam* singing helped bring the deities to the Calanta and Manasa *Deodha*s (Dold 2011). In each case, the women sang a *Nam* of the *Deodha*'s goddess, a Kamakhya *Nam* for the Calanta (who is the deity of the movable image, i.e., of Kameshvari as discussed earlier) and a Manasa *Nam* for the Manasa *Deodha*. As each *Deodha* listened, while also contemplating an altar to their goddess, they began to cry out, scream, and contort their bodies. At this point, the *Namati* increased the tempo of the singing and clapping and switched to a *Nam* refrain listing the Mahavidyas. The *Deodha* continued to twist and shriek as the women continued singing and clapping, stopping only when the *Deodha* picked up his deity's implements (a sign of the deity's presence in him), bowed to the women, and left to go to the main temple to dance before the large crowds gathered there. As Garigliano documents, the singing of *Nam*, the rhythms of the drums, and the blasts of the *kaliyas* all play "a vital role in stirring up the divine presence in *deodhas*' bodies" (2018, 206–7).

It had been traditional for women to sing *Nam* at Tokureshvar, a Shiva temple located to the west of Kamakhya's main temple, during a ceremony that marked the beginning of the *Deodhani* festival and thus the initial public appearance of the deities in their *Deodha*s. For years, the Sati-Mahavidya *Nam* was sung during this ceremony, according to Nani Devi, the *Namati* who led the performance. The *Deodha*s would gather there, moving in and out of the temple, beckoning to the women to sing louder, and eventually receive their deity. The Sati-Mahavidya *Nam*'s emphasis on transformation, its explanation for the *presence* of the Mahavidyas at Kamakhya, would have been vocalized by women as the *Deodha*s themselves transformed, some of them into individual Mahavidyas. Therefore, I suggest, the performance of this *Nam* at Tokureshvar on the first day of *Deodhani* made the ceremony a reenactment of the origin of the Mahavidyas as *the* forms of the goddess Kamakhya who are made present within living human bodies, accessible to worshipers in such an ordinary yet rarified manner.

The Sati-Mahavidya *Nam*'s heightened focus on detailed descriptions of each of the Mahavidyas, be they fearsome or pleasant, Shiva's fearful reactions to each goddess, and the *Nam*'s performance context in the *Deodhani* festival make it an expression of intensification. Clearly, the goddess has multiple distinct identities and, through the singing of *Nam* by women, her presence is powerfully displayed in the bodies of *Deodha*s who likewise enact particular identities, fearsome and benign, raudra and saumya, all of them celebrated by the festival crowds.

In 2009, women disagreed as to which *Nam* should be sung at Tokureshvar and Nani Devi, the *Namati* who previously led the singing there, felt disrespected and did not attend and the Sati-Mahavidya *Nam* was not part of the opening ceremony. Nevertheless, its performance on that first day of the festival seemed to be important for some women. That evening, a large group of women gathered at the main temple and, led by Nani Devi and other *Namati*, the women sang the Sati-Mahavidya *Nam*. This was a larger and more assertive group than the one that regularly gathered to sing for final *arati* (the offering of light to the deity) each evening. Whereas normally women's singing continued even when drowned out by festival musicians or other noise, on that August night, when drummers started to play, women objected and forced them to stop. I suggest the women's perseverance and assertiveness points to the importance they attach to the Sati-Mahavidya *Nam* and perhaps to the importance of the role of women's *Nam* performance in the *Deodhani* festival.

Conclusion

Each of the two *Nam* considered in detail here carry forward currents evident in the Puranas that form part of the textual and historical background of the Kamakhya site and of these specific *Nam*. Parvati Devi's *Nam*, perhaps while retaining some of its function as a *dhyana*, expresses something of the multiplicity of the *Kalika Purana*'s goddess, a goddess who already possesses both raudra and saumya elements. Her *Nam* represents an intensification of the original *dhyana* because it adds raudra characteristics from elsewhere in the *Kalika Purana* and from other *Nam*. Parvati Devi's *Nam* offers and conveys *bhakti* in highly emotional expressions, but I contend that this emotional dimension has part of its foundation in the *bhakti* of the *Kalika Purana*.

The Sati-Mahavidya *Nam* again affirms the goddess's multiplicity and complex character as well as her ten raudra-saumya forms, as Sati transforms and Shiva flees. While it clearly inherits much from the parallel scene in the *Mahabhagavata* and *Brihaddharma Purana*s, it seems uninterested in the devotional relationship between the goddess and Shiva depicted in those texts. Instead, the *Nam* is focused on the fearsome power and presence of the Mahavidyas as well as the protection they provide and the gratitude they therefore inspire. That is, the Sati-Mahavidya *Nam* conveys key themes of the *Deodhani* festival. The intensity of that festival and especially the transformative moment when *Deodha*s receive their deity, an event facilitated by women's performance of Mahavidya *Nam*, including the Sati-Mahavidya *Nam* that highlights the transformation of the goddess from saumya (Sati) to raudra (Kali and other Mahavidyas) forms, points again to the importance for local religion of Kamakhya women's *Nam* ritual performances as vehicles for the preservation of intense, raudra elements, as well as for the expression of *bhakti*.

If the *bhakti* of these *Nam* and also the goddess who inspires it are examples of saumyatization, they are part of a saumyatization process reaching back several centuries, to the time of the composition of the *Kalika* and *Mahabhagavata Purana*s and to centuries of interplay between raudra and saumya elements in those texts and the lived religious experiences that found a basis in them. That Kamakhya women have for generations preserved and performed these *Nam* suggests that they—along with the lived religion of Kamakhya residents—continue to locate religious significance in both saumya and raudra elements.

Notes

1. As McDermott (2001, 230–31) demonstrates for Bengali Shakta song-poems (*padabali*), Vaishnava *bhakti* (devotionalism) also influenced the development of Kamakhya *Nam*. Part of the reformist (and anti-Shakta) neo-Vaishnava movement

founded by Shankaradeva in the sixteenth century were *Nam-ghars* (chanting houses), which remain important centers for congregational worship in Assam. At least one existed at Kamakhya. See Dold (2013, 126–28) on Shakta and Vaisnava *bhakti* in the emergence of Kamakhya *Nam*.

2. Athparia worked as a translator and field assistant, especially for the lived religion of Kamakhya. Here and elsewhere (Dold 2011, 2013), I use her name and the real names of *Namati* at the request and with the permission of these women, whose knowledge and roles in *Nam* performance is thereby recognized.

3. *Nam* use Assamese, Bengali, and Sanskritic vocabulary.

4. On the breadth of Kamakhya oral song traditions, see Rajan-Mishra (2004, 134–43) and Arrago-Boruah (2019).

5. Both texts are later than the *Kalika Purana* and the *Brihaddharma* later than the *Mahabhagavata Purana*. Dating *Puranas* is, according to Axel Michaels, "nearly impossible" in part because of their origins in oral tradition (2004, 59). However, the representations of Mahavidyas in these three *Puranas* help establish relative chronology. The *Kalika Purana* does not yet know the standardized group of ten Mahavidyas while the *Mahabhagavata* and *Brihaddharma Puranas* do. Since the ten Mahavidyas seem to have become a standardized group only by the fourteenth century (Dold 2013, 133–34), those passages of the *Mahabhagavata* and *Brihaddharma Puranas* describing the standard ten cannot be much earlier than the fourteenth century.

6. The Calanta is housed in the main temple, in a section called the Calanta, just to the west of the main *pith*, the "seat" of the goddess where the goddess is present in the aniconic form of a vulva-shaped stone (Rajan-Mishra 2004, 162–63; Garigliano 2018n15).

7. Or, flowers that are love (*prema*).

8. aha e ma kamakhya debi hridaya mandire he ma /1/ prema bhule nayana jale pujibo charane he ma /2/

kahara ramani tumi rangai varana tumi he ma /3/

9. singhata bahi iya achha tate ranga paddo he ma /4/ chhaya vakra dvadasha bhuja ashtadasha netra he ma /5/

10. danuja svarajasane ramaniti kara he ma /6/ rakta padmasane basi ramaniti kara he ma /7/

habarupe achhe shiba padatale jar he ma /8/

11. kumkum pitavarna munimanohara he ma /9/ taruna aruna sama vahanaya para he ma /10/

bara-abhai akhachutra kara charikare he ma /11/

12. Vama could be translated as "woman" or "transgressive one."

13. muktakeśī mṛduhāśī madhura adhare he mā /12/ lollajihvā trinayanī ārādhya savāra he ma /13/

rabiśaśī karṇayuge lukaichhe vāmara he mā /14/ pañcama vadanī tumi pañcarūpa dhari he mā /15/

14. pancapretupare basi thaka ranga kari he ma /16/ kamakhya parameshvari parama prakriti he ma /17/

brahma vishnu shibe yara napai akriti he ma /18/ kamarupa kameshvari kamini kamada he ma /19/

15. See *Kalika Purana* 63.31, which instructs the devotee (*bhakta*). On its tantric *bhakti*, see *Kalika Purana* 58.1–4 in Van Kooij 2022, 37–38.

16. The *gayatri mantra* is a Vedic verse recited in various orthodox brahmanical practices such as the daily ritual at sunrise. The verse, considered by some to be the Vedas in condensed form, is traditionally transmitted from guru to student during the initiation to the student stage of life and therefore to formal study of the Vedas. The *gayatri* honors the Sun as a deity worthy of contemplation who inspires wisdom (Michaels 2004, 95–96). The *Kalika Purana*'s goddess-centered *gayatri mantra* replaces the Sun deity with Kameshvari (Van Kooij 2022, 212–13).

17. Rajrajeshvari sits on five ghosts according to the Sati-Mahavidya *Nam* (the stanza quoted above that begins with "Sati, appearing as Rajrajeshvari").

18. All translation of this *Nam* is by Jayashree Athparia and me, based on performances by Nani Devi (May 1, 2008) and Parvati Devi (August 16, 2009).

19. Parvati Devi accented the velar "k" on *krodha* (angry) and Kali, hitting the consonant hard, as it were, as she did also for a Kali Karalavadani *Nam* (see above). In doing so, I suggest she uses her voice to express intensification.

20. See Kinsley 1997. On the Mahavidyas at Kamakhya, see Dold 2004 and 2011.

21. The last phrase is "*rakha kara krishnachandra bhupe*" or *bhuje* (Nani Devi's version). *Chandra* was explained as an honorific and the line translated as saying that Krishnachandra effects protection with his hand or as king.

22. This arrangement is also used in *kavaca*s, protective talismans containing text, also the name of such texts, that invoke divine beings on the body of one who wears it, in the four cardinal and intermediate directions, above and below, that is, the ten directions.

References

Arrago-Boruah, Emilie. 2019. "Using Verbal Art to Deal with Conflicts: Women's Voices on Family and Kinship in Kāmākhyā (Assam)." *Religions* 10 (8): 455. https://doi.org/10.3390/rel10080455.

Deka, Pranav Jyoti. 2004. *Nilacala Kamakhya: Her History and Tantra.* Self-published.

Dold, Patricia. 2004. "The Mahavidyas at Kamarupa: Dynamics of Transformation in Hinduism." *Religious Studies and Theology* 23 (1): 89–122.

Dold, Patricia. 2005. "The Religious Vision of the Sakta *Mahabhagavata Purana*." PhD diss., McMaster University.

Dold, Patricia. 2011. "Pilgrimage to Kamakhya Through Text and Lived Religion: Some Forms of the Goddess at an Assamese Temple Site." In *Studying Hinduism in Practice*, edited by Hillary Peter Rodrigues, 46–61. Routledge.

Dold, Patricia. 2013. "Re-imagining Religious History Through Women's Song Performance at the Kamakhya Temple Site." In *Reimagining South Asian Religions: Essays in Honor of Professors Harold G. Coward and Ronald W. Neufeldt*, edited by Michael Hawley and Pashaura Singh, 133–54. Brill.

Flueckiger, Joyce Burkhalter. 2015. *Everyday Hinduism*. Wiley Blackwell.

Garigliano, Irene Majo. 2018. "The Dreadful Dance of the Goddess: Creativity and Mimesis in a Possession Cult of Assam." *Cracow Indological Studies* 20: 185–222. https://doi.org/10.12797/CIS.20.2018.01.08.

Goswami, M. C. 1960. "An Annual Shamanistic Dance (Deodha Nach) at Kamakhya, Assam." *Journal of the University of Guwahati (Science)* 11 (2): 37–58.

Kinsley, David R. 1997. *Tantric Visions of the Divine Feminine: The Ten Mahavidyas*. University of California Press.

Kumar, Puspendra. 1983. *The Mahabhagavata Purana: Ancient Treatise on Sakti Cult*. Eastern Book Linkers.

Maa Kamakhya Devalaya. 2023. "Introduction." Accessed July 18. https://www.maakamakhya.org/introduction.php#.

McDermott, Rachel Fell. 2001. *Mother of My Heart, Daughter of My Dreams: Kālī and Umā in the Devotional Poetry of Bengal*. Oxford University Press.

Michaels, Axel. 2004. *Hinduism: Past and Present*. Princeton University Press.

Rajan-Mishra, Nihar. 2004. *Kamakhya: A Socio-Cultural History*. D. K. Printworld.

Shastri, Haraprasad, ed. 1974. *Brhaddharma Puranam*. 2nd ed. Krishnadas Academy.

Urban, Hugh. 2010. *The Power of Tantra: Religion, Sexuality and the Politics of South Asian Studies*. I.B. Taurus.

Van Kooij, K. R. 2022. *Tantric Teachings of the Kalika Purana*. Brill.

11

Sanskritizing and Saffronizing the Rabies Goddess

Sweetening and Intensification in the
Folklore of Hadkai Mata

Darry Dinnell

The lithograph image of Hadkai Mata (see fig. 11.1) is a study in contrast.[1] At first glance, Hadkai resembles goddesses in the Sanskritic, pan-Indian mold such as Durga or Sarasvati, insofar as she is a benevolent-looking young woman with an animal mount. Hadkai's mount, however, is a dog, an animal considered impure according to mainstream brahmanic and Smarta sensibilities.[2] Given her canine mount and oppressed-class followers, nonworshipers frequently associate Hadkai with nonbrahmanic practices typical of other village *mata*s (mother goddesses), including alcohol oblations, possession-like states, and animal sacrifices. Still, the vehicle befits Hadkai Mata, as she is believed to cure dog bites, and her name literally means "rabies mother," as do her other epithets (most notably Hadaksha). Although I regularly saw this lithograph over the course of my fieldwork in Gujarat, devotees often rejected my requests to photograph Hadkai's image. The risk of misuse or misrepresentation, they suggested time and again, was too great. Worshipers in Ahmedabad's Shahpur district, for example, cited a case they had read about in the Gujarati newspaper *Sandesh* in which an outsider had photographed Hadkai and placed her image in a toilet. In this spirit, worshipers strenuously protect Hadkai, believing that she will inevitably be misunderstood by nonworshipers and foreigners.

Figure 11.1. Lithograph image of Hadkai Mata adorned for a festival in the town of Kodava, Gujarat, 2015. *Source:* Photo by the author.

Finding written materials about Hadkai proved equally difficult. While I heard rumors about Hadkai-related publications, my searches for books and pamphlets resembling those dedicated to other deities were fruitless. Hadkai devotees repeatedly told me that such publications did not exist. According to a high-ranking member of a Hadkai temple in Patan, the goddess is wary of anything written about her. If someone creates print material about Hadkai, he claimed, it will quickly disintegrate.

Given this paucity of texts and images, oral narratives become all the more crucial for understanding Hadkai Mata. A rich tradition of oral folklore narratives has developed among Hadkai worshipers, such as the Dalit Valmiki Samaj and especially the Devipujaks. Folklore is a realm in which members of these oppressed-class groups can safeguard the goddess while also defending themselves against stereotypes perpetuated by outsiders. While undertaking a broader ethnography of Gujarati *mata*s in 2015,[3] I visited inner-city communities in Ahmedabad and rural sites such as Angoli and Karadra in order to better understand Hadkai. From these sites, I gathered a number of Gujarati-language stories about Hadkai from her Devipujak and Valmiki officiants and devotees. These stories imagine the goddess as unquestionably pure, or *sattvik*, having originated from the efforts of Sanskritic goddesses and devout Brahmans.

Accordingly, I argue that Hadkai's vernacular folklore has served as a means of Sanskritizing and sweetening the goddess for the Dalits and Devipujaks who worship her, helping them attest to and perform their own *sattvik* nature and thereby challenging their exclusion from "proper" Hinduism. Jürgen Schaflechner has drawn on the notion of "proper" and "improper" Hindu behavior in his study of the Hinglaj Mata temple in Balochistan, Pakistan, a site frequented by many Gujarati Hindu pilgrims. Schaflechner observes that vegetarianism and prohibitions on animal sacrifice are essential to defining "proper Hinduism" for the upper-class Lohanas who run the Hinglaj temple's organizing committee (Schaflechner 2018, 301). I think this emphasis on vegetarianism generally applies to mainline upper-caste Hindu (and Jain) visions of propriety in Gujarat, as do teetotalism and suspicion of spirit possession. Altogether, this is a set of standards that such elites have typecast Hadkai and her devotees as not meeting.

More recently, however, these folkloric efforts to contest marginalization and to Hinduize Hadkai have taken on darker overtones. For example, from the Devipujak community in Shahpur, I uncovered narratives emerging after the 2002 Godhra train-fire riots in Gujarat that depict an intensified Hadkai who takes revenge against Muslims on communal lines. This suggests that, for some Devipujaks, membership in the mainstream Hindu fold may involve the adoption of "saffronized"[4] majoritarian values for themselves and their goddess.

Dogs, Death, Dalits, and Devipujaks

Before discussing Hadkai's folklore, it is first necessary to understand some prevailing stereotypes about the goddess and her worshipers. In popular perceptions among the Gujarati populace, Hadkai is anything but *sattvik*. Like other female divinities bearing the title "Mata," many of whom have undergone their own multilayered "sweetening" processes (Dinnell 2020), Hadkai is considered by relative elites such as caste Hindus and Jains to be a goddess of scheduled castes and Dalits. Moreover, she maintains connections with death, dogs, and disease, all of which are decidedly *tamasik* ("dark" or "impure") from a mainline, Smarta Hindu perspective.

Dogs carry negative associations in Sanskritic and vernacular traditions throughout India. In the Vedas, dogs connote mortality and impurity. Yama, the god of death, is flanked by two canines to which improperly offered dire sacrifices had to be thrown (White 1989, 286). Bhairava, Shiva's fierce manifestation, frequents funerary grounds and, like Hadkai, has a dog for his vehicle. In Gujarat, as in many other regional folk traditions of India, dogs are considered unclean, their touch capable of defiling a Brahman (Kirparam 1901, 377). Furthermore, people who died of rabies were believed to become unfriendly spirits (416). It was thought that dogs were a tell-tale form in which malevolent spirits manifested (Enthoven [1914] 1989, 132). Kal-Bhairava supposedly accepted live animal sacrifices, which were then given to dogs for consumption (70). Comparable beliefs live on today. Rajubhai,[5] for instance, a relatively well-to-do Devipujak banker based in Shahpur, told me that a special Bhairava is associated with the nighttime baying among dogs that portends a death in the family or other misfortunes.[6]

Like dogs, Hadkai bears connections with death. Devipujak funeral grounds are typically located behind Hadkai's shrines (Jadav n.d., 312). The funeral ground is also the setting of Divaso, a summer gathering in which Hadkai figures prominently. Joravarsinha Jadav, whose Gujarati-language book *Divya mandir mara devna re* contains some of the only published material I could find concerning Hadkai, describes the ceremony as follows: "On the day of *Divaso*, people of the Vaghri [a contemptuous name for Devipujaks] caste perform worship of Hadkai, then after having gone into the charnel grounds, weep with many loud cries in memory of their dead kin. This sight puts a tremble in anyone's heart" (312).[7]

Hadkai has long been associated with oppressed-class groups and impoverished areas. Based on fieldwork in the 1970s, David Pocock reports that "this *mātā* is in most cases located in the Untouchable quarter and her *bhuvo* [officiant] is also an Untouchable" (1973, 51). An enduring image in Gujarat is that of dogs roaming around Hadkai's shrines, hoping to eat *prasad* left by devotees (Jadav n.d., 312). Vegetarian temple offerings, however, were assumed to be insufficient for satiating dogs' appetites. Dogs inhabiting the Devipujak and Dalit sections were thought to be fiercer than those in other areas, their taste for meat sharpened by the discarded leftovers of people from marginalized castes presumed to be nonvegetarian (Pocock 1973, 51).

Foremost among Hadkai's followers are the Devipujaks, many of whom identify the goddess as their *kuldevi* (family goddess). Devipujaks are employed in a variety of professions, though they most often work as cultivators or vegetable vendors. Paul D'Souza has classified Devipujaks among Gujarat's "middle backward castes" (2002, 173), but most outsiders consider them tantamount to Dalits. Correspondingly, the Indian government recognizes Devipujaks as a scheduled tribe, and Harald Tambs-Lyche has characterized them as "arch-untouchables" (2004, 22). Devipujaks sometimes claim they were originally Rajputs who declined in social position (Kirparam 1901, 510). Questions of origins aside, a fact of Devipujak life is that poverty, crime, and alcoholism plague their rural and urban sectors (Sheth 2002, 52).

Hadkai worship is also common among members of the Valmiki Samaj.[8] Members of this Dalit group have been glossed as "sweepers," although they were sometimes tasked with cleaning latrines. Franco, Macwan, and Ramanathan (2004) describe the Valmikis' relationship to Hadkai as follows: "The worship of Hadakai Mata is . . . very suggestive of the work they do. Wandering from one place to another as they go about their jobs of cleaning, they are especially vulnerable to attacks from stray dogs and often get bitten. Going to a doctor every time is expensive; and often they do not have faith in the doctor; instead, they prefer to go to their Goddess in whom they have placed their faith" (270). These statements can be extended to Devipujaks. As a principal goddess of oppressed-class communities, then, Hadkai's domain has been established in the Gujarati popular imagination as one of dog-infested disorder and, with that, disease.

Hadkai is both a cause of and cure for rabies. This dual role is typical of disease-related deities in South Asia, as the goddesses Mariamman and Shitala have each been understood as both bringer and remover of smallpox in South India and North India, respectively. Members of the Patan temple told me that symptoms of rabies, such as aversion to water, food, and light, signify Hadkai has entered the human body. Originally, they explained, Hadkai did not have an idol, as she only appeared in the bodies of dogs and rabies patients.[9] Rajubhai, meanwhile, told me that rabies marked a punishment from Hadkai for transgressions such as failing to fulfill an oath. To be sure, these worshipers did not de-emphasize Hadkai's association with this misfortune. It is difficult to know how long Hadkai has served in her rabies-healing role, but Jadav has traced it back to "ancient eras when the quest for a vaccine in opposition to the disease of rabies had not yet begun" (Jadav n.d., 312). Her relation to rabies has persisted "even in the scientific age of today," in which "it is said that when a rabid dog bites, by touching on the foot of Hadkai Ma, the disease of rabies will thereafter be no more" (312). Based on what I observed at Hadkai temples, it appears that this curative technique has endured. At Patan, for instance, officiants tie a string on the wrist of the bite victim, who then keeps a vow of chastity for five weeks before returning to make *prasad*. Other Hadkai sites require offerings with oil lamps, sometimes involving rubbing oil on the wound or even drinking it, as is the case at the Kotha temple. Chastity and oil-drinking indicate that hardship plays a part in properly propitiating Hadkai. Hadkai's rabies-curing role has done little to soften her image for nonworshipers. The folk-healing process for rabies, as with other diseases, is mediated by ritual officiants known as *bhuva*s, who enter into possession-like states called *pavan* to communicate with deities. Many caste Hindus and other elites look askance at *bhuva*s, and Hadkai's *bhuva*s are no exception, as their *pavan* sometimes takes on a ferocious, unrestrained character resembling the symptomatology of rabies.

Jadav documents this sentiment: "If this *avatara* of the *mata* comes in the body of a *bhuva*, then rabies swells up in the *bhuva*" (n.d., 313). Jadav then provides an evocative depiction of a procession of the goddess's platform, or *mandva*, describing a host of marginalized worship styles:

> Then and there, becoming unconscious, the *bhuva* falls on the ground and lies down. His tongue juts out and saliva starts to drop incessantly from his mouth. . . . If the Hadkai *bhuva* cannot be revived by way of a waving feather, and the pacification of the Mata has not commenced, then a girl of sixteen years, holding a sword in her hand, makes a wound on her own body and sprinkles her own blood on the *bhuva*. In this very same manner, the *bhuva* of Shaktmata also makes a wound on his own limb with a sword and sprinkles his own blood on the [Hadkai] *bhuva*. Doing as such, both people make an offering of their own body to the Mata. But if the Mata is still not pacified by these two enjoyments, then, in the end, the *bhuva* of Hadkai Mata also offers a sacrifice of his own self. Five-hundred years previous in Patan, this enjoyment was taken; afterwards, the *mandva* of this Mata was seen to occur only rarely. (Jadav n.d., 313–14)

Jadav's account suggests that Hadkai ceremonies sometimes culminated in bloodletting to mark the end of the goddess's visitation. Such rituals would be highly out of character for a *sattvik* goddess. Jadav's sources are unclear, and the historicity of his account remains up for debate. Apart from *pavan*, I saw no evidence of these sorts of intensive worship styles directly relating to Hadkai in the present day. Nevertheless, the appearance of these ideas in print verifies that, to some extent, Hadkai's supposedly *tamasik* trajectories circulate in public discourse. Accounts such as Jadav's likely arise from and inform the dismissive and derisive attitudes nonworshipers hold toward Hadkai.

Nonworshipers are also skeptical of Hadkai's influence as it relates to biomedicine and healing. Speaking with social workers employed at a women's outreach center in Ahmedabad in March 2015, I heard several stories from the field wherein Hadkai was referenced with no small degree of notoriety. One story involved a family that sought out the goddess instead of going to a hospital after their one year old suffered a dog bite. The family hailed from a relatively prosperous Devipujak community on the outskirts of Ahmedabad, and it was widely agreed that they could afford medical care. As a result of their decision, the child narrowly escaped pneumonia. A more serious story involved a two-year-old dog-bite victim in Surendranagar. When a *bhuva* consulted Hadkai, the goddess advised against medical care, and the child eventually died. Although these stories may simply be urban legends, of sorts, they compel listeners to contemplate the tension between biomedicine and traditional healing that Hadkai embodies. They also catalog the risks that worshipers may sometimes take, even in the face of medical advancement, globalization, and some increasing affluence. Certainly, the well-heeled family in the first story, whether real or legendary, exemplifies this clash between some strains of modernity and tradition. As they are retold by social workers, these stories index nonworshipers' discomfort with the ostensibly backward-looking lifestyle that Hadkai epitomizes.

Her animal mount, environs, followers, and the nature of the disease she causes and cures have all marked Hadkai as a precarious goddess. This has led many nonworshipers to categorize Hadkai among the nonelite *mata*s whose ritual repertoires incorporate nonbrahmanic, *tamasik* practices such as animal sacrifice, liquor oblations, and possession-like states. Indeed, sociologist A.M. Shah lumps Hadkai in with Khodiyar and Shikotar as *mata*s who "were propitiated with non-vegetarian offerings" (2006, 115).[10] These conclusions seem to be based on little more than extrapolations from her worshipers' diets, as well as their endemic difficulties with alcoholism. Moving beyond religious and dietary considerations, social workers view Hadkai as an affront to modern medicine. But Hadkai's worshipers see something quite different, as is evident in the narratives I gathered during my fieldwork among Devipujaks and Valmiki communities in and around Ahmedabad in 2015. Worshipers deny that Hadkai ever took sacrifices or requested liquor oblations. Furthermore, they remain adamant that their goddess is unimpeachably pure and even brahmanic, and this purity marks a pivotal trope in Hadkai's folklore.

The *Sattvik* Hadkai Mata of Folklore

Hadkai's purity comes through strongly in her folkloric narratives. While these stories detail the goddess's associations with rabies and marginalized groups, they are also notable for including Brahmans in critical roles and recurrently affirming Hadkai's *sattvik* nature.

Hadkai's origin stories speak to her timeless purity. In November 2015, I heard one version of Hadkai's inception in an interview with Dasharath Madi, a member of a scheduled caste of weavers and a *pujari* at a Meladi Mata temple in Ahmedabad's Behrampur district. The story goes as follows:

> After the *deva*s (gods) prevailed over the *asura*s (demons) in battle, a big feast was thrown by the goddess Amba. Before the feast, Amba went for a bath in a pond, and took her time doing so. As she waited, Khodiyar Mata became hungry and consumed the plate of food set out for Amba. When Amba finally arrived, she saw there was no food left for her. When Amba demanded the food that was her due, Khodiyar informed her that it was lying in the corner under a fabric cover. Amba overturned the cloth to find only red rose petals. Seeing this, Amba was overcome by anger, another word for which is "Hadakva." She was incensed by the red-colored offering. Khodiyar felt guilty and depressed, and her *svarupa* (form) became Hadaksha. Because blood is red, there is no sacrifice to Hadkai.[11]

Amba is a Gujarati variation of the Sanskritic, pan-Indian goddess Durga who enjoys widespread popularity throughout the state. Amba aligns with brahmanic sensibilities, and this narrative underscores her purity by way of her protracted bath. The blood-colored rose petals, reminiscent of animal sacrifice, prove offensive to Amba. Her subsequent wrath transforms the *tamasik* Khodiyar into a new and purified goddess. Hadkai, then, was born from the righteous anger of a *sattvik* goddess. The subsequent spurning of blood, redolent of the offending rose petals, further emphasizes Hadkai's commitment to upholding this purity by distancing her from *tamasik* sacrifices.

This origin story has a second chapter, involving Hadkai's initial worshipers:

> Khodiyar transferred rabies to a hyena and then rode the animal as her new mount. The hyena became a dog. Hadaksha went at

high speed, first getting down at Kodava, and after that she left a bracelet at Karadra [two Hadkai pilgrimage sites]. The goddess went further into the forest. Here there were trees bearing *mahua* fruits, from which wine is made, and the dog began biting at these. This caused the trees to dry up. Mukhi, the Brahman who owned the forest, decided that the trees should be cut down. When a carpenter cut the trees, milk came out of their trunks. The carpenter tasted the milk and got rabies.

The goddess wanted to come out of the jungle to get exposure, so she introduced herself to a young boy on his way to school and taught him thirty-six *vidya*s (sciences). Normally, the brightest students only know thirty-two *vidya*s. The boy was Udansinh, Mukhi's son. When Udansinh miraculously calculated the numerical date of the universe, his guru was astonished and told Mukhi about it. The goddess then asked Mukhi to boil oil and make *tilak* (a devotional mark), sprinkling *sindura* (lead oxide) powder on the trees to remove the rabies. She made him promise that her *svarupa* would be worshiped by Brahmans as a *kuldevi*. Also, she demanded white garlanding, flowers, sweets, and rice as proof she is pure and brahmanic. Early the next morning, Udansinh sprinkled the powder on the trees, and they all flourished with green leaves. Hadaksha became a goddess worshiped by Brahmans, and people started going to Udansinh to solve rabies-related problems.

This section of the narrative brims with motifs of sweetening and softening. Hadkai's original mount is a hyena, an animal considered in Gujarati folklore to be among the most rabid species of canine. The hyena changes into a dog for an unspecified reason, perhaps suggesting domestication. After stopping at two prominent present-day Hadkai sites, effectively reinforcing contemporary pilgrimage routes, the goddess reaches the forest. Here, her canine mount (or the goddess herself, in some versions[12]) begins biting the trees, transmitting the hydrophobic aspect of the affliction to the foliage. While Hadkai transmits rabies to the trees, she also changes the trees' output from *tamasik* wine into the comparatively purer milk. And while Hadkai spreads rabies, she also removes it. In the process of doing so, she meets her first devotees, who happen to be, quite significantly, Brahmans. With the promise of *sattvik*, brahmanic worship in place, encoded in the all-white offerings, Hadkai restores the vitality of the forest. From then on, she is chiefly worshiped by Brahmans, at least in this primordial, folkloric space.

These themes and motifs are expanded in another story early on in Hadkai's timeline, namely her introduction to oppressed-class groups. I heard the following tale in November 2015 from Mohan Bhuvaji, an Ahmedabad-based member of the Valmiki Samaj and a *bhuva* with *pavan* of Visat Mata. The story picks up just after Hadkai's emergence:

> There were two men called Ramo and Parabo, who hailed from the Devipujak community [in other versions, they are Dalits[13]]. They were skilled thieves who knew where people hid their ornaments. Like other Devipujaks from Patan, they were famous for breaking through thick walls.
>
> Ramo and Parabo were caught by a king and sentenced to be executed in a week's time. Every morning during their imprisonment, they awoke to the sound of *bhajan*s sung by Udansinh. Ramo and Parabo prayed and made a wish for any god to save them. Hadkai honored their request on the condition that they had to give her more priority than their own *kuldevi*. Meanwhile, the king had a dream during prayer time. In it, Hadkai gave the message that Ramo and Parabo were innocent, and that the real treasure of the king's family was buried in a garbage dump. The king searched the dump and found the treasure. On that account, Ramo and Parabo were promptly released.
>
> At this point, Ramo and Parabo tried to find out the name of the goddess who had helped them. They saw that Udansinh was able to withdraw rabies from animals with the goddess's power. They decided to take this goddess back to their home. Meanwhile, the goddess appeared in Udansinh's dreams, giving notice that two Devipujaks would be coming around in the morning to make a demand for her. "Don't let me go to them," the goddess pleaded, "because Vaghris are nonvegetarian and consume liquor." And so Udansinh told Ramo and Parabo, "I will not give my goddess to you because she is brahmanic."
>
> To protest, Ramo and Parabo decided to fast unto death without water or food. They fasted for forty days, getting weak and creating sympathy in Udansinh. Udansinh figured that if he gave the goddess to them and gave her *sindura* powder as compensation, there would be no harm. Around 4 a.m. one morning,

at the time of prayer, Udansinh assumed no one would see him giving the goddess to the two thieves. The goddess appeared and cursed Udansinh and all other Brahmans. "You cannot keep your pure, *sattvik* goddess," Hadkai said. "From today, you will have to beg." Since then, Brahmans have begged for alms. The goddess, meanwhile, was transferred to the Devipujaks.

This narrative conveys ambivalent messages. While it reduces Brahmans to beggars, it also treats Devipujaks (and Dalits) unsparingly, speaking to a self-deprecating streak that I sometimes detected among Hadkai devotees. Thievery, alcoholism, and meat eating among Hadkai worshipers are all out in the open in this tale. Due to their *tamasik* practices, the goddess herself does not want to be worshiped by Devipujaks and Dalits, asking instead for Brahman protection. Via their fast, Ramo and Parabo cultivate some asceticism, and this makes an impression upon the Brahman Udansinh, if not on the goddess herself. The Brahman capitulates and gives up the goddess. As punishment, his entire caste is barred from worshiping Hadkai, despite the close ties Brahmans had with her (even acknowledging her as their *kuldevi*, as per the previous narrative). Although it points out apparent shortcomings among Hadkai's faithful, this tale sees the oppressed-class worshipers ending up with the pure, vegetarian goddess. Ambivalent elements aside, the message is clear: Hadkai is a purely *sattvik* deity who was intended for Brahmans but fell into the hands of Devipujaks and Dalits through Brahman error.

Localized stories also champion Hadkai's *sattvik*, brahmanic facets, and some extend these qualities to her followers. Angoli, a village near Dholka, houses a small temple that stands as a pilgrimage destination for Hadkai devotees today. In May 2015, a man named Jilu, son of the temple's *bhuva*, told me the following origin story of Angoli's Devipujak community: "A lady named Kalari Doshi Mata married a man named Ramji Dada. At the age of eighty, she miraculously had a baby. All followers of Hadaksha Ma trace their lineage from her. Kalari Doshi Mata was a Brahman, her husband a Vaghri. With the blessing of Hadkai, this Brahman lady got pregnant and had many children. As such, Vaghris in Angoli have more of a Brahman influence." Regardless of their mismatched caste backgrounds, Ramji Dada and Kalari married and had children well outside of Kalari's fertile years. Given the significance of this town in Hadkai's pilgrimage circuit, I got the impression that the half-brahmanic foundation of the goddess's followers at Angoli attested to the purity of Hadkai worshipers as a whole. Jilu's story confirmed as much in reporting that it was not only residents of Angoli but *all* Hadkai worshipers who trace their lineage from Kalari. This suggests that some Hadkai devotees see themselves as bonded by a bloodline that is partially brahmanic, the attendant purity living on within them, at least in the context of worshiping Hadkai. In this imagining, Hadkai is sufficiently sweet and *sattvik* to imbue her followers with brahmanic qualities.

Other folktales involving Angoli assert that the goddess actively works against *tamasik* religion. Another leading lady of Angoli lore is Kankuba, an exemplary Hadkai devotee, and Rajubhai shared the following story about her in April 2015:

> Kankuba came from Angoli. She was married to a Thakkor at Kotha [another Hadkai pilgrimage site] and took Hadaksha Ma there. Jhapad Dada, a Dalit in Angoli, had *tamas* power and supported Hadaksha Ma. He was fond of eating the hearts of goats and chickens. He also liked alcohol and was powerful in mantra and tantra. All in all, he was a black *tantrika*. Kankuba, meanwhile, was getting *pavan*. Kankuba went from her husband's home in Kotha to her home in Angoli and did *tapas* [ascetic practices] to Hadaksha by fasting for one week. She managed to dislodge Jhapad from her hometown. Jhapad got quiet and stopped with his black Tantrism.

Once again, a folk narrative affirms that Hadkai will not stand for nonvegetarian rites and alcohol consumption in her name. Working through Kankuba, the goddess manages to purge these practices by combining Sanskritic and village means—that is, *tapas* and *pavan*, respectively. The *sattvik* practices defended by Kankuba and Hadkai have had a lasting influence upon the Angoli temple. While animal sacrifice does happen at this site, Jilu told me that it is only performed in the temple's entrance area. Moreover, it is only offered to the subsidiary Kali and Meladi shrines. While these sacrifices are happening, the shrine to Hadkai is curtained off. This is a custom that has, by Jilu's estimation, "always been." Unlike other *matas* who crave live offerings, Hadkai will not even bear witness to *tamasik* rites.

This persistent motif of characterizing Hadkai as having been "*sattvik*" or "brahmanic" from the beginning is likely a strategy for Sanskritization, to borrow a term from M. N. Srinivas (2002), but it may also be something more. Hadkai worship has not been exclusively undertaken by marginalized groups, and a multigoddess temple at Karadra provides evidence to this effect. This site is presently operated by a Brahman man, Mr. Vaidiki (a pseudonym), and its main temple situates Hadkai in close proximity to several Sanskritic goddesses, including Lalita and Gauri. Mr. Vaidiki treats Hadkai as interchangeable with these goddesses, and he gave no indication of harboring concerns around purity. The site's origin story, which Mr. Vaidiki shared with me in November 2015, would appear to allay any pollution worries. This story, though it does not expressly involve Hadkai, still roots her eventual site in a Sanskritic past:

> The temple plot can be traced back to an ancient *rishi* by the name of Rikhab Muni [from the Sanskrit Rishabha]. Rikhab Muni was a Brahman, and he had a good number of followers. Rikhab meditated at this place and saw the goddess Balatripurasundari in a dream.
>
> The ruler of Gujarat in the twelfth century was Jayasimha Siddharaj [the Chaulukya king who reigned from 1092 to 1142 CE]. His queen wanted to offer *puja* at a banyan tree here with various white powders. As she went along, a dove landed on one of the containers of ingredients and the plate fell down and got dirty. There was a small *havan* pit under the banyan tree. A Brahman with cosmic power sacrificed the dove into the *havan* fire. This was criticized, and the king became unhappy. The Brahman said, "Don't worry," and by chanting mantras and *shloka*s, he gave new life to the dove and it flew away.

The Karadra Hadkai site, then, can be traced back to a powerful Brahman seer and a Sanskritic goddess, namely Balatripurasundari, a mainstay in the *Shri-Vidya* tradition. The goings-on at the site were not always *sattvik*, however. This origin story involves, after all, the corruption of the white (and therefore *sattvik*-coded) powder by the white bird that becomes the victim of sacrifice (which is *tamasik*) performed by a Brahman, who defies his coding as a force of purity. This development may tacitly address ambiguities brought about by the later presence of Hadkai and her oppressed-class devotees at the site. In any event, the Brahman's sacrifice is condemned, but then it is essentially reversed by the Brahman's own efforts, intimating that he alone possesses the ritual apparatuses required to cancel his earlier *tamasik* offering. While the story speaks to a juxtaposition of *tamasik* and *sattvik* ritual at the site, the dove's revivification conveys the triumph of the latter from early on. Again, the brahmanic and the *sattvik* prevail at a Hadkai site, and the rabies mother maintains her position alongside the

Sanskritic goddesses in the temple. Indeed, Mr. Vaidiki reported that temple visitors regularly seek treatment for dog bites.

Beyond establishing pilgrimage sites and rabies associations, the aforementioned stories seem eager to demonstrate Hadkai's unequivocal purity. While Hadkai is pure enough for a Brahman, she is a goddess of Dalits and Devipujaks, drawing attention to the conflicting but not irreconcilable values of elite and nonelite groups. Through Hadkai's folklore, then, marginalized groups push back against the idea that they are "impure." To the contrary, they may even be partly Brahman. As such, Hadkai helps to articulate the possibility of *sattvik* and brahmanic values among her worshipers. Several Hadkai devotees I met have taken up vegetarianism and teetotalism, as was the case for the banker Rajubhai, who had overcome his own struggles with alcoholism. These sorts of adaptations may also advocate for Devipujaks' participation and inclusion in mainstream, "proper" Hinduism. That said, many worshipers, particularly Devipujaks, *do* drink alcohol, consume nonvegetarian food, and perform animal sacrifices to goddesses. Nonetheless, the Devipujaks I met were unanimously adamant that they do none of these things in relation to Hadkai. This goal of aspiring to higher-caste or Smarta sensibilities in whole or in part, however, may have come with some darker consequences, as majoritarian political values have also started to register in the stories told about Hadkai.

Saffronizing Hadkai in Shahpur

The Devipujak section in Ahmedabad's Shahpur district houses dozens of tiny shrines to Hadkai. The risk of dog bites seems particularly imminent in Shahpur, as strays canter through the alleyways at all hours. Many Shahpur Devipujaks live in poverty, subsisting as dealers of rugs, kites, firecrackers, and mangoes. Shahpur has long been a bootlegging hub and, despite Gujarat's "dry state" status, illicit alcohol figures conspicuously in public events here. Shahpur Devipujaks are not unacquainted with forms of religious expression outside the scope of "proper" Hinduism, most notably animal sacrifice.[14] That said, I met several upwardly mobile Devipujaks in Shahpur who were trying to break through these stereotypes of poverty, addiction, and *tamasik* religion. This was reflected in the stories they told about Hadkai, which linked the goddess and Devipujaks not just to the values of upper-caste Hinduism but also with Hindu majoritarian politics.

In April 2015, I met with Yogeshwar and Sundeep, a close-knit pair of Devipujak men in their early twenties. Both were well known in Shahpur by virtue of their involvement with a local gym. They each had bachelor's degrees in accounting, and both were studying law at Gujarat University. They declared Hadkai to be the universal *kuldevi* of Devipujaks, outranking their families' *kuldevi*s in importance. Were they ever to suffer a dog bite, they assured me that they would visit a Hadkai site, preferably the temple at Kotha or the nearby shrine at Delhi Darwaj. Their faith in these healing techniques marks a continued assertion of historical beliefs in which Hadkai worshipers generally take pride. Yogeshwar and Sundeep insisted that Hadkai was more than a rabies goddess, though. Consonant with their legal ambitions, they described Hadkai as a "constitutional deity" (*bhandaran*). Many worshipers I interviewed in Shahpur and elsewhere labeled Hadkai as a "goddess of justice," but this came through most intensely in Yogeshwar and Sundeep's stories.

Their representative narrative was set against the backdrop of the communal strife of 2002. In February and March of that year, riots took place throughout Gujarat in the aftermath of a fatal train fire in Godhra. This incident is widely believed by many among the Hindu majority to have been incited by Muslims against passengers who were devotees of Rama, despite a lack of substantive evidence (Jaffrelot 2021, 476). Yogeshwar and Sundeep narrated as follows:

> During the big communal riot, Shahpur was a key site. Thirty to forty Devipujak communities in the area were forced to vacate, leaving behind houses with small shrines to Hadkai. These were considered strongholds of the goddess's power. The Muslims burnt the houses of Devipujaks. Muslims moved into some of the houses. One by one there was a downfall of the Muslim community because the *tamas* power of the goddess presented itself in their dreams. Political and religious leaders came to this community and requested that the goddess be called off. The Muslims apologized and compensated the Devipujak families. They paid for expensive ceremonies to cool down the three *tamas* goddesses [Hadkai along with, presumably, Kali and Meladi]. Within the surrounding area, Muslims do not damage the shrines. Those Devipujaks who forcibly migrated are now quite wealthy.

Yogeshwar and Sundeep told me additional stories of alleged Muslim recklessness around Hadkai sites, all of which ended in similar punishments. By casting Muslims as the antagonistic and monolithic "other," this kind of story puts Devipujaks on the side of good—that is, as part of the monolithic

"Hindus." Communal lines, then, are rather sharply drawn. The story above contains a rare acknowledgment of Hadkai's *tamasik* potentialities and her connection with less *sattvik* goddesses, but these means apparently justify the end in service of vengeance against the Muslim other.[15] All involved Muslims feel the goddess's wrath, as Hadkai upholds a politically conservative agenda, ruling in favor of Hindus/Devipujaks. This leads to a neat and tidy ending in which all the Muslims apologize, acknowledging the existence and efficacy of the goddess, even going so far as to sponsor rituals in her honor. This newfound Muslim respect for Hadkai persists up to the present day, or so the story goes.

The displaced Devipujaks, meanwhile, are rewarded financially, but at the end of the story, they gain more than just material prosperity. More broadly, the goddess's forceful course of action offers Devipujaks membership in the Hindu majority. With that, they appear to inherit the communalist politics that were gaining momentum under Chief Minister Narendra Modi in 2002, with the post-Godhra riots marking a climactic node on the "saffron wave" of Hindu nationalism in Gujarat and India at large.[16] These majoritarian values protecting "Hindu-ness," or Hindutva, became hallmarks of mainstream Hindu identity for many conservatives supporting the Modi-led Bharatiya Janata Party at the state and national levels. These values may also mark a crucial indicator of Hindu identity for Shahpur Devipujaks.

The above narrative was told to me as a true story based on recent memory, but I submit that it is also a type of folklore, encoding values of the Shahpur Devipujak community. Given that Yogeshwar and Sundeep were children when the 2002 riots took place, they no doubt originally heard the narrative as it was being shaped by adults, and the story has subsequently gained verity through its retellings. Through Yogeshwar and Sundeep, this story lives on like a newly fashioned folktale unto itself, one that pictures Devipujaks quite apart from "arch-untouchables," but rather as members of the mainstream Hindu fold, united in an ongoing struggle against a common enemy. Some degree of Hindutva sympathy, at least in this story, seems to be part of "proper" Hindu-ness. Hadkai's folklore, then, not only sweetens, Sanskritizes, and "brahmanizes" Hadkai, but it also provides opportunities to intensify her along political lines, effectively "saffronizing" her as well.

Conclusion

In Gujarat, Hadkai's devotees have consistently faced negative stereotypes placing them in diametric opposition to mainstream sensibilities that I have heretofore glossed as *sattvik*, Sanskritic, brahmanic, and Smarta. Moreover, because of Hadkai's association with rabies, some nonworshipers see her as a countervailing force against biomedical advancements, and narratives circulate cataloging the hazards of the traditional healing she embodies.

The folklore of Hadkai's faithful puts forward a much different vision of the goddess. Worshipers' narratives abound with attestations to Hadkai's unassailable purity. One prominent origin story contends that she was initially a goddess of Brahmans, while other narratives identify some or all of her followers as (at least) partially Brahman. While Hadkai's folklore sometimes concedes the occurrence of "impure" practices among her Dalit and Devipujak worshipers, it also doggedly advocates for the fundamental purity of a goddess who distinctively belongs to these groups. This follows patterns of sweetening or softening seen among other goddesses in Gujarat and beyond, including Sanskritization. But Hadkai's folklore is unique in that it reiterates a *sattvik*, Sanskritic, and even brahmanic character *that always was*. This counteracts the notoriety around Hadkai and her faithful, and it also sets a *sattvik* precedent for these groups. Along these lines, Hadkai's shrines demarcate spaces in which Devipujaks, Valmikis, and other marginalized groups can cultivate sensibilities corresponding with those of the perceived elites of mainstream, Smarta-styled Hinduism, and this may even help her devotees self-assert as "proper" Hindus. Whether we describe them as brahmanized, Sanskritized, or "Hinduized," these sensibilities are on display at many Hadkai sites. At the shrines near V.S. Hospital and Delhi Darwaj in Ahmedabad, for example, I saw signs barring entry for menstruating women. So while Hadkai's folklore protests some of the discrimination by caste Hindus and other elites against her followers, it also promotes elite values as well. This may explain why some of the most stringent (and gynophobic) of these values are conspicuous at present-day Hadkai shrines.

The efforts to emphasize Hadkai's purity have not, however, led to the downplaying of her function as a rabies goddess in her folk narratives or in practice. While some have argued that disease-related goddesses such as Shitala and Mariamman adopt a more generalized health-related role in the face of biomedical modernity and its vaccinations for diseases like smallpox (Nicholas 1981, 40; Trawick-Egnor 1984, 40), Hadkai injects some doubt into this scholarly narrative. Hadkai has not, after all, undergone a "gentrification" akin to that of Mariamman, in which the goddess changes to reflect the growing affluence of her followers (Waghorne 2004). Rather, the impoverished status of many residents of places like Shahpur means that undertaking postexposure prophylaxis after suffering a dog bite is simply too expensive. For many, Hadkai represents the most readily accessible rabies treatment, and so she remains both cure and cause.

Meanwhile, Hadkai's narratives have in some cases emphasized her fierceness, and this intensification has in part been animated by majoritarian political values. This is evident in the narratives I heard in which the goddess metes out justice based on sharp communal divisions that resonate with pro-Hindu or Hindutva ideologies. This strain of communalism may have afforded Hadkai's devotees, or at minimum the Devipujaks of Shahpur, some degree of participation on the side of the right-wing milieu, itself an increasingly important component of mainline, "proper" Hinduism. This parallels cases in which right-wing forces have reinvented oppressed-class deities in order to bring their worshipers into the Hindu fold. Examples include Salhes, a folk hero of the Dusadhs of Bihar, and Shabari, a female devotee popular among Adivasis in the Dangs region of Gujarat, who were elevated into a Hindu god and goddess, respectively, due to Sangh Parivar efforts (Narayan 2009; Kanungo and Joshi 2009). The case in Shahpur is noteworthy, however, in that the Hinduization appears to be driven from within the community, at least in the context of the Hadkai narrative. Intensifying Hadkai via Islamophobic, Hindutva-styled principles seems to provide some Shahpur Devipujaks with further grounds for self-assertion as Hindus. As these sorts of narratives gain momentum, Hadkai's folklore saffronizes as it Sanskritizes, as both processes may represent avenues of upward mobility for her oppressed-class followers. Hadkai's intensification, then, runs in parallel with her sweetening to serve the same end of making the goddess and her worshipers more amenable for inclusion in mainstream Hinduism.

All told, Hadkai's folklore aptly reflects the mix of *tamasik* and *sattvik*, elite and nonelite, and lower caste and upper caste found in the goddess's iconography and at her worship sites. Indeed, Hadkai is not without upper-caste followers. In May 2015, for instance, I saw a Brahman man hop down from his motorbike to salute the goddess at Delhi Darwaj. Meanwhile, inside the shrine itself, stray dogs lounged in the shadow of the sign barring menstruating women and the intoxicated. These dogs wore the *tilak*, having received *darshan* from the goddess. And at Karadra's patently Sanskritic temple, one particularly esteemed stray was allowed access to the main shrine, barking along at the side of a Brahman, Mr. Vaidiki, during *puja*. Such contrast is commonplace at Hadkai sites, and it is the reconciliation of these apparent incongruities that drives the stories her worshipers tell.

Notes

1. This research was funded by the Social Sciences and Humanities Research Council of Canada (SSHRC).

2. I use "Smarta" here to refer to an upper-caste, Vedanta-inflected, non-sectarian vision of Hinduism that informs mainline notions of Hindu orthodoxy in India and abroad.

3. For my research on Jogani Mata, see Dinnell (2017). For a dissertation on Gujarati *mata*s in general, see Dinnell (2020).

4. "Saffronization" promotes Hindu-centric spirituality and historiography at the expense of other traditions, all in service of a right-wing nationalist political agenda. For a discussion of saffronization and the values undergirding it, see Frykenberg (2008, 205–6).

5. Names of conversationalists provided here are real unless otherwise stated.

6. This resonates with a folk belief that "the barking and howling of a dog with its face turned downwards or towards a man's house foretell the death of one of the occupants" (Kirparam 1901, 377).

7. All translations from Jadav are my own.

8. To better understand the complicated history of the "Valmiki" classification, see Lee (2021).

9. These accounts from Patan parallel descriptions of Mariamman in which symptoms such as pustules mark the manifestation of the goddess through the human body (Srinivasan 2019).

10. Shah promptly qualifies this statement: "However, mythology described them as forms of some great deity or other of Hinduism, and over a period of time non-vegetarian offerings were replaced by vegetarian ones" (2006, 115). While I agree that such a shift occurred for Khodiyar (and likely Shikotar), among other *mata*s, I see little evidence that a movement toward vegetarianism took place for Hadkai; rather, she appears to have been vegetarian all along. The *Gazetteer of the Bombay Presidency* does not count Hadkai among "goddesses to whom blood offerings are made" in Gujarat, a long list that includes Khodiyar, Shikotar, and Meladi (Kirparam 1901, 406). This supports devotees' present-day claims that Hadkai never took sacrifices. In recent times, Fernando Franco, Jyotsna Macwan, and Saguna Ramanathan have observed likewise: "Hadakai is called a pure Goddess because only rice and ghee are offered to her" (2004, 270).

11. I am grateful to Vimal Shukla for helping me render this narrative and those that follow in English.

12. This was the case in the version recounted to me in June 2015 by Mohan Bhuvaji, whom we will soon meet.

13. This was the case in a telling I heard from a Devipujak Hadkai *bhuva* based in Mahemdavad in November 2015.

14. Visiting Shahpur in April 2015, I saw five goat heads lined up inside a Kali shrine. I was told that the goats had been sacrificed the previous day. There is little evidence, however, that Hadkai receives sacrifices at Shahpur or anywhere else, which accords with the lack of evidence in colonial records that Hadkai took sacrifices.

15. Despite Hadkai's vengefulness, Yogeshwar and Sundeep followed other Shahpur residents in asserting that Hadkai never takes blood sacrifices.

16. For more on the "saffron wave," see Hansen (1999).

References

D'Souza, Paul. 2002. "Dalit Identity in Gujarat." In *Pain and Awakening: The Dynamics of Dalit Identity in Bihar, Gujarat, and Uttar Pradesh*, edited by Fernando Franco, 156–261. Indian Social Institute.

Dinnell, Darry. 2017. "Can Tantra Make a Mata Middle-Class? Jogani Mata, a Uniquely Gujarati Chinnamasta." *Religions* 8 (8): 142. https://doi.org/10.3390/rel8080142.

Dinnell, Darry. 2020. "Upwardly Mobile Matas: The Transformation of Village Goddesses in Gujarat, India." PhD diss., McGill University.

Enthoven, R. E. (1914) 1989. *Folk Lore Notes, Volume 1: Folklore of Gujarat*. Asian Educational Services.

Franco, Fernando, Jyotsna Macwan, and Saguna Ramanathan. 2004. *Journeys to Freedom: Dalit Narratives*. Samya.

Frykenberg, Robert. 2008. "Hindutva as a Political Religion: An Historical Perspective." In *The Sacred in Twentieth-Century Politics: Essays in Honour of Professor Stanley G. Payne*, edited by Robert Mallett, John Tortorice, and Roger Griffin, 178–220. Palgrave Macmillan.

Hansen, Thomas Blom. 1999. *The Saffron Wave: Democracy and Hindu Nationalism in Modern India*. Princeton University Press.

Jadav, Joravarsinha. N.d. *Divya mandir mara devna re (Gujaratna lokdevo)*. Pravit Pustak Bhandar.

Jaffrelot, Christophe. 2021. *Modi's India: Hindu Nationalism and the Rise of Ethnic Democracy*. Princeton University Press.

Kanungo, Pralay, and Satyakam Joshi. 2009. "Carving Out a White Marble Deity from a Rugged Black Stone? Hindutva Rehabilitates Ramayan's Shabari in a Temple." *International Journal of Hindu Studies* 13 (3): 279–99.

Kirparam, Bhimbai, compiler. 1901. *Gazetteer of the Bombay Presidency. Vol. IX, Pt. 1. Gujarat Population, Hindus*, edited by James McNabb Campbell. Government Central Press.

Lee, Joel. 2021. *Deceptive Majority: Dalits, Hinduism, and Underground Religion*. Cambridge University Press.

Narayan, Badri. 2009. *Fascinating Hindutva: Saffron Politics and Dalit Mobilization.* SAGE.

Nicholas, Ralph W. 1981. "The Goddess Sitala and Epidemic Smallpox in Bengal." *Journal of Asian Studies* 41 (1): 21–44.

Pocock, David. 1973. *Mind, Body, and Wealth: A Study of Belief and Practice in an Indian Village.* Basil Blackwell.

Schaflechner, Jürgen. 2018. *Hinglaj Devi: Identity, Change, and Solidification at a Hindu Temple in Pakistan.* Oxford University Press.

Shah, A. M. 2006. "Some Further Thoughts on Sanskritization: Response to Nirmal Singh's Rejoinder." *Sociological Bulletin* 55 (1): 112–17.

Sheth, N. R. 2002. "A Spiritual Approach to Social Transformation." In *The Other Gujarat*, edited by Takashi Shinoda, 38–65. Popular Prakashan.

Srinivas, M. N. 2002. *Collected Essays.* Oxford University Press.

Srinivasan, Perundevi. 2019. "Sprouts of the Body, Sprouts of the Field: Identification of the Goddess with Poxes in South India." *Religions* 10 (3): 147. https://doi.org/10.3390/rel10030147.

Tambs-Lyche, Harald. 2004. *The Good Country: Individual, Situation, and Society in Saurashtra.* Manohar.

Trawick-Egnor, Margaret. 1984. "The Changed Mother or What the Smallpox Goddess Did When There Was No More Smallpox." *Contributions to Asian Studies* 18: 24–45.

Waghorne, Joanne Punzo. 2004. *Diaspora of the Gods: Modern Hindu Temples in an Urban Middle-Class World.* Oxford University Press.

White, David Gordon. 1989. "Dogs Die." *History of Religions* 28 (4): 283–303.

12

Sensational Poetics

The Modern Visual Contextualities of Tiruvalluvar's *Tirukkural*

Amy-Ruth Holt

For scholars of modernity, the visual has a particularly strong hold on the modern era, where it often dominates in an effort to control the imagination of the nation (Holt and Pechilis 2019; Benjamin 2008; Anderson [1983] 2006; Levin 1993) through its creation and distribution of sensuous aesthetics (Rancière [2004] 2013, 7–14). In the southeastern Indian state of Tamil Nadu, one popular source of modern political imagery is the poetic text of the enigmatic saint Tiruvalluvar called the *Tirukkural*: a "sacred" collection of "*kurals*" or poetic couplets. Although Tamil tradition claims the *Tirukkural* as a part of ancient Sangam literature (ca. third century BCE–third century CE), most linguistic scholarship places it sometime between 450 CE and 500 CE (Blackburn 2000, 454; Zvelebil 1975, 124). Today, this text frequently appears contextualized within modern visual narratives, even though most of its verses are without clear visual descriptions or plot-oriented situations, being more like proverbs or moral sayings. These modern visuals of the *Tirukkural* either "sweeten" or "intensify" the original verses of this text in an effort to make it more sensationally powerful in its distribution and curation as a model historical text of the state.

With this new visuality of the *Tirukkural*, this chapter will demonstrate how modern narratives of the *Tirukkural* are often depicted in two opposing manners: through the "intensification" of the verse's consequences that appear as visual warnings of "what not to do"; and through the "sweetening" of positive outcomes that romanticize this text, in the manner of Walter Benjamin's "wish" or "dream image," where the envisioned characters and their correct behavior create utopian models for national reverence (Benjamin 1999, 898; also cited in Brosius 2005, 99). Since the agentive context of being in a specific time and space gives material things their meaning (Flueckiger 2020, 164; paraphrasing Ramanujan [1989] 1999), examples in this study will be taken from three different contextualities—national memorial monuments and sculptures sponsored by C. N. Annadurai (1909–1969) and M. Karunanidhi (1924–2018) in Tamil Nadu from 1968 to 1999; religious illustrations in three different editions of the *Tirukkural* distributed by Kauai's Hindu Monastery in Hawaii from 1999 to 2005; and Tamil films that include blockbuster hits spanning from the 1950s to the 2010s.[1] When visually analyzed within these assembled contexts, modern narratives of the *Tirukkural* reveal an underlying sensory teleology, composed of the aesthetic binaries of "sweetening and intensification" that respond to a growing imaging tradition of nationalistic language devotion.

Establishing Context from Translations and Commentaries

The archaic brevity and poetic language of the *Tirukkural*'s phrasing make it only understandable to the reader, either in Tamil or English, when given context through commentary. In ancient times, ten Tamil commentaries were written to help the reader understand these verses, the most prominent of these being Parimelalakar's twelfth-fourteenth century Tamil commentary that gives the main subject chapters and organization of the individual verses that most modern translations and commentaries follow (Cutler 1992, 551). The *Tirukkural* is composed of 1,330 couplets that are divided into three main sections: *aram* (virtue), *porul* (prosperity), and *inpam* (pleasure). Spread among these sections, the verses are divided into 133 individual chapters with ten couplets each that elucidate a particular subtheme within the larger section. Commentaries on the *Tirukkural* highlight the thematic reading of each chapter and fill in the translation of certain words with the author's own cultural understanding, values, or theology (Cutler 1992, 551–53). The earliest European translators of the *Tirukkural* were Jesuits and missionaries, who—until Rev. G. U. Pope in 1886—purposely neglected to translate the third section of this text, due to its focus on premarital sexuality and romance thought to be unsuitable for Christian study (Blackburn 2000, 453; Ebeling 2009, 236–37). Popular modern translators like Satguru Sivaya Subramaniyaswami (1927–2001) continue to ignore this section in order to highlight their religious interpretation of this text,[2] but without it, the *Tirukkural* no longer maintains its original near-correspondence with the four Tamil *urutiporul* or "those things (*porul*) which provide a firm support (*uruti*) [for the world]" (Cutler 1992, 550). This division is a variation of the common four-part Sanskritic discourse on *dharma* (virtue), *artha* (prosperity), *kama* (pleasure), and *moksha* (liberation). Thus, the *Tirukkural*'s three-part division is meant to neatly correspond to the first three of these: *aram* (*dharma*), *porul* (*artha*), and *inpam* (*kama*).

While the *Tirukkural* most likely was either secular or Jain in origin—which could have been the reason for its exclusion of the fourth *urutiporul* on *moksha*—translators and commentators commonly take advantage of the vagueness of these verses to add their own religious interpretations that replace its otherwise missing *moksha* content. One of the most highly debated verses of the *Tirukkural* is the first chapter of the *aram* section called "The Praise of God," which, according to some scholars, might suggest the worship of a Hindu god. G. U. Pope translated verse 3 of chapter 1 in the following manner:

> His feet, "who o'ver the full-blown flower hath past," who gain
> In bliss long time shall dwell above this earthly plain.
>
> [Commentary:] *They who are united to the glorious feet of Him who passes*
> *swiftly over the flower of the mind,*
> *shall flourish long above the worlds.* ([1886] 2020, I.1.1)

Notice the considerable difference when the Shaiva guru, Subramuniyaswami, translates this same verse into modern prose.[3]

> The Supreme dwells within the lotus of the heart. Those who reach
> His Splendid Feet dwell enduringly within unearthly realms.[4]
>   (2000, 7)

Overlooking the change in style that time has caused between these translations, each clearly adds a particular religious context to the sparse poetics of the original verse. Pope's prose commentary appears awkward in its phrasing of "who passes swiftly over the flower of the mind" since the heart-mind (*citta*) of Indic religions has no Christian parallel. Conversely, the heart-mind is a common theme in the later worship of the god Shiva Nataraja (Lord of Dance), who the Sri Lankan-born Subramuniyaswami favored and built a monastery temple for in Kauai, Hawaii. In fact, the translation this guru offers could just as easily be from a Shaiva *bhakti* poem rather than the earlier *Tirukkural*. In his introductory discussion of the *Tirukkural*, Pope even claims that Tiruvalluvar was much like a "Tamil poet Christian" ([1886] 2020, xxi). Today the *Tirukkural*'s varied interpretations make it accessible to any number of faiths as a national source of Tamil reverence, where it is commonly referred to as the "Tamil Bible" as well as the "Tamil Veda."

A recent translation of the *Tirukkural* by Thomas Hitoshi Pruiksma, *The Kural: Tiruvalluvar's Tirukkural*, perhaps gives the most poetically accurate reading of this verse. His version of the *Tirukkural* greatly differs from previous attempts due to his retention of some of the consonance and assonance of classical Tamil poetry, which makes the lines more enjoyable to read and hear in English. He also keeps some of the succinct rhythm of these couplets by giving a longer first line and shorter second. For this debated verse, he provides the following alteration (italics and bolded letters added below to show the repeating poetic sounds).

> At the *f*eet *of* a mind in *f*lower a person
> **L**ives **l**ong upon the earth. (Pruiksma 2021, 3)

> [Tamil:] ***M**alarmicai ēki**ṉāṉ** **m**āṇaṭi cērntār*
> ***N**ilamicai nīṭuvā**ḻ** vār*. (Subramuniyaswami 2000, 8)

His translation also leaves the identity of the divine person unclear, allowing the meaning of the verse to resonate with any reader, which likely was its original intension. For my subsequent discussion of the *Tirukkural*, I will employ the most relevant version that corresponds to the artist's purpose, the image's appearance, and its sociohistorical background. In general, the DMK (Dravidian Progressive Federation) political monuments of C. N. Annadurai and M. Karunandhi refer to G. U. Pope's translation since they both were familiar with it and even honored Pope for it in their political imagery. For Kauai's Hindu Monastery's versions of the *Tirukkural*, I will use Subramuniyaswami's work and their English online descriptions; and for Tamil movies of the *Tirukkural*, I will apply Pruiksma's recent rendition since these are not known in English and are related simply for the reader's reference. Given the *Tirukkural*'s general broadness in meaning, as shown through its various translations, the addition of the visual medium only further increases its possible interpretations according to the artist's or patron's imagination.

National Sculptures as Context: Dravidian Monuments of the *Tirukkural*

Surprisingly in the very long history and widespread popularity of the *Tirukkural*, its quotes as individual context-based narratives were not depicted visually until modern times. While numerous local Tamil stories, deities, and saints have extensive art historical records in sculpture, architecture, and painting, many of which date back centuries in South India, the *Tirukkural* seems to have primarily existed in premodern times as oral and written literature similar to the *Aathichudi* (a collection of 109 single-line quotations) and the *Naladiyar* (a collection of four hundred poems on moral ethics), which are thought to date to the same general period as the *Tirukkural*. The general obscurity of images of Tiruvalluvar and his poetics as visual narratives might have continued until today, if it were not for the considerable enthusiasm they drew from the modern Dravidian movement that began in the early twentieth century.

Following India's Independence in 1947, Tamils were faced with the realization that as a smaller language group of people they were greatly outnumbered by Hindi-speakers in northern India. The underlying anxiety instilled by the sense of being ruled unfairly by North Indians—and by extension brahmanic (or Sanskrit-based) Hindu ideology and the North Indian–derived brahmin caste—continues to this day, but it came to a head in the late 1960s when the central Indian government mandated that all Tamil government schools teach Hindi as the national language of India. Almost instantaneously, riots broke out across the state that included people cutting off their fingers, hair, and tongues and even incinerating themselves in protest of the presumed insult to their distinctive southern culture and ancient mother tongue. Those who died were regarded as martyred-Tamil *bhakta*s or saints (Holt 2019, 246–47; Ramaswamy 1997). At the same time, the Tamil regionalist political parties emerged. The first was the secular social movement called the DK (Dravidian Federation) created by E. V. Ramaswamy (known as "Periyar") in 1944 that led to the creation of the DMK (Dravidian Progressive Federation) in 1949 under the chief minister, C. N. Annadurai, which then split in 1972 under the chief minister, M. G. Ramachandran (commonly called "MGR"), into a second party called the AIADMK (All India Anna Dravidian Progressive Federation). Along with the instigation of regional Tamil parties, focused around the ideology of a purely Tamil state, there came the creation of government-sponsored imagery, where the text and author of the *Tirukkural* took center stage.

Essential to the political imagery of this newly conceived Dravidian nation were the contributions of the past DMK chief ministers, C. N. Annadurai and M. Karunanidhi. In 1968, Annadurai set up eighteen bronze sculptures of Tamil literary heroes that included G. U. Pope, Tiruvalluvar, and Auvaiyar (author of the related *Aathichudi*) along Marina Beach in the capital city of Chennai (then Madras) near the government headquarters of Fort St. George. Following Annadurai's death in 1969, Karunanidhi came to power, and he attempted to rewrite much of Tamil literary history. He produced his own translation of the *Tirukkural* as well as renditions of the epic *Ramayana* and *Cilappatikaram*, where the characters and plot were rearranged to showcase his Dravidian and anti-brahmanic ideals.[5] Having been a screenwriter prior to his political career, he completely revolutionized the manner in which DMK rhetoric and film dialogue were spoken by drawing heavily upon the auditory poetics of past literature like the *Tirukkural* (Krishnan 2013; Bate 2009). His new vision of the state came to fruition through a number of national moments built during his five terms as chief minister between 1969 and 2011.

Karunanidhi's literary and visual achievements are most clearly seen in his commissioning of Chennai's 1976 chariot-temple called the Valluvar Kottam (Tiruvalluvar's Assembly) that is dedicated to the saint Tiruvalluvar, found in the main sanctum. The stone temple stands as an embodied "biopic" of Karunanidhi (Srivathsan 2000, 115): its unusual chariot (*ratha*) form references the temple cart of Karunanidhi's hometown of Tiruvarur. Carved in three rows on the four sides of the chariot's exterior are the 133 chapters of the *Tirukkural*, following their order from the three main sections of this text (*aram*, *porul*, and *inpam*). As a monument to Karunanidhi's extensive political career, a large palace-like audience hall extends from the temple-chariot, where DMK political rallies and Karunanidhi's birthday celebrations were held during his lifetime (Holt 2016, 232, 236). Inside this hall, large granite slabs stand engraved with the entire *Tirukkural*. Crowning Karunanidhi's great reverence for this text was his sponsorship of a massive statue of Tiruvalluvar, completed under his direction in 1999, that stands on a small isle off of Kanyakumari, at the southeastern end of the Indian subcontinent, as a symbol of the Tamil state similar to the US Statue of Liberty or India's more recent Statue of Unity (Holt 2016, 236).[6] Following this statue's completion, Tiruvalluvar's image and quotes from the *Tirukkural* flooded Tamil Nadu, being commonly plastered on government buildings and buses, and from this point on, the *Tirukkural* and its author were invested with the new modern contextuality of political propaganda.

The relief sculptures of Karunanidhi's Valluvar Kottam inaugurated a tradition of depicting the individual proverb-like sayings of the *Tirukkural* as a complete set of visual narratives. These images take on a classical style and format akin to the narrative reliefs commonly sculpted along the base (*adhishthana*) of ancient Tamil temple walls as well as the decorative rows of wooden carvings on processional chariots (*ratha*s). The well-known Tamil sculptor and architect of the Valluvar Kottam, Ganapati Sthapati (1927–2011), created an imagery for the *Tirukkural* verses that at first glance appeared traditional when in fact it was completely different.[7] Within the individual reliefs, the figures appear similar to those sculpted on Chola temples with beautifully coiffed curls and perfectly proportioned curves bedecked in ornaments and draped in flowing garments. Often the bearded ascetic Tiruvalluvar, similar to his form in the main sanctum of the Valluvar Kottam, appears as a narrator figure, without any clear religious affiliation, pointing out objects and characters in the scene in the manner of modern Dravidian politicians.

Of all the narrative reliefs on the Valluvar Kottam, perhaps the images of the third section on *inpam*, which show women lounging, weeping, posing with birds, and embraced by men, resemble most closely the well-known imagery of erotic females and *mithuna*s (loving-couples) found on ancient Indian temples.[8] For example, "Chapter 121, The Visions of the Night," shows a female figure lovingly embraced from behind by her male lover with her left forearm entwined around his (fig. 12.1). The theme of this section is about women dreaming about their absent lovers. Of the verses in this chapter, verse 1218 most likely was the impetus behind this image. It reads,

And when I sleep he holds my form embraced;
And when I wake to fill my heart makes haste!

[Commentary:] *When I am asleep he rests on my shoulders,*
(but) when I awake he hastens into my soul. (Pope [1886] 2020,
    3.2.7)

Figure 12.1. Ganapati Sthapati, "Chapter 121, The Visions of the Night" (Verse 1218). Detail of the west wall of the Valluvar Kottam, Chennai, Tamil Nadu, 1976. *Source:* Photo by the author.

The narrative depicts the dreamed embrace of the lovers, where the touch of the lovers' arms sweetly brings to mind the sensations of pleasure. It shows the "sweetened" and desired outcome of these verses, or what Walter Benjamin coined as "wish images" (Benjamin 1999, 898; cited in Brosius 2005, 104), where an imagined yet classically inspired Dravidian past is brought to life through the archaistic appearance of these sculptures to form a national imagery.

The sculptor Ganapati Sthapati often searched for particularly picturesque descriptions or scenes given in one of the individual verses of the *Tirukkural* to represent the entire chapter on the Valluvar Kottam. Sometimes the images appear as "intensified" narratives of "what not to do" so as to not bring harm to the Tamil state. As the opposite of sweetened "wish images," I call these scenes "warning images." An example of one such "warning image" is the depiction of chapter 50 (verse 500), from the second section on prosperity (*porul*) meant for advising kings and ministers in war.

The jackal slays, in miry paths of foot-betraying fen,
The elephant of fearless eye and tusks transfixing armed men.

[Commentary:] *A fox can kill a fearless, warrior-faced elephant,
if it go into mud in which its legs sink down.* (Pope [1886] 2020,
2.1.12)

In the image for this verse, a battle rages with a charging elephant whose tusks have pierced the chest of a spear-bearing warrior. In the process, however, the elephant has gotten his back legs stuck in the mud, allowing for the foxes around him to attack (fig. 12.2). The position of Tiruvalluvar standing to the upper right and knowingly pointing to the plotted land, marked by squares in reference to the chapter's title, "Knowing the Place," also underscores the chapter's warning tone. A shocking detail of this scene is the mortally pierced soldier raised up in the tusks of the elephant on

Figure 12.2. Ganapati Sthapati, "Chapter 50, Knowing the Place" (Verse 500). Detail of the south wall of the Valluvar Kottam, Chennai, Tamil Nadu, 1976. *Source:* Photo by the author.

the upper left, who brings the physical consequences of this scene back to the human level.[9] Its "intensified" visuality makes this scene more realistic than just reading the verse of the *Tirukkural*. Through these depictions of both intensified "warning images" and sweetened "wish images," the overall imagery of the Valluvar Kottam constructs a useable, educational past of the Tamil state that more vividly and emotionally contextualizes the verses of the *Tirukkural* for modern viewers.

Religious Illustrations as Context: Painted Pictures of the *Tirukkural*

Following the government's interest in political monuments to Tiruvalluvar, Satguru Sivaya Subramuniyaswami and his monks at Kauai's Hindu Monastery published three translations of the *Tirukkural*: *Weaver's Wisdom: Ancient Precepts for a Perfect Life* (1999), *Tirukkural: The American English and Modern Tamil Translations of An Ethical Masterpiece* (2000), and a third 2004–5 version on their Himalayan Academy website through the paintings of the Tamil artist Sundaram Rajam (1919–2010). Subramuniyaswami was given a copy of the *Tirukkural* in 1949 by his teacher, Satguru Siva Yogaswami, in Jaffna, Sri Lanka, with the instruction to bring its wisdom to the West. And this is exactly what he did, albeit through the lens of DMK politics and international Shaivism. All the monastery's *Tirukkural* imagery shows narrative images of the chapter themes similar to the sculptural reliefs of the Valluvar Kottam, and both the Kanyakumari statue and Valluvar Kottam are discussed in the introduction of their second edition. Altogether their printed and online publications of the *Tirukkural* establish another contextuality for this ancient text—modern religious illustration, which even as a separate international enterprise continues to be aligned with the imagery and promotion of the original Tamil state.

An overriding concern for Gurudev (as Subramuniyaswami is affectionally called) was "to make things in the best way possible," according to the arts coordinator of the monastery, Paramacharya Sadasivanathaswami. Generally, for Kauai's Hindu Monastery, this has meant attempting to re-create in the most authentic-looking manner available the Shaiva Shiddhanta tradition of Subramuniyaswami's Tamil heritage and religious training. The monastery's second publication of the *Tirukkural* was meant as an improvement upon the first due to the inclusion of the Tamil text of the *kurals* and the color illustrations of A. Manivelu to replace the earlier black and white drawings of the first edition. The cover image of Tiruvalluvar remained the same for both volumes, being the prized work of the Tamil artist and Karnatic musician Sundaram Rajam. Still unimpressed with these earlier attempts to capture the imagery of the *Tirukkural*'s verses, however, Rajam created his own *Tirukkural* series of 108 paintings in 2004–5 with the monastery's blessings that he donated to their online art gallery, the Himalayan Academy Museum of Spiritual Art.

Rajam's paintings have been a favorite of the monastery; they have been used to decorate their monastery office and conference room for their popular magazine *Hinduism Today*, their website, and many of their books over the past thirty years, including the seminal *Dancing with Siva* and *The Guru's Path* (Gurudev's biography). Rajam painted in the Shanthiniketan tradition of Abanindranath Tagore, who sought to establish a truly Asian style of contemporary painting that was not reliant on Western realism (Subbanna 2009). To make his *Tirukkural* paintings, Rajam developed a technique from the *Chitrasutra* (a sixth-century Sanskrit text on painting) of using ten washed layers of transparent and color paint on cardboard, and he copied the iconography and figural style of Chola bronzes as well as studying the cave paintings of Ajanta, Sigiriya, Ellora, Sittannavasal, and Amaravati. The final result was a modernization of ancient Indian painting that suited the monastery's preference for new techniques, but in a manner that was still authentic to traditional Tamil aesthetics.

Like Subramuniyaswami's translation of these verses discussed earlier, the imagery of the monastery's books and gallery revere the god Shiva and demonstrate their use of the *Tirukkural* as a Hindu devotional text. The opening image of the *Tirukkural*, in all three versions, shows a full-page image of Shiva Nataraja. In Sundaram Rajam's image, he adds the first four letters of the Tamil alphabet as a reference to Shiva's frequent relationship with language devotion in Tamil Nadu (fig. 12.3).[10] As the main deity of Kauai's monastery, Shiva's image illustrates the change in context from one of political secularism, illustrated on the Valluvar Kottam with a seated or pointing Tiruvalluvar, to one of religious instruction.[11] Additional images throughout the monastery's translations and Rajam's paintings show people worshiping various Hindu images, such as other forms of Shiva like his *linga* (a sign of the god) and his feet, the elephant-headed deity Ganesh, goddesses like Sarasvati as well as ascetics, young and old, dressed primarily as Shaiva renunciates with matted hair or shaved heads, *rudhdraksha* (tree seeds sacred to Shiva) prayer beads, *vibhuti* (sacred ash), and sacred threads. Even Rajam's bearded Tiruvalluvar on the monastery's book covers looks strikingly similar to the guru Subramuniyaswami himself.

Figure 12.3. Sundaram Rajam, *Tirukkural*, "Chapter 1, Praising God," from the *Tirukkural* series. Watercolor on cardboard, Himalayan Academy Museum of Spiritual Art, Kauai's Hindu Monastery, Kapa'a, Hawaii, 2004–5. *Source:* Courtesy of Himalayan Academy. Used with permission.

With the deletion of the *inpam* section of this text in all of the monastery's translations, the female figures are meant to appear like Tiruvalluvar's mythical wife, Vasuki, the ideal Hindu wife, who faithfully waits upon her family, husband, house guests, and other male renunciates as noted in Subramuniyaswami's introduction to the *Tirukkural* (2000, xix–xxiv). One such idyllic scene is Rajam's painting of "Chapter 62, Perseverance" (fig. 12.4). The monastery website describes it this way: "An energetic weaver works at his loom, smiling with the joy of working hard to support his family. Behind him his wife is adorned with good clothes and jewelry. She

Figure 12.4. Sundaram Rajam, "Chapter 62, Perseverance," from the *Tirukkural* series. Watercolor on cardboard, Himalayan Academy Museum of Spiritual Art, Kauai's Hindu Monastery, Kapa'a, Hawaii, 2004–5. *Source:* Courtesy of Himalayan Academy. Used with permission.

lovingly takes care of her father as the children are studying industriously. The man's hard work has brought abundance to the family."[12]

Rajam's archaic style and his Chola-esque figures in this painting "sweeten" the original *kural* through the depiction of various family interactions, including the husband joyfully laboring on a traditional Tamil silk loom as a reference to Tiruvalluvar's possible weaver caste.[13] The joint family scene appears recognizably Hindu from the *vibhuti* ash on the weaver's forehead and the sacred thread across the grandfather's chest. Outside of generally "laboring," however, none of these specific actions or the family scene are suggested in the original

Tirukkural verses of this chapter. The painting creates a sweetened "wish image" of the happy Hindu family—the implied keystone of the perfect Tamil nation that also draws parallels with ancient Tamil icons of Shiva with his family or the Somaskanda (Shiva with Uma and Skanda).[14] The lack of an actual Tamil text or translation for this online image allows Rajam's independently conceived visual image (and its modern English description) to replace the *Tirukkural*'s original poetics, creating a heightened dependence on these visuals and their establishment of new meanings for this verse.

Sundaram Rajam's other paintings in the *Tirukkural* series show a similar visual complexity and replacement of the written text for a visual one. Unlike the sculptural images of the *Tirukkural* found on the Valluvar Kottam, the frequent rich coloring of Rajam's images makes the violence of war, men, and in a few cases animals all the more realistic and bloody. Additionally, numerous characters fill many of his scenes, sometimes showing dual outcomes for the same *kural* within the same picture, or through multiple split screens like Amar Chitra Katha (a popular Indian comic book) filmstrips. Yet the need for such complicated narratives is not necessary for Rajam to create an intensified "warning image." Some of his best images have none of these techniques, and instead, depict solitary, suffering individuals. For example, his painting of "Chapter 101, Wealth That Benefits No One" (fig. 12.5), has the following online description: "A man has chosen a lonely life so that he might acquire a great storehouse of wealth. This he has done, but now he must protect his treasure, and so he locks himself in a vault. He is alone, without close friends or family. Despite his efforts, two thieves are walking away with his belongings."[15]

Although the original text of the *Tirukkural* does in one verse mention that the miser "will see it [his wealth] seized by strangers" (verse 1009; Subramuniyaswami 2000, 439) as shown in the background of this image, the rest of the scene is of Rajam's own making. Rajam uniquely places his miser in a prison-like vault with multiple-point-perspective walls enclosing him in a way that draws the viewer's focus to his thin, disheveled, and miserable form, as he embraces himself on the cell's floor, surrounded by his open and discarded treasure trunks. By contrast, previous images on the Valluvar Kottam and in the monastery's earlier versions of this chapter depicted a boisterously large man surrounded by luxury. The cool gray of the trunks and the patterned purple stones of the floor in Rajam's painting also make the room dank. The overall experiential feelings of loss, sadness, and madness that this scene conjures broaden the original *Tirukkural* text, intensifying the scene beyond that of earlier attempts. In doing so, it aptly captures the murky characters who, like the miser, are the antithesis of the

Figure 12.5. Sundaram Rajam, "Chapter 101, Wealth That Benefits No One," from the *Tirukkural* series. Watercolor on cardboard, Himalayan Academy Museum of Spiritual Art, Kauai's Hindu Monastery, Kapa'a, Hawaii, 2004–5. *Source:* Courtesy of Himalayan Academy. Used with permission.

perfect Hindu family and therefore must reform their behavior in order to rejoin the imagined Tamil nation.

Film as Context: Onscreen Imagery of the *Tirukkural*

Films are another way that the *Tirukkural* has become contextualized in the modern Tamil imagination. Since quoting is a standard manner in which this text is used in everyday situations in southern India, the medium of film appears as a natural transition that allows for the auditory effect of the poetics to further sensualize the visual narrative of the film, yet with their inclusion in films comes the additional complexity of these verses being found within complicated plots with often very modern characters (some of which are enacted by popular political stars). Unlike religious illustration and the Valluvar Kottam, however, no one film to date depicts the entire *Tirukkural*; instead, films typically focus their storylines around the meaning of one or two *kurals*. From my conversations with native Tamil speakers about these films, I have noticed that viewers will often recall the entirety of these films simply from the recitation of their particular *Tirukkural* verses.

Rather than narrative depictions of its verses, the earliest imagery of the *Tirukkural* were actually portraits of the saint Tiruvalluvar like the 1968 Tiruvalluvar memorial sculpture on Marina Beach. Oddly, a main source for his imagery was not a movie about himself but Auvaiyar. Auvaiyar is considered to be the author of the *Aathichudi*, which is sometimes called the "sister text" of the *Tirukkural* because both are filled with proverb-like sayings used in elementary school education. Prior to the creation of the film *Avvaiyar* (1953, starring the famous Karnatic vocalist and actor K. B. Sundarambal), Auvaiyar's story was largely unknown and Tiruvalluvar's background was highly debated among scholars. As a result, the film was able to materialize a story for her and Tiruvalluvar that was almost entirely fictitious. Yet in doing so, the film was vastly successful because it was able to present the Tamil language with a desired devotional history (Baskaran [1996] 2013, 23–24) that "provided a translational bridge from the 'mythic' to the 'historical,' allowing [these] previously disavowed individuals and narratives to inhabit the chronotope of truth" (Pinney 2004, 66).

In this film, Auvaiyar appears as an older woman with a walking stick who goes around solving a number of local situations until eventually she finds the Tamil god Murugan and becomes his prime devotee. Along the way, she encounters the sage Tiruvalluvar, who appears as a bearded Shaiva renunciate with *rudhdraksha* prayer beads and sacred thread, teaching his two young followers verse 10 from chapter 1 of the *Tirukkural* in the form of a *bhakti* hymn,

> *piṟavip peruṅkaṭal nīntuvar nīntār*
> *iṟaivaṉ aṭicērā tār.*

[Translation:] A swimmer cannot swim the sea of birth
Without touching the feet of God. (Pruiksma 2021, 3)

This *kural* then becomes the sweetened "wish image" for this subplot of the film, which concerns how Auvaiyar fights to get Tiruvalluvar a position as a classical poet in the historic Madurai Tamil Sangam, or literary committee. She passionately argues before the king, "We are not doing this for our own sake, but for the sake of Tamil!" In the end, she brings the *Tirukkural* to the Golden Lotus Tank at the seventeenth-century Meenakshi-Sundareshwara

Temple in Madurai. Once the text is placed in the water, it disappears and a lotus rises to the surface and opens, bearing the *Tirukkural*—a miraculous sign that the god Shiva (as the official head of the Madurai Tamil Sangam) has accepted this text and Tiruvalluvar into the literary committee. In this film, the saint-like characters, Auvaiyar and Tiruvalluvar, not only represent Tamil literature, but voraciously defend it and quote the *Tirukkural* in the manner of politicized devotion, making it a highly useful propaganda film. Annadurai and Karunanidhi even used the actors' images in this film as models for their Marina Beach sculptures and later monuments.[16]

While *Avvaiyar* featured Tiruvalluvar singing his own verses, it is more typical for films to show a character quoting the *Tirukkural* in order to strategically win an argument at work or home (e.g., *Mudhalvan* 1999, *Ghilli* 2004, *VIP2* 2017, *Natpe Thunai* 2019), bestow advice as a parent, friend, or wise associate to another (e.g., *Ninai Chinnam* 1989, *Boss Engira Baskaran* 2010, and *VIP2* 2017), or sometimes within the lyrics of a devotional song (e.g., *Saraswathi Sabatham* 1966, *Pallandu Vazhga* 1975, and *Raa Raa* 2011). A Tamil film studio, K. Balachander's Kavithalayaa Productions, opened each of their films with the first verse of the *Tirukkural* sung in the background. In the late 1960s and 1970s, films took advantage of the celebrity following of particular actors to recite *Tirukkural* verses, such as Sivaji Ganesan (1928–2001) and M. G. Ramachandran (1917–1987; known as MGR), who were not only actors but political figures. By quoting this text in the context of a film, these actors demonstrated their own Tamil pride and knowledge with the added benefit of further inspiring national devotion toward the *Tirukkural*.

For example, the actor and past chief minister MGR stars in *Pallandu Vazhga* (Long live!), where he fosters six prisoners in his home. As the opening lines of a song, he chants the sweetened "wish image" of this film, *Tirukkural* verses 72 and 619, in the context of a prayer:

> *anpilār ellām tamkkuriyar anputaiyār*
> *enpum uriyar pirarkku.*

[Translation:] Everything belongs to the loveless—for the loving
Bones too belong to others. (Pruiksma 2021, 10)

> *teyvattān ākā teninum muyarcitan*
> *meyvaruttak kūli tarum.*

[Translation:] Even if fate adds nothing effort
Pays the body's labor. (Pruiksma 2021, 66)

As MGR continues to sing, he sits on the floor with the *Tirukkural* as his prayer book, pointing (like Tiruvalluvar) toward all the various images in his *puja* room—Murugan, Buddha, Jesus, Gandhi, the Virgin Mary, a mosque, a south Indian Hindu temple, the Vedantic sage Adi Shankar, and even MGR's political mentor, the past chief minister C. N. Annadurai—as the prisoners watch with little interest, lounging around the room. The inclusion of these various religious images demonstrates MGR's later political motto (which Annadurai originally used to distinguish the DMK party from the DK) of "One Caste; One God," which forms the song's chorus and joins the various religions of Tamil Nadu under a singular governmental slogan. At one point, MGR even sings this chorus while pointing to Annadurai's portrait as Annadurai's statue-like shadow eerily falls across his form. Since MGR eventually names his own political party after Annadurai (the All India "Anna" Dravidian Progressive Federation), this film song and movie were utilized during MGR's political campaign, making the *Tirukkural* a part of his political persona.

From the late 1990s onward, films have continued to add complexity to the contextual meaning of the *Tirukkural* through various quotations in romantic comedies and action-packed thrillers. Although there is no evidence to suggest that Tiruvalluvar's verses were meant to be sung like the verses of later *bhakti* (devotional) poets, many contemporary and Karnatic-styled composers, since the first appearance of the *Tirukkural* in film, have attempted to adapt this text to music. Of these, perhaps the most ambitious and charming application of the *Tirukkural* to date is the song performance of *Anpum Aranum* (Love and Virtue) from the romantic comedy *Raa Raa* (2011), which includes no less than nine *kurals* strung together as a kind of marriage blessing for the theatrical couple, whose families are meeting for the first time.

Before a houseful of family, friends, and children, the film song opens in a *puja* room, where the heroine touches the feet of her intended in-laws, lights a lamp before a large stone sculpture of Tiruvalluvar, and begins singing verse 45, after which the song is titled:

anpum aranum uṭaittāyin ilvālkkai
paṇpum payanum atu.

[Translation:] If a life at home has love and virtue—that
Is its root and flower. (Pruiksma 2021, 7)

The song continues with general verses on friendship sung by her intended groom and his father (verses 786 and 788), followed by verses about avoiding bad speech or gossip sung by other family members and friends (including the girl's rowdy brother who hilariously reads them from a slip of paper) as advice for the couple's communication (verses 127, 129, 200, and 423). The intended bride teaches from a *Tirukkural* book to the assembled children, and the boy's father presents copies of this book on *puja* plates to her grandparents and brother. He then sings a verse on industrious labor to the intended couple (verse 595) as well as a verse similar to the title verse that shows his acceptance of the girl into his family (verse 60):

maṅkalam eṉpa maṉaimāṭci maṟṟu ataṉ
naṉkalam naṉamakkaṭ pēṟu.

[Translation:] A wife with glory is grace—and bearing
Good children its jewel. (Pruiksma 2021, 8)

The song ends with both the girl's and boy's families, now joined together as one happily extended family, singing together and repeating the opening title *kural* of the song outside the mansion of the boy's father. In this film, the united Hindu family appears as the overly sweetened "wish image" of the entire Tamil state due to their careful knowledge and devotion toward the *Tirukkural.*

Another notable use of the *Tirukkural* is in the movie *Mudhalvan* (Chief minister, 1999) where, in an interesting twist of fate, it is the antagonist who quotes the *Tirukkural* that determines his own demise.[17] In this action-packed thriller, an overly zealous reporter, N. Pugazhendi ("Pugazh," played by Arjun Sarja), asks the Tamil chief minister Aranganathar some tough questions about his involvement in local corruption. Irritated by the reporter's gall, the chief minister replies that if he thinks it is so easy to be chief minister then he should try it for a day. When Pugazh calmly refuses him, the chief minister angrily threatens him (pointing like Tiruvalluvar) with verse 691 from the *Tirukkural.*

akalātu aṇukātu tīkkāyvār pōlka
ikalvēntarc cērntoḻuku vār.

[Translation:] With irascible kings move like one who warms
By a fire—neither close nor far. (Pruiksma 2021, 74)

Following this exchange, Pugazh eventually accepts the chief minister's position and immediately gets to work correcting the wrongs of the government. By the end of the day, Chief Minister Aranganathar has lost his position, and Pugazh is set to win in the upcoming election. A now incensed Aranganathar hires a hitman to kill Pugazh, which accidentally leads to the death of Pugazh's parents. Realizing he will never be able to avoid Aranganathar's looming danger, Pugazh invites Aranganathar to his office, where he wounds himself with a gun and then throws it at Aranganathar, who catches it as the police appear and shoot him. The film's plot generates an extreme "intensification" of the "warning image" of the *Tirukkural* recited in the opening scene. As in the *kural*, the "irascible king," Chief Minister Aranganathar, should be handled with care so that the ideal Tamil nation and the struggling hero Pugazh are not its unfortunate victims. The aftermath images of the film further support this verse with a peaceful, highly developed state under Pugazh's rule.

Conclusion: Sensing Devotion in Modern *Tirukkural* Imagery

Modern *Tirukkural* images reveal the significance of context. Since its first English translations and ancient Tamil commentaries, the endless adaptability and interpretation of the *Tirukkural* has resulted in multiple contextualities. Specifically, the modern contextualities of political sculpture, religious illustrations, and Tamil films demonstrate the visual "pull of nation" (Sinha 2007, 215) through two sense-based divergences: the "wish image" that sweetens the text, and its opposite, the "warning image," which intensifies the text. The representational dichotomy of these *Tirukkural*s reflects their modern association with images of *bhakti* or "devotional visuality" (Pechilis and Holt 2023; Holt and Pechilis 2019), which function as a particular mode of nationalistic devotion based upon Tamil's distinctive literary history.

Along with their increasing devotional content, a unique ability of modern visuals themselves is their capacity to more fully express the inner desires, emotions, and intentions of their viewers. As defined by the art historian Christopher Pinney, modern images create a "xeno real" image (2004, 31) through their unique combination of Western realism with local imagery and emotive sentiment whereby "the experience [of the image's] effect is at once its meaning and its power" (2004, 8; quoted from Wagner 1986, 216). While the most sensuously "real" context for the *Tirukkural* is undoubtedly the filmic image with its ability to complicate the text through the visual as well as the auditory, the other examples included in this chapter reveal a significant impact on the sensory development and distribution of its devotional imagery. Religious illustrating, for instance, has an international reach that has further expanded the popularity of the *Tirukkural*, sometimes independent of the Tamil text itself, as seen in the paintings of Sundaram Rajam, to include Tamils living abroad and non-Tamil-speaking foreigners. It, along with film imagery, additionally complicates the *Tirukkural* with imagined narratives and religious sentiment not necessarily explicit to the text like those first sculpted on the Valluvar Kottam; and while Annadurai's and Karunanidhi's political monuments promote the *Tirukkural* as government propaganda, they also build upon the popularity of Tamil devotional characters like Tiruvalluvar already established as "true" from film.

Each of these contextualities ultimately ties back to modern state politics and is evolutionally intertwined with the form of the others. Their new visuality, interpreted through an expansion upon Walter Benjamin's theories on national imaging, shows the aesthetic binaries of "sweetening and intensification" employed to increase the sensational effects associated with the *Tirukkural*'s modern devotion to make it more politically meaningful. As a consequence, the once only oral and written poetics of the *Tirukkural* are now forever embedded and remembered in the visual contextualities of the modern Tamil nation.

Notes

1. In March 2022, I was fortuitously introduced and granted access to Kauai's Hindu Monastery's vast collection of Sundaram Rajam's paintings, while I was there photographing the monastery's temples and speaking with some of the resident monks for another project. All of the films used in this study can be found online, while my study of government monuments draws on more than a decade of fieldwork in South India as well as my past publications.

2. Other than the sculpted reliefs on the Valluvar Kottam reviewed here, it is rare to actually hear someone quote or discuss the third section of the *Tirukkural*. Today, some Indian publications continue to ignore the third section of the *Tirukkural*, especially those that are published for schools or religious institutions. For examples, see Subramuniyaswami 1999 and 2000, as well as www.tamilnation.org. Uniquely, without the third section, there are exactly 108 chapters to the *Tirukkural*, which is a sacred Hindu number.

3. For Tamil quotations from the *Tirukkural*, the standard use of diacritics for Tamil has been applied in order to clarify the sound and meter of this poetry for the reader. In all other instances, Tamil and Sanskrit words are given in their common English spellings without diacritics.

4. This is also the same translation that is given on the Tamil website, aptly called "tamilnation." Accessed September 9, 2022. ttps://www.tamilnation. org/literature/kural/kurale2.

5. Also, see M. S. S. Pandian ([1998] 2014) and Holt (2016). Karunanidhi's movie *Parasakthi* (1952) was a modern retelling of the *Cilappatikaram* (Anklet story), a Tamil epic featuring the queen Kannagi who burns down Madurai with her anklet in her anger against her cheating husband.

6. While certainly not the first massive statue in India, the Kanyakumari Tiruvalluvar statue was the earliest completed example of a government-sponsored symbol of an Indian state that has since been copied numerous times throughout India, most obviously with the Statue of Unity (Vallabhai Patel), sponsored by the Indian federal government under Prime Minister Modi in 2018. For more information about this image and its relationship to Tamil's Tiruvalluvar statue, see Jain 2021, 2–27, 223.

7. Although Ganapati Sthapati today is most reputed for his Hindu temples that are now found around the world, he began as a sculptor for the DMK government. In 1974, he sculpted the narrative scenes of the *Cilappatikaram* in the Art Gallery at Poompuhar, Tamil Nadu, as well as the sculptures of Kannagi and Madhavi (the king's consort) in the building's atrium (Holt 2016).

8. For examples of *mithuna* couples in art, see Huntington 1985.

9. This image also draws a correspondence visually with the Gajendramoksha (Liberation of the Elephant King) narrative commonly depicted in Hindu art; see Huntington 1985, 211.

10. The insertion of Tamil letters in this image also is a literal interpretation of the first verse of the first chapter of the *Tirukkural,* which reads:

"A" is the first and source of all the letters. Even so is
God Primordial the first and source of all the world.

[Tamil:] *akara mutala emuttellām āti*
pakavaṉ mutaṟṟē ulaku. (Subramuniyaswami 2000, 7–8)

11. For images of this Tiruvalluvar, see Holt 2016.

12. www.himalayanacademy.com/hamsa/. The appearance of a family, along with a man at work, most likely comes from verse 615 of chapter 62:

Standing like a pillar, he who prefers work to pleasure
supports his family and sweeps away their every sorrow.

[Tamil:] *iṉpam viḷaiyāṉ viṉaivilaivāṉ taṉkōḷir*
tuṉpam tuṭaittūṉṟum tūṇ. (Subramuniyaswami 2000, 271–72)

13. Subramuniyaswami also identifies Tiruvalluvar as being from the "valluvar" or low-level weaver caste (2000, xxiv–xxxi). For more information about the poet's background, see Blackburn 2000.

14. For an example of the popular Pallava (ca. seventh century) Somaskanda in Tamil history, see Huntington 1985, 311. Such images were thought to be metaphors for the king and his family.

15. The appearance of the miserable miser in this scene with the thieves carrying away his treasure reflects verse 1009 from chapter 101:

He who casts out love and dharma and chooses self-denial
so wealth can pile high will see it seized by strangers.

[Tamil:] *anporiit tarcerru aranōkkātu iṭṭiya
onponuḷ kōḷvār piṛar.* (Subramuniyaswami 2000, 439–40)

16. There was also a portrait of Tiruvalluvar drawn in 1960 by the artist Venugopala Sharma that was hung in the government Assembly and referred to later for the Marina Beach Tiruvalluvar sculpture and the government stamp of this saint (Kolappan 2019). Reflecting the DMK commitment to secular government, these images show the poet-saint in white robes and without any religious markings.

17. The Tamil political artist Shihan Hussaini also quoted this verse from this movie to me in conversation about his contemporary art and his plans to use it to promote his own future in politics (Holt 2018, 83).

References

Anderson, Benedict. (1983) 2006. *Imagined Communities.* Verso.

Avvaiyar. 1953. Directed by Kothamangalam Subbu. Gemini Studios. Accessed November 7, 2023. https://www.youtube.com/watch?v=xHEDEB XaWTw.

Baskaran, S. Theodore. 2013. *The Eye of the Serpent.* Tranquebar Press.

Bate, Bernard. 2009. *Tamil Oratory and the Dravidian Aesthetic: Democratic Practice in South India.* Columbia University Press.

Benjamin, Walter. 1999. *The Arcades Project.* Translated by Howard Eiland and Kevin McLaughlin. Belknap Press of Harvard University Press.

Benjamin, Walter. 2008. *The Work of Art in the Age of Its Technological Reproducibility and Other Writings on Media.* Belknap Press of Harvard University Press.

Blackburn, Stuart. 2000. "Corruption and Redemption: The Legend of Valluvar and Tamil Literary History," *Modern Asian Studies* 34 (2): 449–82.

Boss Engira Baskaran (Boss alias Baskaran). 2010. Directed by M. Rajesh. Vasan Visual Ventures. Accessed November 7, 2023. https://www.youtube.com/watch?v=WG 1tq6BUFKM.

Brosius, Christiane. 2004. *Empowering Visions: The Politics of Representation in Hindu Nationalism*. Anthem Press.

Cutler, Norman. 1992. "Interpreting Tirukkural: The Role of Commentary in the Creation of a Text." *Journal of the American Oriental Society* 112 (4): 549–66.

Ebeling, Sascha. 2009. "The College of Fort St. George and the Transformation of Tamil Philology During the Nineteenth Century." In *The Madras School of Orientalism: Producing Knowledge in Colonial South India*, edited by Thomas R. Trautmann, 233–62. Oxford University Press.

Flueckiger, Joyce Burkhalter. 2020. *Material Acts in Everyday Hindu Worlds*. State University of New York Press.

Ghilli [Gutsy]. 2004. Directed by Dharani. Sri Surya Movies. Accessed November 7, 2023. https://www.youtube.com/watch?v=w10AgaNvRhI.

Holt, Amy-Ruth. 2016. "A Secular Tamil Saint? Karunanidhi's Use of Divine Imagery in Dravidian Politics." *Journal of Hindu Studies* 9 (1): 226–48.

Holt, Amy-Ruth. 2018. "Religious Symbolism in Contemporary Political Art: Hussaini and Popular Tamil Culture." In *Modern Hinduism in Text and Context*, edited by Lavanya Vemsani, 65–83. Bloomsbury.

Holt, Amy-Ruth. 2019. "Symbols of Political Participation: Jayalalitha's Fan Imagery in Tamil Nadu." *Journal of Hindu Studies* 12 (2): 242–69.

Holt, Amy-Ruth, and Karen Pechilis. 2019. "Introduction: Contemporary Images of Hindu Bhakti: Identity and Visuality." *Journal of Hindu Studies* 12 (2): 129–41.

Huntington, Susan L. 1985. *Art of Ancient India: Buddhist, Hindu, and Jain*. Weatherhill.

Jain, Kajri. 2021. *Gods in the Time of Democracy*. Duke University Press.

Kolappan, B. 2019. "How Thiruvalluvar's Portrait Evolved over Time." *The Hindu*, November 19. Accessed September 19, 2022. https://www.thehindu.com/news/national/tamil-nadu/how-thiruvalluvars-portrait-evolved-over-time/article61623716.ece.

Krishnan, Rajan K. 2013. "When Kathavarayan Spoke *His* Mind: The Intricate Dynamics of the Formulations of the Political Through Film-Making Practices in Tamil Nadu." In *New Cultural Histories of India: Materiality and Practices*, edited by Partha Chatterjee, Tapati Guha-Thakurta, and Bodhisattva Kar, 223–45. Oxford University Press.

Levin, David M. ed. 1993. *Modernity and the Hegemony of Vision*. University of California Press.

Mudhalvan [Chief minister]. 1999. Directed by S. Shankar. S Films. Accessed November 7, 2023. https://www.youtube.com/watch?v=4mIWiBAksSo.

Natpe Thunai [Friendship is guidance]. 2019. Directed by Parthiban Desingu. Avni Movies. Accessed November 7, 2023. https://www.youtube.com/watch?v=4mIWiBAksSo.

Ninai Chinnam [Monument]. 1989. Directed by Anu Mohan. Tamilnadu Movies. Accessed November 7, 2023. https://www.youtube.com/watch?v=ixgdAbC8lDY.

Pallandu Vazhga [Long live!]. 1975. Directed by K. Shankar. Udhayam Productions. Accessed November 7, 2023. https://www.youtube.com/watch?v=wmos9Efp5K0.

Pandian, M. S. S. (1998) 2014. "A Rediscovery of Ravana as a Southern Hero Combating Northern Imperialism Is a Fallout of Hindu-Hindi Nationalism," *Outlook India*, November 2. Accessed September 14, 2022. https://dbsjeyaraj.com/dbsj/archives/34856.

Parasakthi [The supreme goddess]. 1952. Directed by Krishnan-Panju. National Pictures. Accessed November 7, 2023. https://www.youtube.com/watch?v=s5Z3rf HeLVw.

Pechilis, Karen, and Amy-Ruth Holt. 2023. *Devotional Visualities: Seeing Bhakti in Indic Material Cultures*. Bloomsbury Academic.

Pinney, Christopher. 2004. *"Photos of the Gods": The Printed Image and Political Struggle in India*. Reaktion Books.

Pope, Rev. George U. (1886) 2020. *Thirukkural: Tiruvalluvar*. W. H. Allen & Co.

Pruiksma, Thomas Hitoshi. 2021. *The Kural: Tiruvalluvar's Tirukkural*. Beacon.

Raa Raa. 2011. Directed by Sandilya. Jaeshan Studios. Accessed November 7, 2023. https://www.youtube.com/watch?v=hZQbjC1xjn0.

Raman, Bhavani. 2010. "Disciplining the Senses, Schooling the Mind: Inhabiting Virtue in the Tamil Tiṇṇai School." In *Ethical Life in South Asia*, edited by Anand Pandian and Daud Ali, 43–60. Indiana University Press.

Ramanujan, A. K. (1989) 1999. "Is There an Indian Way of Thinking? An Informal Essay." In *The Collected Essays of A. K. Ramanujan*, edited by Vinay Dharwadker, 35–51. Oxford University Press.

Ramaswamy, Sumathi. 1997. *Passions of the Tongue: Language Devotion in Tamil India, 1891–1970*. University of California Press.

Rancière, Jacques. (2004) 2013. *The Politics of Aesthetics*. Edited by Gabriel Rockhill. Bloomsbury Academic.

Saraswathi Sabatham [Saraswati's oath]. 1966. Directed by A.P. Nagarajan. Sri Vijayalakshmi Pictures. Accessed November 7, 2023. https://www.youtube.com/watch?v=m ZmMZGUuXg8.

Sinha, A. J. 2007. "Visual Culture and the Politics of Locality in Modern India: A Review Essay." *Modern Asian Studies* 41 (1): 187–220.

Srivathsan, A. 2000. "Politics, Popular Icons, and Urban Space in Tamil Nadu." In *Twentieth-Century Indian Sculpture: The Last Two Decades*, edited by Shivaji K. Panikkar, 108–17. Marg Publications.

Subbanna, S. 2009. "Legacy of Chitrasutra—Sri S. Rajam." *Indian Heritage*. Accessed September 14, 2022. http://www.indian-heritage.org/painting/srajam.html.

Subramuniyaswami, Satguru S. 1999. *Weaver's Wisdom: Ancient Precepts for a Perfect Life*. Himalayan Academy. Accessed February 2, 2025. https://www.himalayanacademy.com/media/books/weavers-wisdom/web/.

Subramuniyaswami, Satguru S. 2000. *Tirukkural: The American English and Modern Tamil Translations of an Ethical Masterpiece*. Abinav Publications. Accessed

February 2, 2025. https://www.himalayanacademy.com/media/books/tirukural/ web/pg_010.html.

VIP2 [The unemployed graduate 2]. 2017. Directed by Soundarya Rajinikanth. V Creations. Accessed November 7, 2023. https://www.youtube.com/watch?v= WG1tq6BUFKM.

Wagner, Roy. 1986. *Asiwinarong: Ethos, Image, and Social Power Among the Usen Barok of New Ireland*. Princeton University Press.

Warrier, Shobha. 2000. "Thiruvalluvar Comes to Life in Kanyakumari," *Rediff: On the Net*, January 29. Accessed September 19, 2022. https://www.rediff.comnews/ 2000/jan/ 29thir.htm.

Zvelebil, Kamil. 1975. *Tamil Literature*. Brill.

Websites

www.himalayanacademy.com/hamsa/
www.tamilnation.org

13

Kali in a Time of Hurt Sentiments

RACHEL FELL MCDERMOTT

Bring it on, BJP! I [am] a Kali worshipper. I am not afraid of anything.
Not your ignoramuses. Not your goons. Not your police. And most
certainly not your trolls. Truth doesn't need backup forces.

—Mahua Moitra

As David R. Kinsely taught many of us in the mid-1970s (Kinsley 1975),[1]
the goddess Kali in Bengal has had a layered history. She began as a
puranic demon-slayer, grew up as a tantric goddess of transformation, and
came into an open, public maturity through patronage, *bhakti*, and public
ritual. In the process, she was maternalized and domesticated, she donned
a nubile body and sweet visage, and she was importuned for saving grace.
To be sure, just like a palimpsest—the reuse of an object by effacing or
smoothing a surface for a new purpose, where vestiges of the original are
never totally obscured—the bloodthirsty, tantric side of the Goddess was
always available.[2] We see this in continuing temple practices of blood sacrifice, as well as in her appropriation by Bengali nationalists after the first
Partition of Bengal, who called upon her votaries to offer her white goats
and who pictured her as dark and emaciated by the depredations of the
British (Chirol 1910; Urban 2003). We also see Kali travel to Western and
principally non-Bengali contexts, where since the 1990s she has stood for
feminine rage against patriarchal oppression (McDermott 1996, 2003). In

309

these cases, the dangerous but freedom-inspiring aspects of Kali have been emphasized.

Could it happen again, that the sweetened Goddess of Bengal could re-reveal the potent underbelly of her wild, tantric, antinomian side? To use the language of this volume, could she become "intensified" again? Could the process of her democratization, by which in the eighteenth century she opened out from her elite, esoteric, fearsome tantric background to become accessible through *bhakti* to a wider public, make way for the revitalization of certain fierce practices or beliefs, or the creation of new ones? And if so, under what circumstances? What could prompt such a change?

In this chapter I examine two related controversies that involved the goddess Kali, one in Toronto and the other in West Bengal, in 2021–2023. These provoke us to wonder what tolerance there may be, and where or by whom in today's India, for a reanimated Karalavadana, the Terrible-Faced One.

The Scandal of Manimekalai's *Kaali*

On July 2, 2022, Leena Manimekalai, an award-winning South Asian film-maker in her forties who was living in Toronto, posted on Twitter a copy of a poster she had made to advertise her short performance documentary called *Kaali* (fig. 13.1). It was one of eighteen short films to be featured by the Toronto Metropolitan University's film series "Under the Tent," a storytelling project in which selected filmmakers were asked to reflect on multicultural-ism, race, and diversity within Toronto. "Under the Tent" was screened at the city's Aga Khan Museum. The poster depicted a woman—Manimekalai herself—dressed as Kali, smoking a cigarette, and carrying an LGBTQ pride flag. In the film,[3] this rebellious Kali walks the streets of Toronto at night, eating meat, drinking liquor, and smoking marijuana.

The Twitter post garnered an immediate, international reaction. Outrage was expressed on social media, Manimekalai received death and rape threats, her effigy was burned, and Mahant Raju Das, a Hindu religious leader in Uttar Pradesh, published a video in which he threatened the filmmaker with beheading (Holland 2022). Legal First Information Reports (FIRs) were filed in India in six different states and Delhi (Xing 2023), alleging "hurt religious sentiment" and demanding imprisonment or fine, under Section 295A of the Indian Penal Code. "For most Hindus, religious tolerance is not just a civic virtue but also a religious value, and respecting other religions is an

Figure 13.1. The poster for Manimekalai's *Kaali*, as posted on Twitter on July 2, 2022. *Source:* Courtesy of Leena Manimekalai. Used with permission.

integral part of being Hindu. We justly demand the same respect to be given to our faith and beliefs," wrote Prem Shukla, national spokesman for the Bharatiya Janata Party, or BJP (Shukla 2022). In Canada, the Indian High Commission in Ottawa exhorted authorities to withdraw the "disrespectful depiction of Hindu Gods" showcased at the Aga Khan Museum (Kumar 2022), and Chandra Arya, a Liberal Member of Parliament (MP) in Ottawa, also passed judgment on the poster on Twitter (Xing 2023). His critique was met with a petition to Prime Minister Justin Trudeau, signed by more than one hundred academics, activists, and members of community organizations, such as PEN Canada, Hindus for Human Rights, the Poetic Justice Foundation, and TMU's Centre for Free Expression, in condemnation of his remarks (Xing 2022b). The furor had proven effective, however: Twitter removed Manimekalai's post within four days, and soon after, the Aga Khan Museum pulled her film (Press Trust of India 2022a).

Manimekalai was unapologetic, enunciating a fivefold defense: (1) the Kali she embodies is the genuine spirit of the Indian Tamil-Telugu goddess, who possesses people and does indeed drink alcohol and eat meat (Moreno 2023); (2) Kali is Mary Magdelene, Rahma, Sappho, and Shekhinah, and hence racially inclusive; (3) Manimekalai's intention was not to provoke but to project the "shared love" of a goddess who "travels in the tram, listens to jazz, drinks cocktails, shares a cigarette, and spends an evening with Torontonians from across cultures"; (4) those who take offense are "misogynists, . . . queer-phobics, [and] . . . absolutists who want to establish a monolithic patriarchal brahmanical Hinduism"; and (5) her poster has been co-opted by the Sangh Parivar, which achieves "a systematic political murder" by fomenting threats and abuse, manufacturing a climate of fear, and filing court cases (Mukherjee 2022).[4]

How can we understand the row over this specific interpretation of *Kaali*, in light of the theme of this chapter? Let me mention three backdrops, or frames of reference. First, *Kaali* was not the first time that Manimekalai had produced a controversial film. In her short documentary *Goddesses* (2007), Manimekalai follows the daily lives of three Dalit women battling caste and gender violence; one of these becomes possessed by the Goddess in a public, frenzied manner. In *Maadathy* (2019), local deities worshiped by subaltern communities are shown to have a subversive power. And *White Van Stories* (2013) centers on seven women who have lost relatives during enforced disappearances in postwar Sri Lanka (Mallik 2022). Her topics focus on South Asian social injustices and feature ameliorating aspects of local traditions. *Kaali* is different because it is a personal statement, Leena Manimekalai's own individual appropriation.

Second, the local, Canada-based furor over the poster and the film were also not unprecedented. Canadian academics have been harassed in the past after critiquing Hindu nationalism in India,[5] and the Indian government is suspicious of "anti-India" sentiments in Canada. Recently, this has been illustrated by the killing of Hardeep Singh Nijjar in Surrey, British Columbia, in June 2023—an execution that Canadian prime minister Justin Trudeau told the House of Commons in September 2023 was credibly alleged to have been ordered by the Indian government, due to Nijjar's claimed support for Khalistan (Schmidt 2023). In other words, the agitation against and for Manimekalai is recognizable within the Canadian political public sphere.

Third, the outcry over "hurt sentiments," as enunciated by watchdog groups in the diaspora, also has a long history.[6] To give examples just since 2017, Kali has been used to sell the following products: "Kali Booty Shorts" (Liquid Dreams); "Blood of Kali Black Tea" (Coffee Shop of Horrors); "Goddess Kali Skirt" and "Goddess Kali Cereal T-Shirt" (Etsy); "Kali Halloween costume" (Bristol Clothing); and "Kali Beer" (Incendiary Brewing Company). Women who have dressed up as Kali or somehow imputed to themselves Kali's image have also come under attack. In early July 2020, the South Indian film actress Anarkali Marikar directed a photo shoot in which she portrayed herself as the dark-skinned low-caste goddess Kali. She later had to apologize for "promoting racism and discrimination over skin color" (Indiaglitz 2022). In another instance, Kathryn Elizabeth Hudson, known as Katy Perry, captioned an image of Kali standing on Siva that she posted on social media, "my current mood," which led to a backlash among Indian fans (Iyer 2022).

In many of these cases a man named Rajan Zed,[7] president of the Nevada-based Universal Society of Hinduism, was the public face of campaigns to eradicate offensive products, depictions, or statements. "The goddess Kali [is] highly revered and [is] meant to be worshipped in temples or home shrines and not to be trivialized in a reimagined version to sell tea. Inappropriate usage of Hindu deities or concepts or symbols or icons for commercial or other agenda [is] not okay as it hurts the devotees" (Sanagala 2020). Further, Kali is "not to adorn one's hips, groin, buttocks, genitals, waist, crotch, thighs, and pelvis for mercantile greed" (Zed 2023). In every instance, in response to Zed, the companies or firms removed the scandalizing merchandise from circulation.

Many scholars and activists "talk back" to the concerns of the watch-dogs.[8] Those who know the background of Kali's history, texts, and rituals understand that the Goddess is primarily nonvegetarian, demands blood and alcohol, possesses men and women, and is known in her textual, often tantric, tradition for being dangerous or threatening to people of the established order. Evidence for such attitudes and rituals is massive. Examples span the considerable blood sacrifice at Assamese temples; the association of Kali with tantrikas and corpses in, for example, Tarapith, West Bengal; the alcoholic offerings to the Goddess, in addition to verbal sexual insults and songs, at the Kodungallur Temple in Kerala; and the offering to Kali of cigarettes and alcohol in Guyanese goddess temples. In addition, Kali worship has sometimes made new social spaces for women, in terms of spiritual leadership in the public sphere (Gupta 1992; Pechilis 2004). Many of those involved in her everyday practice are aware of these attributes of the Goddess. Yet the twin influences of (1) growing Hindu nationalist disapproval of religious diversity and plurality and (2) the diaspora setting, where, since the 1990s, an attempt has been made to bring Hindu religiosity into conformity with the monotheistic, monolithic expectations of "respectable" religion have rendered a conception of Kali such as that by Manimekalai a matter of great concern, or offense.

Indeed, writes Sharanya Manivannan,

> numerous deities of folk origin who have been subsumed over time in Hinduism are propitiated through offerings of tobacco, liquor, animals sacrificed and then cooked and other items that are prohibited or taboo according to some ways of life. . . . A smoking, queer-affirmative Kali is offensive only to those with a very specific and rigid concept of the goddess; one that does not take into account the many other manifestations that She has in other imaginations and cultures. . . . "Hurt sentiment" results in truly disproportionate corollaries, from assassinations to riots and more. Being able to discern between something that bugs us and something that does harm to us, and not reacting to both to the same degree, is a sign of maturity—not just in a person, but in a nation too. (Manivannan 2023)

To turn back to the theme of this volume, is Manimekalai's image a new "intensification" of the Goddess? Is this interpretation of Kali something new, something fierce, something frightening or threatening? In some sense, no; Manimekalai has not created of Kali anything that the Goddess has not already encompassed, for centuries in South Asia and for decades in the South Asian diaspora. Moreover, Manimekalai herself apparently conceives of the Goddess as an empowering, positive force. What seems to be threatening, however, to those who find the filmmaker's conception offensive is the bringing of the Goddess of sacrifice and freedom into a public sphere enabled by a global social media that spreads her image beyond context and control, in the process appearing to denigrate, and hence "hurt," the sensitivities of Hindu people who fear non-Hindu opprobrium. For many in the Asian diaspora, as well as in parts of India where the terrifying Kali is not a home deity (recall that Rajan Zed is not a Bengali), Manimekalai's goddess is understood as intensified, and inappropriately so. In other words, the intensification is in the mind of the scandalized viewer.

"What Does Bengal Have to Do with Ayodhya?" Durga, Kali, and the West Bengal Elections

The furor over *Kaali* had an interesting and unexpected sequel, this time in India itself, in West Bengal, a thriving center of Kali worship. The Goddess, one might say, was caught in the crossfires of political combat between the Bharatiya Janata Party (BJP) and the Trinamool Congress (TMC). The Trinamool Congress, led by Chief Minister Mamata Banerjee (b. 1955), had been in power in the state since 2011. After the BJP was elected as the majority in the Lok Sabha in 2014, the BJP attempted to make inroads into West Bengal. In the 2014 elections, it won only two of the allocated Lok Sabha seats, but in 2019 it increased its edge considerably, winning eighteen. In the lead-up to the 2021 West Bengal Assembly elections, the party hoped to win even more seats. Durga, and then Kali, became talking points in a heated exchange over identity politics and proprietorship (Banerjee 2021a; Datta 2023).

At first, the BJP attempted to argue for the salience of Ram in Bengal, claiming that he had always been worshiped in Bengal; "let the Left-Liberal Cabal not tell you otherwise" (Mozumdar 2020). Moreover, Bengalis were reminded that Hindu nationalism was born in Bengal, with Bankim Chandra Bhatterjee's "Bande Mataram!" and Swami Vivekananda's muscular defense of Indian spirituality (Bhattacharya 2020).

At the same time, the BJP's West Bengal unit president Dilip Ghosh stated that Ram is superior to Durga; after all, Lord Ram is an emperor and an *avatara*, a manifestation of the deity Vishnu. "We know the names of Rama's ancestors. Do we know about the ancestors of Goddess Durga?" (Rajaram 2021). This statement sparked a spirited verbal war between the BJP and the TMC, the latter reacting against what they perceived as the Hindutva insult to their culture and religion, on the sacred soil of Bengal itself. TMC Lok Sabha MP Abhishek Banerjee spoke with pride about the Bengali reverence for divine and human expressions of the feminine, censuring the BJP for its lack of respect for women: he was cited in an online newspaper article, "Disrespect of Women Is Disrespect to Mother Durga," as saying, "Your slogan should not be "Jai Shri Ram," but "Jai Sita Ram" (Indian News Weekly 2021).

Slogans then began flying thick and fast. Reacting to Mamata Banerjee's exhortation to her followers to counter "Jai Shri Ram" with "Jai Ma Durga" and "Jai Ma Kali," the BJP itself began adopting these same slogans. *India Today* exclaimed, "Durga Is the New Ram for Bengal's BJP," an admitted "Bengalisation" of the BJP's core strategy (Datta 2020). A senior BJP leader, requesting anonymity, apparently stated, "We keep evolving and changing policies, depending on the ground level inputs" (Das 2021a).

Further attempting to co-opt the opposition, Amit Shah, minister of home affairs in the BJP government, began to visit Kolkata's Kali temples.[9] BJP spokespeople averred that they were just as faithful interpreters and devotees of Durga and Kali as anyone else in Bengal. This extended to opportunistic interpretations of supposed violence in the state, resulting from Mamata Banerjee's policy of "minority appeasement." BJP MP Arjun Singh blamed local Muslims in Murshidabad for desecrating and burning an image of Kali. He was quoted as saying, "The jihadi nature of Didi's [Mamata Bannerjee's] politics is now hell bent on destroying Hindu religion and culture. See how one religious group has attacked and destroyed a temple and burned the idol of Maa Kali in Murshidabad area of West Bengal. Shameful." No one local lodged any complaint, however, as the image had caught fire by accident (Dwivedi 2020). A tweet posted in response read, "Fascist Amit Shah go back. Bengalis reject CAA-NRC-NPR. #GoBack_Amit_Shah!"[10]

One can see the issues at stake by considering the defensive rhetoric launched by Mamata Banerjee and her ministers against the state and national BJP statements. Here I present an overview of rejoinders. First, Ram prayed to Durga before the war against Ravana, so she is superior to him (ABP News Bureau 2021). Second, we are not the cow belt, and Ayodhya means nothing to us.[11] Ram Navami in Uttar Pradesh is Durga Puja for us, and Diwali in the north is Kali Puja for us. We are different from North India

(Das 2020; ABP News Bureau 2021). Third, we are religiously syncretic, and we do not have Hindu-Muslim discord (Ghosh 2021). Our heroes—for instance, Ramakrishna and Swami Vivekananda, Isvar Chandra Vidyasagar, Rammohan Roy, Rabindranath Tagore, Netaji Subhas Chandra Bose, Mother Teresa, and Kazi Nazrul Islam—are secular, noncommunal, and include Christians and Muslims. Kalyan Banerjee, interviewed for *The Week* (May 16, 2021), stated, "The BJP's problem is that it does not know Bengal's history. It did not know that Kazi Nazrul Islam wrote a thousand songs on goddess Kali and Ramakrishna Paramahamsa read Quran in Dakshineswar Kali temple in Kolkata. Had they known this, they would not have tried to break the secular fabric of Bengal" (Banerjee 2021b).

Such responses are tantamount to claiming a subnational regional identity, to asserting Bengali exceptionalism and pride, and to portraying the BJP as outsiders. Said Mamata Banerjee early in 2022, "Nobody can ignore Bengal. I challenge them. Nobody can wipe out the history of Bengal and India. Those trying it will burn their hands" (Hindustan Times 2022). Even those who felt that Banerjee and her TMC had become authoritarian and corrupt stated that they would prefer to vote for her rather than "encourage an organised fascist party taking over Bengal" (Das 2021b). The Trinamool had a spectacular win in the 2021 West Bengal Assembly elections. Splayed across the headline of the *National Herald* was the jubilant announcement: " 'No Vote to BJP' Echoes in Kolkata, to Be Heard Across Bengal" (Sengupta 2021).

In the case of this show of force against an attempted Hindu nationalist entrée into the state, Durga and Kali were, one might say, mascots for the home team, emblems of a prized and protected Bengali identity. Neither their iconography nor their characters were subjects of discussion; as far as one can tell, they were not publicly prayed to for political salvation from the BJP. Insofar as Bengal needed to be safeguarded against a nationalist platform, they were representative of the state, or were, as such, themselves in need of protection.

This scenario changed when a TMC MP dared to make detailed remarks about her own conception of Kali's image and meaning. The flap occurred in early July 2022, when Manimekalai's *Kaali* poster made its way—instantly—to India across the world of social media. The TMC MP from Krishnanagar, Mahua Moitra (b. 1974), when asked about the poster, stated that she, and others, had every right as individuals to imagine Kali as a meat-eating and alcohol-accepting deity, as each person has his or her unique way of offering prayers. She mentioned Tarapith as proof of the fact that Kali (in her form as Tara) accepts meat and alcohol (The Wire 2022).

There was an immediate backlash by the BJP leaders in West Bengal, who accused her of insulting "traditional Hindu religion," and in an effort to show their own bona fides announced that they would sponsor their own (off-season) Kali Puja, conducted by women priests (Saha 2022). Moitra countered that the BJP should not "impose its agenda of Hindutva, . . . thrusting its monolithic views" on other ethnic groups. "Who is the BJP to teach us how to conduct puja for Goddess Kali in a particular way? Neither Lord Ram nor Lord Hanuman solely belongs to the BJP. Has the party taken the lease of Hindu dharma? Can the Assam CM [Chief Minister] explain in writing to the court what offerings are made to the presiding deity of Kamakhya Temple? Can the CMs of other BJP-ruled states do the same about offerings made to Maa Kali in temples there? Is liquor not part of the offerings in those temples?" (Press Trust of India 2022c).

It was in this context that Prime Minister Narendra Modi entered the scene. On July 10, he announced, at the centenary celebrations of the life of Swami Atmasthananda (1919–2017), fifteenth president of the Ramakrishna Math, that "the blessings of Goddess Kali are always with the country, which is moving ahead with a spiritual energy for the welfare of the world" (Press Trust of India 2022d). BJP leaders used this as an occasion to compare the prime minister's open and flexible views to those of the obnoxious leaders of the TMC. Moitra responded that she would "advise BJP's troll-in-charge for Bengal to tell his masters to stop commenting on things they have no clue about." Trinamool Congress MP Sougata Roy also joined the fray. "The Prime Minister does not know about Kali Puja. He may have come one or two times to Belur Math or Dakshineswar, but how would he know about Kali Puja? Mamata Banerjee has Kali thakur in her residence and she does Kali puja. So we are not going to take lessons of Kali puja from the BJP" (Express News Service 2022).

As several Indian journalists and scholars commented, what Moitra was affirming was twofold: the "acceptance of diversity in worship and a rejection of homogenisation of religion" (Cattopadhyay 2022), and the personal freedom of religious expression. In this vein, Surajit C. Mukhopadhyay, political observer and professor of sociology at Amity University, Chhatisgarh, said, "Mahua Moitra has not slandered anyone, nor has she said anything that scholars have not said *ad nauseum* over the years. Kali is actually a reversal of Durga; it represents the tantrik tradition in Hindu philosophy—everybody knows the rituals and traditions. Mahua Moitra was not inventing them" (Cattopadhyay 2022; Sinha 2022).

Unfortunately for Moitra, her party, the TMC, did not support her. Within hours of Moitra's controversial comments, in response to widespread political and religious protest, the TMC distanced itself from her and issued a Twitter statement that her views were personal and not endorsed by the party (Chakraborty 2022).

The Internet, a Majoritarian Sensibility, and the "Industry of Hurt"

In a real sense, the two intertwined stories I have briefly narrated above are ephemera. Although tempers and bitter emotions have flared, and careers have been temporarily derailed, no one has lost his or her life, and there will be other art pieces, other elections, and other political battles that may repeat the same sort of controversy. At this historical moment, however, there is a particular nexus of contexts, in concert, that illuminates the trajectory of the Bengali Kali (and Durga) and provide commentary on the issue of intensification.

The first context is the burgeoning of electronically enabled world connectivity. The speed at which images, messages, and videos of any conceivable kind can be relayed across the world, without controls of any kind, renders nothing private, nothing cordoned off from potential view. The internet was first introduced into India for educational and research communities in 1986, but the general public gained access to it only in August 1995, through the state-owned telecommunications company, Videsh Sanchar Nigam Limited. For the first ten years, the Internet was slow and dependent on dial-up landlines, making its use frustrating and its penetration into nonurban areas slower than desired. Today, in 2024, internet access in India is provided by public and private companies, using a range of technologies and media; nearly 700 million people use the Internet in some form, and it is anticipated that by 2025 that number will increase to 900 million (Joshy 2023). An image from Toronto can be anywhere in India in moments.

Second, the attempt to dictate or police local religious traditions is not new. Since the rise of the BJP in the mid-1980s, local, often vernacular, and frequently nonmainstream images and conceptions of Ram have become sites of contest. One of the earliest such instances was the outcry over an exhibition mounted by a cultural organization, the SAHMAT Collective,[12] titled Hum Sab Ayodhya (We Are All Ayodhya). In the aftermath of the destruction of the Babri Masjid in December 1992, the exhibition showcased multiple Indian renditions of Ram and the *Ramayana* as a testament to the diversity of narrative and religious traditions in the subcontinent. In the words of Neeti Nair, "The heated parliamentary debates around the exhibition and its subsequent ban reveal the fault lines in civil and political society in the 1990s that would enable the mainstreaming of 'Hindutva' as a way of life" (Nair 2023). This streamlining of Ram, making of him a single and singular image, was noted in an important essay by Anuradha Kapur (1993). The process of narrowing or attempting to restrict acceptable understandings of Ram continued in force over the next two decades. In 2012, Delhi University removed from its syllabus the classic essay by A. K. Ramanujan, "Three Hundred Ramayanas, Five Examples and Three Thoughts on Translation" (Ramanujan 1991). Too numerous to mention here, the instances of historical neglect and revision are still ongoing (Jaffrelot 2019), and after the 2019 Supreme Court decision allocating to Hindus the land on which the Babri Masjid once stood, the glorification of the Hindu right's view of Ram is only likely to consolidate. As stated by Radhika Bordia, "Multiple strands are inconvenient for fundamentalist forces. Their triumph lies in framing a single unchallenged narrative" (Bordia 2020). Whatever groups still exist in India with different views of Ram, their votes are insignificant, and the Rashtriya Swayamsevak Sangh has all but overwhelmed them.

What is being canonized, yet once again, for Kali? For non-Kali-worshiping Hindus—that is, for Hindus who do not live in Kerala, Bengal, or Assam, or who are not part of those diasporas, whether in India or outside—Kali does not belong to the mainly worshiped deities, she is not a major deity in all regions of India, and her own texts, the very short parts of the "Devi-Mahatmya" portion of the *Markandeya Purana* or the various tantras, are either too short or too nonmainstream to be straightforwardly exploited in politicized conversation. So, the homogenization at work during a fracas as seen in 2022–2023 pits a vague, sweetened, *shakti* against things she is not: alcohol-drinking, provocative, threateningly untamed, and projective of the "negative side of Hindu culture" (Indira 2022). Manimekalai was just as guilty as Moitra in defending as liberative, a local—Tamil/Telegu and Bengali—goddess.

It is thus a majoritarian perspective—that is, a vocally predominant Hindu nationalism—that triumphs in cases where posts, films, images, and the like portraying more radical, intensified interpretations are taken down or withdrawn. Any deviation from the majoritarian view will not be permitted (Cattopadhyay 2022), whether regarding Ram or Kali or a host of any other deities.

The third significant context for the current moment (and I suspect, many moments over the years to come) is the culture of offense, the weaponization of the discourse of "hurt sentiments." After Partition, with the uneasy sociopolitical jostling between the Hindu majority and Muslim, Christian, Sikh, and other minorities, Section 295A of the Indian Penal Code, first enacted under the British in 1929, has become increasingly utilized in identity-formation and identity-protection by Indian citizens against each other:

> Deliberate and malicious acts, intended to outrage religious feelings or any class by insulting its religion or religious beliefs—Whoever, with deliberate and malicious intention of outraging the religious feelings of any class of citizens of India, by words, either spoken or written, or by signs or by visible representations or otherwise, insults or attempts to insult the religion or the religious beliefs of that class, shall be punished with imprisonment of either description for a term which may extend to three years, or with fine, or with both. (Section 295A of the Indian Penal Code)

Even if FIRs are not always registered under this law, the law itself contributes to the creation of a "community of sentiment" (Appadurai 1990) or of "emotional subjects" who may be incited to self-justified violence by perceived offenses. Hurt is mobilized by Hindus—many of them nationalists, but the phenomenon applies to "secularists" as well[13]—who view themselves as being marginalized and victimized by minorities; censorship is a tool with which to inhibit the anxiety stimulated by the Other. Comments Laetitia Zecchini, "Expressions such as 'the industry of hurt' or 'the marketplace of outrage' flood the media, where India is repeatedly defined as 'a republic of hurt sentiments'" (Zecchini 2020, 244). Or, in the words of Pratap Bhanu Mehta, "The argumentative Indian is being replaced by the offended Indian" (Mehta 2014). Works of art and scholarship appear to be especially vulnerable to this feeling of offense, and countering them, frequently with threatened or enacted violence, is claimed as a way to return safety and sanctity to society.

This rhetoric of hurt sentiments has become so widespread that in retaliation against the BJP's attempt to co-opt Durga and Kali in the 2021 West Bengal elections, the TMC decried the BJP's comments as an "insult" to the religious sentiments of the Bengali population (Rajaram 2021). Yet, when Moitra incurred critique over her defense of Manimekalai's *Kaali*, in effect standing up for expressions of local culture, the TMC distanced itself from her with the pronouncement that her beliefs were not representative of those of the party. Commented Surajit C. Mukhopadhyay, with some disgust, "The Trinamool has just thrown Mahua Moitra under the bus for their satisfaction" (Cattopadhyay 2022). He continued, "The Trinamool should have stood by Moitra and pointed out with references that she was correct in her statement. Instead, they chose to fight fire with fire and add to the conflagration" (Cattopadhyay 2022; see also Damle, Amod, and Nilu 2023).

To bring these three contexts together, then, in understanding the case of the Goddess in West Bengal, while she can be a specific symbol of Bengali political particularity in conflict with the BJP, and even the Communists,[14] her traditional Bengali iconography and divine persona cannot be too publicly explored or considered, especially in politicized contexts via electronic media. Kali's coincidence of opposites—her blood lust and her motherly mercy, her grisly ugliness as well as her charming beauty, her acceptance of the tantric hero as well as the devotee, and her antinomian and transcendent characteristics—is a difficult package to accept for an orientation championing brahmanical values, whether in Toronto, New Delhi, or anywhere else in our interlinked world. In today's Hindutva-inflected majoritarian environment, what occurs among local publics at Kalighat in Kolkata, West Bengal, or at Kamakhya in Guwahati, Assam, or at the Bhagavathy Temple in Kodungallur, Kerala, can go unexamined as long as it is not utilized for transregional political effect. The fictive public arena, then, curbs freedom of speech.

Conclusion: Who Will Burn Whose Hands?
The Reciprocal Wounding of Offense

Apart from the idea of the palimpsest mentioned at the beginning of this chapter, I am attracted to another way of thinking about elements of a tradition that may get submerged over time and then reemerge at a later point to become predominant again. This is the theory proposed by Jan Assmann (2006).

Assmann posits that there are three principal kinds of memory—that proper to an individual, that which bonds groups together through shared experiences and memories, and what he calls cultural memory (Assmann 2006). This last emerges only through the advent of writing, as a result of which archives of the past are preserved in what he calls the "stream of tradition" (Assmann 2006, 40–41), a flowing repository out of which it is always possible to pick out old resources for use in new times. Competing bonding memories are also carried forward by this stream, which is living and deep.

Censorship has always been a part of Assmann's cultural memory; portions of a tradition are excised by some cultural actors but remain present as possible future assets. Canonization, by contrast, shuts the flow, and damns up the stream, Assmann asserts. A canon leaves no room for change or improvisation: it leads to homogenization and an erasure of multiple strands. The stream still trickles on, and resources are still there. But the act of canonizing renders those left-aside meanings harder to track, to find, and to restore to prominence.

It seems to me that what is happening in India today is the attempt to "canonize" certain ways of thinking about religion, ways that are expressed through the language of upliftment, corroboration of brahmanical orthodoxy, protection from outside contamination, and hurt sentiment. Canonization in Hindu-majority India and its diasporas does not have to happen as it did in the ancient Egyptian or Hebrew traditions, the provenance of Assmann's research. However, the result is the same: the creation of a general rule for theological, iconographic, and historical interpretation that is enforceable and enforced, weaponized by the culture of offense.

More than two decades ago, after cataloguing the emergence of the dread tantric Goddess into the sweetened open of the Bengali *bhakti* sphere, I wondered whether the ferocious Kali was now forever eclipsed. At that time, in 2001, I reflected, "Were a Hindu nationalist party to oust the communists in Bengal, I suspect that one would see a resurgence of interest in Kālī's martial symbolism" (McDermott 2001, 296).[15] As I look at the Goddess from this vantage point in 2024, I agree with this sentiment, but perhaps for a different reason.

Intensification at the hands of vocal Bengali devotees and ritual actors, artists, playwrights, or scholars would seem to provoke ire, consternation, and "insult" to a pan-North-India-dominated, Hindu-nationalist-leaning public. This we saw with Manimekalai and Moitra. Could the TMC or other non-BJP-allied party have the temerity to reinvigorate the angry aspect of the Goddess to fight their political opponents—risking a perhaps national discourse of hurt feeling? How threatened would the TMC have to be in order for the Intensified Goddess to be solicited? Perhaps the intensification will come from the other side. Although the BJP lost the 2021 election, if they were actually to win in West Bengal and become a local majority, as they are gearing up to attempt in every future election (Datta 2023),[16] I would not be surprised to see the Goddess, in their hands, becoming more muscular and threatening to "outsiders," just as, under Savarkar's influence, Ram has changed in that same direction, representing the violent but beneficent unifier of "the whole land from the Himalayas to the Seas under one sovereign sway" (Savarkar 1923, 11).[17]

With a 27 percent Muslim population in the state and a legacy of secular, left-leaning thinking, the BJP might need the strength of the Goddess on its side in order to survive. That such a trajectory might in fact be plausible is indicated by the remarks made by West Bengal BJP leader Suvendu Adhikari on December 8, 2023, when Moitra was expelled from the Lok Sabha. He claimed that her expulsion was the result of "Maa Kali's curse," and said, "You don't have the capacity to belittle Her, but Her rage can raze you completely. Jai Maa Kali" (Roy 2023). This is not the placid, characterless Kali of Narendra Modi, but the Goddess with teeth, who is presented as willing on behalf of the Sangh Parivar to punish her wayward Bengali proponents.

In sum, the double story of this chapter yields three different instantiations of intensification: scandalized devotees react with offense and hurt to forms of the Goddess that they consider to have been falsely intensified; threatened opponents of the BJP might conceivably call (although they have not yet done so) upon a resurgent, violent Kali to fight against Ram and the BJP; and Hindu nationalists, on the offensive once in power in the state (which they have not yet achieved), may use the image of the dread Goddess to assert their own power. In all three cases, an intensified Kali rises in a setting of mutual, public attack.

No one knows the future, except perhaps for the Goddess herself. We watch and wait, to see how her interests are best served.

Notes

1. David often joked, when he telephoned me, "Hello, this is the Father of Kali Studies speaking." He was that to us, in the late 1980s and early 1990s.

2. Goddess is capitalized when she is a singular force, standing in for a known name, but lowercase when a generic goddess. When referring to the goddess Kali, I use lowercase. But I use goddesses when indicating plurality.

3. Almost immediately, the film became unavailable (see Xing 2022a), but Manimekalai kindly shared the film with me, so that I could see it at the time of writing this chapter (January 9, 2024).

4. In February 2023, the Indian Supreme Court ordered that all FIRs be transferred to the IFSO Unit, Special Cell Delhi, for investigation; in the interim, the Court proscribed attempts to harass or coerce her (Xing 2023).

5. Hate speech, threats, and media targeting are widely reported against Canadian academics, including Chinnaiah Jangam of Carleton University in Ottawa and Kristin Plys and Malavika Kasturi at the University of Toronto (Onishi and Isai 2023; Swyers and Trinh 2022;).

6. For examples from the early 1990s, see McDermott 2003.

7. For a discussion of Zed and his concern with the "trivializing" of Hindu deities in the United States, see Zeiler 2018.

8. For example, on November 3, 2022, the Toronto Metropolitan University's Faculty Association organized a "protest and solidarity" screening of both *Kaali* and another of Manimekalai's films. This was joined by PEN Canada, Hindus for Human Rights, the Poetic Justice Foundation, and TMU's Centre for Free Expression (Xing 2022b).

9. He visited the Dakshineswar Kali Temple on November 6, 2020, https://video. search.yahoo.com/search/video?fr=mcafee&ei=UTF-8&p=amit+shah+visits+ dakshieswar&type=E210US739G0#id=0&vid=c705a0187cc046f56b0e95fd4ad 49008&action=click]; Kalighat on December 26, 2023, https://video.search.yahoo. com/search/video?fr=mcafee&ei=UTF-8&p=amit+shah+visits+kalighat&type=E210 US739G0#id=1&vid=e764006587669e1def601245177f8b25&action=click]; he had been to Tarapith, in Birbhum district, on June 28, 2018, https://www.youtube.com/ watch?v=bqun6pa_Z0w].

10. This was a tweet posted from Kolkata on March 1, 2020. See https:// twitter.com/TheKolkataWalla/status/1233987717148692480.

11. "What does Bengal have to do with Ayodhya?" This was asked by West Bengal cabinet minister Firhad Hakim in August 2020 (see Das 2020).

12. The Safdar Hashmi Memorial Trust (SAHMAT) Collective of artists and intellectuals was named after political activist, playwright, and poet Safdar Hashmi, who was murdered in 1989.

13. It was the Congress government that brought charges against SAHMAT in 1993 (Nair 2023, 11).

14. Mamata Banerjee, in January 2023, accused the BJP and the CPM of forging an alliance, commenting, "Now Ram and Bam [Left] have become one" (Gaurav 2023).

15. When I wrote this book, the Trinamool Congress had not yet come to power in the state.

16. Ahead of the 2024 general election, the BJP is trying new tactics to win over Bengal: co-opting people, history, and themes native to the state, resuscitating half-forgotten temples, and reimagining "ancient" pilgrimages. In October 2023, the BJP sponsored a massive Ram Mandir pandal—a replica of the newly dedicated Ayodhya temple—for Durga Puja at Santosh Mitra Square in Kolkata, and Amit Shah came personally to inaugurate it.

17. I am quoting here from the first edition, in May 1923, which Savarkar wrote while in prison in the Andaman Islands in 1921–1922.

References

ABP News Bureau. 2021. "ABP News Shikhar Sammelan: TMC Member Saugata Roy Says 'Bengalis Say Jai Maa Kali Not Jai Shri Ram.'" *ABP News Bureau*, February 18. https://news.abplive.com/news/lok-sabha-tmc-member-saugata-roy-spoke-at-shikhar-sammelan-talked-ma-maati-aur-manush-1444749.

Appadurai, Arjun. 1990. "Topographies of the Self: Praise and Emotion in Hindu India." In *Language and the Politics of Emotion*, edited by Catherine A. Lutz and Lila Abu-Lughod, 92–112. Cambridge University Press.

Assmann, Jan. 2006. *Religion and Cultural Memory: Ten Studies*. Translated by Rodney Livingstone. Stanford University Press.

Banerjee, Rabi. 2021a. "How BJP Is Trying to Gain a Foothold in Kolkata." *The Week*, May 2. https://www.theweek.in/theweek/cover/2021/04/23/how-bjp-is-trying-to-gain-a-foothold-in-kolkata.html.

Banerjee, Rabi. 2021b. "BJP Does Not Know Bengal's History: Kalyan Banerjee." *The Week*, May 16. https://www.theweek.in/theweek/cover/2021/05/06/bjp-does-not-know-bengals-history.html.

Bhattacharya, Snigdhendu. 2020. *Mission Bengal: A Saffron Experiment*. HarperCollins.

Bordia, Radhika. 2020. "How the Sangh Has Waged War to Erase India's Many Ramayanas in Its Quest for Power," *Scroll.in*, August 11. https://scroll.in/article/969983/how-the-sangh-has-waged-war-to-erase-indias-many-ramayanas-in-its-quest-for-power.

Cattopadhyay, Suhrid Sankar. 2022. "In Defence of Kali: Uproar over Comments by Mahua Moitra." *Frontline*, July 24. https://frontline.thehindu.com/politics/in-defence-of-kali-uproar-over-comments-by-mahua-moitra/article65665308.ece.

Chakraborty, Abhishek. 2022. "Mahua Moitra Unfollows TMC on Twitter After Party Condemns Her Comment on Goddess Kaali." *India Today*, July 6. https://www.indiatoday.in/india/story/mahua-moitra-unfollows-tmc-twitter-goddess-kaali-poster-row-1970836-2022-07-06.

Chirol, Sir Valentine. 1910. *Indian Unrest*. Macmillan.

Damle, Amod, and Nilu Damle. 2023. "The Trinamool Congress; Soft Hindutva." In *The Politics of Soft Hindutva: How Culture Matters in Indian Politics*, 169–87. Palgrave Macmillan.

Das, Madhuparna. 2020. "What Does Bengal Have to Do with Ayodhya Bhoomi Pujan, We Have Durga Puja & Eid, Says Minister." *The Print*, August 14. https://theprint.in/theprint-interview/what-does-bengal-have-to-do-with-ayodhya-bhoomi-pujan-we-have-durga-puja-eid-says-minister/481121/.

Das, Madhuparna. 2021a. "With Switch from 'Jai Shree Ram' to 'Jai Ma Durga,' BJP Is Tapping into the Bengali Emotion." *The Print*, January 10. https://theprint.in/politics/with-switch-from-jai-shree-ram-to-jai-ma-durga-bjp-is-tapping-into-the-bengali-emotion/582727/.

Das, Madhuparna. 2021b. " 'Will Suffer Mamata Misrule, Not BJP'—Bengal Intellectuals Don't Want Another 'Poriborton.' " *The Print*, January 25. https://theprint.in/politics/will-suffer-mamata-misrule-not-bjp-bengal-intellectuals-dont-want-another-poriborton/590352/.

Datta, Romita. 2020. "Durga Is the New Ram for Bengal's BJP." *India Today*, November 8. https://www.indiatoday.in/india-today-insight/story/durga-is-the-new-ram-forbengal-s-bjp-1739166-2020-11-08.

Datta, Romita. 2023. "BJP Looks for Breakthrough: Hindutva with a Bengali Accent." *India Today*, June 19. https://www.indiatoday.in/magazine/the-big-story/story/20230619-bjp-looks-for-breakthrough-hindutva-with-a-bengali-accent-2390766-2023-06-09.

Dwivedi, Jyoti. 2020. "Fact Check: The Curious Case of a 'Desecrated' Kali Idol in a Bengal Temple." *India Today*, September 3. https://www.indiatoday.in/fact-check/story/fact-check-the-curious-case-of-a-desecrated-kali-idol-in-a-bengal-temple-1718010-2020-09-02.

Express News Service. 2022. "PM Modi Invokes Goddess Kali, Mahua Hits Back at Him." *Indian Express*, July 11. https://indianexpress.com/article/india/pm-invokes-goddess-kali-mahua-hits-back-at-him-8021364/.

Gaurav, Kunal. 2023. "Mamata's Salvo at the BJP, Left in Bengal." *Hindustan Times*, January 2. https://www.hindustantimes.com/india-news/mamatas-salvo-at-bjp-left-in-bengal-ram-and-bam-have-become-one-101672656573924.html.

Ghosh, Ambar Kumar. 2021. "How Mamata Banerjee Painted the BJP as an "Alien Outsider" to Beat It in Its Own Game." *Scroll.in*, May 13. https://scroll.in/article/994479/how-mamata-banerjee-painted-the-bjp-as-an-alien-outsider-to-beat-it-in-its-own-game.

Gupta, Sanjukta. 1992. "Women in the Śaiva-Śākta Ethos." In *Roles and Rituals for Hindu Women*, edited by Julia Leslie, 193–210. Motilal Banarsidass.

Hindustan Times. 2022. "None Can Change History of Bengal, India, Says Mamata; Slams BJP on Netaji's Birthday." *Hindustan Times*, January 23. https://www.hindustantimes.com/india-news/none-can-change-history-of-bengal-india-says-mamata-slams-bjp-on-netaji-s-birthday-101642958283790.html.

Holland, Oscar. 2022. "Filmmaker Faces Death Threats over Controversial Hindu Goddess Poster." *CNN*, July 8. https://www.cnn.com/style/article/kaali-hindu-goddess-leena-manimekalai/index.html.

IndiaGlitz. 2022. "Anarkali Marikar's 'Kali' Photoshoot Turns Controversial." *IndiaGlitz*, July 10. https://www.indiaglitz.com/anarkali-marikars-kali-photoshoot-turns-controversial-tamil-news-264895.

Indian News Weekly. 2021. "Dilip Ghosh Comment on Devi Durga Creates Political War in West Bengal." *Indian News Weekly*, February 12. https://indiannewsweekly.com/2021/02/14/dilip-ghosh-comment-on-devi-durga-creates-political-war-in-west-bengal-political-disturbance-in-bengal-over-dilip-ghoshs-durga-comment-tmc-attacker/.

Indira, G. 2022. "Mahua Moitra Is Playing the Same Old Liberals' Politics." *MY Voice*, July 21. https://myvoice.opindia.com/2022/07/mahua-moitra-is-playing-the-same-old-liberals-politics/.

Iyer, ShriKrishna. 2022. "When Katy Perry Was Slammed." *Koimoi*, October 4. https://www.koimoi.com/hollywood-news/when-katy-perry-was-slammed-for-sharing-hindu-goddess-kalis-pic-to-express-her-current-mood-angry-netizens-reacted-this-is-a-shameful-offensive-act/.

Jaffrelot, Christopher. 2019. *Modi's India: Hindu Nationalism and the Rise of the Ethnic Democracy*. Translated by Cynthia Schoch. Princeton University Press.

Joshy, Christina. 2023. "Internet Users in India: Statistics and Data." *Grabon*, December 20. https://www.grabon.in/indulge/tech/internet-users-statistics/.

Kapur, Anuradha. 1993. "Deity to Crusader: The Changing Iconography of Ram." In *Hindus and Others: The Question of Identity in India Today*, edited by Gyanendra Pandey, 74–109. Viking.

Kinsley, David R. 1975. *The Sword and the Flute: Kālī and Kṛṣṇa, Dark Visions of the Terrible and the Sublime in Hindu Mythology*. University of California Press.

Kumar, Abhishek. 2022. "Kaali Poster Controversy: Filmmaker Leena Manimekalai Appears in Delhi Court." *ZEE News*, December 3. https://zeenews.india.com/bollywood/kaali-poster–controversy-filmmaker-leena-manimekalai-appears-in-delhi-court-2543560.html.

Mallik, Santasil. 2022. "Leena Manimekalai's Documentary 'Kaali' Challenges Hindutva Nationalism." *The Conversation*, September 14. https://theconversation.com/leena-manimekalais-documentary-kaali-challenges-hindutva-nationalism-189695.

Manivannan, Sharanya. 2023. "The Thin Line Between Harm and Hurt." *New Indian Express*, January 26. https://www.newindianexpress.com/cities/delhi/2023/jan/26/the-thin-line-between-harm-and-hurt-2541547.html.

McDermott, Rachel Fell. 1996. "The Western Kālī." In *Devī: Goddesses of India*, edited by John Stratton Hawley and Donna Marie Wulff, 281–313. University of California Press.

McDermott, Rachel Fell. 2001. *Mother of My Heart, Daughter of My Dreams: Kālī and Umā in the Devotional Poetry of Bengal*. Oxford University Press.

McDermott, Rachel Fell. 2003. "Kālī's New Frontiers: A Hindu Goddess on the Internet." In *Encountering Kālī: In the Margins, at the Center, in the West*, edited by Rachel Fell McDermott and Jeffrey J. Kripal, 273–95. University of California Press.

Mehta, Pratap Bhanu. 2014. "Silencing of Liberal India." *Indian Express*, February 12. https://indianexpress.com/article/opinion/columns/silencing-of-liberal-india.

Moreno, Manny. 2023. "Indian Supreme Court Protects Filmmaker for Depiction of Goddess Kaali." *Wild Hunt*, February 23. https://wildhunt.org/2023/02/indian-supreme-court-protects-filmmaker-for-depiction-of-goddess-kaali.html.

Mozumdar, Jaideep. 2020. "Bhagwan Ram Has Always Been Revered and Worshipped In Bengal, Let The 'Left-Liberal' Cabal Not Tell You Otherwise." *Swarajyamag*, August 4. https://swarajyamag.com/politics/bhagwan-ram-has-always-been-revered-and-worshipped-in-bengal-let-the-left-liberal-cabal-not-tell-you-otherwise.

Mukherjee, Anusua. 2022. "'The Moment Reflected in the Poster Is About Shared Love.'" *Frontline*, July 24. https://frontline.thehindu.com/society/interview-leena-manimekalai-kaali-movie-the-moment-reflected-in-the-poster-is-about-shared-love/article65653273.ece.

Nair, Neeti. 2023. *Hurt Sentiment: Secularism and Belonging in South Asia*. Harvard University Press.

Onishi, Norimitsu, and Vjosa Isai. 2023. "Modi's Hindu Nationalism Stokes Tension in Indian Diaspora." *New York Times*, September 30. https://www.nytimes.com/2023/09/30/world/canada/modi-canada-hindu-nationalism.html.

Pechilis, Karen, ed. 2004. *The Graceful Guru: Hindu Female Gurus in India and the United States*. Oxford University Press.

Press Trust of India. 2022a, "Twitter Removes Filmmaker Leena Manimekalai's 'Kaali' Poster Tweet." *Indian Express*, July 6. https://indianexpress.com/article/india/twitter-removes-filmmaker-leena-manimekalai-kaali-poster-tweet-8012735/.

Press Trust of India. 2022b. "Party Leader Claims TMC Doesn't Support Goddess Kali's Portrayal in 'Bad Taste.'" *Outlook*, July 7. https://economictimes.indiatimes.com/news/politics-and-nation/tmc-doesnt-support-goddess-kalis-portrayal-in-bad-taste-party-leader/articleshow/92732374.cms.

Press Trust of India. 2022c. "BJP Not Custodian of Hindu Deities, Shouldn't Teach Bengalis How to Worship Goddess Kali: Mahua Moitra." *Indian Express*, July 8. https://indianexpress.com/article/cities/kolkata/mahua-moitra-goddess-kali-controversy-bjp-8016725/.

Press Trust of India. 2022d. "Goddess Kali's Blessings Are with Country: PM Modi." *Indian Express*, July 10. https://indianexpress.com/article/cities/kolkata/goddess-kalis-blessings-are-with-country-pm-modi-8020617/.

Rajaram, Prema. 2021. "TMC Supporters Tonsure Their Heads in Protest Against Bengal BJP Chief Dilip Ghosh's Remark on 'Durga.'" *India Today*, February 14. https://www.indiatoday.in/india/story/tmc-supporters-tonsure-their-heads-bengal-bjp-chief-dilip-ghosh-durga-remark-1769197-2021-02-14.

Ramanujan, A. K. 1991. "Three Hundred Ramayanas, Five Examples and Three Thoughts on Translation." In *Many Ramayanas: The Diversity of a Narrative Tradition in South Asia*, edited by Paula Richman, 22–49. University of California Press.

Roy, Manisha. 2023. "Mahua Moitra's Expulsion Result of 'Maa Kali's Curse': BJP's Suvendu Adhikari." *Republican World*, December 8. https://www.republicworld.com/politics/mahua-moitra-s-expulsion-result-of-maa-kali-s-curse-bjp-s-suvendu-adhikari/.

Saha, Pritam. 2022. "Kali Poster Row: BJP's Counter to Mahua Moitra: Women Priests and 'Dhaki' to Perform Kali Pua in Bengal on THIS Day." *Zee News*, July 20. https://zeenews.india.com/india/kaali-poster-row-bjps-counter-to-mahua-moitra-women-priests-and-dhaki-to-perform-kali-puja-in-bengal-on-this-day-2487629.html.

Sanagala, Naveen, 2020. "Upset Hindus Urge Orlando Firm to Withdraw 'Blood of Kali' Tea and Apologize." *Hindupad*, July 10. https://hindupad.com/upset-hindus-urge-orlando-firm-to-withdraw-blood-of-kali-tea-apologize/.

Savarkar, V. D. 1923. *Hindutva*. V. V. Kelkar.

Schmidt, Samantha. 2023. "Masked Gunmen, an Ambush, a Chase: The Execution of Hardeep Singh Nijjar." *Washington Post*, September 20. https://www.washingtonpost.com/world/2023/09/20/hardeep-singh-nijjar-killing/.

Section 295A of the Indian Penal Code. 2025. Center for Internet and Society. https://cis-india.org/internet-governance/resources/section-295a-indian-penal-code.

Sengupta, Amit. 2021. " 'No Vote to BJP' Echoes in Kolkata, to Be Heard Across Bengal." *National Herald*, March 15. https://www.nationalheraldindia.com/india/no-vote-to-bjp-echoes-in-kolkata-to-be-heard-across-bengal.

Shukla, Prem. 2022. "Viewpoint: Tolerance of Hindus Has Been Tested . . . And It Continues." *Asian Newstable*, July 28. https://newsable.asianetnews.com/india/opinion-tolerance-of-hindus-is-being-continuously-tested-rfqio5.

Sinha, Satkirti. 2022. "Mahua Moitra's Kali Embodies the Diversity of Hinduism: The People in Power Don't Like That." *Live Wire*, July 25.

Swyers, Katie, and Judy Trinh. 2022. "Hate Speech and Death Threats: Canadian Academics Harassed After Criticizing Hindu Nationalism in India." *CBC News*, April 7. https://www.cbc.ca/news/canada/academics-harassed-criticism-india-politics-1.6402486.

The Wire. 2022. "Mahua Moitra Says People Can Imagine Gods as They Like, Rattled TMC Distances Itself." *The Wire*, July 6. https://thewire.in/politics/kaali-row-mahua-moitra-says-people-can-imagine-gods-as-they-like-tmc-distances-itself.

Urban, Hugh B. 2003. " 'India's Darkest Heart': Kālī in the Colonial Imagination." In *Encountering Kālī: In the Margins, at the Center, in the West*, edited by Rachel Fell McDermott and Jeffrey J. Kripal, 169–95. University of California Press.

Xing, Lisa. 2022a. "Toronto Filmmaker Receives Backlash, Death Threats over Hindu Goddess Poster." CBC, July 14. https://www.cbc.ca/news/entertainment/leena-manimekalai-kaali-film-poster-hindu-right-1.6519758.

Xing, Lisa. 2022b. "Director Got Death Threats over Film Poster Featuring Hindu Goddess: Now She's Getting a Protest Screening." CBC, November 3.

Xing, Lisa. 2023. "India's Supreme Court Grants Protection to Filmmaker Attacked for Movie Poster Featuring Hindu Goddess." CBC, February 22. https://www.cbc.ca/news/entertainment/kaali-goddess-leena-manimekalai-court-order-1.6755493.

Zecchini, Laetitia. 2020. "Hurt and Censorship in India Today: On Communities of Sentiments, Competing Vulnerabilities and Cultural Wars." In *Emotions, Mobilisations, and South Asian Politics*, edited by Amélie Blom and Stéphanie Tawa Lama-Rewal, 243–63. Routledge.

Zed, Rajan. 2023. "After Hindu Protest, Etsy Removes Goddess Kali Skirt." *MyIndMakers*, January 13. https://www.myind.net/Home/viewArticle/after-hindu-protest-etsy-removes-maa-kali-skirt.

Zeiler, Xenia. 2018. "Digital Journalistic Uses of the Terms 'Sacred' and 'Trivial': Online Press Releases on Portrayals of Hindu Deities in the USA." *Journal of Religion, Media, and Digital Culture* 7: 300–318.

Contributors

Amy L. Allocco is Professor of Religious Studies at Elon University, where she is also the founding director of the Multifaith Scholars program. Allocco is an ethnographer of South Asian traditions whose research focuses on everyday Hinduism in Tamil Nadu, South India. Her current field research analyzes the story, song, and ritual repertoires of three generations of hereditary Tamil Hindu drummer-priests called *pampaikkārar* to understand a vernacular performance tradition in transition. A book in progress based on her previous project, *Living with the Dead in Hindu South India*, focuses on the family-sponsored Hindu invitation rituals performed to domesticate dead relatives known as *pūvāṭaikkāri* as permanent, protective household deities in northern Tamil Nadu. She is the coeditor of *Ritual Innovation: Strategic Interventions in South Asian Religion* (with Brian K. Pennington, 2018) and of a double issue of *Fieldwork in Religion* (with Jennifer D. Ortegren, 2020). Her work on divine embodiment, narrative and ritual healing, snake goddess worship, ritual relationships with the dead, and class and gender in urban Hinduism has been published in the *Journal of the American Academy of Religion, International Journal of Hindu Studies, Journal of Feminist Studies in Religion, Religions of South Asia*, and the *Journal of Hindu Studies*.

Indira Arumugam is an anthropologist who works in Tamil Nadu, South India, and among the Tamil diaspora in Singapore and Southeast Asia. She is an Assistant Professor in the Department of Sociology and Anthropology at the National University of Singapore. Her research interests include ritual theories and practices, intimate economics of (re)production, gendered rituality, play and pleasure, and popular Hinduism. Her writings on animal sacrifice, divine agency, monstrosity and sacrality, rituals, the gift, and kinship have appeared in *Hau: Journal of Ethnographic Theory, Social Anthropology,*

Anthropological Forum, Anthropology and Humanism, Material Religion, and *Modern Asian Studies.* Her monograph, *Visceral Politics: Imaginaries of Power in South India,* is forthcoming.

Darry Dinnell received his PhD in Religious Studies from McGill University. He has taught at McGill and St. Thomas More College, University of Saskatchewan. He served as coeditor for the volume *Intersections of Religion and Astronomy* (2021).

Patricia Dold is an Associate Professor in the Department of Religion and Culture at Memorial University of Newfoundland and Labrador and Associate Dean, Curriculum and Programs, in the Faculty of Humanities and Social Sciences. Her teaching and research focus on Hindu Shakta traditions but include South Asian religious history and areas such as religion and gender and religion and violence.

Carter Hawthorne Higgins is a Lecturer in Religious Studies at the University of Kansas. He holds a PhD in Asian Literature, Religion, and Culture from Cornell University and was previously a Postdoctoral Research Fellow at the National University of Singapore.

Amy-Ruth Holt is an independent scholar and art historian who has taught at Washington & Lee University, the University of Alabama, Birmingham, and Ohio State University, Newark. Her research focuses on the symbolic and political relationship between historical and contemporary forms of Hindu art and architecture in southern India and the global Tamil diaspora. Her recent publications include an edited volume with Karen Pechilis (Drew University), *Devotional Visualities: Seeing Bhakti in Indic Material Cultures* (2023), and articles in the *Journal of Hindu Studies* such as "A Secular Tamil Saint? Karunanidhi's Use of Divine Imagery in Dravidian Imagery" (2016), "Symbols of Political Participation: Jayalalitha's Fan Imagery in Tamil Nadu" (2019), and a special edition with Karen Pechilis, "Contemporary Images of Hindu Bhakti: Identity and Visuality" (2019). She also has contributed chapters to *Modern Hinduism: In Text and Context* (2018), *A Cultural History of Hinduism* (2024), and *A History of Hindu Architecture in India* (2022).

Aftab S. Jassal is an Associate Professor of Anthropology and an Affiliate Faculty in the Program for the Study of Religion and Global Health at the University of California, San Diego. He previously taught at Duke

University and Colgate University. He received his PhD in West and South Asian Religions from the Graduate Division of Religion at Emory University. His ethnographic research focuses on ritual performance traditions and human-divine relations in Uttarakhand, North India, a region facing the combined pressures of tourism, neoliberal development, and Hindutva. Jassal's first book, *Gods in the World: Placemaking and Healing in the Himalayas* (2024), was awarded the Claremont Prize for the Study of Religion. The book explores key themes in the anthropology of religion, including the dynamics of caste, gender, possession, ritual healing, and placemaking. Jassal's work offers critical insights into everyday Hinduism as a terrain of ongoing negotiation and struggle.

Seth Ligo is an Assistant Teaching Professor of Asian Studies, South Asian Religions, and Buddhism at Pennsylvania State University. Initially driven by an interest in oral cultures and Asian languages, he specializes in the material and visual cultures of Hinduism, Buddhism, and pan-Asian tantra—especially traditions related to the "horrifying" deity Bhairava. Other research interests include the study of tantra, yoga, margins and marginalization, art history, ethnography and ethnomusicology, plural religious spaces, and indigenous religions. Having lived in South Asia and southern Appalachia, Seth has a love of both Bollywood music and bluegrass. He plays the banjo to untangle his mind when it gets snarled in his scholarship, and his commitment to experiential learning means his courses often involve community-building Bollywood dance sessions.

Rachel Fell McDermott is Professor in the Department of Asian and Middle Eastern Cultures, Barnard College, Columbia University. She studies the goddesses of Bengal, principally Kālī, Durgā, and Umā, in their literary, ritual, and festival traditions, spanning the mid-eighteenth century to the present. Her books include *Mother of My Heart, Daughter of My Dreams: Kālī and Umā in the Devotional Poetry of Bengal* (2001), *Singing to the Goddess: Poems to Kālī and Umā from Bengal* (2001), *Revelry, Rivalry, and Longing for the Goddesses of Bengal: The Fortunes of Bengali Festivals* (2011), and two coedited volumes: *Encountering Kālī: In the Margins, at the Center, in the West*, with Jeffrey Kripal (2003), and *Breaking Boundaries with the Goddess: New Directions in the Study of Śāktism*, with Cynthia Ann Humes (2009). She is currently involved in two research projects on the "Rebel Poet" of Bengal and the national poet of Bangladesh, Kazi Nazrul Islam (1899–1976). This new focus has led her to expand her research field from

West Bengal to Bangladesh. Additional interests include comparative theology, particularly between Hindus and Christians and Hindus and Jews. Her most recent book is *A Hindu-Jewish Conversation: Root Traditions in Dialogue*, cowritten with Daniel Polish (2024).

Brian K. Pennington is the Director of the Elon University Center for the Study of Religion, Culture, and Society and Professor of Religious Studies there. A historian of religion in modern India, he is the author of *Was Hinduism Invented? Britons, Indians, and the Colonial Construction of Religion* (2005), editor of *Teaching Religion and Violence* (2012), and coeditor with Amy L. Allocco of *Ritual Innovation: Strategic Interventions in South Asian Religion* (2018). His current book in progress, *God's Fifth Abode: Entrepreneurial Hinduism in the Indian Himalayas*, is based on more than a decade of field research in the pilgrimage city of Uttarkashi. He has served on the Board of Directors of the American Academy of Religion, the Board of Directors of the Society for Hindu-Christian Studies, the Advisory Council for the Conference on the Study of Religions of India, and as President of the American Academy of Religion, Southeast Region.

Tracy Pintchman is Professor of Religious Studies and Director of the Global Studies Program at Loyola University of Chicago. Her scholarly publications include more than two dozen articles and book chapters and five edited and coedited volumes: *Seeking Mahādevī: Constructing the Identities of the Hindu Great Goddess* (2001); *Women's Lives, Women's Rituals in the Hindu Tradition* (2007); *Goddess and Woman in Hinduism: Reinterpretations and Re-envisionings* (with Rita Sherma, 2015); *Hindu Ritual at the Margins: Transformations, Innovations, Reconsiderations* (with Linda Penkower, 2011); and *Sacred Matters: Materiality in Indian Religions* (with Corinne Dempsey, 2015). She is also the author of three monographs: *The Rise of the Goddess in the Hindu Tradition* (1994), *Guests at God's Wedding: Celebrating Kartik Among the Women of Benares* (2005), and *Goddess Beyond Boundaries: Worshipping the Eternal Mother at a North American Hindu Temple* (2024).

R. Jeremy Saul received his PhD from the University of Michigan, and conducted Fulbright-endorsed PhD fieldwork in India. He recently retired as a lecturer in the College of Religious Studies, Mahidol University, Bangkok, having long taught about Asian and tribal/folk religions. He will shortly begin an American Institute of Indian Studies–funded year of Hindi-based ethnographic fieldwork in India for a book project. He has published journal articles and chapters on folk deities of Rajasthan and northwestern India, and the sociocultural context of contemporary deity devotion, including "The Ayodhya Decision and Marwari Merchants: Financing Ram Devotion Through Hanuman," in *Contemporary South Asia* (2024); "Merchant Patronage and Royal Hanumans: A Modern Devotional Visuality," in *Devotional Visualities: Seeing Bhakti in Indic Visual Cultures*, edited by Karen Pechilis and Amy-Ruth Holt (2023); and "Merchants, Ritualists, and Bifurcated Hanumans: A Cultural History of Miracle Deities in Rajasthan," in *International Journal of Hindu Studies* (2022). His book project research takes this inquiry further, especially focusing on the recent trajectory of devotion among urban merchants throughout India for miracle-promising village deities of Rajasthan, such as manifestations of Hanuman, and even new deities derived from them.

Caleb Simmons, PhD, is the Vice Provost of Arizona Online, overseeing the University of Arizona's online campus with over 10,000 students, 4 distance locations throughout Arizona, and Continuing and Professional Studies. He is also Professor of Religious Studies and a Center for University Education Scholarship Distinguished Fellow at University of Arizona. He specializes in digital and online learning and religion in South Asia, especially Hinduism. His religious studies research spans from religion and state-formation in medieval and colonial India to contemporary transnational aspects of Hinduism. His book *Devotional Sovereignty: Kingship and Religion in India* (2020) examines how the late early modern/early colonial court of Mysore reenvisioned notions of kingship, territory, and religion, especially its articulations through devotion. His second monograph, *Singing the Goddess into Place: Locality, Myth, and Social Change in* Chamundi of the Hill, *a Kannada Folk Ballad* (2022), examines popular local folk songs that engage the mythology of Mysore's Chamundeshwari and her consort Nanjundeshwara to critique social inequalities. He also edited (with Moumita Sen and Hillary Rodrigues) and contributed to *Nine Nights of the Goddess: The Navarātri Festival in South Asia* (2018).

Xenia Zeiler is Professor of South Asian Studies at the Department of Cultures, Faculty of Humanities, University of Helsinki. For many years, she has combined her background in classical Indology with her interest in contemporary and mediatized Hindu traditions. In order to understand how digital spaces such as social media and video games, and more traditional media formats such as film and TV, shape and are shaped by various actors, she researches and teaches digital religion, popular culture, and cultural heritage. She has published numerous articles and book chapters on these themes. Her larger publications include the edited volume *Digital Hinduism* (2020), the coedited volume *Mediatized Religion in Asia* (2019), and the coedited special journal issue "Digital Tantra" in *International Journal of Hindu Studies* (2022). Her larger coedited publications also include work on digital culture beyond specific geographical borders, such as the special journal issue "Video Games and Cultural Heritage," *International Journal of Heritage Studies* (2021); *The Routledge Handbook of Religion and Journalism* (2020); and a special journal issue titled "Video Game Development in Asia," *Gamevironments* (2018).

Index